Condemned To Repeat?

Condemned to Repeat?

The Paradox of Humanitarian Action

Fiona Terry

CORNELL UNIVERSITY PRESS

ITHACA AND LONDON

Copyright © 2002 by Cornell University

All rights reserved. Except for brief quotations in a review, this
book, or parts thereof, must not be reproduced in any form without
permission in writing from the publisher. For information, address
Cornell University Press, Sage House, 512 East State Street, Ithaca,
New York 14850.

First published 2002 by Cornell University Press
First printing, Cornell Paperbacks, 2002

Printed in the United States of America

Library of Congress Cataloging-in-Publication Data

Terry, Fiona.
    Condemned to repeat? : the paradox of humanitarian action / Fiona
Terry.
       p. cm.
Includes bibliographical references and index.
    ISBN-13: 978-0-8014-8796-5 (pbk. : alk. paper)
    1. Refugee camps—Case studies. 2. Humanitarian assistance—Political
aspects. 3. Refugees—International cooperation. 4. Civil war—Case
studies. I. Title.
    HV640 .T47 2002
    361.2'6—dc21
                                2001008176

Cornell University Press strives to use environmentally responsible
suppliers and materials to the fullest extent possible in the publishing
of its books. Such materials include vegetable-based, low-VOC inks
and acid-free papers that are recycled, totally chlorine-free, or partly
composed of nonwood fibers. For further information, visit our website
at www.cornellpress.cornell.edu.

Paperback printing   10 9 8 7 6 5 4

For my mother, Judyth, and her soulmate, Richard, who opened my eyes to the best of this world and gave me the freedom to discover the rest.

Contents

Maps

Acknowledgments

I wrote a first draft of this book in the Department of International Relations at the Australian National University, which I entered after several years working in emergency relief programs in different parts of the world. I am deeply grateful to the ANU for the generous scholarship and field research funds they provided, and to the Evans-Grawemeyer Award for an additional grant. I owe a great debt to Ramesh Thakur, William Maley, and Philip Pettit for their enthusiastic guidance of the original project, and to Roger Haydon and Louise E. Robbins from Cornell University Press for their encouragement and patience during revisions. Thanks also to Kay Dancey for her technical assistance with the maps, and to Kay Scheuer for her editing skills.

A number of people have helped shape my thinking about humanitarian issues and the cases presented here, particularly Rony Brauman, Fabrice Weissman, Peter Hakewill, Tony Jackson, Gérard Prunier, Jean-Hervé Bradol, François Jean, Marc Le Pape, Mauro De Lorenzo, and Patrick Vial. I appreciate the access that UNHCR gave me to their files on the Great Lakes Region of Africa, and the hospitality of ICRC and MSF missions in the field. Mathilde Creignou and Christine Dufour at the MSF documentation center in Paris were helpful in tracking down sources, and I am grateful to Odile Hardy for assisting in the search for elusive documents. Special thanks to everyone involved in MSF Sydney and Paris for their support, patience, and understanding of my "other" commitment, and for the enthusiasm they showed for this project.

My greatest appreciation is to my family: Judyth, Richard, and Alex, whose love and encouragement are limitless. Writing in the calm of Australia gave me the precious opportunity to be near them, and to share the last years of Richard's life. My deepest regret is that he is not with us to see the publication of this book.

F. T.

Paris and Brisbane

Abbreviations

AFDL	Alliance des Forces Démocratiques pour la Libération (de Congo) (Alliance of Democratic Forces for Liberation [of Congo])
CGDK	Coalition Government of Democratic Kampuchea
CRS	Catholic Relief Services
CZSC	Contingent Zaïrois de Sécurité dans les Camps (Zairean Contingent for Security in the Camps)
DK	Democratic Kampuchea
DPKO	Department of Peacekeeping Operations (of the United Nations)
ECHO	European Community Humanitarian Office
ECOMOG	Economic Community of West Africa Monitoring Group
FAR	Forces Armées Rwandaises (Rwandan Armed Forces)
FMLN	Frente Farabundo Martí para la Liberación Nacional (Farabundo Martí National Liberation Front)
FUNCINPEC	Front Uni National pour un Cambodge Indépendent, Neutre, Pacifique et Coopératif (United Front for an Independent, Neutral, Peaceful, and Cooperative Cambodia)
ICRC	International Committee of the Red Cross
IDP	Internally displaced person
IFRCRC	International Federation of Red Cross and Red Crescent Societies
IRC	International Rescue Committee
ISI	Inter-Services Intelligence Directorate (of the Pakistani military)
KPNLF	Khmer People's National Liberation Front
MSF	Médecins sans Frontières
NGO	Nongovernmental organization

NWFP	Northwest Frontier Province (of Pakistan)
OAU	Organisation of African Unity
RDR	Le Rassemblement pour le Retour et la Démocratie au Rwanda (Rally for the Return and Democracy in Rwanda)
RPA	Rwandan Patriotic Army
RPF	Rwandan Patriotic Front
RTLM	Radio-Télévision Libre des Mille Collines
SAF	Salvadoran Armed Forces
UNAMIR	United Nations Assistance Mission for Rwanda
UNBRO	United Nations Border Relief Operation
UNHCR	United Nations High Commissioner for Refugees
UNICEF	United Nations Children's Fund
UNPROFOR	United Nations Protection Force (in the former Yugoslavia)
USAID	United States Agency for International Development
WFP	World Food Programme

Condemned to Repeat?

Introduction

In October 1996, the Rwandan refugee camps on the banks of Lake Kivu in eastern Zaire were attacked by Zairean rebels and their Rwandan army allies. Narcisse, a Rwandan refugee, survived.

It was during the day, around 3 P.M. We heard gunfire, two shots far from us, and we were afraid it was the start of an operation. We took the possessions we could carry and fled. . . . in the meantime, the soldiers encircled the group left in the forest with the children and took them away to massacre them, even the babies. . . . Every time refugees erected camps, others [soldiers] would come and destroy them. There was a little camp near Kibumba where I found many dead. The Banyamulenge [Zairean rebels] destroyed all the camps to disperse the refugees. All the dead [in Kibumba] had been shot.[1]

What Narcisse experienced near the town of Goma was replicated at hundreds of sites across Zaire. Refugees were rounded up in camps, in the forest, or on the road and either taken away and shot or macheted where they stood—men, women, and children. The killing continued for months. Some refugees reached a makeshift camp at Biaro, 500 kilometers west of Goma, but even there they were not safe. One night the camp was emptied, including the hospital. Aid workers returned in the morning to find intravenous lines hanging limply from their stands. There was no sign of the patients.

The license to slaughter these men, women, and children was premised on their "guilt by association" with the authors of the 1994 Rwandan genocide, who had been ensconced in the refugee camps for the past two years. The camps had been used as a base from which the former extremist government, army, and Interahamwe militias launched raids on Rwanda to continue the killing they had started in April 1994. The Rwandan gov-

---

[1] *Zaire: "Attacked by All Sides": Civilians and the War in Eastern Zaire*, Human Rights Watch Africa, vol. 9, no. 1 (A) (New York: Human Rights Watch, 1997), p. 9.

ernment had warned on several occasions that it would break up the camps if nothing was done to control this threat on its border, but no outside state was willing to send armed forces into this dangerous quagmire. Hence those responsible for genocide, the greatest crime against humanity, remained living with impunity in camps run by the United Nations, and the very system established to protect the refugees became the source of their peril.

The history of the Rwandan refugee camps graphically illustrates the paradox of humanitarian action: it can contradict its fundamental purpose by prolonging the suffering it intends to alleviate. Relief agencies rushed to avert immediate disaster among the refugees pouring into Tanzania and Zaire, but inadvertently set the scene for the eventual disaster that Narcisse described. Former leaders manipulated the aid system to entrench their control over the refugees and diverted resources to finance their own activities. In short, humanitarian aid, intended for the victims, strengthened the power of the very people who had caused the tragedy. The consequences were devastating.

I first came face to face with this dilemma in the Rwandan camps in Tanzania toward the end of 1994. I was the head of the French section of the humanitarian medical association Médecins sans Frontières (MSF)[2] in Tanzania when we took the controversial decision to withdraw our assistance from the camps. The moral quandary we faced and the intense, emotional, and sometimes acrimonious debates that surrounded our decision left an indelible mark on my conscience. It pushed all of us in MSF to reflect deeply upon what humanitarian action represents, and at what point it loses its sense and becomes a technical function in the service of evil. It invoked a basic question: Can we, in the name of moral principles, cease to aid a population in need? And it prompted us to think about what our responsibility is for the fate of people under our care when we are unable to influence the overall context. As an aid organization we had to choose between only two options: to participate or to refuse.

I would like to claim that these questions were as clear in my mind then as they are now, but unfortunately they were not. The bigger picture, although omnipresent, was not always so clear from the field, where analysis was clouded by details and, at times, strong emotion. Everyone in the team felt deep discomfort about assisting people who had murdered others, particularly as few of the killers expressed remorse. The genocide against the Tutsi and those who were seen as supporting them had continued in the

---

[2] The organization is also known by its English name, Doctors without Borders.

camps, and bodies were frequently dragged from the lake. In the MSF hospital we strongly suspected that Tutsi children were given minimal care, or left to die, when we were not around to supervise. We wondered how many of our Rwandan staff—working in the feeding center, the hospital, even in our house—had blood on their hands.

But these thoughts were pushed aside in the daily battles to combat a shigellosis epidemic and rising malnutrition and to minimize the diversion of supplies. They would reappear around the table at night, after a couple of beers, and divide the team. Should we respect conventional medical ethics, treating anyone who needed it regardless of their history, or should we recognize our wider responsibility for what was happening in the camps? The latter concern was heightened by reports of military training not far away, generating concern that an attack on Rwanda was imminent. But at the same time in Tanzania some progress was being made toward reducing the perverse effects of aid: a census had permitted the number of food rations to be reduced from 350,000 to 230,000, thereby curtailing the excess diverted by the leaders. Furthermore, the Tanzanian government had approved a deployment of police to the camps to help provide security.

It took a visit from headquarters to provide the perspective we needed to see things in a clearer light. A meeting of all MSF coordinators in the region—from the French, Dutch, Belgian, Swiss, and Spanish sections—was convened in Kigali in October 1994 to discuss the situation. With the emergency phase of the relief operation over, it was time to consider our future in the camps. It soon emerged that we all shared the same diagnosis about the unacceptable conditions with which we were confronted, but considerable difference of opinion arose over how MSF should react.

The areas of debate within MSF centered predominantly around two questions: To what extent were *we* responsible for the manipulation of humanitarian aid in the camps? How could we best assume such responsibility? Some people argued that our participation in the aid system implicated us in all its outcomes, that everything from our presence in the camps to the resources we lost from theft made us direct accomplices in whatever harmful acts ensued. Lacking the power to ensure what is just, we should at least not participate in what is obviously unjust; thus our only recourse was to refuse the unacceptable and withdraw from the camps. One participant followed this argument to its logical conclusion and advocated dismantling the structures we had built.

Others vehemently opposed such a position. The impact of MSF's medical services was marginal compared with that of organizations in charge of distributing food, they believed, and responsibility for what happened in the camps lay with states which had the capacity to intervene but had so far refused to do so. Why should we feel responsible when others failed to prevent the militarization of the camps? There were genuine refugees in the camps who needed our help; what would be their fate if we left? Those who took this position felt that MSF's responsibility was to remain present and work to minimize the negative impact of humanitarian aid while continuing to lobby governments to carry out their responsibilities for the security and humanitarian status of the camps. Thus they advocated staying longer to document the manipulation of aid and pressure the "international community" into action.

By the end of the meeting many of us were convinced that we should withdraw, but saw value in postponing such a move a few more weeks to try to bring all MSF sections into agreement. A united front, we believed, would strengthen the impact of MSF's stance and might force governments to respond to questions which they preferred to ignore. Serious differences of opinion at headquarters, however, dampened any hope of consensus. The French section decided to follow its convictions and leave, whereas the other sections decided to stay. This rupture undermined the coherence of our claims that the situation was untenable for humanitarian organizations, and our withdrawal made few waves in the aid community, among donor governments, or in the press. But at a tactical level it did add weight to the attempts of several aid agencies, including the remaining MSF sections, to curb abuses of aid by the camp leaders. MSF-France provided an example that other agencies implied they would follow if improvements were not forthcoming. For those of us who left, however, the decision was far more than tactical; it was a question of ethics and responsibility.

This book explores questions about the negative consequences that can result from well-intentioned humanitarian action. An important factor in determining whether we act responsibly in a given situation is the knowledge we have at our disposal when making decisions. I analyze several cases of militarized refugee camps that preceded the Rwandan crisis—the Afghan refugee camps in Pakistan, the Salvadoran and Nicaraguan refugee camps in Honduras, and the Cambodian refugee camps in Thailand—to ascertain how humanitarian action has benefited combatant forces in the past, and what knowledge aid organizations had of the "side effects" of their action. I then examine the Rwandan camps in Zaire and suggest some reasons why the paradoxes of humanitarian action recur and persist in spite of the experience aid organizations have acquired.

In adopting a historical approach to the study of "refugee-warriors"[3] and humanitarian action, this book challenges two assumptions of the contemporary international aid regime which are fast becoming axiomatic. The first, epitomized by the term "complex emergency," depicts the post–Cold War environment as more complicated than that of the past, and filled with new dilemmas for aid organizations. While acknowledging that there have been changes in the nature of warfare that impact upon humanitarian action, I show that the dilemmas confronting aid organizations today are essentially the same as in the past. It is the international response that is more "complex"; proliferation in the number and type of actors in the field has exacerbated dilemmas inherent in the provision of humanitarian assistance.

The second assumption, which follows from the first, is the growing but unsubstantiated assertion that "aid is becoming a major factor in the continuation of conflicts."[4] Although it is impossible to determine the precise effect of aid or the absence of it on a given conflict, there have been surprisingly few attempts to back up such claims with assessments of the impact of humanitarian aid in comparison to that of other political, economic, and military resources available to belligerents. Hence the following chapters situate humanitarian action within the broader political and military context to avoid the aid-centricity of most studies, and to shed light on the circumstances in which humanitarian action might be said to prolong conflict.

The Role of Refugee Camps in War

The tragedy of the Rwandan refugee camps is still fresh in the UN's memory. Since then, the razing of Palestinian refugee camps in Gaza by Israeli tanks and bulldozers, attacks on camps housing Sierra Leonean refugees in Guinea, and the cross-border raids into East Timor by Indonesian militias from camps in West Timor have revived international concerns about the involvement of refugee camps in conflict and its implications for regional security and the safety of refugees. In his March 2001 report on the protection of civilians in armed conflict, the UN sec-

[3] The term "refugee-warriors" was first used in Aristide R. Zolberg, Astri Suhrke, and Sergio Aguayo, *Escape from Violence: Conflict and the Refugee Crisis in the Developing World* (New York: Oxford University Press, 1989).

[4] Barry Munslow and Christopher Brown, "Complex Emergencies: The Institutional Impasse," *Third World Quarterly* 20, no. 1 (1999): 207–222 at p. 221. See also Mary B. Anderson, *Do No Harm: How Aid Can Support Peace—or War* (Boulder, Colo.: Lynne Rienner, 1999), p. 161.

retary-general listed the "separation of civilians and armed elements" in refugee contexts as one of four priority measures for the Security Council to undertake to enhance civilian protection, and recommended that the Security Council support the development of clear criteria and procedures to facilitate this task.[5] This statement was preceded in the report by an indictment of the increased threats to civilians posed by today's wars. Indeed, one could be forgiven for imagining that the use of refugee camps by combatants was a recent phenomenon, another symptom of the new world "disorder." Yet refugee-warriors have been a widespread feature of the international scene for the last fifty years, and while renewed attention to this issue is laudable, proposals to address the militarization of refugee camps are likely to be futile in the absence of a deeper understanding of the problem.

The Palestinian refugees in the Middle East constituted the first refugee-warrior community[6] and are undoubtedly the best known owing to Israeli attacks on the Sabra and Shatilla refugee camps in Lebanon in 1982. Other early refugee-warrior communities were formed on the African continent: Tunisia and Morocco were host to the Algerian resistance opposing the French colonial government in the 1950s, and Tutsi refugees who fled postindependence violence in Rwanda after 1959 found sanctuary in Uganda. After thirty years in exile, this community and its descendants successfully reinvaded Rwanda in 1994 under the banner of the Rwandan Patriotic Front, with the ensuing refugee exodus providing the base for the genocidal regime to create a new refugee-warrior community in the camps of Tanzania and Zaire. Eritrean insurgents opposing successive Ethiopian governments operated elaborate bases in refugee camps in Sudan throughout the 1960s, 1970s, and 1980s, and Ethiopia has been host to Sudanese refugees and rebels opposing Khartoum. The armed branch of the South-West African People's Organization maintained bases beside Namibian refugee camps in Angola, and refugee camps in many of the front-line states bordering South Africa provided recruitment grounds for the African National Congress (ANC) resistance. Algeria played host to refugees and Polisario guerrillas from Western Sahara; guerrillas from northern Chad mixed with refugees in Libya; and the Somali refugee camps in Kenya fulfilled some functions of a humanitarian sanctuary for a

[5] *Report of the Secretary-General to the Security Council on the Protection of Civilians in Armed Conflict*, S/2001/331 (New York: United Nations, 30 March 2001), pp. 6–9.

[6] Zolberg, Suhrke, and Aguayo, *Escape from Violence*, p. 277. For more detailed discussion of the Palestinian refugee issue, see Benny Morris, *The Birth of the Palestinian Refugee Problem, 1947–1949* (Cambridge: Cambridge University Press, 1987).

few of Somalia's warring factions in the early 1990s. Currently, Burundian refugee-warriors in Tanzania engage in military activities against their home state, and Sierra Leonean camps in Guinea have come under attack for allegedly harboring rebel forces.

In Asia, refugees from East Pakistan were trained and equipped in refugee camps in India before their victorious return to form the state of Bangladesh in 1971, and Pakistan provided sanctuary for Afghan refugees and *mujahideen* opposing the Soviet-backed regime in Kabul. Refugee camps in Thailand provided sanctuary for rebels trained by the U.S. Central Intelligence Agency from the Hmong hill tribes in Laos and for Cambodian opponents of the Vietnamese-installed regime in Phnom Penh. More recently, the Burmese refugee camps in Thailand have been attacked by the Rangoon-sponsored Democratic Karen (Kayin) Buddhist Army for allegedly assisting insurgents from the Karen National Liberation Army. Refugee camps to the east of Papua New Guinea's border with the Indonesian province of Irian Jaya have also provided sporadic sanctuary for resistance fighters from the Organisasi Papua Merdeka (Free Papua Movement), and Indonesian militia sheltering among refugees in West Timor today form a significant threat to the newly independent territory of East Timor.

In the Americas during the 1980s, Guatemalan refugee camps in Mexico were attacked for allegedly sheltering opponents of the right-wing Guatemalan regime, and Salvadoran refugee camps in Honduras were targeted by El Salvador's notorious death squads. Nicaraguan refugee-warrior communities formed in Costa Rica and Honduras in opposition to the Sandinista government in Managua.

In spite of the serious implications of militarized refugee camps for regional peace and security, refugee protection, and humanitarian action, the issue has received surprisingly little attention in the international relations, peacekeeping, or refugee literature, beyond being recognized as one of several security implications of refugee flows.[7] The UN body responsible for the protection of refugees, the office of the High Commissioner for Refugees (UNHCR), has addressed the question in a legal sense, deliber-

---

[7] See Myron Weiner, "Introduction: Security, Stability, and International Migration," in Myron Weiner (ed.), *International Migration and Security* (Boulder, Colo.: Westview, 1993), pp. 1–35, and Gil Loescher, *Refugee Movements and International Security*, Adelphi Paper 268 (London: IISS/Brassey's, 1992). Sporadic articles like that of Ben Barber have also appeared in international relations literature, but a survey of prominent works in the peacekeeping literature conducted by Howard Adelman found that the issue is virtually ignored. Ben Barber, "Feeding Refugees, or War? The Dilemma of Humanitarian Aid," *Foreign Affairs* 76, no. 4 (1997): 8–14; Howard Adelman, "Why Refugee Warriors Are Threats," *Journal of Conflict Studies* 18, no. 1 (1998): 49–69 at n. 11.

ating whether the principal onus lies with asylum countries to ensure the civilian nature of refugee camps, or with neighboring states to abstain from attacking them.[8] But only two works of note analyze why and how refugee camps are of benefit to combatant forces, Jean-Christophe Rufin's 1986 book *Le piège humanitaire*[9] and Aristide Zolberg, Astri Suhrke, and Sergio Aguayo's *Escape from Violence*. Both identify the refugee-warrior phenomenon as a by-product of the simultaneous emergence of an effective international refugee regime and democratic nationalism. Refugee camp structures and humanitarian aid became useful assets in guerrilla struggles to gain political control over civilians.

Rufin identifies the use of refugee camps as the most successful of three organizational arrangements employed by guerrilla movements. The first and least sustainable strategy is to operate exclusively within the borders of a country, depending upon the local population for food and cover in accordance with Mao Zedong's dictum that the people are to guerrillas as the sea is to fish. While this mode of functioning was successful in populous China, Rufin cites the failures of the Biafran secessionists in Nigeria, the Mau Mau in Kenya, and the Hux in the Philippines as examples of its limitations.[10] In fact, this strategy has all but disappeared in the "new wars" of the current age,[11] in which combatants increasingly exploit global connections—whether to international markets to sell diamonds and other precious resources, to the media to broadcast ransom demands for kidnapped tourists, or to international aid agencies operating in the heart of conflicts.

A second and more successful strategy is establishing a military base in a neighboring country sympathetic to the guerrilla cause. Having crossed an international border, combatants are less vulnerable to attack by virtue of norms of state sovereignty and the concomitant risk of interstate confrontation. The military sanctuary serves as a base for cross-border assaults and facilitates resupply and rearmament. This strategy also has limitations, however, principally stemming from the vulnerability of the guerrilla movement to political fluctuations in the host country. The

---

[8] See Elly-Elikunda Mtango, "Military and Armed Attacks on Refugee Camps," in Gil Loescher and Laila Monahan (eds.), *Refugees and International Relations* (Oxford: Oxford University Press, 1989), pp. 87–121, and M. Othman-Chande, "International Law and Armed Attacks in Refugee Camps," *Nordic Journal of International Law* 59, nos. 2 and 3 (1990): 153–177.

[9] Jean-Christophe Rufin, *Le piège humanitaire, suivi de Humanitaire et politique depuis la chute du Mur*, revised and updated edition (Paris: Jean-Claude Lattès, 1993). The original title was *Le piège: Quand l'aide humanitaire remplace la guerre* (Paris: Jean-Claude Lattès, 1986).

[10] Rufin, *Le piège humanitaire*, p. 118.

[11] Mary Kaldor, *New and Old Wars: Organized Violence in a Global Era* (Cambridge, U.K.: Polity, 1999).

Palestine Liberation Organization (PLO), for example, lost its sanctuary in Jordan when it was expelled in Black September of 1970, and the bases of the ANC in Mozambique were disbanded after Maputo signed the Nkomati Agreement with South Africa in 1984. More recently, the Sudan People's Liberation Army lost its military sanctuary in Ethiopia as a consequence of the rapprochement between Addis Ababa and Khartoum during the Ethio-Eritrean War (1998–2000).

Humanitarian sanctuaries created by the international refugee regime provide three major advantages to guerrilla factions over purely military sanctuaries. First, refugees have protected status under international law from which combatants illegally benefit by mixing among them. To be eligible for asylum, a refugee, according to the 1951 Refugee Convention, must have a "well-founded fear of persecution" in his or her country of origin, which the Organisation of African Unity extended in 1969 to include people who fled more generalized "external aggression, occupation, foreign domination or events disturbing public order." International norms oblige states to accept refugees on their territory and to refrain from returning them to their country of origin against their will. Thus guerrilla movements are not only safer from their opponents' reprisals by virtue of the international condemnation that armed attacks on refugee camps invoke, but are less dependent upon the political backing of the host state. Refugee-warriors are, of course, more tolerated by states sympathetic to their cause: in fact, Zolberg, Suhrke, and Aguayo argue that to exist, refugee-warrior communities "require sanctuary in a neighboring country permitting military operations from its territory" and that "without a friendly base, the community in exile can only be refugees."[12] But the Salvadoran refugee camps in Honduras, discussed in chapter 3, show that this is not always the case: even on hostile territory, refugee camps can provide sanctuary to combatants.

Second, refugee camps attract humanitarian assistance that provides guerrillas with an economic resource independent of external patrons. Most host states prefer to share the cost and administration of refugee camps with international donors and aid organizations, and a myriad of nongovernmental aid organizations (NGOs) and specialized UN agencies are invariably present to provide services in the areas of food and nutrition, water and sanitation, health, education, and shelter and site maintenance. In addition to appropriating food and medical supplies for military use,

[12] Zolberg, Suhrke, and Aguayo, *Escape from Violence*, p. 276.

guerrilla groups can raise revenue from a variety of sources including taxes on the salaries of refugees employed by international organizations.

Third, and most important, refugee camp structures provide mechanisms through which a guerrilla movement can control the civilian population and legitimize its leadership. Refugee camps were, in the words of refugee specialists Barbara Harrell-Bond and Eftihia Voutira, "invented as the most efficient method of distributing aid to a constituency that has been labelled as requiring it,"[13] and it is through the distribution systems that control over the population can be exerted. Aid organizations seek to identify "leaders" to act on behalf of the refugees, thereby imbuing certain individuals with legitimacy and power over their "constituency." This power is particularly significant in closed refugee camps where the refugees are entirely dependent upon international aid: the people who control the aid control the refugees.

Thus in direct contrast to military sanctuaries, which are militarized, secret, and political, humanitarian sanctuaries are civilian, public, and "neutral."[14] The benefits of humanitarian sanctuaries that Rufin points to are not specific to refugee camps, but can be identified to varying degrees whenever humanitarian action occurs in a conflict zone. For that reason, chapter 1 elaborates on these four areas of paradox concerning humanitarian action (protection, war economy, population control, and legitimacy) within a broader context than that of refugee camps, before I assess each in the individual contexts of chapters 2–5. Rufin's distinction between military and humanitarian sanctuaries provides a framework for examining the individual cases and thus a way to assess the relative importance of humanitarian action to the conflicts waged by guerrilla movements.

The Creed of the New Humanitarians

One of the most tenacious myths of the contemporary aid regime is that the end of the Cold War ushered in a barbarous "new world disorder" that created unprecedented challenges for aid organizations in addressing the humanitarian consequences of this perceived new instability. Encapsulating these challenges under the label "complex emergency," the prevailing

[13] Eftihia Voutira and Barbara E. Harrell-Bond, "In Search of the Locus of Trust: The Social World of the Refugee Camp," in E. Valentine Daniel and John Chr. Knudsen (eds.), *Mistrusting Refugees* (Berkeley: University of California Press, 1995), pp. 207–224 at pp. 209–210.
[14] Rufin, *Le piège humanitaire*, p. 121.

discourse laments "how much more complex humanitarian work [is] now than it had been in the past,"[15] basing its position on clichés about the changed nature of warfare. Contemporary conflicts are frequently characterized as more barbaric and irrational than those of the past, "little more than rampages by groups within states against one another with little or no apparent ennobling purpose or outcome."[16] There is allegedly a dwindling of respect for human values and the laws of wars, leading to an upsurge in the number of civilian casualties and persons displaced as a result of ethnic and religious hatred. Humanitarian actors have supposedly lost immunity: "shooting at the Red Cross used to be unthinkable."[17] The originality of the contemporary context even extends to refugee issues, as seen in the summary of an international workshop on the crisis in the African Great Lakes Region, which noted that "today, humanitarian assistance has to operate in a very different context. . . . though plainly unintended, humanitarian assistance has de facto *become* highly politicized."[18] The special envoy of the European Union to the Great Lakes Region, Ambassador Aldo Ajello, concurred, stating that "we were confronted with a situation which was *completely abnormal:* the coexistence in the HCR camps of civilian refugees and military forces."[19]

Despite the ubiquity of these notions, a cursory glance at history raises doubts about the originality of the evidence underpinning them. I have already said enough about refugee-warriors to refute the view that the status of the Rwandan refugee camps was completely abnormal, and shooting at the Red Cross was not previously unthinkable: Red Cross ambulance units were deliberately targeted and destroyed by Italian planes in Ethiopia in 1935–36.[20] The distinction between combatants and noncombatants disappeared with the advent of aerial warfare: bombs dropped on

[15] Comments attributed to former European Commissioner for Humanitarian Affairs Emma Bonino in the final report from an ECHO-ICRC seminar, "Humanitarian Action: Perceptions and Security," Lisbon, 27–28 March 1998, p. 6.

[16] Donald Snow, *Uncivil Wars: International Security and the New Internal Conflicts* (Boulder, Colo.: Lynne Rienner, 1996), pp. 1–2.

[17] Bonino, final report from ECHO-ICRC seminar "Humanitarian Action: Perceptions and Security," p. 4.

[18] Winrich Kühne, "Executive Summary and Recommendations," in Winrich Kühne (ed.), *Improving African and International Capabilities for Preventing and Resolving Violent Conflict: The Great Lakes Region Crisis. 2nd International Workshop, Berlin, July 3–5, 1997* (Ebenhausen: Stiftung Wissenschaft und Politik, 1997), pp. 13–27 at p. 14 (my emphasis).

[19] Aldo Ajello, "Opening Statements," in Kühne (ed.), *Improving African and International Capabilities for Preventing and Resolving Violent Conflict*, pp. 35–39 at p. 35 (my emphasis).

[20] See Marcel Junod, *Warrior without Weapons*, trans. Edward Fitzgerald (Geneva: International Committee of the Red Cross, 1982), pp. 22–83.

cities throughout the Second World War did not discriminate between targets.[21] And the fact that international humanitarian law is now invoked during conflicts, rather than after they have ended, is at odds with its image of eroding pertinence. Moreover, respect for the laws of war was not uppermost in the minds of combatants during the Cold War conflicts in Vietnam or Central America.

Even more serious than the collective historical amnesia is the failure of international observers to recognize that the international system is experiencing a period of relative stability with regard to political causes of mortality. Data compiled by the Center for Systemic Peace demonstrate that the rates of global warfare and ethnopolitical rebellion, and the incidence of autocratic authority around the world have steadily declined since 1992, as has the number of refugees.[22] The number of internally displaced people appears to have increased dramatically in the post–Cold War era, but the extent to which they were identified and counted in the past is open to question. The center's data show that "the magnitude of violence in the world has *decreased* very sharply and steadily since the Cold War ended in 1990."[23]

Changes in the post–Cold War period are overemphasized as an explanation for the difficulties that humanitarian actors face today, and in spite of attempts to construct typologies[24] of "complex emergencies," the term blurs rather than illuminates the contemporary context. It confuses the specificities of war, famine, epidemics, drought, population displacement, massacres, and genocide, and renders irrelevant the precedents from the "simple" past. One observer recently remarked that the vogue for labeling crises "complex emergencies" is a means to conceal "that one does not

---

[21] In fact some observers argue that the combatant–noncombatant distinction blurred as far back as the nineteenth century, when small professional armies were replaced by enormous conscript armies, and casualty rates among noncombatants rose dramatically. See Chris af Jochnick and Roger Normand, "The Legitimation of Violence: A Critical History of the Laws of War," *Harvard International Law Journal* 35, no. 1 (1994): 49–95 at p. 63 n. 52.

[22] The analysis is based on data by the Minorities at Risk Project, U.S. Committee for Refugees, the Polity Project, and work by Ted Robert Gurr; see Center for Systemic Peace, *Global Conflict Trends*, http://members.aol.com/CSPmgm/conflict.htm.

[23] Ibid.

[24] It is difficult to see the point of these typologies. One produced by Raimo Väyrynen is at odds with conventional usage of the term, arguing that Bosnia was a "simple humanitarian emergency" because it contained only two of the four criteria of "complex emergencies," war, displacement, disease, and hunger. The typology of Lionel Cliffe and Robin Luckman is more insightful in illuminating the characteristics of contemporary conflicts, but as they admit, the exercise represents a simplification of specific complex realities. See Väyrynen, *The Age of Humanitarian Emergencies* (Helsinki: World Institute for Development Economics Research, United Nations University, 1997), and Cliffe and Luckman, "Complex Political Emergencies and the State: Failure and the Fate of the State," *Third World Quarterly* 20, no. 1 (1999): 27–50.

know what is going on."[25] But, what is more insidious, the term actually distorts understanding, making no distinction among causes of suffering, instead defining a crisis in terms of the required "multifaceted response." The causes of most crises are political; some consequences may be humanitarian. But labeling them "complex emergencies" and "humanitarian crises" disconnects the consequences from the causes and permits the international response to be assigned—and confined—to the humanitarian domain.

There are more lucid explanations for the increased prominence of humanitarian aid in today's conflicts than increased barbarity.[26] Changes in the nature of conflict coincided with the rapid expansion of the international aid regime, and aid has become integrated into the dynamics of conflicts in regions that were previously off limits to international organizations. During the Cold War, respect for norms of state sovereignty usually relegated aid organizations to refugee camps on the periphery of conflicts, and few ventured inside a country at war before the advent of "negotiated access" in Sudan in 1989. The end of the Cold War and emergence of "a right to intervene" opened the door to a vast new array of "humanitarians," and there are now more aid workers in the field than ever before, negotiating with combatants and witnessing abuses against civilians.

This expansion of the aid system coincided with the erosion of ordered war economies into "fragmented patterns of violence and asset stripping,"[27] partially as a result of the loss of superpower patronage to warring factions. Combatants increasingly turned to two strategies to sustain their war economies: the predatory appropriation of local resources, and the criminalization of economic activity, defined as the production, exploitation, or illegal commercialization of goods and services for private, as opposed to state, benefit.[28] Neither strategy is new; the looting of property, for instance, has been a characteristic of wars for centuries. Contracts

[25] Gwyn Prins, "Modern Warfare and Humanitarian Action," final report from ECHO-ICRC seminar "Humanitarian Action: Perceptions and Security," p. 13.

[26] Paul Richards, *Fighting for the Rainforest: War, Youth, and Resources in Sierra Leone* (Oxford and Portsmouth, N.H.: International African Institute in association with James Currey and Heinemann, 1996); François Jean and Jean-Christophe Rufin (eds.), *Économie des guerres civiles* (Paris: Hachette, 1996); Jean-François Bayart, Stephen Ellis, and Béatrice Hibou, *The Criminalization of the State in Africa*, trans. Stephen Ellis (Oxford and Bloomington: International African Institute in association with James Currey and Indiana University Press, 1999); Mark Duffield, "The Political Economy of Internal War: Asset Transfer, Complex Emergencies, and International Aid," in Joanna Macrae and Anthony Zwi (eds.), *War and Hunger: Rethinking International Responses to Complex Emergencies* (London: Zed Books in association with Save the Children Fund [U.K.], 1994), pp. 50–69; and Kaldor, *New and Old Wars*.

[27] Mark Duffield, "Complex Emergencies and the Crisis of Developmentalism," *IDS Bulletin* 25, no. 4 (1994): 37–45 at p. 42.

[28] Jean-Christophe Rufin, "Les économies de guerre dans les conflits internes," in Jean and Rufin (eds.), *Économie des guerres civiles*, pp. 19–59 at p. 41.

signed by English military commanders in the Hundred Years War between England and France included the "spoils of war" as a payment of
service, and pillage was a key source of finance for armies in seventeenth-
century France.[29] In the past, however, such practices could not sustain
war indefinitely; once stripped of assets, the local population was of little
value. But the provision of humanitarian assistance provides a renewable
source of exploitation, thereby becoming a factor in conflicts.

Humanitarian organizations have also become both direct and indirect
targets of criminal practices, with everything from their presence to the
rental of warehouse space potentially incurring a tax or fee for the armed
group controlling the territory. Compared to the revenue gained from the
production and trade in internationally banned goods—such as opium in
Afghanistan and cocaine in Colombia—or the uncontrolled exploitation of
legal goods—like diamonds in Sierra Leone and Angola[30] and rubber and
timber in Liberia—humanitarian assistance may not appear lucrative. Within
six months of commencing his offensive in Liberia, Charles Taylor had
earned over $3.6 million from timber exports to the European Union alone.[31]
Similarly, after capturing the Cuango Valley in Angola in 1992, rebels from
the National Union for the Total Independence of Angola (União Nacional
para a Independência Total de Angola—UNITA) generated some $3.7 bil-
lion in revenue from the high-quality diamonds the region produces.[32] Nevertheless, aid organizations have become another source of exploitation.

As reliance on external support has given way to the exploitation of local resources, many rebel movements have fragmented and compete for
control of resources. This fragmentation of structures of authority has left
aid organizations with fewer reliable interlocutors in the field to ensure
their safety. Acceptable conditions and security guarantees may be successfully negotiated with faction leaders, traditional elders, and local government representatives, but their control may not extend to all armed elements. These changes legitimately cause new concerns for aid agencies in
the field. But pursuing the discourse associated with increased barbarity,

[29] David Keen, "A Rational Kind of Madness," *Oxford Development Studies* 25, no. 1 (1997): 67–75 at p. 69.

[30] UN Security Council Resolution 1173 of 12 June 1998 and UNSC Resolution 1306 of 5 July 2000 imposed embargoes on the unofficial export of diamonds from Angola and Sierra Leone to curb this source of funding for UNITA and the Revolutionary United Front, re-spectively.

[31] "Britain Helps Turn Logs into Rebel Arms," *Guardian*, 25 June 1991, p. 9, as cited in Max Ahmadu Sesay, "Collective Security or Collective Disaster? Regional Peace-keeping in West Africa," *Security Dialogue* 26, no. 2 (1995): 205–222 at p. 215.

[32] *A Rough Trade: The Role of Companies and Governments in the Angolan Conflict* (London: Global Witness, 1998).

irrational warfare, and the erosion of respect for humanitarian norms neglects the fact that aid is now injected into the core of disintegrating states in which authority and the state's monopoly of violence are contested, giving aid greater prominence as a potential source of exploitation. More aid workers have been killed and injured in the 1990s than previously, but aid organizations and resources are present in greater numbers than ever before. Much of the "complexity" of contemporary crises resides in the changed response to crises, particularly the competing agendas of the multitude of actors from NGOs, the UN, donor governments, and international military forces. Some 250 NGOs were present in Rwanda after the 1994 genocide, working beside at least eight UN agencies, three branches of the Red Cross and Red Crescent movement, and military contingents from eight different countries.[33] Emphasizing the complexity of crises has become a convenient way of deflecting responsibility for the negative consequences of humanitarian action from the international aid regime to the context in which it operates.

The increasing conspicuousness of the relationship between humanitarian action and conflict has generated a growing number of studies analyzing the side effects of such action. Although several excellent works preceded it,[34] the November 1994 African Rights discussion paper *Humanitarianism Unbound?* is widely considered to have "opened the debate on humanitarianism" as it assertively declares.[35] Several prescriptive works aimed at reducing the negative impact of humanitarian action have also gained attention, the best-known of which has commandeered the slogan of the Hippocratic oath of Western medicine, "First, do no harm" (*primum non nocere*).[36] Embraced as a response to the growing criticism of humanitarian action, this idea has been received as a "new paradigm" of aid in

[33] John Borton, Emery Brusset, and Alistair Hallam, "Humanitarian Aid and Effects," Study 3 of *The International Response to Conflict and Genocide: Lessons from the Rwanda Experience* (Copenhagen: Steering Committee of the Joint Evaluation of Emergency Assistance to Rwanda, 1996), p. 159.

[34] Morris Davis (ed.), *Civil Wars and the Politics of International Relief: Africa, South Asia, and the Caribbean* (New York: Praeger, 1975); Rufin, *Le piège humanitaire*; B. E. Harrell-Bond, *Imposing Aid: Emergency Assistance to Refugees* (Oxford: Oxford University Press, 1986); William Shawcross, *The Quality of Mercy: Cambodia, Holocaust, and Modern Conscience* (New York: Simon and Schuster, 1984); François Jean (ed.), *Populations in Danger* (London: John Libbey, 1992); Alain Destexhe, *L'humanitaire impossible, ou Deux siècles d'ambiguïté* (Paris: Armand Colin, 1993).

[35] *Humanitarianism Unbound? Current Dilemmas Facing Multi-Mandated Relief Operations in Political Emergencies*, Discussion Paper No. 5 (London: African Rights, 1994), pp. 36–39. Thomas Weiss also credits this paper with having initiated the debate: Weiss, "Principles, Politics, and Humanitarian Action," *Ethics and International Affairs* 13 (1999): 1–28 at p. 2.

[36] This dictum is associated with the work of the American aid consultant Mary Anderson. The idea developed through several stages, in isolation from the work of British and French

some quarters,[37] joining other reconceptualizations of the purpose and priorities of aid in the era of "complex emergencies."[38]

But the unsubstantiated nature of the claims that frequently underpin these analyses has provoked a backlash within some sections of the humanitarian community. John Borton, for example, criticizes the emphasis on humanitarian action in conflicts in isolation from other factors:

> Whilst there have been many instances where humanitarian aid has been hijacked and diverted to the benefit of warring factions, the empirical evidence is simply not available to warrant a focus upon humanitarian aid "doing no harm" as against harm done by, say, other states, business interests, illegal and semi-legal trading activities (tropical hardwoods, drugs, precious stones, etc.) and arms traders. The manipulation and occasional diversion of relief aid have wrongly been equated with an analysis of the war economy. In most, if not all, conflicts the role of humanitarian aid as a source of support for warring factions has probably been slight.[39]

Borton is justified in his concern about the lack of evidence to support claims that aid prolongs conflict. But his suggestion that the relative harm of aid is slight compared to other factors does not in itself absolve aid organizations of responsibility for the repercussions of their acts. Political, business, and military actors hold primary responsibility for the pursuit and outcome of conflicts, and their contributions are undoubtedly more significant than those of humanitarian actors. But the raison d'être of humanitarian assistance is the alleviation of suffering. If such action contradicts this purpose by causing harm, then a focus on the issue is indeed warranted.

---

writers on the same subject. For its genesis see Mary B. Anderson and Peter J. Woodrow, *Arising from the Ashes: Development Strategy in Times of Disaster* (Boulder, Colo.: Westview, 1989); Mary B. Anderson, "International Assistance and Conflict: An Exploration of Negative Impacts," (n.p., 1994 mimeo); Mary B. Anderson, *Do No Harm: Supporting Local Capacities for Peace through Aid* (Cambridge, Mass.: Collaborative for Development Action, 1996); and Anderson, *Do No Harm: How Aid Can Support Preace—or War.*

[37] A recent article claimed that the "Do no harm" maxim emerged in 1996 as "a new development in the thinking behind relief aid." Munslow and Brown, "Complex Emergencies: The Institutional Impasse," p. 210.

[38] For critiques of the current paradigms in the literature see Cindy Collins, "Critiques of Humanitarianism and Humanitarian Action," paper prepared for UN Office for the Coordination of Humanitarian Affairs (OCHA) Seminar on Lessons Learned on Humanitarian Coordination, Stockholm, 3–4 April 1998; *Humanitarian Assistance and Conflict*, report prepared for the Norwegian Ministry of Foreign Affairs (Bergen: Chr. Michelsen Institute, 1997); and Weiss, "Principles, Politics, and Humanitarian Action."

[39] John Borton, *The State of the International Humanitarian System*, briefing paper (London: Overseas Development Institute, March 1998), p. 3.

1

Humanitarian Action and Responsibility

Concerned with preserving the dignity of humanity, the term "humanitarian" encompasses constraints, or things that individuals and governments must not do, and obligations, or things that they should do. International humanitarian law imposes limits on permissible behavior during war; human rights law sets the minimum standards to which individuals are entitled by virtue of their membership in humanity; and humanitarian action seeks to restore some of those rights when individuals are deprived of them by circumstance. Hence the "duty" to provide humanitarian assistance occurs only once the duty to avoid depriving and to protect from deprivation have failed to be performed.[1] Governments hold the primary responsibility for the safety and well-being of their citizens, and combatants are obliged by the Geneva Conventions to respect civilian immunity in times of conflict. Humanitarian assistance is necessary only once governments or combatants have been unwilling or unable to shoulder their respective responsibilities.

Aid organizations do not inherit the responsibilities that others have failed to uphold, but the very need for their intervention and the impact of their assistance depend upon the extent to which higher-order responsibilities have not been met. Aid agencies cannot be held responsible, for example, for the militarization of the Rwandan refugee camps because it was neither their task nor within their capacity to ensure the civilian character of the camps. But the failure of the UN and its member states to ensure this influenced the context in which aid was provided and placed the onus on aid organizations to deal with the problems posed by the presence of *génocidaires*. Likewise, the failure of the UN Protection Force (UNPROFOR) to protect the "safe area" of Srebrenica in Bosnia in 1995 forced MSF to consider to what extent its presence in the enclave contributed to the illusion of protection that encouraged the population to

[1] Henry Shue, *Basic Rights: Subsistence, Affluence, and U.S. Foreign Policy* (Princeton: Princeton University Press, 1996).

stay, and hence what share of responsibility it ought to assume for the tragedy.

Responsibility is a complex notion with several connotations: responsibility as task and duty; responsibility as accountability and liability; responsibility as virtue in terms of behaving responsibly; and causal responsibility for a certain outcome.[2] Ideas about the responsibility of humanitarian actors for the consequences of their actions and what constitutes responsible behavior are intrinsically linked to conceptions of the purpose and limits of humanitarian action. While responsible behavior for some actors might be judged in relation to the efficiency with which they undertook their tasks, for others it might be judged according to the overall impact of their work. Whereas for some the task of humanitarian action is limited to the short-term alleviation of suffering, others advocate integrating it within a broader approach to conflict management.

The divergent views on the purpose of humanitarian action have obvious implications for the possibility of promoting an ethical framework that is applicable or acceptable to all aid organizations. Three of the seven fundamental principles of the Red Cross movement, humanity, impartiality, and neutrality, provide the most broadly accepted principles to guide humanitarian action[3] and form the basis of the various codes of conduct[4] that have appeared in recent years; thus I look in detail at the issues surrounding them. Although the other four principles—independence, universality, voluntary service, and unity—apply more to the Red Cross's internal mode of functioning, I examine independence here along with the first three because it is a precondition for genuinely upholding the other principles.

[2] Mark Bovens also adds responsibility as capacity in terms of *compos mentis* (soundness of mind), but it is less relevant to this discussion. Bovens, *The Quest for Responsibility: Accountability and Citizenship in Complex Organisations* (Cambridge: Cambridge University Press, 1998), pp. 24–25.

[3] UN General Assembly resolution 46/182 of 19 December 1991, which created the UN Department of Humanitarian Affairs, stated that humanitarian assistance must be provided in accordance with the principles of humanity, neutrality, and impartiality.

[4] The most widely acknowledged is the Code of Conduct for the International Red Cross and Red Crescent Movement and NGOs in Disaster Relief, developed in 1994. National NGO umbrella organizations, such as the Australian Council for Overseas Aid and the American InterAction, have developed a "Code of Conduct" and an "NGO Field Cooperation Protocol" respectively; and the World Conference on Religion and Peace drafted the Mohonk Criteria in 1994. In addition, academics have published guidelines such as the Providence Principles of the Humanitarianism and War Project of Brown University. In the field specific guidelines have been formulated by agencies including the Principles and Protocols of Operation in Liberia in 1995; the Somali Aid Coordination Body Code of Conduct for International Rehabilitation and Development Assistance to Somalia; the Code of Conduct for Humanitarian Agencies in Sierra Leone; and Principles of Engagement for Humanitarian Assistance in the Democratic Republic of Congo.

Universality for the Red Cross refers to the sharing of common humanitarian values by the different branches of the Red Cross movement; the equivalent, I believe, is represented for the wider humanitarian community by both the humanitarian imperative and the principle of impartiality.

Most humanitarian organizations have signed on to codes of conduct, but the extent to which they apply these principles to guide operations in the field varies greatly.

Operational Principles of Humanitarian Action

Humanitarian action posits a universal ethic founded on the conviction that all people have equal dignity by virtue of their membership in humanity.[5] The Red Cross principles of humanitarian action aim to embody this maxim and promote its universal acceptance. The "humanitarian imperative" declares that there is an obligation to provide humanitarian assistance wherever it is needed, and is predicated on the right to receive, and to offer, humanitarian aid. Impartiality implies that assistance is based solely on need, without any discrimination among recipients because of nationality, race, religion, or other factors. The principle of neutrality denotes a duty to refrain from taking part in hostilities or from undertaking any action that furthers the interests of one party to the conflict or compromises those of the other. Independence is an indispensable condition to ensure that humanitarian action is exclusively concerned with the welfare of humanity and free of all political, religious, or other extraneous influences.

These principles, based on the Geneva Conventions, are predominantly aimed at convincing belligerents that all sides are equally entitled to humanitarian assistance and that humanitarian action does not constitute interference in conflict. They aim to create a "humanitarian space" in war which is detached from the political stakes of the conflict. The term "humanitarian space" has been used to invoke a space "separate from the political,"[6] but, as later chapters illustrate, such a separation is seldom possible in practice. Here it implies the existence of certain conditions that permit humanitarian aid to be given in accordance with its purpose.

For the International Committee of the Red Cross (ICRC), adhering to these principles provides an important means to carry out its mandate—

[5] Rony Brauman, "L'assistance humanitaire internationale," in Monique Canto-Sperber (ed.), *Dictionnaire de philosophie morale et politique* (Paris: Presses Universitaires de France, 1996), pp. 96–101 at p. 96.

[6] Daniel Warner, "The Politics of the Political/Humanitarian Divide," *International Review of the Red Cross* 833 (March 1999): 109–118.

bestowed by international law—to assist victims of war, visit political prisoners, organize the exchange of prisoners-of-war, and disseminate international humanitarian law, among other duties. But the multifaceted nature of its mandate can, on occasion, provoke conflicts between these principles, particularly when satisfying one task compromises another. Other aid organizations also face tradeoffs between competing principles in proportion to the scope of the mission they have set for themselves in their organizational charters. Aid agencies concerned only with saving lives are likely to face fewer dilemmas from competing principles than those aiming to alleviate suffering and promote justice and human rights. When tensions arise between various principles, and between honoring these principles and acting in the best interests of victims, the disparate multitude of aid organizations respond very differently, according to their mandates, structures, and conception of what humanitarian action represents.

NEUTRALITY

Because much of ICRC's actions is directed toward influencing the behavior of states and belligerents, retaining the confidence of these entities is of paramount importance for opening dialogue and achieving access to prisoners or victims of conflict. Thus ICRC privileges the principle of neutrality as an operational tool for securing access and dialogue. But maintaining a neutral stance can involve concessions elsewhere in its functions and principles. Although ICRC is the custodian of international humanitarian law, for example, its delegates are not permitted to testify in court about abuses they have witnessed in the field, because that could jeopardize the safety of ICRC personnel and their reputation for confidentiality and neutrality, on which future access is thought to depend. In general, ICRC prefers to be discreet about abuses, preferring to influence parties to the conflict behind closed doors, and to speak publicly only when all diplomatic avenues have been exhausted and it is in the interest of the victims to do so.[7] The dictates of neutrality also necessitate obtaining permission from both sides to a conflict before intervening, thereby compromising the humanitarian imperative to save lives if such permission is not forthcoming.

It was this latter constraint that led some former Red Cross doctors to create MSF. Frustrated by delays in obtaining permission to ease the suffering of starving Biafrans during the Nigerian Civil War (1967–70), these

---

[7] See Massimo Lorenzi, *Le CICR, le coeur et la raison: Entretiens avec Cornelio Sommaruga, Président du Comité international de la Croix Rouge* (Lausanne: Favre, 1998).

doctors created a new kind of humanitarian organization *sans frontières*, which put the needs of victims above concerns of state sovereignty and neutrality. Not having the same diplomatic role or range of activities as ICRC, MSF rejects the necessity of discretion, considering that informing the public of the causes of suffering is part of its responsibility, rather than a last resort. MSF speaks publicly only when its personnel have been direct witnesses, and only if it is likely to help the victims to do so. But this can itself involve a difficult choice between denouncing abuses against victims and the humanitarian imperative to assist them, since a public statement criticizing a faction or regime may compromise the security and hence the presence of MSF in the field. But in extreme circumstances, when victims are at greater risk of losing their lives to violence or oppression than to starvation or a lack of medical care, humanitarian action loses its sense. In such cases, MSF considers that aid organizations have only one tool left to them, the freedom of speech, and that it has a responsibility to denounce the violence and oppression, even at the cost of expulsion.

Although neutrality is viewed as an operational tool to gain access to populations in need, the question of whether it is morally acceptable to remain neutral when faced with absolute wrong warrants consideration. Can aid agencies be bystanders to abuses and avoid making judgments in the name of not taking sides? Although Elie Wiesel is hardly the model of universal values given his characterization of a Jewish state as "more human than any other,"[8] what he writes in his novel *The Town beyond the Wall* about the Holocaust survivor's thoughts toward the man at the window watching his Jewish neighbors deported provides a poignant reminder of a perverse side of neutrality:

> This was the thing I had wanted to understand ever since the war. Nothing else. How a human being can remain indifferent. The executioners I understood; also the victims, though with more difficulty. But the others, all the others, those who were neither for nor against, those who sprawled in passive patience, those who told themselves, "The storm will blow over and everything will be normal again," those who thought themselves above the battle, those who were permanently and merely spectators—all those were closed to me, incomprehensible. And as often happens I saw all those neutrals in the features of a single face: the spectator across from the synagogue.[9]

[8] In Kansas City in 1970, Wiesel said, "There is a State, it is different from all others. It is Jewish, and as such is more human than any other." Cited in Vladimir Rabi, *Un peuple de trop sur la terre?* (Paris: Les Presses d'aujourd'hui, 1979), p. 17.

[9] Elie Wiesel, *The Town beyond the Wall*, trans. Stephen Becker (London: Robson Books, 1975), p. 149.

But aid organizations are not merely bystanders; they are active participants in attempts to alleviate suffering. Thus is their responsibility greater or less if their intentions are good? ICRC argues that humanitarians cannot play judge and jury in the field and cannot hold a population collectively responsible for the actions of its leaders by choosing to aid only one side. But refusing to make a judgment about who is right and who is wrong in many ways assumes a legal and moral equality between oppressors and their victims. Even the UN's official report on the fall of Srebrenica in 1995 concludes that the UN's global commitment to ending conflict does not preclude moral judgments, but makes them necessary.[10] Moreover, neutrality ratifies the law of the strongest.[11] Bosnian Muslims recognized this when they shouted at humanitarian organizations, "we have no need of you, we need arms to defend ourselves, your food aid and medicines only allow us to die in good health."

The Bosnian context also raises the question of whether neutral humanitarian action is possible in situations of total war, where the displacement or death of segments of the population is a goal of the war itself. Any assistance brought to such populations which permits their survival and allows them to remain in situ necessarily affects the course of the conflict;[12] humanitarian action cannot subscribe to the notion of "noninterference" in this type of conflict since the provision of assistance, like the absence of assistance, results in some winners and some losers. An ICRC delegate expressed the limits of neutrality in the former Yugoslavia: "neutrality, of which we are so proud, is for them something impossible. We hear even from ministers: if you are not with us, you are against us."[13]

The desires to act in an impartial fashion and to retain an image of neutrality can also be in tension. The perceptions of neutrality held by belligerents are the practical measure of neutrality,[14] and if the needs on one side of a conflict are greater than on the other, as they often are, aid will be directed disproportionately to one side. Given the paradoxes of aid discussed below, one party to the conflict is likely to gain greater benefits from aid than the other. States that declare neutrality in an international

[10] *Report of the Secretary-General pursuant to General Assembly Resolution 53/35: The Fall of Srebrenica,* UN General Assembly Document A/54/549 (New York: United Nations, Nov. 1999), paragraph 506.

[11] Rony Brauman, *L'action humanitaire* (Paris: Dominos/Flammarion, 2000), p. 107.

[12] See Mark Duffield and John Prendergast, *Without Troops and Tanks: The Emergency Relief Desk and the Cross Border Operation into Eritrea and Tigray* (Lawrenceville, N.J.: Red Sea Press, 1994), p. 162.

[13] Beat Schweizer as cited in Alain Maillard, "Nous sommes arrivés aux limites du tenable," *L'Hebdo* 16 (18 April 1996), pp. 16–18 at p. 16.

[14] Adam Roberts, *Humanitarian Action in War: Aid, Protection, and Impartiality in a Policy Vacuum,* Adelphi Paper 305 (Oxford: IISS/Oxford University Press, 1996), p. 52.

conflict face a similar problem. Under international law they are permitted to retain normal patterns of trade with both belligerents, but since trade is rarely equal between states, one side benefits more than another. To cease trade with both sides will simply reverse the advantage.[15]

IMPARTIALITY AND INDEPENDENCE

Although in theory impartiality is a less controversial principle among aid organizations than neutrality, in practice it is seldom applied in line with the universal values underpinning humanitarian action. Impartiality is based on the conviction that all people have equal rights to certain standards, but only those aid organizations that are financially and politically independent can ensure that they base their allocations of aid solely on need. ICRC receives much of its funds from governments but insists that no conditions be imposed on where or to whom its activities are directed. MSF ensures that the majority of its funds come from donations from the general public, and although crises receiving media attention attract more funds than forgotten tragedies away from the spotlight, MSF obtains sufficient non-earmarked funds from regular donors to enable it to respond where the need is greatest. The majority of NGOs, however, do not have this margin of maneuver and are dependent upon the discretion of government donors to support their activities.

A glance around the globe shows that far from giving in accordance with the greatest need, most donor governments allocate aid funds according to their political priorities, creating major differences between crises. Despite pledges by Bill Clinton during his 1998 Africa trip to increase U.S. support for measures to halt tragedies like that of Rwanda, by mid-1999 the United States had committed only $15 million to this end in Sierra Leone, compared with $13 billion in Kosovo.[16] And the United States was not alone in its priorities: donor governments gave $207 per person in response to the 1999 UN appeal for Kosovo and the former Yugoslavia, compared with $16 per person to the UN appeal for Sierra Leone.[17] Yet on the basis of all objective criteria, civilians in Sierra Leone were in greater need of assistance than those in the Balkans: life in one country clearly held greater value for donor governments than life in the other. UNHCR is particularly affected by funding discrepancies between

[15] See Michael Walzer, *Just and Unjust Wars: A Moral Argument with Historical Illustrations* (New York: Basic Books, 1992), pp. 234–238.

[16] "Kosovo and Sierra Leone," *International Herald Tribune*, 16 June 1999, p. 6.

[17] *An End to Forgotten Emergencies?* briefing paper (Oxford: Oxfam, May 2000), http://www.oxfam.org.uk/policy/papers/gemg/fgemgsum.htm.

those refugee emergencies that are perceived to hold important stakes for major donor governments and those that are not.

Acting independently of local authorities in the field is also a prerequisite to ensuring that aid is given in accordance with the greatest need, causing tensions for those aid organizations whose mission is to promote "local capacity building." If guided by "minders" as in North Korea, or the "humanitarian" branch of a local faction as in South Sudan, aid organizations cannot be certain that their assessment has been objective and that aid will go without discrimination to those most in need. Aid might be directed to certain groups above others in accordance with the political project pursued by the government or faction.

Similarly, aid organizations that aspire to link humanitarian action to conflict prevention and resolution and peace-building activities find tensions arising between these objectives and that of giving impartial assistance. Either aid is given without discrimination and in accordance with the greatest need, or it is given in the interests of peace. The former UN special representative to Liberia made this abundantly clear in 1993 when explaining why jets of the regional peacekeeping force, ECOMOG, bombed an MSF convoy that was bringing food to civilians suffering from the effects of an embargo imposed on the region. "Certain organizations have the task of bringing relief to those in need. We have a more important task: bringing peace. If relief gets in the way of peacemaking then there will be no relief."[18]

HUMANITARIAN IMPERATIVE

The Code of Conduct of the Red Cross and Red Crescent Societies and NGOs in Disaster Relief specifies that "the humanitarian imperative comes first," hence privileging the duty to alleviate human suffering over all other considerations. Although recognizing that the provision of humanitarian assistance may have adverse side effects, strict advocates of the right to give and receive aid subordinate other concerns to this fundamental task. Humanitarian action at its inception aimed to protect and heal wounded combatants; whether they returned to combat, hence potentially prolonging the conflict, was for politicians and rule-makers to decide. The task of humanitarian action was to relieve their suffering, and the responsibility of aid organizations was limited to accomplishing this task.

But increased recognition of the negative consequences of humanitar-

---

[18] "Liberia: Leave It to the Neighbours," in François Jean (ed.), *Life, Death, and Aid: The Médecins sans Frontières Report on World Crisis Intervention* (London: Routledge, 1993), p. 55.

ian action has led some aid organizations to try harder to assess the good versus potential harm that aid engenders. Whether decisions should be based on doing more good than harm, doing no more than a minimum amount of harm regardless of the total good, or ensuring that no harm is done, is open to debate. Mary Anderson, author of several works on the negative consequences of aid, posits that it is possible to do no harm if aid organizations learn and employ lessons from past experience.[19] Yet what if the harm outweighs the good? Few aid agencies are ready to abandon the humanitarian imperative and stop providing aid, even then. Anderson argues that "it is a moral and logical fallacy to conclude that because aid can do harm, a decision not to give aid would do no harm. In reality, a decision to withhold aid from people in need would have unconscionable negative ramifications."[20]

Apart from the obvious problem with the zero-sum nature of this argument, it denies the possibility that in some cases aid can be turned against the people it was intended to assist. Rony Brauman, former president of the French section of MSF, makes a compelling argument in favor of the positive ethical implications of refusing to act. Recalling Solzhenitsyn's question throughout the *Gulag Archipelago*, "Oh, why didn't we ever say no?" Brauman demonstrates that acquiescence may be submission and refusal may be courage; that "any plan of action must incorporate the idea that abstention is not necessarily an abdication but may, on the contrary, be a decision."[21] Some of the most abhorrent episodes in history have depended upon the silent acceptance of the status quo and mechanical obedience to authority, and aid can become part of the mechanisms of oppression and violence, as it did in the Rwandan refugee camps.

African Rights also criticizes the aversion of aid organizations to setting limits of acceptable compromise, instead prioritizing operationality and access over considerations of human rights and advocacy. It argues that "a silent witness to an abuse is necessarily a complicit witness."[22] Hence the organization advocates a rights-based approach to humanitarian action which privileges solidarity with the victims of oppression. It calls for human rights objectivity and a greater sharing of risk with the people with

[19] Mary B. Anderson, *Do No Harm: How Aid Can Support Peace—or War* (Boulder, Colo.: Lynne Rienner, 1999), p. 3.

[20] Ibid., p. 2.

[21] Rony Brauman, "Refugee Camps, Population Transfers, and NGOs," in Jonathan Moore (ed.), *Hard Choices: Moral Dilemmas in Humanitarian Intervention* (Lanham, Md.: Rowman and Littlefield, 1998), pp. 177–193 at p. 192.

[22] *Humanitarianism Unbound? Current Dilemmas Facing Multi-Mandated Relief Operations in Political Emergencies*, Discussion Paper No. 5 (London: African Rights, 1994), pp. 26–27.

whom solidarity is expressed. Whether objective solidarity is possible is open to conjecture, however.

Recent UN and donor initiatives to integrate humanitarian assistance into political endeavors aimed at "a just and sustainable peace," such as the Strategic Framework for Afghanistan,[23] create additional tensions between acting in the best interests of victims and applying conditions on the provision of aid to induce peace. The framework specifies that the humanitarian imperative prevails, but asserts that since aid "clearly has not contributed, and is unlikely to contribute, to peace-building . . . a more structured, coherent, coordinated and principled approach is required."[24] The UN stipulates that its international partners must agree to speak with one voice on all issues of principle and collectively apply human rights conditionality to the assistance program. But whose principles is the UN upholding, and how can the humanitarian imperative or the requirement that assistance be impartial prevail alongside the need to ensure that certain human rights are upheld before aid is given? Humanitarian principles were designed to guard against the use of humanitarian assistance to induce political or any other compliance.

The foregoing discussion has highlighted some of the tensions among the traditional principles of humanitarian action that can appear when these principles are applied to contemporary crises by a multitude of aid organizations with different conceptions of the purpose of humanitarian action and of their responsibilities. Deliberations about whether aid organizations have acted responsibly and can be held to account for the consequences of their actions also involve considerations of prior knowledge and of their capacity to have acted differently. Decisions are made on the basis of available information, and aid organizations are only fully responsible for actions decided on accordingly. However, if necessary information did exist and the agency did not obtain it when it could reasonably have been expected to do so, then it is guilty of avoidable ignorance.[25] Similarly, although aid agencies are morally responsible for an outcome only if they had the capacity to have acted differently, the full range of possible action needs to be taken into account—including the choice of refusal which, as noted above, is often overlooked.

---

[23] *Strategic Framework for Afghanistan Endorsed by UN Agencies* (New York: United Nations, 4 January 1999), http://www.reliefweb.int.

[24] Ibid.

[25] Hugo Slim, "Doing the Right Thing: Relief Agencies, Moral Dilemmas, and Moral Responsibility in Political Emergencies and War," *Disasters* 21, no. 3 (1997): 244–257 at p. 253.

The Paradoxes of Humanitarian Action

Elaborating on the side effects of humanitarian action in areas outlined in the introduction will more deeply expose some of the tensions inherent in trying to assist populations without contributing to the forces responsible for their suffering. What unintended benefits does humanitarian assistance supply to combatants, and how do they take advantage of procedures that aid organizations follow in the best interests of the victims of armed conflict and oppression?

PROTECTION

Combatants benefit from refugee camps, "safety zones," and other humanitarian sanctuaries in times of war by virtue of the protected status of the area, or of the civilians residing therein, under international humanitarian law and refugee law. Their presence in such places violates the law that inadvertently protects them. As Michael Walzer remarks, "if civilians had no rights at all, or were thought to have none, it would be of small benefit to hide among them."[26] The notions of "humanitarian sanctuaries" and "refugee-warriors" are "a contradiction in terms and proscribed"[27] in international law, but in the absence of enforcement mechanisms, the protected space can be manipulated to serve military purposes. This abuse violates the principles on which the protected space is based, to the detriment of the civilians it is created to protect.

All provisions of international humanitarian law as codified in the Geneva Conventions of 1949 and Additional Protocols of 1977 hinge on the fundamental distinction between "combatants" and "protected persons."[28] Civilians are entitled to protection under international humanitarian law as long as they do not take part in hostilities. Not only are attacks against civilians forbidden, but so are "acts or threats of violence the primary purpose of which is to spread terror among the civilian population."[29] Indiscriminate attacks, reprisals against the civilian population, and the use of civilians as a shield from attack or to shield military operations are also prohibited.[30] In addition to those that protect individuals, the Geneva Conventions contain measures designed to protect areas or insti-

---

[26] Walzer, *Just and Unjust Wars*, p. 186.
[27] Aristide R. Zolberg, Astri Suhrke, and Sergio Aguayo, *Escape from Violence: Conflict and the Refugee Crisis in the Developing World* (New York: Oxford University Press, 1989), p. 276.
[28] Hans-Peter Gasser, "International Humanitarian Law: An Introduction," offprint from Hans Haug, *Humanity for All* (Geneva: Henry Dunant Institute/Haupt, 1993), p. 24.
[29] Additional Protocol I, Article 51, para. 2.
[30] Additional Protocol I, Article 51, para. 4, 5, and 7.

tutions, including demilitarized zones, medical establishments, and neutral zones that might be instituted by agreement or an ad hoc declaration.[31]

Combatants are obliged under international law to distinguish themselves from the civilian population, except "where, owing to the nature of hostilities an armed combatant cannot so distinguish himself."[32] According to Hans-Peter Gasser, this refers to exceptional situations of belligerent occupation and wars of national liberation, in which case combatants are permitted to "go underground" and hide among civilians as guerrilla fighters.[33] However, they are required to carry arms openly preceding an offensive and during each military engagement so that they are recognizable as combatants.[34]

International humanitarian law is applicable during times of international and internal[35] armed conflict, and extends to refugees as long as they flee to a belligerent or occupied country, or one that is beset by an internal conflict. International humanitarian law does not protect refugees who flee to the territory of a state that is not taking part in armed conflict.[36] Jean-Philippe Lavoyer notes that this was the situation of, among other groups, the Afghan refugees in Pakistan and Iran, Iraqi refugees in Iran after the Gulf War, and Rwandan refugees in Zaire, Burundi, and Tanzania.[37]

Refugees are protected under refugee law, although protection is predominantly framed in legal rather than physical terms.[38] The refugee regime is premised on the principle that if a state cannot or will not uphold its responsibility to provide protection to its nationals, then a country of asylum, with the assistance of UNHCR if requested, will provide such protection. The core principle of protection is *non-refoulement*, the obligation of host governments to refrain from returning refugees to their coun-

---

[31] See Frédéric Maurice and Jean de Courten, "ICRC Activities for Refugees and Displaced Civilians," *International Review of the Red Cross* 280 (January–February 1991): 9–21 at p. 12.

[32] Additional Protocol I, Article 44, para. 3.

[33] Gasser, "International Humanitarian Law," p. 55.

[34] Ibid.

[35] The provisions relevant to internal armed conflict are contained in Article 3 common to the 1949 Geneva Convention and Additional Protocol II. See Denise Plattner, "The Protection of Displaced Persons in Non-international Armed Conflicts," *International Review of the Red Cross* 291 (November–December 1992): 567–580.

[36] Jean-Philippe Lavoyer, "Refugees and Internally Displaced Persons: International Humanitarian Law and the Role of the ICRC," *International Review of the Red Cross* 305 (March–April 1995): 162–180 at p. 168.

[37] Ibid., p. 168 n. 22.

[38] International refugee law is predominantly based on the 1951 Convention on the Status of Refugees; the 1967 Protocol relating to the Status of Refugees; the 1969 Convention of the Organisation of African Unity Governing the Specific Aspects of Refugee Problems in Africa; the 1984 Cartagena Declaration on Refugees; and resolutions adopted by the Executive Committee of UNHCR and the UN General Assembly.

tries of origin against their will. The right to seek asylum is also recognized in Article 14 of the Universal Declaration of Human Rights.

The distinction between combatants and noncombatants is also a central tenet of refugee protection, and the concept of a refugee and the mandate of UNHCR are embedded in a discourse that is humanitarian, apolitical, and civilian. The granting of asylum by a state has been pronounced "a peaceful and humanitarian act and . . . , as such, it cannot be regarded as unfriendly by any other State,"[39] and refugee camps should have an "exclusively civilian and humanitarian character."[40] Exclusion clauses contained in the 1951 and 1969 Conventions disqualify from refugee status persons alleged to have committed war crimes, serious nonpolitical crimes, and acts "contrary to the purposes and principles of the United Nations," and the Organisation of African Unity (OAU) Convention prohibits the engagement of refugees in subversive activities against their home countries. The protection bestowed on refugee camps is also derived from broader norms of state behavior, particularly respect for state sovereignty.[41]

The lack of protective provision in international law for civilians displaced within their national borders has been the subject of increased attention in the 1990s. Although such persons are protected by international humanitarian law during times of armed conflict and by international human rights law at other times, specific initiatives have been proposed to enhance their protection—in particular the Guiding Principles on Internal Displacement that were presented to the UN Commission on Human Rights in 1998 by the UN Representative for Internally Displaced Persons, Francis Deng.[42] The 1990s have also seen the advent of "safety zones" created in conflict areas, designed to protect victims in situ and facilitate humanitarian access to them. Such safety zones include the "safe

---

[39] Noted in the Preamble of the *United Nations Declarations on Territorial Asylum*, UN General Assembly Resolution 2312 (XXII) of 14 December 1967, and reaffirmed in Article 2 (2) of the Organisation of African Unity *Convention Governing the Specific Aspects of Refugee Problems in Africa* of 1969.

[40] In 1987 the Executive Committee of UNHCR urged host and other states to do all within their capacity to ensure the civilian and humanitarian character of refugee camps. See "No. 48 (XXXVIII) Military or Armed Attacks on Refugee Camps and Settlements" (Executive Committee—38th Session, 1987), in *Conclusions on the International Protection of Refugees Adopted by the Executive Committee of the UNHCR Programme* (Geneva: UNHCR, 1991), pp. 109–111.

[41] See *Note on the Protection of Refugees in Armed Conflict Situations*, EC/SCP/25, Sub-committee of the Whole on International Protection, Executive Committee of the High Commissioner's Programme, 33rd session, Geneva, 4 October 1982.

[42] See Roberta Cohen, "Recent Trends in Protection and Assistance for Internally Displaced People," in Janie Hampton (ed.), *Internally Displaced People: A Global Survey* (London: Earthscan and Norwegian Refugee Council, 1998), pp. 3–9.

haven" established in northern Iraq in 1991; the "open relief centers" in Sri Lanka that provide protection, shelter, and relief to people displaced temporarily by military action; the French military *zone humanitaire sure* (safe humanitarian zone) in southwest Rwanda in 1994; and the "safe areas" established by UNPROFOR in Bosnia and Herzegovina in 1993 (see Box 1).[43] Other variations include "corridors of tranquillity" negotiated between the warring parties in Sudan, and "humanitarian corridors" to protect relief supplies.

Although refugee camps and safety areas must, according to the law, retain a purely civilian or demilitarized nature, in practice this has seldom been ensured. The introduction noted the widespread incidences of refugee-warrior communities over the past fifty years, and "safety zones" have similarly harbored insurgents. Box 1 discusses the Bosnian government's use of safe areas in Bosnia and Herzegovina in spite of the presence of international forces, and the "safe humanitarian zone" established by the French Opération turquoise also hosted a military force.

Box 1: Safe Areas in Bosnia-Herzegovina

The "safe areas" created during the Bosnian War (1992–95) to protect predominantly Muslim civilians from Serb attack played an important role for Bosnian government forces as a strategic base in the midst of enemy territory. The UN established six safe areas in April and May 1993, in the towns of Srebrenica, Sarajevo, Tuzla, Zepa, Gorazde, and Bihac. The creation of protected areas was prompted by the Bosnian Serb siege of Srebrenica in early 1993, which cut off all humanitarian supplies to the town, resulting in many deaths.

These safe areas were located in Bosnian Serb–held territory and surrounded by artillery, but placed under the protection of UNPROFOR. Security Council Resolution 836 of 4 June authorized UNPROFOR "to use force in self-defense or in deterring attacks against the safe areas," and authorized UN member states, acting nationally or through regional organizations, to employ all necessary means, including airpower, to support UNPROFOR. The resolution also charged the peacekeepers with promoting the withdrawal of military

---

[43] For further discussion on "safety zones" see Yves Sandoz, "The Establishment of Safety Zones for Persons Displaced within Their Country of Origin," in Najeeb Al-Nauimi and Richard Meese (eds.), *International Legal Issues Arising under the United Nations Decade of International Law* (Dordrecht: Martinus Nijhoff, 1995), pp. 899–927; B. S. Chimni, "The Incarceration of Victims: Deconstructing Safety Zones," in ibid., pp. 823–854; and Karin Landgren, "Safety Zones and International Protection: A Dark Grey Area," *International Journal of Refugee Law* 7, no. 3 (1995): 437–458.

and paramilitary units from the safe areas other than those of the Bosnian government. However, since the removal of forces from only the Bosnian Serb side would have been considered a hostile military act, the UNPROFOR force commander preferred a negotiated demilitarization of the safe areas.[a]

In reality, however, UNPROFOR had the capacity neither to demilitarize nor to defend the safe areas. Of the 34,000 troops the force commander requested to implement the protection scheme, only 7,600 had materialized after one year. The Bosnian government allegedly used the safe areas as bases for rest, recuperation, and resupply of troops, and launched attacks from the enclaves into the surrounding territory, such as the Bihac offensive in November 1994. Susan Woodward claims that these offensives were aimed at provoking Serbian artillery fire in order to call for NATO air attacks against Serb positions, and to "reinforce their propaganda strategy of being the victims of Serb aggression and deserving military assistance."[b] There were also reports that the Bosnian government did not assist in the defense of Gorazde in order to encourage increased NATO involvement in the conflict.[c]

To the Bosnian Serbs, these safe areas were not humanitarian enclaves, but strategic zones of the Bosnian Muslims, and in July 1995 Serb forces overran two of them, Srebrenica and Zepa. Thousands of civilians died in Srebrenica; up to 20,000 people were killed in or around safe areas in 1995.[d] Woodward says that "the creation of safe zones, motivated largely by the humanitarian objective, thus made possible an escalation of the war and further exposure of civilians to bombardments."[e] The obvious lack of demilitarization of the safe areas gave the Bosnian Serbs a pretext to attack. They knew that, even if bombed as a consequence, they would either regain the territory or pressure the UN to ensure the neutrality of the safe areas, thereby depriving the Bosnian government of strategic bases. But Adam Roberts claims that there was no way that the zones could have been neutralized since neither the Bosnian government nor the civilian inhabitants would have been willing to trust their security to the UN forces.[f]

---

[a] Oliver Ramsbotham and Tom Woodhouse, *Humanitarian Intervention in Contemporary Conflict: A Reconceptualization* (Cambridge, U.K.: Polity, 1996), p. 185.
[b] Susan L. Woodward, *Balkan Tragedy: Chaos and Dissolution after the Cold War* (Washington, D.C.: Brookings Institution, 1995), pp. 320–321.
[c] Ramsbotham and Woodhouse, *Humanitarian Intervention in Contemporary Conflict*, p. 186.
[d] *Report of the Secretary-General pursuant to General Assembly Resolution 53/35: The Fall of Srebrenica*, UN General Assembly Document A/54/549 (New York: United Nations, 1999). The report states that there is no credible evidence to substantiate claims that the attack on Srebrenica was provoked by Bosnian Muslim offensives from the enclave.
[e] Woodward, *Balkan Tragedy*, p. 321.
[f] Adam Roberts, "The Role of International Issues in International Politics in the 1990s," *International Review of the Red Cross* 833 (March 1999): 19–43.

The infiltration of refugee camps and safety zones by combatants has generated violent consequences on many occasions. Some 4,000 displaced persons were massacred at the Kibeho camp in southwest Rwanda in April 1995 as a result of the violent forced closure of camps because insurgents were suspected to be inside. Radovan Karadzic imposed a blockade of safe areas in Bosnia, declaring that "if the Muslims continue to use the enclaves, the UN Safe Havens, to attack us, we shall cut off all humanitarian aid, and they may count on counter-attacks."[44] Srebrenica and Zepa were overrun in 1995. Many refugee camps have suffered armed attacks, the majority from colonial armies in Africa. Rhodesian forces attacked Zimbabwean refugee camps in Mozambique, and the South African Defence Forces attacked camps housing South African and Namibian refugees in Botswana, Lesotho, Swaziland, Zimbabwe, and Angola.

The difficulty of enforcing compliance with the law to prevent combatants using refugee camps and safety zones and belligerent forces attacking them is the major constraint on effective protection of civilian populations. "Safety zones" have predominantly been declared by the UN Security Council and "protected" by international troops, so that the responsibility of enforcing the rules falls mainly to the international force and is variously carried out in accordance with its mandate, capabilities, and political will to act. In fact, if they are imposed upon the parties, rather than being established as the result of consent, the protected zones fail to meet the requirements of international humanitarian law.[45]

The issue of armed attacks on refugee camps is a more complicated question, principally because of contending views as to whether the primary onus lies with asylum countries to ensure the exclusively civilian nature of refugee camps, or with states to abstain from attacking them. This debate paralyzed attempts in the Executive Committee of UNHCR between 1982 and 1987 to forge a consensus in favor of prohibiting armed attacks against refugee camps, with asylum states advocating categorical condemnation of attacks under all circumstances, and the "Western caucus" arguing that camps harboring military elements may constitute a legitimate target of attack.[46]

---

[44] As cited in Stephan Oberreit and Pierre Salignon, "Bosnia: In Search of a Lasting Peace," in Médecins sans Frontières, *World in Crisis: The Politics of Survival at the End of the Twentieth Century* (London: Routledge, 1997), pp. 122–143 at p. 130.

[45] Lavoyer, "Refugees and Internally Displaced Persons," p. 176.

[46] In 1981 Ambassador Felix Schynder was appointed by the Executive Committee of UNHCR to survey the problem of armed attacks on refugee camps in the hope that this "would lead to the adoption of measures which would make refugee camps and settlements safer from military attacks than they so far have been." "No. 27 (XXXIII) Military Attacks of Refugee Camps and Settlements in Southern Africa and Elsewhere" (Executive Committee—33rd Session, 1982), in *Conclusions on the International Protection of Refugees Adopted by the*

The Conclusion reached in 1987 was a compromise based on "reciprocal concessions": it expressly recognized that attacks against refugee camps cannot be justified, but it was predicated on the assumption that refugee camps and settlements had an exclusively civilian and humanitarian character.[47]

Embedded in this debate were opposing claims of a "just war" waged by the refugees to secure a return home versus the right of states to respond in self-defense to external aggression. Camps housing refugees and combatants who had fled colonial repression were generally perceived to have a just cause, and attacks on them generated condemnation, as exemplified by the outrage that followed the 1958 French bombing of the camp at Sakiet-Sidi-Youssef in Tunisia.[48] The fact that the camps provided sanctuary to combatants from the Algerian Front de Libération Nationale garnered little sympathy for the actions of the French government. Under the African Charter for Human and Peoples' Rights, in fact, African states are obliged to support armed struggles conducted by national liberation movements, and the clauses of the OAU Convention prohibiting subversive activities were not intended to contradict this commitment.[49] "Freedom fighters" were one of three categories of refugee recognized by the OAU: in the inaugural address to a conference on African refugees in 1979, President Julius Nyerere of Tanzania stated that "the OAU recognises their [the "freedom fighters' "] right to pursue the struggle for liberation, and the right of the host country to aid them with the full approval and support of the OAU if its Government so decides."[50]

Executive Committee of the UNHCR Programme, p. 61. The polarized discussion of Schnyder's report is contained in *Informal Meeting on Military Attacks on Refugee Camps and Settlements in Southern Africa and Elsewhere*, EC/SCP/27, Sub-committee of the Whole on International Protection, Executive Committee of the High Commissioner's Programme, Geneva, 6 June 1983. For comprehensive discussions of the debate see Elly-Elikunda Mtango, "Military and Armed Attacks on Refugee Camps," in Gil Loescher and Laila Monahan (eds.), *Refugees and International Relations* (Oxford: Oxford University Press, 1989), pp. 87–121, and M. Othman-Chande, "International Law and Armed Attacks in Refugee Camps," *Nordic Journal of International Law* 59, nos. 2–3 (1990): 153–177.

[47] "No. 48 (XXXVIII) 1987: Military or Armed Attacks on Refugee Camps and Settlements," in *Conclusions on the International Protection of Refugees*.

[48] The bombing polarized public opinion in France, caused an international stir, and led to a French ministerial crisis. Jean-Christophe Rufin, *Le piège humanitaire, suivi de Humanitaire et politique depuis la chute du Mur*, revised and updated edition (Paris: Jean-Claude Lattès, 1993), pp. 119–120.

[49] Mtango, "Military and Armed Attacks on Refugee Camps," p. 88.

[50] Julius K. Nyerere, "Inaugural Speech," in L.-G. Erikson, G. Melander, and P. Nobel (eds.), *An Analysing Account of the Conference on the African Refugee Problem, Arusha, May 1979* (New York: Africana Publishing Company, 1981), 65–71 at p. 67.

Effective protection of refugee camps is heavily dependent on the influence of international opinion to condemn armed attacks against them. Hence perceptions of the justness of the refugee-warrior cause, the popularity of the victims, and the international standing of the perpetrating regime are important variables. States already internationally considered "pariahs," such as the apartheid regime in South Africa, the Heng Samrin government in Cambodia, and to a lesser extent the Israeli government, had less reason to fear the moral wrath of the "international community"· than states with reputations to protect. Each of these regimes conducted attacks on refugee camps. Similarly, during the Bosnian war shaming the parties through publicly denouncing human rights violations was one of the major tactics international agencies employed to try to curb such abuses. But as Susan Woodward notes: "Those parties who already had widespread international support were more vulnerable to international opinion but less likely to be exposed, whereas those who were most accused of such atrocities and on whom media attention focused—the Bosnian Serbs in the case of Bosnia-Herzegovina—were far less susceptible because they had little international support to lose or to try to maintain."[51]

The refugee-warrior phenomenon and the military use of safety zones bring the obligations of civilians, combatants, host governments, the UN, donor governments, international aid organizations, and peacekeepers sharply into conflict. At the field level, the difficulty of reconciling the legitimate desire of refugees or oppressed populations to fight for their freedom with the need to ensure the physical safety of civilian refugees is compounded by practical constraints. Even if the purely civilian and humanitarian nature of refugee camps and safety zones is ensured in theory, can it be in practice? Host states and UNHCR are urged to establish refugee camps "a reasonable distance" from international borders,[52] but the cost of moving camps, opposition from refugees, and fears of permanent settlement held by host governments often make this impossible to accomplish.[53]

[51] Susan L. Woodward, *Balkan Tragedy: Chaos and Dissolution after the Cold War* (Washington, D.C.: Brookings Institution, 1995), p. 322.

[52] "No. 48 (XXXVIII) Military or Armed Attacks on Refugee Camps and Settlements," in *Conclusions on the International Protection of Refugees*, p. 111.

[53] For some of the constraints to physical protection which endured after the 1987 Conclusion, see *Note on International Protection*, General Assembly document A/AC.96/7, Executive Committee of the High Commissioner's Programme, 39th session, New York, 15 August 1988.

Table 1. The contribution of humanitarian aid to the economy of war

Type of Contribution	Level		
	Macro	Meso	Micro
Legal	Import taxes	Housing rental	Assistance to local authorities
	Immigration fees	Car rental	
	Warehouse rental	Truck rental	
	Purchase of food	Purchase of locally manufactured products	Purchase of local raw materials
	Taxation of salaries	Taxation of salaries	Taxation of salaries
	Airport/port charges		
	Administration fees		
	Exchange rates		
Gray Area	Obligatory employment of certain staff	Obligatory employment of certain staff	Employment of guards
		Taxation of recipients	Taxation of recipients
Illegal	Government misuse of aid	Checkpoint extortion	Checkpoint extortion
	Bribery and corruption	Looting materials from aid agencies	Looting recipients after distribution
	Black market purchase and currency exchange	Protection rackets	Trading in looted goods
		Inflated population numbers	

HUMANITARIAN AID AND THE ECONOMY OF WAR

Humanitarian aid contributes to the war economy of belligerent parties, in both legal and illegal ways, at three different levels. Table 1, adapted from Philippa Atkinson's typology of the war economy in Liberia,[54] provides an overview. The macro level denotes central government departments or the administrative equivalents of factions; the meso represents regional or local

[54] Philippa Atkinson, *The War Economy in Liberia: A Political Analysis*, Paper 22, Relief and Rehabilitation Network (London: Overseas Development Institute, May 1997), p. 8.

government, local commanders, or traditional authorities or elders; and the micro signifies individual combatants, civilians, and merchants. Many of the contributions of humanitarian aid to the war economy occur in a legal—although not necessarily a legitimate—sense, violating neither laws of the country nor international laws. Some fall into a gray area in which precise laws may not apply but the activity "forms a relatively unthreatening part of local survival strategies."[55] Other activities are illegal. The theft of humanitarian assistance is increasingly specified as violative of the law: in the Abuja II peace agreement of August 1995 in Liberia, for example, adverse interference with relief constituted a cease-fire violation, and UN Security Council Resolution 794 affirmed that those who deliberately impeded the delivery of food and medical supplies in Somalia would be held individually responsible.[56]

Although taxing local salaries is legal under a legitimate government—and a lucrative revenue earner at the macro level during large operations—the taxing of aid recipients is categorized as "gray area" here to indicate that the practice may have legitimate purposes or may be predatory. Aid organizations do not generally compensate for taxation; thus the practice potentially deprives recipients of a minimum acceptable ration. Beyond a certain point, or according to the nature of the regime, "taxation" is simply theft and is illegal. Similarly the compulsory employment of certain staff falls into a gray area when it is innocuous, but becomes illegal, for example, when armed guards must be hired as part of a protection racket (see Box 2). The development of security rackets like those in Somalia can multiply the number of employees agencies hire. One NGO in Baidoa paid $28,000 per month for security in 1993.[57]

Directing aid through the "humanitarian branch" of a local faction can also have beneficial or harmful consequences. During the 1980s, the consortium of aid agencies called the Emergency Relief Desk had a successful partnership with the Relief Society of Tigray and the Eritrean Relief Association, which were affiliated with the Tigrayan People's Liberation Front (TPLF) and the Eritrean People's Liberation Front (EPLF) respectively. The Fronts had a strong commitment to the public welfare of civilians in

---

[55] Ibid., p. 7.

[56] For a discussion of S/Res/794 declaring "a right to humanitarian relief" in Somalia, see David P. Forsythe, "Choices More Ethical Than Legal: The International Committee of the Red Cross and Human Rights," *Ethics and International Affairs* 7 (1993): 131–151 at p. 146.

[57] The NGO administrator specified that this payment was for 178 guards at $160 per month to guard 2 warehouses, 30 vehicles, 7 houses, and 2 offices. See John Sommer, *Hope Restored? Humanitarian Aid in Somalia, 1990–1994* (Washington, D.C.: Refugee Policy Group, 1994), p. 85 and p. 108 n. 93.

their areas of control.[58] The Sudan People's Liberation Army (SPLA), by contrast, has a predatory relationship with the local population, and its humanitarian branch, the Sudan Relief and Rehabilitation Agency (SRRA), is much the same. Officially empowered by the UN-led massive relief effort Operation Lifeline Sudan to participate in the targeting and distribution of humanitarian assistance, the SRRA misappropriated aid and employed discriminatory distribution practices during the 1998 famine, creating major constraints to reducing mortality, according to MSF.[59]

Box 2: MSF and the Economy of War in Somalia

The Paris office of MSF conducted a detailed evaluation of activities undertaken in Somalia between January 1991 and May 1993,[a] and specifically questioned the extent to which MSF activities potentially contributed to the war economy. Somalia was not the first country in which MSF had worked with armed guards; clandestine missions into Afghanistan were undertaken with Afghan resistance fighters who guarded against Soviet attack. It was, however, the first time such security had been paid for.

Arriving in Mogadishu for the first time in January 1991, MSF commenced working in the Digfer General Hospital, which was under government control until Siad Barre was forced to flee Mogadishu at the end of that month. General insecurity and shots fired at the team forced MSF to evacuate twice in January, but by early February security guarantees from the victorious Hawiye forces enabled a return, this time to Medina Hospital. Insecurity was rife: in the hospital patients were armed; vehicles with mounted machine guns (known as "technicals" or "Mad Max") drove into the hospital grounds, right to the operating theater; and MSF workers were forced at gunpoint to tend to the wounds of certain patients in preference to others. The team decided that it was impossible to continue unless a system of security were established to control entry to the hospital and, since the Hawiye had divided into two opposing subclans, one under Ali Mahdi (Abgal) and the other under Mohammed Farah Aidid (Habir Gedir), both were approached to provide protection. Aidid provided "police" at the entrance to the hospital, but when they proved ineffective, MSF accepted the proposal of Osman Ato, one of Aidid's top officials, to supply armed guards.

Humanitarian organizations had previously employed armed guards in Somaliland, and the only other aid agencies present in Mogadishu at that time, ICRC and SOS-Kinderdorf International, also found it impossible to protect

---

[58] For a comparison between the EPLF and TPLF and the SPLA see Duffield and Prendergast, *Without Troops and Tanks*, pp. 164–167.

[59] *A Review of the Famine in Southern Sudan and the Organization of Relief Assistance* (Paris: Médecins sans Frontières, January 1999).

lives and property without resort to this method. But what started as a concession to enable MSF to operate the only surgical facility in the war zone developed into an entire security industry, not only contributing to the war economy,
but creating a vicious circle of dependence from which it was difficult to escape.
The role of armed guards was extended to protecting vehicles once the first
MSF car was stolen in April 1991, and this became a permanent fixture in July.
The question of whether such guards should be paid was debated, but what
other method could ensure reliability and some element of independence from
their political source? The revenue Osman Ato gained made him dangerous,
however; if MSF tried to organize a trip without his security, the team risked attack from his own men. The racket had commenced. Guards demanded higher
pay, and NGOs had no recourse to alternative sources of protection. This problem grew in July–August 1992 when scores of new agencies and the media arrived in earnest, launching an entire security industry. Lack of coordination and
agreement on salary scales among NGOs led to exorbitant salary demands, and
some organizations were literally held hostage by their own guards.

MSF estimates that in the three-month period from October to December
1991, the organization paid some $60,000 to Osman Ato in the form of house
and "technical" rental, truck hire, and guards. Excluding inflation caused by
the fluctuation of the Somali shilling, this figure can be extrapolated to yield
an estimate that MSF paid some $400,000 to Ato in Somalia.

[a] Virginie Raisson and Serge Manoncourt, *MSF-France en Somalie, janvier 1991–mai
1993: Evaluation de la mission* (Paris: Médecins sans Frontières, 1994).

At the macro level, exchange rates imposed on local currency are one
of the largest areas of revenue earnings. In the relief operation for the
Kurds in northern Iraq, for example, the UN was required to conduct
all transactions at the official exchange rate, generating some $250 mil-
lion in profit for the central government in 1992 alone.[60] Import duties,
visas, airport and port charges, travel permits, licenses, and other "administrative fees" can also generate substantial sums of money for authorities, from the 5,000 Liberian dollars ($10) berthing fee for boats at
the port of Greenville in southeast Liberia[61] to the $150 per tonne
levied on aid flights to the interior of Mozambique.[62] House, office, and

[60] P. Vallely, "How He Is Getting Cash," *Daily Telegraph*, 25 August 1993, as cited in
François Jean, "Aide humanitaire et économie de guerre," in François Jean and Jean-
Christophe Rufin (eds.), *Économie des guerres civiles* (Paris: Hachette, 1996), pp. 543–589 at
p. 568 n. 2.
[61] Fabrice Weissman, *L'aide humanitaire dans la dynamique du conflit libérien* (Paris: Fonda-
tion Médecins sans Frontières, May 1996), p. 45.
[62] *Conspicuous Destruction: War, Famine, and the Reform Process in Mozambique* (Africa Watch,
1992) as cited in Jean, "Aide humanitaire et économie de guerre," p. 570.

warehouse rental and vehicle hire also generate revenue for local contractors, companies, and individual merchants and feed into systems of patronage.

The principal impact of humanitarian assistance on the economy of war at the meso and micro levels occurs through the pillage, diversion, and extortion of aid supplies by local authorities, militias, bandits, and merchants. At the simplest level, direct theft of food and nonfood items before, during, and after distribution is common during times of conflict. Food and medical supplies can be used by combatants or sold locally or in a neighboring country. Woodward says that more than half of all aid in the former Yugoslavia supported the war effort because it was diverted to feeding and supplying soldiers,[63] and much of the food and medical supplies looted in Somalia was sold across the border in Kenya.

Vehicles and equipment belonging to aid organizations are valuable commodities. In 1994, aid organizations in Liberia had more than $5 million worth of materials stolen during interfactional clashes, including 74 vehicles, 27 trucks, 18 motorcycles, communication equipment, computers, and thousands of tons of food.[64] This was surpassed in 1996 by the loss of $20 million in equipment during clashes in Monrovia.[65] Aid organizations curtailed their operations after each incident, and several debated stopping assistance to the country when aid supplies so blatantly reinforced the operational capacity of the warring factions.[66]

Other methods used to divert aid supplies include demanding payment as a condition of access and inflating beneficiary numbers. Charles Taylor demanded 15 percent of all aid entering the territory he controlled in Liberia in 1995, to be paid in cash or in kind. In the zone controlled by the regional peacekeeping force ECOMOG (Economic Community of West Africa Monitoring Group), the numbers of displaced persons was exaggerated by the local authority responsible for registration, the Liberian Refugee Repatriation and Resettlement Commission. The World Food Programme (WFP) and Catholic Relief Services (CRS) distributed food in camps around Buchanan for 200,000 persons although the epidemiological information collected by the medical organizations suggested that no more than 130,000 resided in the camps. Empty trucks were in evidence at

[63] Woodward, *Balkan Tragedy*, p. 319.
[64] Weissman, *L'aide humanitaire dans la dynamique du conflit libérien*, p. 48.
[65] Atkinson, *The War Economy in Liberia*, p. 21.
[66] See, for example, Jean-Daniel Tauxe, "Libéria, la logistique humanitaire en question," *Revue Internationale de la Croix Rouge* 819 (May–June 1996): 379–381.

the outskirts of the camps during each distribution, waiting to collect the excess food and resell it in Monrovia.[67] Furthermore, a food-basket monitoring survey undertaken by MSF in 1995 found that the displaced did not receive the ration to which they were entitled, but on average 20 percent less. Fabrice Weissman estimated that up to 60 percent of aid was diverted in the camps of Buchanan.[68]

The banditry in Somalia took the diversion of food aid to unprecedented levels. Not only were beneficiary numbers inflated by local factions or authorities, but fictitious villages were registered for distribution. According to Alex de Waal, false committees were also formed to represent real villages and divert the food, and real villages were coerced into signing for receipt of aid that did not arrive or did so only partially.[69] Estimates of the quantity of food stolen in Somalia vary from 20 to 80 percent: most Somali Red Crescent staff interviewed by de Waal believed that half of the food distributed by the Red Cross was looted, diverted, or extorted.[70]

In spite of the increased attention in the literature to the implication of aid in the dynamics of conflict, aid organizations and donors rarely attempt to quantify the contribution of aid to the war economy. A guide to evaluating humanitarian assistance produced by the Organisation for Economic Co-operation and Development (OECD) in 1999 notes that "reliable empirical evidence of the degree to which humanitarian assistance is diverted is often lacking even though such knowledge may be fundamental to understanding the impact of the assistance provided either on the intended target group or in potentially providing warring factions with additional resources."[71]

In fact some evaluations ignore the broader impact of the war economy altogether. The Dutch government's relatively detailed evaluation of its $42 million of aid to Somalia between 1991 and 1993, for example, specifically addresses the side effects of the aid delivered through various UN agencies, NGOs, and ICRC, yet concludes that the largest negative side effect was "the slow return to food production because relief supplies had

[67] Personal observations in 1995.

[68] Weissman, *L'aide humanitaire dans la dynamique du conflit libérien*, p. 71.

[69] Alex de Waal, "Dangerous Precedents? Famine Relief in Somalia 1991–93," in Joanna Macrae and Anthony Zwi (eds.), *War and Hunger: Rethinking International Responses to Complex Emergencies* (London: Zed Books in association with Save the Children Fund [U.K.], 1994), pp. 139–159 at p. 146.

[70] Ibid.

[71] *Guidance for Evaluating Humanitarian Assistance in Complex Emergencies* (Paris: Development Assistance Committee, Organisation for Economic Co-operation and Development, 1999), p. 8.

flooded the market."[72] Although security payments made to factions are mentioned, the wider repercussions of this were excluded from the assessment of the effectiveness and efficiency of the aid provided.

Considering the amount of aid money and supplies that directly contributed to the arsenal of warring factions in Liberia and Somalia, aid organizations are understandably reluctant to publicize such information. Not only might it jeopardize the "good" image of aid among individual donors, but it fuels arguments against giving aid or in favor of military intervention. Claims of 80 percent losses in food aid in Somalia by senior officials of the UN and CARE were a major influence in the U.S. decision to intervene militarily. The intervention occurred several months after the peak of deaths, and, at a cost to the United States alone of over $1.5 billion,[73] saved between 10,000 and 25,000 lives. Aid organizations were estimated to have saved some 90,000 lives prior to December 1992,[74] yet the failings of the aid organizations are still invoked to justify the intervention. According to Michael Kelly:

> The point being made in relation to the NGO effort prior to the UNITAF [Unified Task Force] deployment is that, without military intervention, relief efforts in Somalia were not effective enough. In many ways they were counterproductive. . . . The military intervention was justified, necessary and extremely successful in reducing and preventing excess mortality from famine, war and genocide. The debate over where the military intervention went wrong goes to matters beyond this fundamental core of the mission.[75]

Yet notwithstanding the ways opponents of aid use information about the impact of assistance on war economies, quantitative evaluations are essential if aid organizations are to minimize their negative effects. Whether it is of direct military benefit to combatants or contributes indirectly

---

[72] *Humanitarian Aid to Somalia: Evaluation Report 1994* (The Hague: Operations Review Unit, Ministry of Foreign Affairs, Netherlands, 1994), p. 302.

[73] The United States spent $1.5 billion on military intervention, as opposed to $311 million on humanitarian assistance, and $470 million on UN contributions (paid and unpaid) between April 1992 and July 1994. The incremental costs of Operation Restore Hope were estimated at $1.97 billion in Defense Department spending and assessments for subsequent UN military efforts. Sommer, *Hope Restored?* p. 72 and appendix C5.

[74] Refugee Policy Group estimated that some 50,000 lives were saved between 1991 and August 1992; 40,000 were saved between September and December 1992; and 10,000–25,000 from December to March 1993. Steven Hansch et al., *Lives Lost, Lives Saved: Excess Mortality and the Impact of Health Interventions in the Somalia Emergency* (Washington, D.C.: Refugee Policy Group, 1994), pp. 28–32.

[75] Michael Kelly, *Peace Operations: Tackling the Military Legal and Policy Challenges* (Canberra: Australian Government Publishing Service, 1997), paras. 722–723.

through its fungibility in releasing resources for military use, humanitarian aid has the potential to fuel conflict.

LEGITIMACY

Humanitarian action, through its media appeal and the services it brings, can bestow legitimacy on individuals, organizations, rebel movements, and governing regimes, from the local village level to the international arena. While much of the legitimacy thus conferred may pass unnoticed by the aid organizations and be genuinely unintended, governments and rebels have long been aware of the political credibility that accompanies aid. The Biafran leadership, for example, exploited the legitimizing qualities of humanitarian action during the Nigerian Civil War (Box 3).

Box 3: Humanitarian Action and Legitimacy in Biafra

The Nigerian Civil War (1967–70) provides one of the most insidious examples of the manipulation of suffering and humanitarian action to gain international legitimacy. In May 1967, Colonel Emeka Odumegwu Ojukwu, governor of the oil-rich province of Biafra, declared independence, provoking a secessionist war with Nigerian government forces. The Nigerian government imposed a blockade of the territory, effectively employing starvation as a weapon of war given Biafra's inadequate productive capacities. Widespread famine resulted. By the time that news was broadcast internationally in mid-1968 in what was the world's first televised famine, the federal forces had defeated the secessionists militarily. But by using the famine to mobilize international public opinion in Biafra's favor, Ojukwu continued the struggle for independence and engaged humanitarian action as a key player.

International opinion was important to both sides of the conflict. The federal government invited international observer teams to Nigeria to inspect the conduct of the war, eased enforcement of the blockade on relief supplies following international pressure, and sought international reinforcement of its claims by insisting that relief organizations recognize Nigeria's sovereignty over Biafra and submit relief flights to inspection in federal territory before entering Biafra. For the Biafran leadership, however, international opinion constituted the key to its primary objective, sovereign independence, and was "assiduously courted."[a] While using the plight of his people to gain international sympathy and attention, Ojukwu hindered efforts to bring relief to Biafra. Not only was it in his interests to keep the starvation issue alive, but he preferred to receive arms and politically supportive assistance rather than just humanitarian relief.

Aid organizations devised complicated programs of relief delivery to circumvent the prohibitions of the federal government and the Biafran leadership. Ojukwu refused a federal proposal to establish a relief corridor through the blockade, arguing that this might weaken Biafra's claim to sovereign status and would facilitate Nigerian attacks once roads and bridges were repaired; he also said that the Nigerians might poison the food.[b] Thus all supplies had to be airlifted in and landed at night since the federal authorities did not grant approval. Concerned that the flights provided cover for arms shipments, the aid organizations requested different landing times, but the Biafran leadership refused. Moreover, the Biafrans imposed charges for landing rights for relief flights and local supplies and services, which constituted a major source of the secessionists' foreign exchange: $3.5 million according to one official.[c]

Ojukwu's intransigence increased with the extent of external support. Aid organizations and activists flew to the defense of the Biafran cause, accusing the Nigerian government of genocide, although 7 million Ibo people lived without persecution in government-held regions. At the height of the famine, which claimed over 1 million victims, Ojukwu chose to print new legal tender and stamps while aid organizations struggled to save starving civilians. He appeared on television stating "in the long term we have achieved quite a lot. No matter what one says, indeed, if the 14 million people, Biafrans, are killed, the notion of Biafra will persist until the end of time. That is an achievement."[d] His flight to the Ivory Coast in January 1970 put an end to the fighting.

---

[a] Alvin Edgell, "Nigeria/Biafra," in Morris Davis (ed.), *Civil Wars and the Politics of International Relief: Africa, South Asia, and the Caribbean* (New York: Praeger, 1975), pp. 50–73 at p. 53.
[b] Ibid.
[c] John de St. Jorre, *The Nigerian Civil War* (London: Hodder and Stoughton, 1972), p. 250, as cited in ibid., p. 68.
[d] As cited in *La pitié dangereuse*, a French documentary by Rony Brauman and François Margolin, Arte, June 1996.

The reluctance of the United States to recognize the Bolshevik regime in 1921 similarly delayed decisions to provide aid in spite of the catastrophic famine that threatened 40 million lives. Lenin overcame his initial unwillingness to request external assistance and issued an appeal in July 1921 amid reports of mass starvation, cannibalism, and the sale of human flesh. In contrast to the European aid organized by the Norwegian explorer Fridtjof Nansen, the United States attached conditions to minimize the support its aid would lend to the Bolsheviks and the Red Army.[76] Nevertheless, the famine relief bolstered the regime, enabling Russia to resume exporting cereals in 1922, while "disloyal" areas like the Ukraine were still affected by famine. Alain Destexhe argues that Western aid not only permitted the Soviet regime to survive the most difficult point of its brief history, but it "opened the way for the resumption of commercial and diplomatic exchanges with the West, which had always been the principal objective"[77] of the Soviet regime.

Local and international legitimacy and recognition are important objectives of any political movement, whether it holds power or is contesting the authority of a governing regime. Humanitarian action can legitimize movements and individuals in several ways. First, negotiations with faction leaders and local commanders that aid organizations undertake to gain access and security guarantees implicitly recognize those groups' authority over a territory or population. The need to gain the consent of local commanders for aid shipments entering regions of the former Yugoslavia, for example, reinforced the authority of the faction over that territory. Woodward says that the Bosnian Serbs had few other sources of legitimacy, having been branded as aggressors by the international community.[78] The recognition of military leaders is magnified if the international media are present. When U.S. Special Envoy to Somalia Robert Oakley shook hands with Mohammed Farah Aided and Ali Mahdi in front of the international press, he accorded them recognition as the legitimate representatives of the Somali people. In doing so, Oakley undid months of thoughtful negotiation by the former representative of the UN Secretary-General, Mohamed Sahnoun, who was promoting traditional elders and grassroots associations as alternative sources of authority.[79]

Second, by participating in relief activities, individuals and political movements can gain local and international kudos. Gayle Smith says that in the Horn of Africa, liberation movements gained international status "not because their claims or demands have been accepted, but because they became active players in international relief operations."[80] Local lead-

---

[76] See Alain Destexhe, *L'humanitaire impossible, ou Deux siècles d'ambiguïté* (Paris: Armand Colin, 1993), pp. 40–46, for a more detailed discussion of aid to Russia at this time.

[77] Ibid., p. 45.

[78] Woodward, *Balkan Tragedy*, p. 319.

[79] See Mohamed Sahnoun, *Somalia: The Missed Opportunities* (Washington, D.C.: United States Institute of Peace Press, 1994), p. 40.

[80] Gayle E. Smith, "Relief Operations and Military Strategy," in Thomas G. Weiss and Larry Minear (eds.), *Humanitarianism across Borders: Sustaining Civilians in Times of War* (Boulder, Colo.: Lynne Rienner, 1993), pp. 97–116 at p. 108.

ers can claim credit for attracting a health center, water supply, or food to an area, and may direct aid toward supporters and away from opponents to consolidate political power. Channeling food through the "humanitarian branch" of a rebel faction helps to legitimize the force.

Third, the presence of an international organization in itself can accord legitimacy to a faction or regime, whether it publicly comments on humanitarian concerns or remains discreet. One party to justify its own acts, for example, can exploit public denunciations of the actions of an opposing party: labeling "victims" creates "perpetrators." But remaining silent about atrocities and abusive policies can also lend countenance to them: as organizations professing to uphold certain principles of humanity, international aid agencies just by their presence and participation can be a strong propaganda tool in the service of governments or insurgents. This is particularly true of ICRC, whose mandate, reputation, and discretion imbue its presence with a particularly affirming quality. ICRC often confronts contexts in which it must weigh the legitimacy its presence bestows upon a regime or faction against the benefits it can bring to individuals in needs of protection and assistance. David Forsythe discusses the compromise that ICRC made in South Africa between 1969 and 1987, where it was granted access to prisoners like Nelson Mandela, who were serving sentences, but not to those under interrogation and awaiting trial.[81] Noting that prisoners are usually subjected to worse treatment in military or police detention facilities immediately after arrest than when transferred to the normal penal system, Forsythe points out that ICRC was unable to visit those at the highest risk of mistreatment. Yet the organization's presence in South Africa accorded the government some respectability, implying that the regime cooperated with international inspection. Mandela remarked in his autobiography that the prison authorities respected and feared ICRC because "avoiding international condemnation was the authorities' principal goal."[82] In 1987 ICRC withdrew from South Africa, considering that the limitations imposed on its actions outweighed the benefits of remaining. But as Forsythe says, "that took a quarter of a century, during which time the government was allowed both to claim cooperation with the ICRC and to torture and mistreat prisoners, sometimes fatally—as in the case of Steve Biko."[83]

The fourth way in which humanitarian action bestows legitimacy on, and potentially sustains, a state or local authority is by fulfilling the social obligations normally required of a regime toward its citizens. This prob-

[81] Forsythe, "Choices More Ethical Than Legal," pp. 139–140.
[82] Nelson Mandela, *Long Walk to Freedom* (London: Little, Brown, 1994), p. 396.
[83] Forsythe, "Choices More Ethical Than Legal," p. 139.

lem was recognized at the birth of humanitarian action: Florence Nightingale disagreed with Henri Dunant's proposal to create a civilian medical service, arguing that it would relieve states from part of the burden of going to war.[84] Walzer explains the importance of the social contract: "The moral standing of any particular state depends upon the reality of the common life it protects and the extent to which the sacrifices required by that protection are willingly accepted and thought worthwhile. If no common life exists, or if the state doesn't protect the common life that does exist, its own defense may have no moral justification."[85]

The increasing "internationalisation of public welfare," in the words of Mark Duffield,[86] has seen a transfer of "state" responsibilities for the welfare of citizens to the international community, particularly to NGOs. Not only does this process have repercussions for postemergency state building, but by fulfilling such responsibilities, humanitarian action potentially allays local dissent that might otherwise challenge the legitimacy of the local power. It is not unreasonable to suggest that without the presence of NGOs in Afghanistan to meet the basic needs of the population in Kabul and the south, for example, the Taliban might have faced earlier opposition to their rule when the populations under their control, particularly widows and children of "martyred" warriors, were not cared for.

The legitimacy that humanitarian action can inadvertently bestow upon warriors or local officials is in many respects the negative side of the popular development notion of "empowerment." Authors like Mary Anderson advocate empowering local players during emergency relief operations and criticize the contemporary relief system for making aid recipients "passive dependents on the competence of outsiders" by relying upon external aid providers to establish, manage, and control the emergency response.[87] Although she recognizes the bestowal of legitimacy on warriors as a negative consequence of aid in her later work *Do No Harm*,[88] she overlooks the subjectivity inherent in labeling one action "empowerment" and the other "legitimacy." Calls for local empowerment assume that aid or-

[84] Dunant's proposal threatened to undermine the efforts of Nightingale to improve British Army medical services after her return from the Crimea. After reading his book, *A Memory of Solferino*, she wrote to him expressing her opposition to the establishment of a volunteer corps. See Caroline Moorehead, *Dunant's Dream: War, Switzerland, and the History of the Red Cross* (London: HarperCollins, 1998), pp. 29–32.

[85] Walzer, *Just and Unjust Wars*, p. 54.

[86] Mark Duffield, "The Political Economy of Internal War: Asset Transfer, Complex Emergencies and International Aid," in Macrae and Zwi (eds.), *War and Hunger*, pp. 50–69 at p. 57.

[87] Mary B. Anderson, "Development and the Prevention of Humanitarian Emergencies," in Weiss and Minear (eds.), *Humanitarianism across Borders*, pp. 23–38 at p. 30.

[88] Anderson, *Do No Harm*, pp. 50–53.

ganizations arriving at the scene of a crisis have the capacity and right to judge who merits legitimacy and power and who does not.

Legitimacy and the next paradox of humanitarian action to be examined, population control, are two sides of the same coin. The possession of legitimacy of authority is an important aspect in gaining influence and control of civilian populations, and having control and influence over civilian populations is an important aspect of gaining legitimacy.

POPULATION CONTROL

The control of populations and territory is a key objective of conflict, and food has been used as a weapon of war for thousands of years. Just as destroying food supplies in a region will force the occupants to move, so providing or denying humanitarian relief can control the movement of civilian populations. The converse is also true: detaining a malnourished population in a particular location attracts humanitarian assistance to that locale, which may serve strategic, political, or economic objectives. Charles Taylor's demand of 15 percent of aid supplies entering his territory in Liberia, for example, came after he invited NGOs to witness the malnutrition among segments of the population under his control. Aid organizations had stayed out of his territory since the massive theft of aid supplies the year before. Another Liberian faction, the Kromah branch of the United Liberation Movement for Democracy in Liberia, also used this tactic in July 1996, detaining 350 civilians without food in a camp thirty kilometers from Monrovia to attract humanitarian assistance to the region.[89]

The use of humanitarian assistance as a lure was illustrated starkly in Ethiopia during the devastating famine of 1983–85 (Box 4), where food distribution sites became traps at the service of the Ethiopian government. Aid also influenced population movements in the former Yugoslavia, where forced migration was an essential feature of the war. While less a tool of population control per se there than in Ethiopia, the provision of humanitarian aid to towns encouraged the occupants to stay, while depriving them of aid forced the occupants to leave. Aid organizations faced a quandary: whether to assist the residents to remain, thereby risking their physical safety, or to assist them to leave, thereby aiding the policy of ethnic expulsion. One MSF report noted: "In Bosnia, forced population displacements are not simply the consequence of war, they are its main purpose, and the relief organizations are not only reduced to impotence by

---

[89] *Civilians Trapped in Hunger Camp: Abuse of Humanitarian Aid by Liberian Warlords Must Stop*, press release, Médecins sans Frontières, Monrovia and Brussels, 10 July 1996.

this strategy of terror, they are actually trapped into becoming its unwilling accomplices, as they sometimes endeavour to evacuate those whose lives are most at risk."[90]

Aid organizations were divided over the best strategy to pursue with regard to the evacuation of civilians. According to Kathleen Newland, UN-HCR was reluctant to evacuate any but sick or injured civilians from conflict zones to avoid forwarding the racial objectives of the belligerents; it advocated bringing safety to people rather than taking people to safety.[91] ICRC, by contrast, argued that this was a secondary concern to saving lives. Neither position was without repercussions: ICRC was accused of having participated in the Bosnian authorities' ethnic expulsions,[92] and the UN safe areas gave a false sense of security, shattered by the fall of Srebrenica and the murder of over 7,000 of the town's residents.

Box 4: Famine and Population Control in Northern Ethiopia

The principal causes of the devastating famine in northern Ethiopia in 1983–85, contrary to the views prevailing at the time, were the counterinsurgency campaign of the Ethiopian army and air force directed against opponents of the government of Colonel Mengistu Haile Mariam, and the disastrous economic policies of Mengistu's regime. Famine was a weapon of war; drought, harvest failure, and unsound government agricultural policies were secondary causes.[a] Although the regime was initially reluctant to allow Western aid organizations and media into the country, it changed its position as it began to turn the international humanitarian action to its economic, diplomatic, and military advantage. Relief was thoroughly manipulated, denied to areas not held by the government, and used as a weapon to control populations in the north.

Relief supplies and equipment became particularly effective tools in the government resettlement plan. Ostensibly designed to relocate northerners away from the "famine-prone" region for their benefit, the plan served to deprive the opposition movements of a base of local support and to advance the government policy of collectivization. Humanitarian aid and equipment was used to orchestrate these goals. Food distribution centers became traps, attracting populations to a central location at which many were forcibly recruited into the army or signed up for transfer to the south in accordance with quotas set by Addis Ababa.[b] Aid was the bait, and the presence of international

---

[90] François Jean (ed.), *Populations in Danger 1995: A Médecins sans Frontières Report* (London: La Découverte, 1995), p. 80.

[91] Kathleen Newland, "Ethnic Conflict and Refugees," *Survival* 35, no. 1 (1993): 81–101 at p. 98.

[92] Maillard, "Nous sommes arrivés aux limites du tenable," p. 16.

NGOs gave the program an element of legitimacy and security; some NGOs and UN agencies even assisted in the deportation process, espousing the government rationale about preventing future famines. To facilitate the deportations the government requisitioned trucks and cash meant for famine relief in the north, and food was withheld from those who refused to leave. Jason Clay noted that "in some camps the Ethiopian government did not allow children to receive food from Western agencies until their parents agreed to be resettled. MSF eventually left Ethiopia after an estimated 6,000 children died in a camp where they had adequate materials for assistance but were not allowed to distribute them because, according to government officials, a sufficient number of adults had not agreed to be resettled."[c]

The people were transported in deplorable conditions to the south. No effort was made to keep families, villages, or ethnic groups together. Many died en route. Almost all destination villages lacked infrastructure, and the new arrivals were required to clear land and construct their shelter. Due to the lack of health care and sanitation, tropical disease inflicted a high toll on the weakened population. A USAID survey in two sites in Pawe found mortality rates to be 7–15 deaths per 10,000 people per day from illness and malnutrition, and subsequent data indicated that between October 1985 and January 1986, nearly one quarter of the 85,000 people in Pawe died.[d] The aid agency Concern recorded a similar statistic for other sites and estimated that 100,000 of the 500,000 people transferred had died.[e] Many other settlers fled to Sudan as refugees. Clay suggests that resettlement may have been the single most important cause of mortality in Ethiopia in 1985.[f]

---

[a] Alex de Waal, *Famine Crimes: Politics and the Disaster Relief Industry in Africa* (Oxford and Bloomington: African Rights and the International Africa Institute in association with James Currey and Indiana University Press, 1997), p. 115.

[b] François Jean, *Ethiopie: Du bon usage de la famine* (Paris: Médecins sans Frontières, 1986), p. 57. Also see Rony Brauman, foreword to Médecins sans Frontières, *World in Crisis: The Politics of Survival at the End of the Twentieth Century* (London: Routledge, 1997), pp. xix–xxvi at p. xxiii.

[c] Jason Clay, "Ethiopian Famine and the Relief Agencies," in Bruce Nichols and Gil Loescher (eds.), *The Moral Nation: Humanitarianism and U.S. Foreign Policy Today* (Notre Dame: University of Notre Dame Press, 1989), pp. 232–277 at p. 264.

[d] As documented in Jean, *Ethiopie: Du bon usage de la famine*, p. 73. A crude mortality rate of above one death per 10,000 people per day is considered to be an "emergency."

[e] The results of the population transfers remain controversial, with some aid officials, particularly Kurt Jansson, former director of the UN Office for the Emergency Operations in Ethiopia, refuting the mortality figures and discrediting the agencies that produced or cited them. Kurt Jansson, Michael Harris, and Angela Penrose, *The Ethiopian Famine* (London: Zed Books, 1990), pp. 24–26.

[f] Clay, "Ethiopian Famine and the Relief Agencies," p. 262. See pp. 271–273 n. 13 for a discussion of how mortality figures were estimated.

Humanitarian assistance can be most effectively used as a tool of control when the civilian population is dependent upon it, as is often the case in refugee camps. The transfer of goods and principles of reciprocity bind refugees in relationships of power that increase in strength with the proximity of the assistance to its intended recipients. "The ultimate authority in the chain of distribution lies with the person, whether foreign aid worker or refugee, who performs the penultimate act in the chain of handlers, 'tipping' the grain into the sack of the kneeling beneficiary."[93] Aid becomes an important tool of control; reducing or withholding food and other rations pressures refugees to conform to the wishes of the aid distributors.

Textbook prescriptions of refugee camp management stress that "the level of refugee participation will determine the success or failure of a project."[94] Refugees are encouraged to elect or appoint representatives to speak on their behalf, and competition for such a role can be fierce. The social hierarchy can change in refugee camps as humanitarian aid becomes a source of patronage and refugees with a Western education are sought to advise and work with aid organizations. Eftihia Voutira and Barbara Harrell-Bond state that there is rarely a sense of political solidarity among refugee populations despite the apparent commonality of their experience in the country of origin.[95] The refugees are often highly factionalized, and control of the aid distribution channels can be essential in securing support for one faction over another. Information networks such as radio broadcasts, newspapers, and community meetings are also avenues through which to disseminate messages and propaganda, and the curricula at schools can indoctrinate the younger generation with a particular version of history and events.[96] Refugee camps also provide an environment conducive to recruiting combatants. In January 2000, Tanzanian officials reported that Burundian rebels were recruiting refugees from five camps in western Tanzania and slipping them out of the country for military training.[97]

[93] Eftihia Voutira and Barbara E. Harrell-Bond, "In Search of the Locus of Trust: The Social World of the Refugee Camp," in E. Valentine Daniel and John Chr. Knudsen (eds.), *Mistrusting Refugees* (Berkeley: University of California Press, 1995), pp. 207–224 at p. 211.

[94] Médecins sans Frontières, *Refugee Health: An Approach to Emergency Situations* (London: Macmillan, 1997), p. 31.

[95] Voutira and Harrell-Bond, "In Search of the Locus of Trust," p. 218.

[96] Liisa Malkki conducted an excellent study of the way that Hutu refugees from Burundi living in camps in Tanzania constructed and reconstructed their history as a "people." Malkki, *Purity and Exile: Violence, Memory, and National Cosmology among Hutu Refugees in Tanzania* (Chicago: University of Chicago Press, 1995).

[97] Rodrique Ngowi, "Burundi Rebels Recruiting Refugees," Associated Press, 19 January 2000.

Finally, some donor governments actively use humanitarian action to influence a population. The U.S. Food for Peace Program was created not to reduce hunger but to increase U.S. influence abroad and reduce U.S. agricultural subsidies,[98] and donors and host governments sometimes use aid to encourage refugee repatriation. Food rations are reduced, camp closure threatened, and assistance packages offered as incentives to stimulate refugees to return to their country of origin.

Recent Measures to Enhance Accountability

The conspicuously negative consequences of humanitarian action in the Rwandan refugee camps, and to a lesser extent in Bosnia and Somalia, provoked a backlash against aid agencies. Fearing a loss of the public confidence on which fundraising heavily depends, a group of established aid organizations launched initiatives aimed at increasing their accountability to the people in whose name they intervene (or at least at appearing to do so). The initiatives aim to promote ethical and technical standards in relief efforts and to develop a mechanism through which "beneficiaries" can express criticisms and complaints. Codes of conduct and a Humanitarian Charter deal with the ethical standards; the Sphere Project for Minimum Standards in Disaster Response addresses technical benchmarks for assistance; and the Humanitarian Ombudsman Project (recently renamed the Humanitarian Accountability Project) aims to be a voice of "clients, beneficiaries, and claimants" of humanitarian assistance.

While these initiatives have undoubtedly raised awareness in the humanitarian community of the need for competent staff and appropriate resources when responding to life-threatening situations, they have several serious shortcomings. I have already discussed some of the difficulties involved in promoting a common set of ethical principles within the diverse aid community; here I briefly raise some concerns regarding the other two initiatives.

The first and most serious shortcoming of the Sphere and Ombudsman projects is that they do not address the problems they claim to address; rather, they obscure the real problems and their sources. According to Nicholas Stockton, chair of the interagency group that presided over its development, the Sphere Project was launched in response to

[98] Smith, "Relief Operations and Military Strategy," p. 99.

three crises in the humanitarian domain, in protection, in the quality of humanitarian space, and in resources, necessitating a new search for legitimacy by aid agencies.[99] Yet each of these "crises" is framed in a purely technocratic manner. The Sphere guidelines do not refer to the legal or physical protection of civilians, but misleadingly equate the right to a certain level of technical assistance with protection. Stockton claims that the "articulation of food, water, sanitation, health and shelter, defined as rights founded in international legal norms rather than negotiable relief needs, does speak directly to certain essential qualities that a protective environment should fulfill, and without which civil and political freedoms would be merely academic."[100] But pretending that the fulfillment of biological needs is a form of protection is dangerous. In Liberia and Somalia, combatants forcibly seized relief items from civilians after distribution; in the Democratic Republic of Congo, rebel forces followed aid vehicles at a distance and slaughtered refugees who emerged from hiding to receive aid. The victims of these attacks first required not civil and political freedoms but physical safety. Humanitarian action in these cases not only failed to ensure but actually jeopardized their safety.

The deterioration in the quality of "humanitarian space" to which Stockton refers is also conceived of in a purely technical sense. The proliferation of well-meaning but underqualified NGOs has resulted in negligence and harmful practices, which the Sphere Project aims to rectify by setting technical benchmarks. But even if we put aside the fact that technical guidelines (from Oxfam, MSF, ICRC, UNICEF, and UNHCR) were widely circulated before the advent of Sphere, the idea that the quality of humanitarian space can be measured in technical terms neglects crucial issues such as the conditions of access negotiated with combatants and the relationship between combatants and civilians in areas where aid agencies are working. The achievement of technical standards risks becoming an objective in itself. Sphere ignores the importance of evaluating the overall impact of aid: technical standards may be perfectly achieved, but they are counterproductive if they work against rather than for the victims.

In the search for increased legitimacy for aid agencies, Sphere reduces

[99] Nicholas Stockton, *Performance Standards and Accountability in Realising Rights: The Humanitarian Case,* paper presented at the Overseas Development Institute, London, 17 March 1999, http://www.odi.org.uk/speeches/sumstockton.html.
[100] Ibid.

humanitarian action to its technical components for the sake of "proving" efficiency to donors, thereby demeaning the ideas on which humanitarian action is based. Moreover, Sphere, the codes of conduct, and the Ombudsman Project hand over means of control to the very powers from which aid agencies should strive for independence. Many donor governments have made adherence to these initiatives a prerequisite for funding. In the current climate, where the UN and donors increasingly bind humanitarian aid to peace and other political processes, it is not unreasonable to envisage the use of these standards as a way to marginalize aid organizations whose views do not conform to the prevailing discourse. The Ombudsman Project has taken this risk one step further by accepting $800,000, almost half its budget of $1,860,416 for field trials, from the department for international development of the British government.[101]

The Ombudsman Project faces a similar distortion in the problems and solutions it professes to address. The most obvious begins with the very language it uses. The term "beneficiary" implies that aid is of benefit, even though the project itself was conceived in recognition of the fact that this might not always be so. Even more problematic are the references to "clients," which depict humanitarian action as a commercial enterprise that can be judged according to market forces. The "clients" to which this initiative refers, however, are not consumers but victims of abuse that has left them powerless to meet their own needs. To imagine that they will organize of their own volition to oppose the people who came to assist them is not only utopian, it ignores the real source of their distress. It is not the aid agencies which overlook the dietary preferences of victims that pose the greatest constraints on effective relief, but local power-holders who in most cases cause the suffering. A more likely scenario is that those in control will use the Ombudsman mechanism to oppose aid agencies that do not act in their interests—increasing the pressure on victims in the process.

Placing the onus on victims to identify the problems of humanitarian action shifts responsibility away from aid agencies; it does not make them more responsible for their actions. As the following chapters show, the most serious challenges that face humanitarian groups in alleviating the suffering of victims are not technical but political: How does one assist vic-

---

[101] *Humanitarian Ombudsman Project Meeting: Outcome and Next Steps*, Geneva, 16 March 2000, http://www.oneworld.org/ombudsman/outcome-en.html.

tims without strengthening their oppressors? Signing on to codes of conduct, technical guidelines, or the Ombudsman initiative gives an illusion of enhanced responsibility. Just as it is not always possible to achieve minimum standards of relief assistance, so the attainment of minimum standards does not guarantee that aid is humanitarian.

2

The Afghan Refugee Camps in Pakistan

Pakistan was one of the most generous and compliant asylum
states of the 1980s. After the Soviet invasion of Afghanistan in
1979 and during the ten years of Soviet occupation, Pakistan
hosted over three million Afghan refugees and resistance fighters. The
Afghan refugee camps, situated close to the Afghan border, served a
dual purpose as a refuge for victims of conflict and as a sanctuary in
which *mujahideen* ("Warriors in the Way of God") could rest, recuperate, and recruit new combatants. Zolberg, Suhrke, and Aguayo dubbed
the Afghans in Pakistan "the world's most effective refugee-warrior
community."[1]

One of the striking features of this case is that aid organizations recognized aspects of the dual role of the camps, yet there was little debate concerning the ethical issues this raised or the implications for the safety of
the refugees. Instead the aid community, journalists, and academics alike
exhibited broad tolerance of the ambiguous camp functions.[2]

Pakistan as a Military Sanctuary

The Afghan resistance movement of the mujahideen had all the necessary
criteria for an armed insurgency. A loyal support base inside Afghanistan
provided food, shelter, information, and recruits to the resistance; the terrain of Afghanistan favored guerrilla warfare; ideological unity in Islam in-

---

[1] Aristide R. Zolberg, Astri Suhrke, and Sergio Aguayo, *Escape from Violence: Conflict and the Refugee Crisis in the Developing World* (New York: Oxford University Press, 1989), p. 254.

[2] The unquestioned acceptance of the politicization of humanitarian aid is well shown by its absence from the agenda and from discussion at an international symposium held in 1987 on the domestic and foreign implications of the Afghan refugee crisis. The symposium at-tracted some 180 participants from twenty countries who were directly and indirectly in-volved in the refugee issue. See "The Crisis of Migration from Afghanistan: Domestic and Foreign Implications," Summary of the Proceedings of an International Symposium, co-sponsored by the Refugee Studies Programme and the Department of Ethnology and Prehis-tory at Oxford University, 29 March to 2 April 1987, Oxford.

spired the ultimate dedication of combatants;[3] external patrons financed and promoted the cause internationally; and neighboring countries provided sanctuaries to which the guerrillas could withdraw and resupply.[4] While Iran gave refuge and backing to Shi'ite resistance groups during the Soviet occupation of Afghanistan,[5] it was Pakistan that comprehensively filled the role of sanctuary to the mujahideen.

Pakistan harbored exiled opponents to regimes in Kabul several years before the Soviet invasion of Afghanistan. In 1973 a coup d'état led by Prince Mohammad Daoud, a secular Pashtun nationalist, provoked militant Islamists to exile themselves in Pakistan where they received training from the Pakistani military. Among these Islamists were two men who were to play an increasingly important role in Afghan resistance: Ahmad Shah Massoud and Gulbuddin Hekmatyar. Using Pakistan as a base, they began organizing clandestine missions into Afghanistan in mid-1975 and tried to incite the people into a popular rebellion against the government. Only in the northeast, however, was there local support, and the uprising failed, resulting in the capture, imprisonment, execution, or disappearance of hundreds of militant Islamists and intellectuals. Important lessons for future insurgencies were gleaned during this period, including the necessity of involving traditional leadership ('ulama) in the campaigns, increasing contacts with the rural population, and gaining the support of the army.[6] The surviving militant leadership established offices in Peshawar, the capital of Northwest Frontier Province (NWFP), which borders Afghanistan (see Map 1). There they divided into two opposing groups: one moderate Is-

[3] For a detailed discussion of the history, ideology, and politics of Islam in Afghanistan see Asta Olesen, *Islam and Politics in Afghanistan* (Richmond, U.K.: Curzon, 1995).

[4] Mohammad Yousaf and Mark Adkin, *The Bear Trap: Afghanistan's Untold Story* (London: Leo Cooper, 1992), p. 64.

[5] Iran was also host to more than 2 million refugees. Although Iran helped to establish and finance four Shi'ite resistance groups which operated primarily in the western and central regions of Afghanistan, Anwar-ul-Haq Ahady suggests that Iran played a minor role in the Afghan conflict for two reasons. First, the Iran-Iraq war erupted within a year of the Soviet invasion, and Iran did not want to provoke Soviet involvement on Iraq's side. Second, radical clerics had just gained power in Iran and concentrated on strengthening the Shi'ite cause rather than on the anti-Soviet struggle in Afghanistan. Anwar-ul-Haq Ahady, "Saudi Arabia, Iran, and the Conflict in Afghanistan," in William Maley (ed.), *Fundamentalism Reborn? Afghanistan and the Taliban* (London: Hurst, 1998), pp. 117–134 at p. 119. John Merriam also notes that Soviet bombing of villages inside Iran in 1980 probably dissuaded Iran from actively providing sanctuary to the Afghan resistance. See Merriam, "Arms Shipments to the Afghan Resistance," in G. M. Farr and John G. Merriam (eds.), *Afghan Resistance: The Politics of Survival* (Boulder, Colo.: Westview, 1987), pp. 71–101 at pp. 91–92.

[6] Olivier Roy, *Islam and Resistance in Afghanistan* (Cambridge: Cambridge University Press, 1986), p. 76.

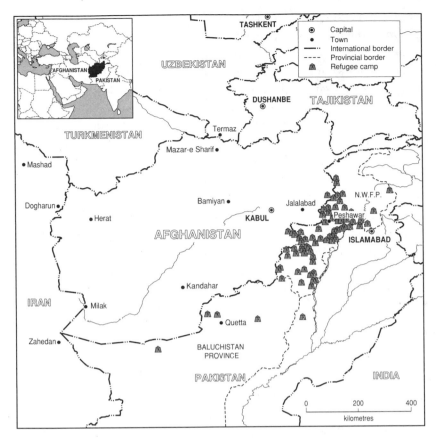

Map 1. Afghan refugee camps and settlements in Pakistan. From UNHCR, as modified by author.

lamist under the leadership of Burhanuddin Rabbani, and one radical Islamist, predominantly Pashtun, under the leadership of Hekmatyar.

The number of exiled Afghans during this period remained low; only some 1,500 moved to Pakistan between 1973 and early 1978. But after a communist coup that brought Nur Mohammad Taraki to power in Kabul in April 1978, the exodus increased to 100,000, and rose to 190,000 following an internal struggle in September 1979 which installed Hafizullah Amin as president. The Pakistani-based groups aided opponents of the Taraki-Amin regime, although their contribution was negligible in comparison with opposition within the country.[7] It was not until the 1979 So-

[7] Zolberg, Suhrke, and Aguayo, *Escape from Violence*, p. 151.

viet invasion that opposition groups based in Pakistan began to play a crucial role in the resistance movement.

Pakistan performed three vital functions as a military sanctuary to the Afghan resistance following the Soviet invasion. First, Pakistani territory was a relatively secure and well-equipped rear base for the resistance, and the Inter-Services Intelligence Directorate (ISI) of the Pakistani military coordinated and trained mujahideen units. Second, Pakistan was a conduit for weapons and financial support supplied to the Afghan resistance. And third, Pakistan facilitated political organization among the resistance parties. Although actively strengthening the Afghan resistance, Pakistani authorities maintained almost complete control over mujahideen activities in Pakistan and often pursued contradictory policies, enhancing unity among the parties on the one hand and using discriminatory practices to divide them on the other.

Throughout the 1980s, Pakistan's Afghan policy was principally determined by the ISI, with strong influence in political matters from the main Pakistani Islamic party, Jama'at-e Islami. The ISI allocated weapons to the various resistance factions and, according to the former head of the Afghan division of the ISI, Mohammad Yousaf, trained as many as 80,000 mujahideen on Pakistani territory between 1983 and 1987.[8] Yousaf claims that the number of training camps in Pakistan grew from two in 1983 to seven in 1987—four near Peshawar and three near Quetta in Baluchistan Province—catering to as many as 20,000 mujahideen per year from 1984.[9]

The bulk of arms and ammunition channeled to the mujahideen through Pakistan before 1985 was purchased in China to reduce the visibility of Western aid to the resistance. After 1985, supplies were augmented by shipments from Egypt, Saudi Arabia, the United States, and, surprisingly, Israel.[10] The United States and Saudi Arabia were the largest financial backers of the resistance. Washington viewed the invasion of Afghanistan—the first instance of Soviet aggression outside Eastern Europe—as a prelude to Soviet expansion throughout southwest Asia.[11] The Carter administration launched covert support to the Afghan resistance

---

[8] Yousaf and Adkin, *Bear Trap*, p. 117. It is possible that this figure has been inflated for political reasons.

[9] Ibid. See pp. 115–127 for details of the training programs.

[10] Apparently the weapons sold by Israel were captured during Israel's invasion of Lebanon. They were purchased with American funds in secrecy since the Arab nations would not have agreed to fight a jihad with weapons bought from Israel. See ibid., pp. 81–96 for more details of arms shipments to the resistance. Also see J. Bruce Amstutz, *Afghanistan: The First Five Years of Occupation* (Washington, D.C.: National Defense University Press, 1986), pp. 202–214.

[11] Declassified Soviet documents now show such fears to have been unwarranted.

and increased military aid to Pakistan. Thirty million dollars was allocated to the mujahideen in 1980, and $50 million in 1981. Under the Reagan administration, the sum grew to $120 million by 1984, $250 million in 1985, $470 million in 1986, and $630 million in 1987.[12] Pakistan's loyalty was also ensured by a massive injection of funds: despite its former objections to Pakistan's plans to develop a nuclear weapons capability, Washington offered a $400 million short-term military aid package to President Zia ul-Haq's government, which was increased to a five-year $3.2 billion military aid program in 1981.[13]

Funds from Saudi Arabia to the Afghan resistance closely matched those given by the United States.[14] Saudi motives for such support were tied to concerns about Soviet intentions in the Persian Gulf, aggression against an Islamic state, and Saudi Arabia's leadership in the Muslim world, which was threatened by the Islamic Revolution in Iran.[15] Actively financing the Afghan resistance was a way to assert Saudi leadership among Islamic countries and provided an opportunity to promote the Sunni Islamist parties through cooperation with the Jama'at-e Islami in Pakistan.

The ISI was predominantly concerned with Afghan military affairs, but these were closely linked to the political organization of the resistance after 1983. The discovery of a lucrative smuggling operation involving several mujahideen commanders and the Quetta branch of the ISI precipitated a major change from direct ISI allocations of weapons and finance to field commanders in Afghanistan, to the channeling of all supplies through the seven recognized political parties based in Peshawar.[16] Thereafter mujahideen commanders were required to declare allegiance to a party in order to receive supplies. Few of the party leaders had ever fought in Afghanistan, however, and only Mohammad Yunis Khalis and Rabbani[17]

---

[12] Barnett R. Rubin, *The Fragmentation of Afghanistan: State Formation and Collapse in the International System* (New Haven: Yale University Press, 1995), p. 180.

[13] Ted Galen Carpenter, "The Unintended Consequences of Afghanistan," *World Policy Journal* 11, no. 1 (1994): 76–87 at p. 77.

[14] Rubin, *The Fragmentation of Afghanistan*, p. 180.

[15] Ahady, "Saudi Arabia, Iran, and the Conflict in Afghanistan," p. 118.

[16] The parties were Jamiat-e Islami, led by Rabbani; Hezb-e Islami (H) led by Hekmatyar; Hezb-e Islami (K), led by Mohammad Yunis Khalis; Harakat-e Inqilab-e Islami, led by Mohammad Nabi Mohammadi; the National Islamic Front for Afghanistan, led by Sayyid Ahmad Gailani; and the Afghanistan National Liberation Front, led by Sebghatullah Mojadeddi. The seventh party, Abdul Rasul Sayyaf's Islamic Union for the Liberation of Afghanistan, was later recognized by the ISI because of its significant backing from Saudi Arabia. For more information on the parties and the profiles of the leaders see Olesen, *Islam and Politics in Afghanistan*, pp. 283–292.

[17] Rabbani's relationship with Massoud accorded him a territorial base in the Panjshir Valley.

had territorial bases for their power. Most of the two hundred or so commanders in the field were, in the words of one analyst, "disdainful of party officials who have sat out the war in Peshawar."[18] Nevertheless, they became dependent on the parties for arms and finance, and their allegiances were forged on the basis of ethnic or tribal loyalty, religious conviction, and, to a considerable extent, opportunism.

The empowerment of the Peshawar-based political leaders with discretionary allocation of weapons and finance to field commanders helped forge an image of a united resistance while maintaining Pakistan's strong influence through government controls and the Jama'at-e Islami. Although more than twenty Afghan resistance parties had formed in Peshawar and Quetta by 1980,[19] the Pakistani government recognized only the seven based in Peshawar. The others were incorporated into recognized parties or disbanded. Four of the parties were strongly Islamist[20] and three were traditionalist, advocating a return to the clan and tribal ties of the past. Pakistan forbade any secular political parties to operate on Pakistani soil and denied the exiled king, Mohammad Zahir Shah, or any member of the royal family access to the resistance movement or the refugees in Pakistan.[21] The Pakistani government also refused to allow the resistance to form a government-in-exile.

Pakistan's rationale for controlling the resistance movement on its soil was twofold. First, General Zia had personal experience of the potential security threat posed by a strong and united resistance movement to a host country, having been a military adviser in Jordan during Black September in 1970. The Palestine Liberation Organization (PLO) had been a unified, almost autonomous organization and nearly succeeded in overthrowing the monarch of the host nation, King Hussein.

Second, an irredentist movement had been active in Pakistan since the 1950s which claimed the NWFP of Pakistan as "Pashtunistan." Pashtun nationalism was strong among many in Afghanistan, and Pakistan was keen to suppress such movements. It refused to recognize the Pashtun Nationalist Party, Afghan Millat, and gave preference to the Islamist parties over the traditionalist parties partly in the belief that an ideologically

[18] Marvin G. Weinbaum, "The Politics of Afghan Resettlement and Rehabilitation," *Asian Survey* 29, no. 3 (1989): 287–307 at p. 291.

[19] Edward Girardet, *Afghanistan: The Soviet War* (New York: St. Martin's, 1985), p. 167.

[20] Roy argues that the term "Islamist" is preferable to "fundamentalist," since the latter invokes the return to a former state based on the pure meaning of the Koranic Scriptures, while the Islamists aim to create a modern political state based on Islamic ideology. See Roy, *Islam and the Resistance in Afghanistan*, pp. 3–6.

[21] Rubin, *The Fragmentation of Afghanistan*, p. 199.

minded Islamist regime installed in Kabul would be less supportive of the irredentist demands.[22] Olivier Roy contends that the preference for the Islamic parties had less to do with ideological affinities of the Pakistani government than with the influence of highly placed individuals in Jama'at-e Islami.[23] Nevertheless, all observers recognize the special position accorded by the ISI to Hekmatyar's radically Islamic party, Hezb-e Islami, which received a disproportionate share of military and financial aid, and international recognition.

The Pakistani authorities, through according recognition to certain parties over others and allocating disproportionate funds and weapons to favored groups, were pursuing a policy of divide and rule to avoid "another Palestine." For the United States and Saudi Arabia, however, the diplomatic war against the Soviet Union was as important as the military one, and unification of the parties was a vital component of such a strategy. Saudi Arabia made funding conditional upon the formation of an alliance of unity. Hence, in 1980, an alliance of five parties (which Hekmatyar's refused to join) formed, but soon disintegrated, polarizing along Islamist and traditionalist lines. Other attempts to form a union were plagued by ethnic, tribal, and religious differences among the parties, but in 1985, under pressure from external supporters and Pakistan,[24] a broad alliance was formed and named the Islamic Unity of Afghan Mujahideen.[25] The Soviet withdrawal from Afghanistan demonstrated the fragility of the alliance as the parties turned their weapons on one another.

Thus Pakistan performed a crucial role for the Afghan resistance as a conduit for arms and finance from external supporters, and in facilitating the political organization of the resistance. But a crucial factor in Pakistan's ability to fulfill such a role was the presence of millions of Afghan refugees who had fled to Pakistan. Militarily, they performed an invaluable service, as Yousaf suggests:

> Our [ISI] interest in the camps was that they provided a safe refuge from
> the war for the families of the Mujahideen, who could fight in Afghanistan
> in the knowledge that their relatives were immune from reprisals. They

[22] Richard P. Cronin, *Afghanistan after the Soviet Withdrawal: Contenders for Power* (Washington, D.C.: Congressional Research Service Report for Congress, 1989), p. 12.

[23] Roy, *Islam and the Resistance in Afghanistan*, pp. 209–210.

[24] According to Yousaf, President Zia personally intervened to insist on the 1985 alliance, and imposed ultimatums on the parties. See Yousaf and Adkin, *Bear Trap*, p. 39.

[25] For details about the political parties and their differences in Pakistan see Anthony Hyman, "The Afghan Politics of Exile," *Third World Quarterly* 9, no. 1 (1987): 67–84.

also acted as places to which the Mujahideen could return for a rest and to see their families without compromising themselves. Also, inside these camps was a huge reservoir of potential recruits for the Jehad. Thousands of young boys came to the camps as refugees, grew up, and then followed their fathers and brothers to the war.[26]

Relative to the extent of the direct military support that the resistance received, the role of the refugee camps may not have been essential to the overall success of the struggle. Nevertheless, the camps did play an important role in the resistance movement, as Yousaf attests, and also in more subtle ways than the purely military dimension, as the next section demonstrates.

Pakistan as a Humanitarian Sanctuary

The Soviet invasion of Afghanistan provoked a massive exodus of Afghans across the border into Pakistan, initially at a rate of 1,000 per day, but increasing to an average of 4,700 per day between January and June 1981 in response to Soviet tactics aimed at depopulating rural areas.[27] According to Pakistani statistics, there were an estimated 500,000 refugees in Pakistan in mid-January 1980, more than 1 million by July 1980, 2 million by May 1981, and 2.5 million by December 1984. By 1989 the number was estimated at 3.5 million. These figures remained only a rough estimate, however, because of difficulties inherent in refugee registration and the existence of a porous border.[28] On the one hand the United Nations thought that the numbers in the camps were inflated by false or multiple registrations,[29] and on the other hand an estimated 200,000 to 400,000 refugees remained unregistered since they had settled outside the government-designated refugee sites and thus did not qualify for registration or food and nonfood rations.[30] The "official" refugees settled in camps (or "refugee tented villages," as they were known) that were established for an average of 10,000 inhabitants, although some camps

[26] Yousaf and Adkin, *Bear Trap*, p. 138.

[27] Louis Dupree and Nancy Hatch Dupree, "Afghan Refugees in Pakistan," in *World Refugee Survey: 1987 in Review* (Washington, D.C.: U.S. Committee for Refugees, 1988), pp. 17–21 at p. 17.

[28] Nancy Hatch Dupree, "Demographic Reporting on Afghan Refugees in Pakistan," *Modern Asian Studies* 22, no. 4 (1988): 845–865.

[29] Marvin G. Weinbaum, *Pakistan and Afghanistan: Resistance and Reconstruction* (Boulder, Colo.: Westview, 1994), p. 54.

[30] Pierre Centlivres and Micheline Centlivres-Demont, "The Afghan Refugees in Pakistan: A Nation in Exile," *Current Sociology* 36, no. 2 (1988): 71–92 at 73.

were much larger. By 1986 there were 350 such camps, 72 percent of which were located in the NWFP, 24 percent in Baluchistan, and 4 percent in the Punjab.[31]

All the advantages that Rufin suggests guerrilla movements accrue from humanitarian sanctuaries were evident in the Afghan camps in Pakistan: international protection, diverse and neutral sources of resupply, and mechanisms through which to exert influence over the civilian population. The camps also served another crucial function described by Zolberg, Suhrke, and Aguayo, the bestowal of legitimacy upon the resistance movement: "Refugees constitute a legitimizing population for the warriors. The presence of a large population in exile is taken as a physical testimony of support for the warriors, at least in the sense that they represent a rejection of the other side in the conflict."[32] This was arguably the most important role the camps played in the Afghan conflict for the resistance and for Pakistan as host. The more legitimate the cause, the greater the justification in the West for continuing active support for the guerrilla war.

PROTECTION

The Soviet forces intentionally provoked refugee flows into Iran and Pakistan to deprive the guerrillas of support bases within Afghanistan for shelter, food, and information, essential ingredients in guerrilla strategy. They pursued policies of blanket bombing and infrastructural destruction, particularly in the provinces bordering Pakistan.[33] These tactics compounded the general condemnation of the Soviet invasion,[34] and the refugees gained widespread sympathy in the West. Other simultaneous crises occurring in the world, such as the thousands of Iranians fleeing to Pakistan to escape the Khomeini regime and conscription into the war against Iraq, did not attract the same attention. Their case was equally life threatening,

[31] Hatch Dupree, "Demographic Reporting," p. 846.

[32] Zolberg, Suhrke, and Aguayo, *Escape from Violence*, p. 277.

[33] Marek Sliwinski notes that "from 1978 to 1981, the Soviets gave priority to isolating the resistance movements by creating a cordon sanitaire along the Pakistan border, and consequently this strip was depopulated by aerial bombings." Sliwinski, "Afghanistan: The Decimation of a People," *Orbis* 33, no. 1 (1989): 39–56 at p. 50.

[34] In a special session, the United Nations General Assembly overwhelmingly adopted a resolution calling for "the immediate, unconditional and total withdrawal of the foreign troops from Afghanistan." United Nations General Assembly, *Resolution* ES-6/2, 14 January 1980, as cited in William Maley, "The Geneva Accords of April 1988," in Amin Saikal and William Maley (eds.), *The Soviet Withdrawal from Afghanistan* (Cambridge: Cambridge University Press, 1989), pp. 12–28 at p. 13.

but for them there were no camps, no mass relief, and very little international attention.[35]

The international focus on the refugees in Pakistan enhanced the security of the camps, providing a safe haven to the mujahideen and their families in which they could rest and recuperate. The presence of the refugee camps was not vital to the protection of the combatants, as both "bachelor camps" and training camps existed in Pakistan, separate from the refugee camps. Nonetheless, without the presence of such a large population of refugees, it is doubtful that Pakistan could have provided such extensive military support to the Afghan resistance. The refugee camps supplied a cover for military activities and the involvement of Pakistan, and the international attention focused on the refugees reduced the chances of retaliatory attacks by the Soviet forces. Several aerial attacks against refugee camps did occur in early 1987 in NWFP, killing and wounding hundreds of refugees, mujahideen, and Pakistanis,[36] and cross-border incursions and infiltrations of the refugee camps by Soviet/Afghan government forces and agents occurred, particularly in mid-1984.[37] But no major military reprisals were ever undertaken against Pakistan, although this may have had more to do with avoiding direct confrontation with Pakistan's allies than with the presence of refugees among combatants.

The humanitarian sanctuary was further enhanced in Pakistan by provision of treatment facilities for wounded mujahideen who survived the journey to the border. The International Committee of the Red Cross (ICRC) ran two fully equipped surgical hospitals, one in Peshawar and one in Quetta, for the treatment of Afghan war wounded. The paradox of humanitarian action rehabilitating combatants, thereby enabling them to return to battle, can be seen at health posts in Afghanistan today, as men wearing prostheses fitted in the 1980s come for treatment of their latest war wounds.

WAR ECONOMY

The contribution of humanitarian aid to the war economy in Afghanistan is difficult to assess. Several sources allege that millions of dollars of funds for the refugee program were diverted by resistance parties and Pakistani

---

[35] Zolberg, Suhrke, and Aguayo, *Escape from Violence*, p. 154.

[36] See *By All Parties to the Conflict: Violations of the Laws of War in Afghanistan* (New York: Helsinki Watch/Asia Watch, March 1988), pp. 81–83.

[37] See Allen Jones, *Afghan Refugees: Five Years Later* (Washington, D.C.: U.S. Committee for Refugees, 1985), p. 13.

officials,[38] but whether these funds flowed to combatants or lined the pockets of Afghan party members and Pakistani officials is impossible to gauge. Material supplies meant for the refugee camps may also have crossed the border into Afghanistan, although the volume was limited by logistical constraints: all materials were carried personally or transported by animal across the mountains. As there was a cross-border aid program, it probably contributed more to the war economy than aid from the refugee camps. Helga Baitenmann noted that inside Afghanistan "humanitarian aid has frequently been stolen before reaching the intended beneficiaries, reports have been falsified, and . . . some rebels have given the right to work in their areas to the highest-bidding NGO."[39]

Aid to the refugee camps did indirectly benefit the resistance, however, through easing the responsibility of combatants to provide for their families, thereby permitting more energy and resources to be committed to the war effort. The aid distribution system in the camps was also structured to support the resistance. Recruits who left the camps to participate in *jihad* (struggle for the faith) did not lose their entitlements to food rations, even if they were away for months at a time. A specific jihad book registered absences and allowed a designated local official to act on behalf of the mujahid, collecting all the commodities distributed in his absence.[40] Humanitarian aid also fed mujahideen fighters when food was diverted to the "bachelor" camps,[41] but this was not a systematic or regular occurrence.

Thus the humanitarian sanctuaries aided the resistance indirectly through the provision of protection and some contributions to the war economy. It was, however, in the political rather than the military realm that the refugee camps made their greatest contribution to the guerrilla war.

LEGITIMACY

Pakistan was the first beneficiary of the legitimacy that often flows from international humanitarian action. As host to millions of refugees, the Pakistani government became pivotal as interlocutor between the interna-

---

[38] Ibid., p. 67. Also see Edward Girardet, "Corrupt Officials Reap Spoils of Afghan War," *Christian Science Monitor,* 7 September 1988, as noted in Weinbaum, *Pakistan and Afghanistan,* p. 59.

[39] Helga Baitenmann, "NGOs and the Afghan War: The Politicisation of Humanitarian Aid," *Third World Quarterly* 12, no. 1 (1990): 62–85 at p. 73.

[40] Centlivres and Centlivres-Demont, "The Afghan Refugees in Pakistan: A Nation in Exile," p. 83; and Amstutz, *Afghanistan: The First Five Years of Occupation,* p. 229.

[41] Pierre Centlivres and Micheline Centlivres-Demont, "The Afghan Refugees in Pakistan: An Ambiguous Identity," *Journal of Refugee Studies* 1, no. 2 (1988): 141–152 at p. 150.

tional community and the refugees. The Pakistani president, General Zia, rapidly capitalized upon this, and, like Mobutu Sese Seko of Zaire fifteen years later, Zia was turned by the refugee flow from an international pariah into a "respectable" statesman. Prior to the refugee influx, many countries ostracized Zia for Pakistan's poor human rights record, particularly the 1979 execution of the former prime minister, Zulfikar Ali Bhutto, at Zia's directive. But Pakistan's public image greatly improved as a result of its role as host to some three million refugees, and the hospitality accorded to the predominantly Pashtun[42] refugees helped to defuse the Pashtunistan issue. Moreover, the loyalty accorded to Zia by the refugees under the Pashtun tribal code, *Pashtunwali*, obliged them to defend their host in times of difficulties or hostilities. Pierre Centlivres and Micheline Centlivres-Demont reported that several Afghan leaders affirmed their commitment to fight for Zia if conflict with India arose.[43]

General Zia's political power was also enhanced by the financial package offered by the United States, which enabled Zia's government to modernize the Pakistani military with sophisticated weaponry.[44] Furthermore, the flood of refugees provided a pretext for maintaining the domestic "state of emergency," thereby restraining political opponents, who were forbidden to operate their own political parties or run a free press.[45] Many Pakistani opposition members thus deeply resented the government tolerance of Afghans operating exile resistance organizations, publishing newspapers, and holding meetings on Pakistani territory.[46]

Zia also gained stature in the Muslim world by supporting the more Islamic resistance parties operating in Pakistan, and, as mentioned earlier, U.S. objections to Pakistan's pursuit of a nuclear program were repeatedly postponed in the face of the more pressing issues of Pakistan's loyalty to the United States. Thus the Afghan resistance benefited from having such a compliant host, and General Zia benefited from the international recognition and military support that accompanied the roles of host to the world's largest refugee population and bastion of opposition to communist oppression.

While international sympathy for the Afghan refugees helped to legit-

---

[42] Until 1984, 80–94 percent of refugees were from the Pashtun ethnic group. See Hatch Dupree, "Demographic Reporting," p. 848, and Centlivres and Centlivres-Demont, "The Afghan Refugees in Pakistan: A Nation in Exile," p. 73.

[43] Centlivres and Centlivres-Demont, "The Afghan Refugees in Pakistan: An Ambiguous Identity," p. 147.

[44] Dupree and Hatch Dupree, "Afghan Refugees in Pakistan," p. 21.

[45] Jones, *Afghan Refugees: Five Years Later,* p. 16.

[46] Girardet, *Afghanistan: The Soviet War,* p. 207.

imize General Zia and the mujahideen, it was through the refugees in Pakistan that the leaders of the Afghan political parties gained legitimacy—legitimacy which they might not have otherwise been accorded, owing to their general lack of military prowess or territorial bases inside Afghanistan. And, as with the military aid to the resistance, it was the strong arm of Pakistan that created the conditions through which the political parties could utilize the mass of humanity to their political advantage. Pakistan was not a signatory to the 1951 Refugee Convention or 1967 Protocol, and invited United Nations High Commissioner for Refugees (UNHCR) participation only in the coordination of relief activities. Pakistani authorities were appointed to administer the camps. A Pakistani Chief Commissionerate for Afghan Refugees was assigned to supervise the overall refugee situation, and Pakistani officials held various positions in the administrative apparatus of the camps. To assist in the camp management, they established committees of public order (*Islahi komite*) and appointed a refugee representative (*malik*) in each camp to distribute relief goods to the families he represented. Although maliks were supposed to be traditional representatives of the Afghan refugees, the individuals filling this role were often the choice of the Pakistani authorities, since the Pakistanis preferred an interlocutor with whom they were assured cooperation.[47] Thus the Pakistani government exercised authority in the camps at every level and also met approximately half of the cost of the refugee assistance, estimated in excess of $1 million per day in 1984.[48]

The Peshawar-based political parties used the refugees to gain international recognition and funding by posing as their legitimate representatives. The more "support" the parties could show, the more weight they carried in their fundraising and diplomatic sojourns abroad. Hence the parties obliged the refugees arriving from Afghanistan to become affiliated with one of the Pakistani-recognized parties in order to be certified as refugees.[49] Edward Girardet describes how party activists waited at the frontier villages and enlisted entire families, clans, and tribes into political parties.[50] Those who were not affiliated in this way joined parties through

[47] Lynn Carter and Kerry Connor, "A Preliminary Investigation of Contemporary Afghan Councils" (Peshawar: Agency Coordination Body for Afghan Relief, ACBAR mimeo, 1989), pp. 18–19, as cited in Weinbaum, *Pakistan and Afghanistan*, p. 57.

[48] Girardet, *Afghanistan: The Soviet War*, p. 204, and Hatch Dupree, "Demographic Reporting," p. 845.

[49] A Helsinki/Asia Watch report noted that this system gave political parties "a veto over whether a refugee will receive assistance and turns refugee aid into a political patronage plum." *By All Parties to the Conflict*, p. 90.

[50] Girardet, *Afghanistan: The Soviet War*, p. 173.

the malik, and many refugees were registered by more than one party. Unable, for the most part, to read, they initially had little idea of what they had joined,[51] but camp life soon rectified that; in the course of their research, Centlivres and Centlivres-Demont met hardly anyone who did not have allegiance to a party and did not know the name of their party leader. They found that allegiance had little to do with ideology, being rather a result of the intense propaganda in the camps in the form of posters, iconography, martyr worship, religious schools, and the distribution of membership cards.[52]

Pakistan collaborated fully in this process. Party affiliation was imperative to receive a refugee identity card, without which an Afghan could be suspected of being a KhAD[53] agent and have constant problems with the Pakistani police.[54] Travel within Pakistan and abroad was impossible without an identity card, and employment in Pakistan, even for highly educated Afghans, could be found only through the political parties, particularly Hekmatyar's Hezb-e Islami. Even Western aid organizations accepted the party card as the refugee identity card, so entrenched was the practice.[55] In addition, the revenue collected from membership fees was a source of income for the parties.

The legitimacy of the political leaders thus derived from their assumed representation of the refugee population. Since support from the West was proportional to the representation claimed, factional competition for refugee allegiance was strong. The refugee camp structures, therefore, became useful tools in gaining influence over the refugee population.

POPULATION CONTROL

Unlike in many other refugee camps around the world, the influence exerted over the refugee population was more normative than coercive.[56] The Afghan resistance had the overwhelming support of the refugees, and

---

[51] Ibid.

[52] Centlivres and Centlivres-Demont, "The Afghan Refugees in Pakistan: A Nation in Exile," p. 86.

[53] The KhAD was the secret police of the Afghan government, the local equivalent of the KGB.

[54] Dr. Haider Reza, personal interview, 4 June 1997.

[55] Centlivres and Centlivres-Demont, "The Afghan Refugees in Pakistan: A Nation in Exile," p. 83.

[56] After the Soviet withdrawal, however, the increased tension between the parties spilled over to their supporters, and increasingly coercive means were employed, particularly by the extremist Islamic parties against refugees aligned with the relatively secular parties. See *Afghanistan: The Forgotten War. Human Rights Abuses and Violations of the Laws of War since the Soviet Withdrawal* (New York: Asia Watch, February 1991), pp. 99–123.

pictures of martyrs from the jihad adorned various buildings throughout the camps. Recruitment of combatants, for example, was not forced, but expected of male refugees. A survey conducted in the camps of the NWFP in 1991 found that 83 percent of people who had visited Afghanistan since becoming refugees had returned for jihad.[57] "Every family is obliged to send a member to take part in the jihad who is expected to spend up to three months at the battle front. When the three months are over, the Mujahed returns and is replaced by another member of the family, his brother, father or cousin."[58]

Enjoying universal refugee support, the resistance did not need to manipulate the relief distributions in the camps to that end per se, but did so to cultivate support for one faction over another. The Islamic parties, particularly Hezb-e Islami, benefited from preferential access to the aid programs between 1980 and 1983, due to the influence of the Pakistani refugee commissioner, Sheikh Abdullah Khan.[59] Educational programs became a primary instrument of indoctrination, and some 250 schools with 43,000 students and 1,500 teaching and administrative staff were operated by the Hezb-e Islami. The graduates of these schools formed the new generation of *Hezb*, including the majority of the soldiers of Hekmatyar's military force, the Army of Sacrifice (Lashkar-e Isar).[60] School curricula included paramilitary training and emphasized concepts surrounding jihad and anti-Soviet sentiment.[61] Hezb-e Islami also had its own police, courts, and prisons, and opponents were "persecuted, criminals tried and convicted, and the infrastructure maintained, all on the alien territory of Pakistan."[62]

The food distribution system initially conducted by the maliks was also instrumental in the control of refugees, enabling the establishment of patron-client relationships between the maliks and refugee families. The maliks kept the ration books between distributions, charged a fee for facilitating distributions, and accumulated extra rations for their favored clients.[63]

[57] Mamoona Taskinud-Din, *UNHCR-IRC Survey of Socio-economic Conditions of Afghan Refugees Living in NWFP Camps* (Peshawar: UNHCR Sub-office, February 1992), p. 45.

[58] Ibid.

[59] Amstutz, *Afghanistan: The First Five Years of Soviet Occupation*, p. 229; Weinbaum, *Pakistan and Afghanistan*, p. 59. General Zia replaced Abdullah with an apolitical official in 1983, after relations between his government and the Jama'at-e Islami became strained. See Roy, *Islam and Resistance in Afghanistan*, p. 210.

[60] Rubin, *The Fragmentation of Afghanistan*, p. 215.

[61] Centlivres and Centlivres-Demont, "The Afghan Refugees in Pakistan: A Nation in Exile," p. 89.

[62] Cheryl Benard, "Politics and the Refugee Experience," *Political Science Quarterly* 101, no. 4 (1986): 617–636 at 630.

[63] Pierre Centlivres and Micheline Centlivres-Demont, "Hommes d'influence et hommes de partis: L'organisation politique dans les villages de réfugiés afghans au Pakistan," in Erwin

UNHCR considered these practices corrupt and discontinued distributions through the maliks, instead giving rations directly to the heads of families in the camps. Nevertheless, the maliks retained influence by acting as interlocutors between the refugees and the Pakistani authorities or aid organizations and remained involved in the transportation of supplies. In many areas they also conducted a redistribution of relief goods after the official distribution was complete.[64]

The refugee camp structures thus empowered certain elements of society, often to the detriment of the traditional leaders. In rural Afghan villages there was traditionally no single malik, but a collective leadership of elders through a village council, each member having a different area of responsibility.[65] But in the refugee camps the maliks possessing liaison skills became prominent through dealing with the Pakistanis and aid organizations, as did the maliks appointed by the Pakistani authorities. Consequently, competition erupted between the new maliks (called "ration" or "rupiyah" maliks among the refugees) and the traditional Afghan leadership. The political parties that sought to optimize their influence in the camps by appointing as their representative either the respected *ulema* or the young educated militant exacerbated this competition.[66]

A survey published by the Afghan Information Centre Monthly Bulletin suggested that legitimacy of leaders was not widely accepted, with more than 70 percent of Afghan refugees interviewed preferring the king to any of the political leaders as a future head of state. Barnett Rubin, however, suggests that the survey methodology was not accurate and, although the result was representative of the position of the elders, it did not take into account that the younger generation would not have contradicted the elders in front of strangers whether they agreed or not.[67] Either way, it was Pakistan that determined the political orientation of the refugees by oblig-

---

Grötzbach (ed.), *Neue Beiträge zur Afghanistanforschung* (Liestal: Stiftung Bibliotheca Afghanica, 1988), pp. 29–46 at p. 36.

[64] Centlivres and Centlivres-Demont, "The Afghan Refugees in Pakistan: A Nation in Exile," p. 82.

[65] For a more detailed discussion of the societal changes see Louis Dupree, "Cultural Changes among the Mujahidin and the Muhajerin," in Bo Huldt and Erland Jansson (eds.), *The Tragedy of Afghanistan: The Social, Cultural, and Political Impact of the Soviet Invasion* (London: Croom Helm, 1988), pp. 20–37.

[66] Centlivres and Centlivres-Demont, "The Afghan Refugees in Pakistan: A Nation in Exile," p. 83.

[67] Rubin, *The Fragmentation of Afghanistan*, p. 249, and n. 5 to chapter 11, p. 339. Louis Dupree also doubted the validity of polls conducted among the refugees that showed a preference for the return of Zahir Shah. See Louis Dupree, "Post-Withdrawal Afghanistan: Light at the End of the Tunnel," in Saikal and Maley (eds.), *Soviet Withdrawal from Afghanistan*, pp. 29–51 at p. 43.

ing adherence to one of the Pakistani-recognized political parties and denying the royal family entry into Pakistan.

In summary, the refugee camps served several purposes in the resistance to Soviet occupation of Afghanistan. They provided a military sanctuary in which combatants could receive protection, food, medical attention, and security for their families, and the presence of three million refugees provided a shield behind which the Pakistani government could channel military aid and training to the mujahideen fighters. With military means, General Zia and the Peshawar-based political parties were empowered, and with humanitarian means they were legitimized. Without this support, the political parties might have remained on the fringes of Afghan political life. But as Ted Carpenter argues, with the backing of the United States and the Pakistanis "they were not only able to dominate the Afghan exile community, they acquired even more influence than many of the military commanders who were waging the armed struggle against the Soviet and Afghan communist forces."[68]

Overt manipulation of the refugee community through the aid structures empowered the party leaders at the expense of the traditional leadership, the repercussions of which are visible in the continuing civil war. It is interesting to note that many of the Taliban who recently held power in Afghanistan were born in the refugee camps in Pakistan and educated in their particularly repressive brand of Islam[69] in Pakistani *madrassas* (Islamic colleges). The rival Islamic party in Pakistan, the Jama'at-e Ulema-i Islami, was largely behind the creation of the Taliban movement, having built up a support base in Baluchistan and the NWFP by "opening up madrassas and carrying out relief work in the refugee camps."[70]

Humanitarian aid was instrumental in the political manipulation of the refugee population. While most actors accepted this in the name of a just cause during the Soviet occupation of Afghanistan, the repercussions of the absence of humanitarian space were increasingly realized when the Soviet army withdrew.

The Relief Response: In the Name of a Just Cause

In an article entitled "Military and Armed Attacks on Refugee Camps," Elly-Elikunda Mtango wrote that clear evidence of what occurred in the

---

[68] Carpenter, "The Unintended Consequences of Afghanistan," p. 79.

[69] For a discussion of the origins and doctrine of the Taliban see William Maley, "Interpreting the Taliban," in Maley (ed.), *Fundamentalism Reborn?* pp. 1–28.

[70] Ahmed Rashid, "Pakistan and the Taliban," in Maley (ed.), *Fundamentalism Reborn?* pp. 72–89 at p. 75.

refugee camps in Pakistan is difficult to obtain.[71] In condemning an attack in the Kurram district of Pakistan in 1987 which killed forty-two people, the majority of whom were Afghan refugees, he states that "there is no justification for attacking refugees on the mere suspicion that (from time to time) some guerrilla fighters may be living among the civilian refugees."[72] Similarly, Asia Watch denounced such attacks, stating that "even if the mujaheddin were present in the camps in force . . . the rule of proportionality requires the DRA [Democratic Republic of Afghanistan] to refrain from striking there because of the large number of civilians present."[73]

Now that clearer evidence of the involvement of the refugee camps in the war is available, can such attacks be legally justified as self-defense? Given that Soviet and Afghan agents infiltrated the camps, it is perhaps surprising that more attacks did not occur. But whether the attacks were legal or illegal is of less interest here than the fact that they did occur as a consequence of the presence of mujahideen fighters among the refugees. Why was there so little discussion of the potential repercussions of the role of the refugee camps in the war?

Two main factors help to explain the humanitarian community's acceptance of the status quo in the camps. The first concerns the persuasions of the aid organizations working there, which can be divided into two categories, politically oriented and technically focused. The second stems from the first and relates to the difference between the normative perception of the refugee community held by the international aid organizations and the way the refugees perceived themselves.

DIFFERENT APPROACH, SAME ENDS

The Afghan resistance was idealized among the Western public, and the notion of a "just war" was emphasized in the minds of many aid workers operating in the camps. Nineteen international NGOs were formed specifically to respond to the Afghan crisis, the majority of which were "solidarity NGOs" with an overtly political focus.[74] Some of them restricted their activities to lobbying, but most became operational in either

---

[71] Elly-Elikunda Mtango, "Military and Armed Attacks on Refugee Camps," in Gil Loescher and Laila Monahan (eds.), *Refugees and International Relations* (Oxford: Oxford University Press, 1989), pp. 87–121 at p. 95.

[72] Ibid.

[73] *By All Parties to the Conflict*, p. 81.

[74] Nigel Nicholds with John Borton, *The Changing Role of NGOs in the Provision of Relief and Rehabilitation Assistance: Case Study 1—Afghanistan/Pakistan*, Working Paper 74 (London: Overseas Development Institute, 1994), pp. 73–78.

the refugee camps or the cross-border program, or both. These "solidarity" NGOs joined approximately fifty established international NGOs that had programs in other parts of the world. With humanitarian relief activities largely restricted to the periphery of conflicts during the Cold War, most humanitarian activity was undertaken in refugee camps, assisting, for the most part, refugees who had been uprooted from their homes by oppressive policies and human rights abuses carried out by totalitarian regimes. Hence the 1980s saw some aid organizations taking an increasingly active stance on the side of the "victims" over the "oppressors" and directing their relief aid accordingly. For Médecins sans Frontières (MSF), which worked in the refugee camps and was the first NGO to work clandestinely inside Afghanistan in 1980,[75] this was certainly the case: "in Afghanistan, MSF never sought to take a neutral stance. . . . we had implicitly picked our side."[76]

Even if other organizations did not feel so strongly or express their opinions so bluntly, the fact that a superpower was using brutal and disproportionate strength to crush a popular resistance movement invoked a moral imperative to aid the victims. The Soviet forces razed villages and hospitals and dropped napalm and explosive devices, some of which resembled toys, to terrorize, maim, and kill civilians and combatants alike. The resistance was armed with only basic weapons until the 1986 introduction of the Stinger antiaircraft missile. Thus the majority of aid organizations felt assistance to the resistance was just.

The "justness" of the resistance cause was further enhanced by restrictions the government in Kabul placed on aid to the civilian populations in Afghanistan. The Kabul regime occupied Afghanistan's seat at the UN, and any proposal that UN relief agencies intervene in the mujahideen areas faced an effective veto from the Soviet Union. UN agencies and ICRC were restricted to working in areas approved by Kabul, which were predominantly around major cities, not in rural and resistance-held areas. As a consequence, a few NGOs mounted clandestine missions into these areas from Pakistan. Most, like MSF, Aide Médicale Internationale, and the Swedish Committee for Afghanistan, provided medical assistance to casualties of war, but some, like American Aid for Afghans, also engaged in the

---

[75] See Asger Christensen, *Aiding Afghanistan: The Background and Prospects for Reconstruction in a Fragmented Society* (Copenhagen: Nordic Institute of Asian Studies, 1995), p. 127.

[76] Rony Brauman, foreword to Médecins sans Frontières (ed.), *World in Crisis: The Politics of Survival at the End of the Twentieth Century* (London: Routledge, 1997), pp. xix–xxvi at p. xxii. Also see *Les French Doctors dans le piège afghan*, a film by Joël Calmettes, État Urgence et FR3-GMT Productions, 1996.

provision of clothing, boots, and equipment for the clandestine Radio Free Kabul.[77] Until 1986, only some ten to fifteen NGOs conducted cross-border operations from Pakistan, and they were limited in the scale of activities that they could undertake.[78] But numbers rose significantly once the introduction of the Stinger missile reduced the risk from air attack and once the United States provided funding for cross-border activities.[79]

Not all aid agencies chose to "politicize" their work, and particularly before 1986 the majority focused on the technical aspects of relief provision in the camps, turning a blind eye to the use of the camps by the Afghan resistance. Girardet states that some agencies restricted their activities to "official" areas for fundraising purposes and cites a CARE official as saying that "we are not into clandestine relief."[80] However, the extent to which they acknowledged the vested interests of many of their institutional donors, and reduced their dependence on them accordingly, varied. UNHCR, for example, was limited in its capacity to guarantee the civilian character of the camps since its leverage with Pakistan was weakened by Pakistan's not being a party to the 1951 Refugee Convention. UNHCR did, however, try to prohibit the carrying of arms in the refugee camps and attempted, sometimes in vain, to prevent the diversion of aid to "bachelor" camps of the mujahideen.[81] In addition, UNHCR became aware of the obligation of refugees to join political parties in 1982, but the United States allegedly placed strong pressure on the organization to avoid interfering in Pakistani policy.[82] The United States, as the largest donor of what it termed "nonlethal" aid, providing one-third of UNHCR's special budget for Afghanistan and one-half of the commodities of the World Food Programme (WFP),[83] had considerable leverage over aid policy.

UNHCR was not the only agency to be strongly influenced by U.S. funding; many NGOs were direct tools of U.S. foreign policy. Whether they believed they were neutral or not, NGOs that received U.S. funding either in Pakistan or for cross-border operations were assisting the foreign

---

[77] John H. Lorentz, "Afghan Aid: The Role of Private Voluntary Organizations," *Journal of South Asian and Middle Eastern Studies* 9, nos. 1 and 2 (1987): 102–111 at p. 106.

[78] S. Barakat and A. Strand, "Rehabilitation and Reconstruction of Afghanistan: A Challenge for Afghans, NGOs, and the UN," *Disaster Prevention and Management* 4, no. 1 (1995): 21–26 at p. 23.

[79] The first U.S. funds available for cross-border programs inside Afghanistan were an $8 million allocation for 1985. In 1986 this rose to $15 million and in 1988 to $45 million. Lorentz, "Afghan Aid: The Role of Private Voluntary Organizations," p. 107, and Baitenmann, "NGOs and the Afghan War," p. 75.

[80] Girardet, *Afghanistan: The Soviet War,* p. 210.

[81] Centlivres and Centlivres-Demont, "The Afghan Refugees in Pakistan: An Ambiguous Identity," p. 150.

[82] Baitenmann, "NGOs and the Afghan War," p. 68.

[83] Amstutz, *The First Five Years of Occupation,* p. 227.

policy strategy of the U.S. government. In Pakistan, U.S. aid aimed to placate Pakistan to avoid, in the words of a U.S. State Department cable, "the chances that Pakistan might abandon its stalwart opposition to the Soviet intervention in Afghanistan in favor of accommodation with the USSR."[84] The U.S. administration provided funding to American NGOs such as CARE, Catholic Relief Services, the International Rescue Committee, and Church World Services in the camps, many of which coordinated their relief efforts with U.S. policy in return.[85]

The U.S. cross-border program of nonlethal aid was even clearer in its aim: to bring essential supplies to Afghans living in resistance-controlled regions so that the resistance would be able to organize genuine base areas.[86] Baitenmann argues that NGOs were direct instruments of this policy: "when the USA has wanted to strengthen certain commanders, it has done so through NGOs."[87] She cites Afghanaid as an example, stating that it received 65–70 percent of its funding from U.S. government sources, including State Department funding specifically for aid to the Panjshir Valley where General Massoud was based.[88] Some NGOs refused U.S. government finance to retain some measure of independence from government policy. These NGOs, however, were the exception rather than the rule, and aid served to bolster the prestige and legitimacy of certain commanders inside Afghanistan over others. "Aid resources were after all, an important means by which these leaders expected to insure the loyalty of groups and individuals."[89]

Thus whether NGOs adopted a position of solidarity with the mujahideen, became channels of U.S. anticommunist policy, or simply focused on the technical provision of humanitarian assistance, it was difficult to remain apart from the highly political context of the Afghan refugee camps. The direct involvement of Pakistani authorities in all levels of the relief apparatus exacerbated the constraints of providing impartial relief to the refugee population.

CONTENDING IMAGES OF "REFUGEEHOOD"

The difference in the way the aid organizations perceived the refugees and the way the refugees saw themselves provides the second explanation for

---

[84] U.S. State Department Cable A-67 from Islamabad, 8 September 1981, as cited in Baitenmann, "NGOs and the Afghan War," p. 69.

[85] Baitenmann, "NGOs and the Afghan War," p. 69.

[86] Rubin, *Fragmentation of Afghanistan*, p. 224.

[87] Baitenmann, "NGOs and the Afghan War," p. 76.

[88] Ibid.

[89] Weinbaum, *Pakistan and Afghanistan*, p. 60.

the lack of condemnation of the violation of the refugee camps. The normative definition of refugees constructed by aid organizations is of dependent, dispossessed victims who are forced to flee their homeland. Fundraising imperatives exacerbate the "victim discourse," generally portraying the recipients of aid as helpless and deprived, and in need of immediate Western aid. Images such as that painted by ISI leader Yousaf are typical. He characterized the refugee camps as "squalid places, teeming with humanity. Overcrowding has put impossible strains on rudimentary water, sanitation, and medical facilities. Refugees arrive weak and exhausted, many are sick or wounded, all are virtually destitute."[90] I have no wish to trivialize the suffering that the refugees underwent, but the conceptualization of them as dependent, vulnerable victims masked the reality that they were also a highly politicized population, many of whom chose to flee an infidel government, and who above all wanted to return to their homeland.

For the Afghan refugees, fleeing a communist regime in Kabul held a different connotation from that of non-Muslim populations escaping communist regimes elsewhere. According to Islamic teachings, Muslims are encouraged to leave Muslim territory which is occupied by infidels or in which the free practice of Islam is forbidden. Following the practice of the Prophet Mohammad, who fled from Mecca to Medina in 622 C.E. when persecuted for his beliefs and teachings, the Koran states that "those who believed and left their homes and strove for the cause of Allah . . . these are the believers in truth."[91]

The term in Arabic for refugee is *mohajir* and has the same root as the word *hejra*, which refers to Mohammad's flight into exile. A mohajir is a person who voluntarily takes exile and has severed ties with relatives and possessions, thus denoting courage for sacrificing comfort and family, rather than shame at taking flight. Nazif Shahrani states that the original hejra was an obligation: "not joining the migration resulted in exclusion from the society."[92]

In Medina, Mohammad built up his support base and prepared for war, marching victoriously into Mecca several years later. Accordingly, for the Afghans, "the conditions of refugee does not imply renunciation of armed battle, but on the contrary, falling back temporarily to make preparations

[90] Yousaf and Atkin, *Bear Trap*, p. 138.
[91] Cited in Roy, *Islam and Resistance in Afghanistan*, p. 165.
[92] M. Nazif Shahrani, "Afghanistan's Muhajirin (Muslim 'Refugee Warriors'): Politics of Mistrust or Mistrust of Politics," in E. Valentine Daniel and John Chr. Knudsen (eds.), *Mistrusting Refugees* (Berkeley: University of California Press, 1995), pp. 187–206 at p. 192.

for a reconquest."[93] *Mohajir* is thus the other side of *mujahed*, and the resistance movements regularly cited passages from the Koran to this effect: "those who believe and have emigrated, and have struggled in the way of God with their possessions and their selves are mightier in rank with God; and those—they are the triumphant."[94] As Centlivres and Centlivres-Demont argue, the conception of mohajir was a powerful motivational force in the construction of identity: "from a personal point of view, it renders a refugee almost a fighter and, from a collective point of view, it binds the group to the very sources of Islam."[95]

Thus for the refugees, the humanitarian and the political were inseparable: as Shahrani writes, "what distinguishes the Afghan refugee-warriors' situation in Pakistan from refugees elsewhere is the recognition of and respect for the mutually reinforcing relationship between the humanitarian and political dimensions of their refugee life."[96] The notions of choice and refugee agency were for the most part overlooked by the Western refugee regime operating in Pakistan. Moreover, the images of refugeehood depicted in fundraising campaigns deny such a role. Understanding the political nature of refugees would have necessitated the recognition of a dilemma and the reconceptualization of the applicability of Western refugee norms to the Afghan case. It might also have prompted a search for a way of preserving a purely humanitarian space in a context in which the lines between the political and the humanitarian were obviously blurred. It was in the interests of very few aid organizations to do so. The cause was just.

Conclusion: From Warriors to Warlords

Pakistani, Western, and Arab interest in the mujahideen was insignificant before the Soviet intervention in Afghanistan, but this event galvanized anticommunist and Islamic support for Afghan self-determination. The invasion of an independent Islamic state by a communist superpower and the flight of millions of refugees provided a potent mix of incentives. While the presence of refugees generated sympathy in the West, thereby

[93] Centlivres and Centlivres-Demont, "The Afghan Refugees in Pakistan: A Nation in Exile," p. 87.
[94] Sûra IX, 20 as cited in Centlivres and Centlivres-Demont, "The Afghan Refugees in Pakistan: An Ambiguous Identity," p. 146.
[95] Centlivres and Centlivres-Demont, "The Afghan Refugees in Pakistan: An Ambiguous Identity," p. 147.
[96] Shahrani, "Afghanistan's Muhajirin," p. 201.

strengthening public support for the resistance, direct financial support to the mujahideen from the United States and Saudi Arabia ($1 billion combined in 1986) and logistical, training, and material support from Pakistan gave aid a complementary, though in no way determinant, role in the conflict. Humanitarian sanctuaries assisted the resistance by supporting the mohajir and mujahideen when they were in Pakistan, though they cannot be said to have prolonged the Afghan conflict.

Nevertheless, humanitarian action fueled aspects of the conflict, the effects of which reverberate to this day. With the benefit of hindsight, we can appreciate the role that the camps played in empowering Peshawar political leaders and the importance of Pakistani influence in the process. The Western policy of tying funding to proportional representation among refugees allowed political leaders to manipulate the aid program for political ends, thus inevitably implicating the refugees in power politics among leaders. The primary beneficiary of influence generated through the refugee camps was Hekmatyar's Hezb-e Islami, the party whose attacks on the postcommunist Rabbani government in Kabul wrought more destruction on the capital than it had suffered during the entire Soviet period. But the greatest irony is reserved for the United States, which ended up at war with the very forces it had been instrumental in creating. Its response to the 11 September 2001 attack on the World Trade Center repeated many of the errors that both it and the Soviets had committed in Afghanistan. One "lesson" that it had learned is that refugee camps are dangerous breeding grounds of dissent. Rather than limit the political use of camps, however, the United States tried to prevent an exodus of Afghan civilians by dropping food in addition to cluster bombs from its aircraft. Clearly, little has been learned about refugeehood in Islam.

The legitimacy gained by Pakistan as host to both refugees and resistance, and the profound role that the country assumed in Afghan affairs during the Soviet occupation, entrenched Pakistani interference. Although other neighboring states such as Iran, Uzbekistan, and Russia have been implicated in the continuing Afghan conflict, Pakistan's support for the Taliban, as Anthony Davis observes, "has unquestionably been broader in its scope and ultimately far more ambitious in its goals than that of other regional powers for their Afghan candidates."[97] Although Pakistan was the principal backer of the Taliban in its rise to power in Afghanistan, the United States has again courted the Pakistani leadership with offers of mili-

[97] Anthony Davis, "How the Taliban Became a Military Force," in Maley (ed.), *Fundamentalism Reborn?* pp. 43–71 at pp. 70–71.

tary aid to help defeat it. Once again the Pakistani leadership became a major beneficiary of the West's expediency, in spite of the continued development of its nuclear program and its ambiguous stand in the regional conflict.

Humanitarian aid organizations operating in the refugee camps in Pakistan in the 1980s had little scope to reduce the influence of Pakistani authorities. It is, after all, primarily the responsibility of the host state to care for refugees on its territory. But aid agencies accepted conditions imposed both by Pakistan and by the mujahideen while there was a just cause against an identifiable "oppressor," and their acceptance would haunt these agencies once the Soviet army had left.

The aid organizations involved in cross-border assistance into Afghanistan were clearly supporting one side of the conflict. Claiming that only ICRC and, later, the UN agencies were consistently present on both sides, Antonio Donini remarked that "although the civilian populations in the government-held cities suffered from the effects of the war, none of the NGOs based in Peshawar felt a humanitarian imperative to provide aid to these innocent victims."[98] He is critical of the way in which "the humanitarians usually operated in a political space instead of actively promoting humanitarian space and respect for humanitarian values. While this course of action may have been understandable but not excusable during the years of the Soviet invasion, the absence of a peace discourse remained a distinguishing feature of the Afghan scene well after the Soviet departure."[99]

Some of his criticism is valid for reasons discussed further below, but Donini overlooks the fact that the Afghan context generated a clash of principles that obviated the possibility of respecting the two most fundamental tenets of humanitarian action. Strict neutrality in aid operations was not consistent with the proportionality prescript embedded in the principle of impartial relief. Impartiality requires that aid be given without discrimination, in accordance only with the greatest need. The needs of the civilian populations on the mujahideen side were greater than those on the government-held side, but no aid agency was officially authorized to operate in mujahideen areas. ICRC's "presence on both sides" entailed working in Pakistan with war wounded and in government-held areas after 1988.[100] Thus aid agencies venturing to provide aid across the border sac-

[98] Antonio Donini, *The Policies of Mercy: UN Coordination in Afghanistan, Mozambique, and Rwanda*, Occasional Paper no. 22 (Providence, R.I.: Thomas J. Watson Institute for International Studies, Brown University, 1996), p. 54.

[99] Ibid.

[100] See John Borton with Nigel Nicholds, Charlotte Benson, and Sanjay Dhiri, *NGOs and Relief Operations: Trends and Policy Implications*, ESCOR Research Study R47774 (London: Overseas Development Institute, 1994), p. 45.

rificed perceptions of neutrality in the conflict in order to meet a profound humanitarian need in mujahideen-held areas. They provided the civilian populations with solidarity and a choice of whether to seek refuge outside the country or remain in their homes.

The lack of neutrality in cross-border relief was less problematic than the compromises involved in supplying it. The aid agencies were dependent on the protection and assistance of the mujahideen; negotiations for the practical application of humanitarian values, such as ensuring that aid reached the most needy, were tainted by support for "the cause." The absence of standards led to manipulation of aid, which became a source of conflict among the factions in the wake of the Soviet withdrawal. Each faction tried to maximize territorial claims in anticipation of a post-Soviet carve-up of the country, and aid was an important source of legitimacy. Disillusionment crept into aid organizations as "freedom fighters" became "warlords" and the moral crusade against communism was replaced by "ethnic conflict."

Thus Donini makes a valid point when he asserts that "humanitarian activities have played into the fragmentation of Afghanistan society rather than promoting reconciliation." Promoting reconciliation, however, was never the purpose of humanitarian action: creating a genuine humanitarian space, in which aid could alleviate suffering with minimal negative consequences, would have been enough. Because this was not achieved, humanitarian aid continued to fuel aspects of the conflict. The primary responsibility of aid organizations was to curb the negative consequences of aid, not to engage in the discourse of peace.

The situation in Afghanistan, more clearly in the wake of the terrorist attacks against the United States than ever before, raises the question whether the "good" guerrillas who benefit from humanitarian sanctuary today will still be the "good" movement, faction, or government tomorrow. Most Western observers believed that aiding the resistance was just, not necessarily in terms of the Reagan Doctrine but because of the Afghan right to self-determination. Richard Falk, for example, argued about two of the theaters of the Reagan Doctrine, Afghanistan and Nicaragua, that "helping the Afghan resistance has been a contribution to self-determination, whereas helping the Contras is an obstruction to self-determination."[101]

It may have appeared that American policy supported Afghan self-determination during the Soviet occupation, but the reality became apparent after the Soviet withdrawal. Amin Saikel points out that "the United

---

[101] Richard A. Falk, "The Afghanistan 'Settlement' and the Future of World Politics," in Saikal and Maley (eds.), *Soviet Withdrawal from Afghanistan*, pp. 142–170 at p. 146.

States made little effort to link its anti-Soviet stand to a commitment to ensure a viable resolution of the Afghan conflict."[102] Afghanistan lost its strategic value to the United States, prompting abrupt disengagement from a renewed conflict the United States had been instrumental in generating. Furthermore, the U.S. Agency for International Development withdrew funding from hundreds of health clinics, a medical supply system, and training programs in rural Afghanistan,[103] leaving the NGOs that had been conduits of U.S policy with limited financial support to continue their activities. Allowed to fester for another twenty years, the Afghan conflict gave rise to extremists and a ready pool of recruits and sympathizers who have known little else than hardship and suffering. The United States is now facing the consequences of its past self-interested policies.

In its renewed involvement in Afghanistan, the United States is again turning to so-called humanitarian action as a key component of its strategy. Again, it is calling upon U.S. NGOs to be agents of its foreign policy. In remarks to the National Foreign Policy Conference for Leaders of Nongovernmental Organizations in October 2001, U.S. Secretary of State Colin Powell said "the problems that this world has brought to our door make cooperation between government and NGOs not only highly desirable, but absolutely essential and necessary." Being careful to note that cooperation does not mean cooptation, Powell nevertheless outlined the crucial role that NGOs were expected to play:

> I have made it clear to my staff here and to all of our ambassadors around the world that I am serious about making sure we have the best relationship with the NGOs who are such a force multiplier for us, such an important part of our combat team. . . . Few people know better than you how important sustained American diplomatic engagement is to the world. And few are better positioned here at home to get that message out to the American public. I know that you do that, but I ask you to do even more. I ask you to help me take the message to the American people, that the front line of our defense, the front line of our efforts is the American diplomatic effort, use of foreign aid, use of our diplomats and Peace Corps volunteers, and others from so many American governmental agencies, out doing the job for the American people. This is important work. . . . [We are] all committed to the same, singular purpose to help humankind, to help every man and woman in the world who is in need, who is hungry, who is without hope, to help

---

[102] Amin Saikal, "The UN and Afghanistan: A Case of Failed Peacemaking Intervention?" *International Peacekeeping* 3, no. 1 (1996): 19–34 at p. 26.

[103] Donini, *Policies of Mercy*, p. 51.

every one of them fill a belly, get a roof over their heads, educate their children, have hope, give them the ability to dream about a future that will be brighter, just as we have tried to make the future brighter for all Americans.[104]

Will aid organizations consider the negative repercussions of their past role as adjuncts of Western foreign policy and assert their independence, so that they can act solely in the interests of victims of this conflict? Or will they consider that this "war against terrorism" justifies advancing U.S. interests through their aid? Given the collective amnesia of most aid agencies today, and the funding opportunities this conflict presents, I doubt that many will ignore the rallying cry of Secretary Powell.

[104] Conference held at the U.S. Department of State, Washington, D.C., 26 October 2001, http://www.state.gov/secretary/rm/2001/index.cfm?docid=5762.

3

The Nicaraguan and Salvadoran Refugee Camps in Honduras

Central America was the scene of large refugee movements from the late 1970s to the end of the 1980s as state repression, guerrilla warfare, and human rights abuses drove millions from their homes to become displaced people within their own countries or asylum seekers in neighboring states. El Salvador, Nicaragua, and Guatemala were the three main refugee-producing countries, and the United States, Mexico, Honduras, and Costa Rica were the principal countries of asylum.

Sharing borders with three countries torn by civil strife, Honduras housed refugees fleeing U.S.-backed regimes in El Salvador and Guatemala in the west of the country, and refugees fleeing the Sandinista regime[1] in Nicaragua in the east (see Map 2). As an ally of the United States in a region enmeshed in superpower rivalry, Honduras welcomed Nicaraguan refugees and *contra*[2] insurgents opposing Managua, but was reluctant host to Salvadoran and Guatemalan refugees and was opposed to the Farabundo Martí National Liberation Front (Frente Farabundo Martí para la Liberación Nacional— FMLN) in El Salvador. Refugees throughout the region were intensely politicized, their presence considered "evidence" by leftists and rightists alike of the brutality and injustice of the opposing regime, and refugees were treated according to the political allegiance their presence implied.

The highly politicized context had repercussions for refugee protection. Most refugee settlements in Central America were accused of posing a security threat either to the host nation or to the regime from which they fled, by providing sanctuary for subversive forces and being sources of political organization and ideological contagion. The Costa Rican authorities alleged that camps housing Salvadoran refugees "may have served as train-

---

[1] The Sandinistas were named after a Nicaraguan nationalist, Augusto Cesar Sandino.

[2] The term "contras," short for *contrarevolucionarios*, denotes the various groups opposing the Sandinista government in Nicaragua from bases in Honduras and Costa Rica and within Nicaragua.

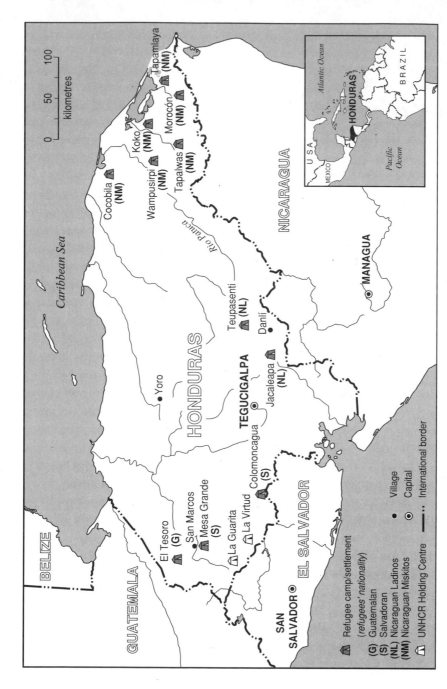

Map 2. Nicaraguan and Salvadoran refugee camps and settlements in Honduras. From James Morsch, *Summary of Refugee Conditions in Costa Rica, Honduras, and Mexico* (Washington, D.C.: Refugee Policy Group, 1987), p. 1, as modified by author.

ing grounds for extremists who return to El Salvador as well trained guer-rillas,"[3] and harassed the 6,000 refugees present, while concurrently per-mitting Nicaraguan guerrilla forces to train and operate on Costa Rican soil.[4] The Guatemalan military attacked refugee camps in Mexico,[5] and the Salvadoran Armed Forces (SAF) attacked camps in Honduras, alleging that they harbored members of the FMLN. The contras openly lived among refugees along the Honduran-Nicaraguan border.

The humanitarian aid community was not impervious to the politically charged environment of Central America, even if organization charters proclaimed neutral and impartial intent. Just as the refugees were tainted by the ideological identification of the regimes they were fleeing, so the aid agencies were tainted by the refugees with whom they chose to work. And while for some this categorization may have been an unfortunate by-product of the provision of humanitarian assistance in conflict, for most, humanitarian assistance was a tool in a "just" war against tyranny, whether communist or conservative. With the acquiescence or support of the aid community, the refugees became pawns in the political strategies pursued by all sides.

Honduras as a Military Sanctuary

The complexity of the refugee situation in Honduras was intrinsically linked with historical relations in the region. Honduras traditionally viewed El Salvador as its principal security threat, and tensions caused by population density and migration issues led to an outbreak of conflict in 1969. Atrocities committed by Salvadoran soldiers during the conflict ex-acerbated public hostility toward Salvadoran nationals, and the two coun-tries remained officially at war one decade after the combat ceased. De-spite strong U.S. encouragement to settle the border dispute, the Honduran military remained reluctant to cooperate with the Salvadoran military, even in their common fight against communist insurgencies.

Nicaragua, by contrast, was not viewed as a security threat to Hon-duras, despite border clashes in the 1950s and 1960s. Nevertheless, Hon-duras was implicated in much of the conflict in Nicaragua, first providing a

[3] Quote from *La República* (San José, Costa Rica), 7 October 1982, as cited in Liisa North and Canada-Caribbean-Central American Policy Alternatives (CAPA) (eds.), *Between War and Peace in Central America: Choices for Canada* (Toronto: Between the Lines, 1990), p. 147.
[4] North and CAPA, *Between War and Peace*, p. 148.
[5] See Gil Loescher, "Humanitarianism and Politics in Central America," in Bruce Nichols and Gil Loescher (eds.), *The Moral Nation: Humanitarianism and U.S. Foreign Policy Today* (Notre Dame: University of Notre Dame Press, 1989), pp. 154–191 at p. 158.

military sanctuary for the forces which overthrew the Somoza regime (1933–79), and then, ironically, hosting the contra opposition to those same forces once they had come to power. In fact, the Sandinista National Liberation Front (Frente Sandinista de Liberación Nacional—FSLN) was founded in Honduras in 1961 and, according to a U.S. State Department document, conducted the first armed incursions into Nicaragua in 1962.[6] But it was when the United States in 1979 lost Nicaragua, its closest ally in Central America, to a regime that favored ties to Havana and Moscow over Washington, that Honduras was transformed into a "Pentagon Republic," a military sanctuary from which to launch a covert war against Nicaragua.[7]

THE NICARAGUAN OPPOSITION FORCES

The Nicaraguan contras consisted of a diverse range of combatant groups whose only shared objective seems to have been the overthrow of the Sandinista government. The initial core of this resistance were members of Somoza's former National Guard who managed to flee the country in the wake of the overthrow of the government.[8] They were later joined by combatants who had opposed Somoza but became disaffected from the Sandinista regime, and by indigenous Indian opposition groups. Despite efforts to unite the assemblage into a coherent opposition force, the contras remained far from homogeneous, plagued by internal rivalry and corruption.

U.S. support to the contras began toward the end of President Jimmy Carter's term in office in response to suspicions that the Sandinistas were supplying arms to the FMLN in El Salvador.[9] This support expanded markedly when Ronald Reagan assumed the U.S. presidency in 1981; by December, $19.5 million had been allocated to assemble, train, arm, and direct a commando force of 500 mostly Cuban exiles to conduct paramilitary operations against Nicaragua from Honduras.[10] According to a former contra spokesperson, U.S. support ensured the existence of the con-

[6] "Revolution beyond Our Borders": Sandinista Intervention in Central America, Special Report No. 132 (Washington, D.C.: U.S. Department of State, September 1985), p. 3.

[7] Richard Lapper and James Painter, Honduras: State for Sale (London: Latin American Bureau, 1985), p. 88.

[8] The U.S. military helped to evacuate commanders of the Nicaraguan National Guard by disguising a DC-8 jet with Red Cross markings and landing it in Managua. See Peter Kornbluh, "The Covert War," in Thomas W. Walker (ed.), Reagan versus the Sandinistas: The Undeclared War on Nicaragua (Boulder, Colo.: Westview, 1987), pp. 21–38 at p. 21.

[9] Marlene Dixon, "Reagan's Central America Policy: A New Somoza for Nicaragua," in Marlene Dixon (ed.), On Trial: Reagan's War in Nicaragua: Testimony of the Permanent Peoples' Tribunal (London: Zed Books, 1985), pp. 111–152 at pp. 116–117.

[10] William M. LeoGrande, "The Contras and Congress," in Walker (ed.), Reagan versus the Sandinistas, pp. 202–227 at p. 203.

tras and transformed the fighters from "a collection of small, disorganized and ineffectual bands of ex–National Guardsmen . . . into a well-organized, well-armed, well-equipped and well-trained fighting force of approximately 4,000 men."[11]

The U.S. assistance enabled daily raids from Honduras by the end of 1982, which were aimed at political, economic, and military targets in Nicaragua. The extent of these attacks raised questions in the media concerning the intentions of the U.S. government, and prompted the U.S. Congress to pass a bill in December prohibiting government aid to paramilitary groups for the purpose of overthrowing the Nicaraguan government.[12] The Reagan administration denied that this was the purpose of the contra support, instead justifying the attacks as necessary in order to "turn their [the Sandinistas'] attention away from subversion beyond Nicaragua's borders and reduce the availability of material to be sent to the FMLN."[13] Although arms shipments, some of which were obtained from Cuba, are widely believed to have been sent from Nicaragua by air, sea, or overland via Honduras in preparation for the failed "final offensive" of the FMLN in El Salvador,[14] no credible evidence of shipments after early 1981 was ever provided.[15]

Military operations from Honduras intensified in 1983, and by June the contra force was 8,000 strong.[16] Military offensives included the invasion of Nicaragua by some 2,000 contras in March 1983; the bombing of Managua in September 1983; and air and sea attacks against oil storage tanks and pipelines in September and October 1983 in which the CIA played a

[11] Affidavit of Edgar Chamorro at International Court of Justice (ICJ) case *Nicaragua v. United States*, as cited in Holly Sklar, *Washington's War on Nicaragua* (Boston: South End Press, 1988), p. 117.

[12] For a detailed discussion of the congressional debates over Central American policy from the late 1970s to the late 1980s, see Cynthia J. Arnson, *Crossroads: Congress, the Reagan Administration, and Central America* (New York: Pantheon, 1989).

[13] "*Revolution beyond Our Borders*," p. 23.

[14] See Marc Edelman, "Soviet-Cuban Involvement in Central America: A Critique of Recent Writings," in Bruce D. Larkin (ed.), *Vital Interests: The Soviet Issue in U.S. Central American Policy* (Boulder, Colo.: Lynne Rienner, 1988), pp. 141–167 at p. 152.

[15] The *Washington Post* (13 June 1984) reported that after four years of trying, the Reagan administration was unable to prove its case or produce evidence of arms shipments to El Salvador. David MacMichael, a former CIA analyst, testified that there was no successful interdiction or verified report of arms movement after April 1981. See Dixon, "Reagan's Central America Policy," p. 131, and the Testimony of David MacMichael, "The Involvement of the CIA," in Paul Ramshaw and Tom Steers (eds.), *Intervention on Trial: The New York War Crimes Tribunal on Central America and the Caribbean* (New York: Praeger, 1987), pp. 82–84.

[16] According to CIA figures, the force grew from 500 in 1981 to 4,000 by December 1982, 5,500 by February 1983, and 8,000 by June. See Edward Best, *U.S. Policy and Regional Security in Central America* (Aldershot, U.K.: International Institute of Strategic Studies and Gower, 1987), p. 58.

direct role.[17] Between February and April 1984, mines were laid in or close to three Nicaraguan harbors upon the written authorization of President Reagan, an act which the International Court of Justice (ICJ) ruled was in violation of the principles of customary international law.[18] The harbor mining ignited a debate which had been simmering in Congress since the beginning of U.S. support to the contras, and culminated in a vote banning all direct and indirect aid to the guerrilla force in October 1984.

Anticipating the financial obstruction to his foreign policy goals, earlier that year President Reagan had authorized the National Security Council (NSC) to create a surrogate supply network to continue aiding the contras, which operated from the basement of the White House.[19] Oliver North, an aide to NSC Chief Robert McFarlane, worked with retired senior U.S. military officials to establish a covert network consisting of three key components. First, the governments of Saudi Arabia, Israel, South Korea, South Africa, and Singapore became surrogate suppliers of weapons and funds to the guerrillas. From July 1984 to May 1986 the Saudi government alone contributed $32 million to the contras.[20] Funds from allied governments were augmented by profits from the secret U.S. arms sales to Iran that had secured Iranian assistance in the release of U.S. hostages held in Lebanon.

Second, former U.S. military officials established a covert supply system, purchasing arms in Portugal and Poland with false documents provided by the Guatemalan military, through real and fictitious companies in Canada, the United States, and Switzerland. Over 800 tons of weapons were allegedly supplied to El Salvador and Honduras in 1985 and 1986 for the covert war from these sources.[21] The third component of the covert network consisted of private American organizations whose activities ranged from fundraising and charity drives to paramilitary activities, often under the guise of "humanitarian" support. These are discussed in more detail below.

Having Honduras as a compliant host for the contras, the Reagan ad-

[17] New York Times, 18 April 1984, and Washington Post, 18 April 1984, as cited in Dixon, "Reagan's Central America Policy," p. 119.

[18] For a detailed account of proceedings before the ICJ, see Terry Gill, Litigation Strategy at the International Court: A Case Study of the Nicaragua v. United States Dispute (Dordrecht: Martinus Nijhoff, 1989), part 2, pp. 123–346. For a summary of the ICJ judgment of June 1986, see World Court Digest, volume 1: 1986–1990 (Berlin: Max-Planck Institute for International Law, Springer-Verlag, 1993), pp. 264–274.

[19] See Peter Kornbluh, "Test Case for the Reagan Doctrine: The Covert Contra War," Third World Quarterly 9, no. 4 (1987): 1118–1128 at p. 1121.

[20] See ibid., pp. 1121–1122, for details of these transfers. Also see Sklar, Washington's War on Nicaragua, pp. 223–233, for details of the arms and finance pipelines.

[21] Kornbluh, "Test Case for the Reagan Doctrine," pp. 1122–1123.

ministration was also able to circumvent some of the restrictions imposed by Congress in other ways. The United States and Honduran military undertook annual joint maneuvers which involved the construction of military facilities, the allocation of communication equipment, and the expansion of airstrips in Honduras. Much of these facilities and equipment was left in Honduras for use by the contras once the exercises terminated.[22] Furthermore, direct U.S. aid to the contras continued in increasingly veiled forms, such as the designation of military equipment as "surplus to requirements," thereby avoiding the imposition of a dollar value and hence the need for Congressional approval.[23]

Congress reversed its ban on funding for the contras in June 1985, approving $27 million of so-called humanitarian assistance in the wake of a visit by Nicaraguan President Daniel Ortega to the Soviet Union and Soviet-allied states. The "humanitarian" proviso, described by Henry Shue as "one of the most shameful episodes of mendacity in recent American politics,"[24] appeased those members of Congress opposed to resuming contra support by limiting aid to "food, clothing, medicine and other humanitarian assistance." It specifically excluded "the provision of weapons, weapons systems, ammunition or other equipment, vehicles or material which can be used to inflict serious bodily harm or death."[25] Debasing the term "humanitarian" by using it to describe nonlethal logistical support to a military force was bad enough. But even then the funds were not spent as Congress specified.

The Nicaraguan Humanitarian Aid Office that was established to manage and disperse the $27 million became a vehicle for supplies to the contras. In addition to payments for arms flights to the contras,[26] a General Accounting Office audit conducted in 1986 found a trail of corruption, including one bribe of $450,000 to the Honduran military commander-in-chief.[27] Two-thirds of the money had vanished, much of it into bank accounts in the Cayman Islands,[28] and the funds were also linked to co-

---

[22] *United States–Honduran Relations: A Background Briefing Packet* (Central American Historical Institute, May 1994), p. 1, as cited in Dixon, "Reagan's Central America Policy," p. 125.

[23] Sklar, *Washington's War on Nicaragua*, p. 147.

[24] Henry Shue, "Morality, Politics, and Humanitarian Assistance," in Nichols and Loescher (eds.), *The Moral Nation*, pp. 12–40 at p. 23.

[25] Sklar, *Washington's War on Nicaragua*, p. 268.

[26] *New York Times*, 15 August 1987, as cited in Sklar, *Washington's War on Nicaragua*, p. 269.

[27] *Investigation of U.S. Assistance to the Nicaraguan Contras*, Hearings and Markup before the Committee on Foreign Affairs and Subcommittee on West Hemisphere Affairs, U.S. House of Representatives, April 9, May 1, May 8, and June 11, 1986, p. 64.

[28] Leslie Cockburn, *Out of Control* (New York: Atlantic Monthly Press, 1987), pp. 45, 159.

caine-running activities of the contras.[29] Despite the appearance of the GAO report before Congress and attempts by some members to halt all payments to the contras until the full $27 million was accounted for, fund allocations continued, culminating in the congressional decision in June 1986 to approve Reagan's request for an additional $100 million. One estimate suggests that $200 million was allocated in public and private funds to the Nicaraguan opposition in the previous seven years, bringing the total in 1986 to $300 million.[30] By the time the contra camps began to be dismantled in February 1989, the guerrilla force had received an estimated $400 million.[31]

As in Pakistan during the Soviet occupation of Afghanistan, Honduran authorities greatly benefited from playing the role of sanctuary to U.S.-backed guerrilla forces. Economic aid to Honduras doubled from $24 million to $50.7 million between 1979 and 1980[32] following the overthrow of Somoza, and by 1982 Honduras had become the second highest recipient of U.S. military aid in Latin America (receiving $31.3 million in 1982, compared with $32.5 million for the entire period 1946–81).[33] By 1984, military aid to Honduras reached $78.5 million, and economic aid $168.7 million.[34] The Honduran military also received training with the aid of U.S. military personnel, whose numbers stationed in Honduras rose from 25 in 1980 to 700–800 in 1983.[35] In addition, the joint military exercises undertaken between 1982 and 1984 contributed some $150 million to air and naval bases on the Atlantic Coast[36] and involved some 4,000 U.S. combat troops.[37] Individuals within the Honduran military also gained personally through the corruption surrounding contra activities.

The role of Honduras in the war against Nicaragua was thus of crucial importance to the Nicaraguan resistance movement, providing a secure base through which the United States and its allies could comprehensively undertake resupply, training, and rearmament. The compliance of the

[29] Ibid., pp. 159–167.

[30] E. Bradford Burns, *At War in Nicaragua: The Reagan Doctrine and the Politics of Nostalgia* (New York: Harper and Row, 1987), p. 61.

[31] John A. Booth and Thomas W. Walker, *Understanding Central America* (Boulder, Colo.: Westview, 1989), p. 66.

[32] U.S. Congressional Hearing on Honduras, February 1985, as cited in Lapper and Painter, *Honduras: State for Sale*, p. 87.

[33] Lapper and Painter, *Honduras: State for Sale*, p. 88. Also see Best, *U.S. Policy and Regional Security in Central America*, pp. 59–60, for details of U.S. support to Honduras.

[34] Lapper and Painter, *Honduras: State for Sale*, p. 87.

[35] Ibid., p. 88.

[36] *New York Times*, 23 July 1983, as cited in Dixon, "Reagan's Central America Policy," p. 125.

[37] Best, *U.S. Policy and Regional Security in Central America*, p. 60.

Honduran authorities even permitted the United States to portray the Nicaraguans as the aggressors while simultaneously displaying the full weight of American backing to the contras and Honduras. One of the primary roles of the contras was to "provoke border attacks by Nicaraguan forces and thus serve to demonstrate Nicaragua's aggressive nature."[38] Then, when Sandinista forces in hot pursuit of contras did cross the border, as occurred in early 1986, U.S. troops and helicopters mobilized with the Honduran military in a large and threatening show of force.[39] Under the umbrella of the U.S. military, Honduras was a well-protected military sanctuary.

THE SALVADORAN OPPOSITION FORCES

It is difficult to assess the extent to which Honduran territory played the role of military sanctuary to Salvadoran guerrillas opposing the U.S.-backed government. Richard Lapper and James Painter suggest that Honduras was a staging post for arms supplies to the guerrillas which were bought in Europe and landed on Honduras's Atlantic Coast,[40] but whether or not this was with the complicity of members of the Honduran armed forces is unclear. Historical animosities between the armed forces of the two countries are alleged to have split the Honduran military into two camps. U.S.-trained soldiers perceived the left-wing guerrillas to be the greatest threat to Honduran stability, while veterans of the 1969 conflict considered the Salvadoran army to be the greater danger.[41] Hence individuals in Honduras may have assisted the FMLN to maintain a constant pressure on the Salvadoran military forces in order to reduce the potential threat posed to Honduras.

As mentioned earlier, shipments of arms may have crossed Honduras from Nicaragua in the early days of the Sandinista regime, but no evidence exists of transfers after early 1981. Marc Edelman surmises that the Nicaraguans stopped them after this time owing to the failure of the FMLN offensive.[42] Scant information exists concerning support to the Salvadoran guerrillas, and what is available is mostly conjecture and speculation. This lacuna is attested to by the number of times an article by Jiri

---

[38] David MacMichael's testimony before the World Court, 13 September 1985, p. 8 of transcript, as cited in Kornbluh, "The Covert War," p. 23.

[39] Eva Gold, "Military Encirclement," in Walker (ed.), *Reagan versus the Sandinistas*, pp. 39–56 at p. 51.

[40] Lapper and Painter, *Honduras: State for Sale*, p. 76.

[41] Loescher, "Humanitarianism and Politics in Central America," p. 168.

[42] Edelman, "Soviet-Cuban Involvement in Central America," p. 153.

Valenta was reprinted,[43] even though it did not substantiate claims that "the Cuban orchestration of the supply of armaments from Soviet allied countries has been significant," and that "Soviet-backed involvement of Cuba has significantly strengthened the guerrillas in El Salvador."[44] A better idea of the source of weapons for the FMLN was provided in 1984 by the U.S. under-secretary of defense, Fred Iklé, who conceded that official estimates suggested that half the guerrillas' arms were captured from the SAF.[45]

Several factors militate against the conclusion that Honduras was used to any great extent as a military sanctuary for the Salvadoran guerrillas. First, crossing the border into Honduras did not ensure protection, either from the host country, which was officially opposed to their cause, or from incursions by the SAF. Such incursions by the SAF and the notorious death squads are well documented.[46] Second, the guerrillas held considerable territory within El Salvador from which they launched attacks on the capital, and they therefore had less need of an external base. The FMLN strategy consisted of establishing "zones of control" or "liberated zones" which, by 1984, constituted over 20 percent of the country and contained some 250,000 inhabitants.[47] But although Honduras was unlikely to have benefited the FMLN as a purely military sanctuary, a humanitarian sanctuary has several advantages over a military one, and the refugee camps in Honduras were able to perform some functions for the guerrilla forces.

Honduras as a Humanitarian Sanctuary

THE SALVADORAN REFUGEE CAMPS

UNHCR officials maintain today that no proof ever surfaced to confirm that the Salvadoran refugee camps sheltered guerrilla fighters, or that humanitarian aid was filtered to the FMLN in El Salvador.[48] From a visit to

[43] Jiri Valenta, "The U.S.S.R., Cuba, and the Crisis in Central America," in Larkin (ed.), *Vital Interests*, pp. 321–350. This article was reprinted from Jiri Valenta, "The U.S.S.R., Cuba, and the Crisis in Central America," *Orbis* 25, no. 3 (Fall 1981): 715–746, which was itself an adaptation of "Soviet and Cuban Responses to New Opportunities in Central America," in Richard Feinberg (ed.), *Central America: International Dimensions of the Crisis* (New York: Holmes and Meier, 1982), pp. 127–159.

[44] Valenta, "The U.S.S.R., Cuba, and the Crisis in Central America," pp. 345–346.

[45] Edelman, "Soviet-Cuban Involvement in Central America," p. 154.

[46] See, for example, Jeremy Adelman, "The Insecurity of El Salvadorean Refugees," *Refuge: Canada's Periodical on Refugees* 3, no. 1 (October 1983): 1–4 at p. 4; North and CAPA (eds.), *Between War and Peace in Central America*, pp. 133–137; and Elizabeth Ferris, *The Central American Refugees* (New York: Praeger, 1987), p. 102.

[47] Helen Schooley, *Conflict in Central America* (Essex, U.K.: Longman, 1987), p. 185.

[48] Personal interviews with UNHCR officials, Geneva, March 1998.

Colomoncagua in 1986, Gil Loescher also concluded that it was physically impossible to smuggle significant quantities of aid past the Honduran military that patrolled the border.[49] Honduran and U.S. officials, by contrast, firmly asserted that such activities were occurring, and advocated relocating the camps further inland accordingly.[50] Examining each of the potential sources of support provided by the refugee camps makes it evident that, in comparison with refugee camps based on friendly territory, the Salvadoran camps did not function significantly as a source of resupply or protection to the guerrilla forces. Nevertheless, norms of refugee asylum and the presence of aid organizations provided some benefits.

Protection

The hostility of at least an important segment of the Honduran military toward the Salvadoran guerrillas and refugees limited the effectiveness of refugee camps as a protected zone. Animosity toward the refugees was evident from the outset, with the military repelling all but the first refugee influx of 2,000 Salvadorans in 1980. The first refugees settled with the border populations with whom they had retained good relations in spite of the 1969 conflict. But the Honduran army brutally prevented further influxes, and in one incident in May 1980 combined Salvadoran and Honduran troops killed hundreds of refugees as they crossed the Sumpul River.[51] By 1981, the government's policy changed to permit refugees to enter Honduras, but the newly formed National Refugee Commission was effectively placed under the jurisdiction of the military through the appointment of a retired army colonel, Abraham Turcios, to head it.[52]

The proximity of the refugee camps to the border—in some cases only a few kilometers away—and suspicions of guerrilla infiltrations of the area provoked heavy military surveillance. Frequent searches of the camps were

[49] Loescher, "Humanitarianism and Politics in Central America," p. 170.

[50] Different accounts in the literature of the Honduran attitude toward camp relocation suggests that the military was divided over the issue. William Stanley, for example, claims that the Honduran military "consistently opposed" U.S. proposals to move the refugee camps further from the border, fearing the contagion of radical political ideology among Honduran peasants. Patricia Weiss Fagen and Sergio Aguayo, however, cite Honduran support for such a move. See Stanley, "Blessing or Menace? The Security Implications of Central American Migration," in Myron Weiner (ed.), *International Migration and Security* (Boulder, Colo.: Westview, 1993), pp. 229–260, at p. 245, and Fagen and Aguayo, *Fleeing the Maelstrom: Central American Refugees*, Occasional Paper No. 10, Central American and Caribbean Program (Baltimore: School of Advanced International Studies, Johns Hopkins University, 1986), p. 64.

[51] North and CAPA (eds.), *Between War and Peace in Central America*, p. 133.

[52] Mandy Macdonald, "Salvadorean Refugees in Honduras," Appendix 3 in Lapper and Painter, *Honduras: State for Sale*, p. 130.

undertaken, and the military stationed around Colomoncagua were allegedly ordered to shoot and kill anyone leaving the camp after 5 P.M.[53] The refugees had no freedom of movement outside the camps and no possibility of working. But in spite of the constant patrols and military surveillance, the nature of the terrain and the unfenced perimeter of the camps made movements in and out impossible to fully control.

Evidence of numerous incidents of violence against refugees and aid personnel existed, including the killing of two members of the Catholic aid organization Caritas by the Salvadoran military in the reception center of La Virtud in 1981; the discovery of the bodies of fourteen Salvadorans twenty-five kilometers from Mesa Grande in 1984; the killing of at least twenty refugees by Honduran troops between January and July 1984; and the shooting of a Spanish doctor and two Salvadorans in June 1984.[54] The most publicized incident took place in August 1985 when a Honduran military raid on Colomoncagua resulted in the death of two refugees, the injury of thirteen others, and the arrest of ten more. Such incidents illustrate that the camps did not provide a safe haven in which combatants were immune from attack. But the outrage expressed by international organizations following military incursions into the camps limited military impunity and in that sense did provide some form of protection to the refugee camp inhabitants. Indeed, some international organizations sent their personnel to live in the camps specifically to provide protection by confronting death squad members who entered to abduct and kill camp occupants.[55]

The most significant indication that the camps did play a role for the Salvadoran insurgents was provided by refugee reaction to attempts to relocate the camps further inland, away from the insecurity of the border. UNHCR was strongly in favor of such a move since, in addition to the insecurity generated by military suspicions of guerrilla infiltrations in the camps, the proximity of some camps (La Virtud in particular) to the border subjected them to "collateral damage" from heavy fighting in El Salvador. But in spite of the danger to the camp inhabitants, the forced closure of La Virtud in early 1982 and the relocation of the refugees to Mesa Grande, the farthest camp from the border, provoked vehement protest from the refugees, aid agencies, and human rights organizations working

[53] James Morsch, *Summary of Refugee Conditions in Costa Rica, Honduras, and Mexico* (Washington, D.C.: Refugee Policy Group, 1987), p. 9.

[54] Schooley, *Conflict in Central America*, p. 210.

[55] Testimony of Father Henry Atkins, Jr., "The Policy of Displacement and the Flight of Refugees," in Ramshaw and Steers (eds.), *Intervention on Trial*, pp. 24–25.

in the area. Their stated reasons for opposition were twofold. First, they claimed that the motive for such a move was to militarize the border and prevent the influx of more Salvadorans, which violated the refugees' rights to asylum. Second, they claimed that the proposed relocation sites were unacceptable to the refugees and aid workers for reasons of security and refugee well-being. Mesa Grande, to which further transfers were proposed, was overcrowded, and alternative sites in the interior departments of Olancho and Yoro were allegedly populated by Hondurans who had persecuted Salvadoran migrants following the 1969 war. Agencies insisted that there was a high degree of hostility to Salvadorans in the interior, and cited the return of 4,000 refugees from La Virtud to El Salvador to avoid the move to Mesa Grande as proof of refugee fears of the interior.[56]

This sudden repatriation, however, can just as readily support the claim that the camps housed Salvadoran guerrillas and their supporters since any relocation further from the border would have reduced the utility of the camps for the insurgents. The camps provided protection to the guerrillas if only in deterring the further militarization of the border: a U.S. State Department "non-policy paper" stated that the closure of Colomoncagua would make the border area more secure and render it "easier for the Honduran military to make sweeps of the area and to disrupt any regional insurgency activity there."[57] To counter claims that the refugees would be less subject to harassment away from the border, aid agencies argued that at Mesa Grande accusations of guerrilla infiltration by the Honduran military abounded despite the camp's distance from the border.[58] But despite the opposition, UNHCR remained firm in its support for relocation, stressing that as long as the camps remained where they were, the Honduran authorities "have ample justification in their view to act as they had [in the August 1985 raid on Colomoncagua]."[59] Moreover, a senior UNHCR official asserted that "UNHCR could do little to prevent the Honduran authorities from exercising their legitimate right to carry out policing operations in the camps, especially when they maintained that national security was at stake."[60] Nevertheless, the support of international agencies

<hr/>

[56] Fagen and Aguayo, *Fleeing the Maelstrom*, p. 64.

[57] U.S. State Department Non-Policy Paper, February 1985, as cited in Macdonald, "Salvadorean Refugees in Honduras," p. 130.

[58] The remarks of the Oxfam representative, as noted in Jennifer Waugh and Flora Liebich, "Debriefing for NGOs on Situation in Honduras, Friday, 13 September 1985, UNHCR," UNHCR "note for the file" mimeo, 17 September 1985, p. 4.

[59] Waugh and Liebich, "Debriefing for NGOs on Situation in Honduras," p. 4.

[60] Robert Muller, head of the Regional Bureau for the Americas and Europe, UNHCR, as cited in ibid., p. 2.

and the readiness of the refugees to resist relocation at all costs prevented any further camp relocations. UNHCR recognized that any new attempts to move the refugee camps forcibly would result in loss of life since the camps were sufficiently well organized to ensure the solidarity of the entire refugee population.

The refugees' vehement aversion to camp relocation despite incursions by Salvadoran and Honduran forces, together with the enduring accusations that the camps sheltered guerrilla fighters, suggests that the camps did serve a dual purpose. Mixing with the refugees, many of whom were family members,[61] guerrillas were impossible to distinguish from the civilians. Despite the heavy patrols, the camps were not impenetrable, and the presence of international aid workers inhibited the military's ability to pursue counterinsurgency operations free from scrutiny. Hence the camps served to protect the FMLN forces to a certain extent. Once penetrated, the camps became a source of provisions to the rebel forces in El Salvador.

War Economy

The raid on Colomoncagua in August 1985 was allegedly undertaken after a deserter from the FMLN testified that substantial amounts of food and medicine routinely left the camp for El Salvador. He also alleged that the camp was a rest and recreation facility for the guerrillas.[62] The plausibility of a testimony reported by the Honduran military is questionable, but the allegation is supported by the experiences of Médecins sans Frontières (MSF), which worked in the camps from 1980 to 1988. Dr Bernard Pécoul, who was medical coordinator for MSF in Honduras, confirms that the camps were a source of resupply for the guerrillas, often with the assistance of the aid organizations. He claims that most organizations were "infiltrated" to varying degrees by expatriate volunteers who were highly politicized and considered the insurgency to be a just war against the brutal Salvadoran government and military. A Spanish doctor who arrived in Honduras for MSF, for example, disappeared with medical supplies across the border into El Salvador to assist the FMLN. She reappeared six months later but was killed by the Honduran military before reaching safety.[63]

---

[61] Gilles Bataillon, "L'action humanitaire des ONG françaises en Amérique centrale: Entre bureaucratie humanitariste et nouvelle vision de l'humanité," *Cultures et Conflits* 11 (autumn 1993): 65–76 at p. 69.

[62] Waugh and Liebich, "Debriefing for NGOs on Situation in Honduras," p. 2.

[63] Bernard Pécoul, former MSF medical coordinator in Honduras, personal interview, 25 April 1998.

The strong ideological convictions of many aid agency employees influenced the relief system and levels of aid in the camps, as the experience of MSF in the health sector attests. MSF assumed responsibility from Caritas for the medical coordination of all the camps in 1986 and tried to standardize the quantity and type of medical assistance in accordance with public health guidelines used in refugee camps throughout the world. MSF was concerned by the elevated drug consumption rate and the levels of health care and caloric consumption, which were higher in the camps than among the surrounding population. Data were produced to substantiate these concerns, including a census, not a survey, of the nutrition level of the children in the camps, in which not one child was found to be malnourished.[64] MSF recommended that the feeding center, which was operated by Concern, be closed, but Concern refused, arguing that the need still existed. MSF met intense opposition from the refugee committees in the camps who, far from accepting reduced levels of assistance, demanded that larger quantities and a wider range of drugs be made available to the Salvadoran health staff and sought an increase in the training of local health workers. Cognizant of the disappearance of trained personnel into the guerrilla forces and the superior health status in the camps, MSF refused to meet these demands.

Hence although difficult to quantify, evidence suggests that food, medical supplies, and health staff trained in the refugee camps routinely left for the Salvadoran guerrillas. Humanitarian assistance was provided by many NGOs in excess of requirements, to enable a portion to be skimmed off and sent across the border. As the total Salvadoran refugee population in Honduras was only 20,000, however, the overall quantities of aid leaving the camps was limited in its potential impact on the war economy.

Population Control and Legitimacy

The most important contributions of the Salvadoran refugee camps to the guerrilla insurgency were the mechanisms they provided to derive benefits from the civilian population. As mentioned above, sectoral committees of refugee leaders were formed in each of the camps, and their control over the aid distribution channels enabled them to exert considerable influence over the refugee population. Committee members were approved by the guerrilla leadership and assisted in conscription for the guerrilla forces,[65]

---

[64] Ibid. Ordinarily it is deemed sufficient to conduct a survey to attain a representative sample of the nutritional status of the population, but in this case all children were measured to avoid any doubt concerning the results.

[65] Bataillon, "L'action humanitaire des ONG françaises en Amérique centrale," p. 69.

allegedly coercing women to give up their children once they reached the age of ten, through threats to reduce their food rations, harassment, and punishment.[66] All correspondence in the camps was controlled by the committees, and refugees were prevented from repatriating since their presence was imperative to ensure the continuation of humanitarian assistance. While some refugees requested help from the aid agencies to escape the leaders, Gilles Bataillon suggests that the majority recognized the authority of the guerrillas as legitimate, or at least tolerated it as the least bad to be expected.[67] UNHCR, unable to ensure the protection of the refugees in such an environment, resorted to extreme measures. One staff member was quoted as saying, "We have had to conduct departures at night in the hope of escaping the vigilance of the committees. We have ourselves, as a consequence, been physically threatened at the committees' orders."[68]

The refugee committees were also accused of exploiting the suffering of the refugees for propaganda purposes. In an interview with the French newspaper *La Croix*, Rony Brauman, president of MSF in Paris, cited two occasions in which refugees injured by the Honduran military had their dressings and intravenous lines removed by members of the committees. He argued that "for their propaganda, a dead refugee is more useful than an injured refugee" and accused the committees of having hidden dehydrated children to exacerbate the gravity of their affliction.[69] Brauman considered the committees had a "totalitarian hold" over the camps reminiscent of the Khmer Rouge, and used humanitarian aid for their own purposes.[70] His views were not broadly supported, however, because of the political allegiance of aid workers who tolerated or even supported this system, disagreement that the committees posed a problem, or the reluctance of aid agencies to challenge the status quo.[71] When questioned about the diversion of aid supplies to the guerrilla forces in El Salvador, for example, Patrick Ahern, country director of Catholic Relief Service (CRS) in Honduras said: "It's the price of our success. The refugees become actors in their own development. By respecting their form of organization, we

[66] Bertrand de la Grange, "L'organisation Médecins sans frontières renonce à assister les réfugiés salvadoriens au Honduras," *Le Monde*, 16 November 1988, p. 8.

[67] Bataillon, "L'action humanitaire des ONG françaises," pp. 69–70.

[68] De la Grange, "L'organisation Médecins sans frontières," p. 8.

[69] Alain Hertoghe, "Des limites supposées de l'aide humanitaire," *La Croix*, 25–26 December 1988, p. 6.

[70] Rony Brauman, "Les camps de réfugiés salvadoriens au Honduras," Letter to the editor, *Le Monde*, 26 November 1988, p. 6.

[71] Bataillon, "L'action humanitaire des ONG françaises en Amérique centrale," p. 70.

are accused of serving the forces supposedly hidden behind the committees. It's very serious for our security and that of the refugees."[72]

The risk of opposing the system was far greater than that of accepting it: MSF's refusal to meet the demands of the committees and Brauman's sharp criticisms of the transformation of the camps "into small gulags"[73] provoked the committees to organize hostile protests against MSF's "insensitivity." In 1988 the committees blocked access of MSF personnel to the refugee camps and demanded their replacement by an organization "more sympathetic." MSF decided to withdraw from the camps in November 1988.

To further complicate the possibility of objective discussions about the camp structure, the dispute immediately assumed the discourse of the dominant Cold War polemic, and accusations that MSF staff were mercenaries in the service of American imperialism ensued. Once UNHCR publicly backed the MSF position, it too was accused of having a U.S. agenda, this time to force the refugees to return to El Salvador.[74] Only four years earlier, the Heritage Foundation had published a report accusing UNHCR of sympathizing with the FMLN guerrillas and recommended that U.S. funding be withheld as a consequence.[75] Such accusations of political allegiance abounded in Central America, but ironically MSF and UNHCR were two of only four organizations that worked with both the Salvadoran and Nicaraguan refugees.[76] For UNHCR, such action was required under its mandate, but for MSF, working with both sides was an attempt to assert the neutrality and impartiality of humanitarian action in the region. Hence when continued access to the Salvadoran camps was denied, MSF decided also to terminate its work with the Nicaraguan refugees in the east of the country, phasing out through transferring activities to other aid organizations.

THE NICARAGUAN REFUGEE CAMPS

As a major sponsor and base of contra rebels, Honduras was naturally a welcoming host to Nicaraguan refugees, whose very presence bolstered

[72] Hertoghe, "Des limites supposées de l'aide humanitaire," p. 6.

[73] As cited in De la Grange, "L'organisation Médecins sans frontières," p. 8.

[74] Ibid.

[75] Juliana Geran Pilon, Are the United Nations Camps Cheating Refugees in Honduras? (Washington, D.C.: Heritage Backgrounder, 23 July 1984).

[76] The other two organizations were CRS and Caritas. See Fagen and Aguayo, Fleeing the Maelstrom, pp. 58–62, for the locations and programs of the NGOs in the camps in Honduras.

convictions that the Sandinistas were an unpopular regime. In contrast to the treatment of Salvadoran and Guatemalan refugees as security threats in Honduras, the two groups of Nicaraguan refugees, the Ladinos and the indigenous Miskito, Rama, and Suma Indians[77] were accorded freedom of movement and employment opportunities.[78] The Miskitos were even permitted to settle permanently, if they so desired, in the sparsely populated region of Gracias a Dios.

The creation of refugee flows from Nicaragua generally followed the pattern described by Jean-Christophe Rufin:[79] guerrilla attacks triggered government reprisals against the local population, which provoked the flight of civilians across the border. In the case of the Miskitos, this process was superimposed on a simmering issue of minority rights which identified the local population with the cause of the rebel forces and gave them added legitimacy in the eyes of international observers. Conflict between the Sandinistas and the Miskitos began in the early days of the Sandinista regime, when a campaign for Atlantic Coast autonomy provoked clashes and several indigenous leaders were arrested. Upon release these leaders exiled themselves in Honduras and, joining the growing contra forces, conducted incursions into Nicaragua. To deny the guerrillas a sympathetic population, the Sandinistas forcibly moved 8,500 Miskito and Suma Indians eighty kilometers to the south and destroyed their villages and crops. As a consequence 10,000 refugees crossed into Honduras in 1981, and by the end of 1983, 13,500 Miskitos were living in six settlements along the Mocorón, Patuca, and Warunta Rivers.[80] This figure had grown to an estimated 25,000 by 1987.[81] Although some of the Miskitos joined the contras, the vast majority were bona fide refugees fleeing repression by the Sandinista regime.

The majority of the Nicaraguan Ladino population in Honduras, by contrast, fled Nicaragua to avoid conscription into the Sandinista armed

[77] Since the Indian refugees were predominantly from the Miskito ethnic group, the literature tends to cluster all indigenous groups under this name. To avoid confusion I shall do the same.

[78] See Comptroller General, *Report to the Congress of the United States. Central American Refugees: Regional Conditions and Prospects and Potential Impact on the United States*, GAO/NSIAD-84-106 (Washington, D.C.: U.S. General Accounting Office, 20 July 1984), pp. 8–9.

[79] Jean-Christophe Rufin, *Le piège humanitaire, suivi de Humanitaire et politique depuis la chute du Mur*, revised and updated edition (Paris: Jean-Claude Lattès, 1993), pp. 124–126.

[80] Fagen and Aguayo, *Fleeing the Maelstrom*, p. 53.

[81] UNHCR *Central American Facts Sheet*, as cited in Morsch, *Summary of Refugee Conditions*, p. 1.

forces,[82] and constituted the bulk of the contra forces. Only half of those estimated to have resided in Honduras lived in the UNHCR-assisted refugee camps, the rest choosing to stay along the border. By 1987 UNHCR estimated the total population of Ladinos in Honduras to be 18,000.[83]

Equipped with a secure base in Honduras, the contras did not require the presence of refugee camps to provide cover and international protection for the combatants. The refugees were given the choice of whether to remain at the border, living in ad hoc settlements initially without any humanitarian aid, or be transported inland to a UNHCR-assisted refugee camp. They were accorded refugee status and hence legal protection only if they moved to one of the UNHCR camps;[84] nevertheless, many chose to reside along the border. The presence of the refugees did, however, contribute in other ways to the contra insurgency, primarily through the legitimacy they bestowed upon the contra cause and the propaganda potential this induced, and through their ability to attract "humanitarian" aid to the border regions. The UNHCR-assisted camps, by concentrating populations together and offering humanitarian support, also gained the attention of the guerrillas, although to a lesser extent than seen elsewhere.

Population Control and Legitimacy

UNHCR's decision to locate the refugee camps away from the border reduced the ability of the contra forces to control the refugee populations. UNHCR deployed protection officers to the camps, and although they were unable to prevent refugees from leaving to fight or to hide, they did try to prevent forced recruitment. UNHCR personnel also tried to isolate the aid distribution system from the political agendas of the refugee leadership.[85] Nevertheless, both the Ladino and Miskito contra groups undertook recruitment drives, and the contras appointed local coordinators to take charge of the relief supplies provided by the international agencies.[86]

As an important symbol of Sandinista oppression, the refugees became pawns in the propaganda campaign waged by the Reagan administration to generate support among the American public and in Congress for the contra war. Although Reagan attained high opinion poll ratings for his overall

---

[82] Morsch, *Summary of Refugee Conditions*, p. 14.
[83] UNHCR *Central American Facts Sheet*, as cited in ibid., p. 1.
[84] Fagen and Aguayo, *Fleeing the Maelstrom*, p. 58.
[85] Ibid., p. 7, and Morsch, *Summary of Refugee Conditions*, p. 14.
[86] Ferris, *The Central American Refugees*, p. 107.

performance as president, his Nicaragua policy did not enjoy widespread support, frequently being disapproved of in the polls by a two-to-one margin.[87] Hence Reagan went to great lengths to convince the American public and Congress that the U.S. engagement was vital to protect American interests from the communist scourge. The Sandinista regime was thoroughly demonized with the assistance of a biased press,[88] and the refugees were the visible embodiment of the administration's rhetoric. The litany of alleged Sandinista crimes included genocide against the Miskito Indians, anti-Semitic pogroms that drove the Jewish community into exile, massive and widespread human rights abuses, drug smuggling to poison the youth of America, and providing a base for international terrorism.[89] By emphasizing the oppressiveness and communist leanings of the Sandinistas and continually assaulting the regime's character, the administration managed to shift attention away from the debate over the merits of Reagan's policy and the abuses and corruption committed by the contras.

The predicament of the refugees was exploited to influence the congressional debate on aid to the contras. Americas Watch documented one such instance in 1986 which was timed to coincide with a congressional vote.[90] The U.S. embassy in Honduras invited sixty journalists to visit the Mosquita region and allegedly staged a new refugee influx to coincide with the visit. Americas Watch claims that the refugee flow was the result not of repressive activities of the Sandinistas as U.S. authorities alleged, but of a deliberate campaign by one of the contra organizations to spread fear in parts of Nicaragua to encourage the exodus. Reporters from the *Boston Globe* and the *Philadelphia Inquirer* concurred with this analysis, saying that the refugees were obviously coached in their testimonies and were rarely left unaccompanied when speaking to journalists.[91] Americas Watch concluded that:

> Coming at a moment when the U.S. Congress is voting on aid to the *contras*, the flight of thousands of Indians across the border gives a very bad

[87] Eldon Kenworthy, "Selling the Policy," in Walker (ed.), *Reagan versus the Sandinistas*, pp. 159–181.

[88] See Jack Spence, "The U.S. Media: Covering (Over) Nicaragua," in Walker (ed.), *Reagan versus the Sandinistas*, pp. 182–210 at p. 183.

[89] LeoGrande, "The Contras and Congress," p. 222.

[90] *With the Miskitos in Honduras* (New York: Americas Watch, 1986).

[91] See Steve Stecklow, "Fearing Sandinistas, Indians Flee to Honduras" and "A Media Event—With No Audience," *Philadelphia Inquirer*, 6 April 1986; and Pamela Constable, "Nicaraguan Indians Move to Honduras," 7 April 1986, as cited in *With the Miskitos in Honduras*, p. 3.

impression of Sandinista-Miskito relations, which were supposed to be on the mend. . . . The picture that has already been painted by the Reagan Administration is that serious new abuses provoked this massive exodus, although Americas Watch has not learned of such abuses. The exodus gives the Congress more reasons to vote for aid to the *contras*, especially "humanitarian" aid which could be thought to benefit these refugees.[92]

The symbolic importance of the refugee population made their repatriation undesirable, and the contras employed coercive measures to ensure that the refugees remained in Honduras. In one such incident in December 1984, a group of thirty-five refugees who had registered for repatriation with UNHCR were confronted by three hundred fellow refugees armed with machetes.[93] The U.S. government was also implicated in this process: members of the International Council of Voluntary Agencies visiting Honduras witnessed three of the most prominent members of the contra leadership conducting rounds of the refugee camps in a military helicopter accompanied by CIA and U.S. State Department personnel to dissuade the refugees from repatriating.[94] Spreading rumors of an imminent new offensive against the Sandinistas was another method employed to encourage the refugees to remain in Honduras.

Thus in the Nicaraguan refugee camps it was not the presence of aid organizations or the assistance that they provided that lent legitimacy to the guerrilla cause, but the presence of the refugees, manipulated to exaggerate images of suffering. Once successfully enticed to the region, however, the aid served the guerrillas in other ways.

War Economy

Since UNHCR would provide assistance to refugees only in the camps located away from the border, thus catering to refugees, not combatant forces, the Nicaraguans living along the border had no initial access to humanitarian relief. Some 3,000 Nicaraguans lived among the contra groups.[95] But in 1984, Congress authorized the U.S. Agency for International Development (USAID) to spend $7.5 million for Miskito and other Indians living outside the UNHCR camps and, seriously undermining the UNHCR program, actually stipulated that the funds be administered "in-

[92] *With the Miskitos in Honduras*, p. 14.

[93] Fagen and Aguayo, *Fleeing the Maelstrom*, p. 85.

[94] Hansruedi Peplinsky and Martin Diskin, *Report of the ICVA Mosquita Mission* (Geneva: International Council of Voluntary Agencies, 1987), pp. 9–10.

[95] Fagen and Aguayo, *Fleeing the Maelstrom*, p. 86.

dependently from United Nations relief agencies."[96] A large proportion of the funds was allocated to infrastructural improvements to roads and bridges, which inevitably served more than just the relief community along the border. Budget allocations were also made to health care in the border area, and seeds and tools were allegedly distributed through a right-wing American private aid organization, Friends of the Americas (FOA).[97]

The sudden infusion of aid to the border region and the promise of jobs through the USAID projects came at a time when UNHCR was reducing humanitarian assistance in the camps to encourage refugee self-sufficiency. Some 2,000–3,000 refugees abandoned crops and houses to move back to the border region. The policy was clearly intended to support the contra effort since neither the promised jobs on road works nor the assistance offered by FOA were sustainable: according to Fagen and Aguayo, "Nobody pretends that this organization [FOA] is interested in, or capable of, administering a long-term refugee settlement project. . . . The presence of a large civilian population helps to attract assistance which, in reality, is intended for the contras."[98] In a similar vein, a report by CRS concluded: "The border relief programs are not designed to meet the long or short-term interests of the Miskitos, but rather are designed for political purposes as a conduit of aid to the contras."[99]

But while many of the established aid organizations opposed such a misuse of aid for political objectives, other organizations were more than willing supporters of such policies. As mentioned above, the 1984 U.S. congressional ban on aid to the contras prompted the establishment of private aid networks in the United States to channel private assistance to them. Some of these groups were openly military, supplying arms, equipment, and financial support to the contra groups in Honduras. Others, however, established a humanitarian front to avoid openly violating the Neutrality Act[100] or to benefit from legislation loopholes and public support. The United States Council for World Freedom, which is a paramilitary group associated with the World Anti-Communist League, for example, benefited from tax-exempt status as an educational organization to

---

[96] House Appropriations Report, Second Supplemental Appropriations Bill, 1984, pp. 88–89, as cited in Larry Minear, *Helping People in an Age of Conflict: Toward a New Professionalism in U.S. Voluntary Humanitarian Assistance* (New York: American Council for Voluntary International Action [InterAction], 1988), p. 77 n. 8.

[97] *Inter-Hemispheric Education Resource Centre Bulletin* 3, no. 1 (1986): 2.

[98] Fagen and Aguayo, *Fleeing the Maelstrom*, pp. 87–88.

[99] *Nicaraguan Miskito and Sumo Indian Refugees in Honduras: A Report* (CRS, 14 March 1985), as cited in *The Inter-Hemispheric Education Resource Centre Bulletin*, p. 4.

[100] Kornbluh, "The Covert War," p. 32.

recruit people with skills in intelligence and psychological warfare to train the contras and the Salvadoran police and military.[101] Refugee Relief International adopted a humanitarian persona but advertised for donations in *Soldier of Fortune,* a magazine that also advertises mercenary services. Other groups which allegedly supported the contras included the relief branch of the Christian Broadcasting Network (Operation Blessing), World Medical Relief, Knights of Malta, Americares, and the Reverend Sun Myung Moon's Unification Church, through their affiliates, the Confederation of Associations for the Unity of the Societies of America, and the Nicaraguan Freedom Fund.[102] A 1985 report of the Congressional Arms Control and Foreign Policy Caucus stated:

> close to 20 privately incorporated U.S. groups have reportedly sent (or plan soon to send) aid, supplies or cash contributions to Nicaraguan refugees in Honduras and to the contras themselves. . . . [The] driving forces behind the major groups are a small group of about half a dozen men, most of whom have military or paramilitary backgrounds or mercenary experience. . . . While many of the groups work closely together, they have different stated purposes. . . . Most groups call their aid "humanitarian," but either privately or publicly acknowledge that some of it (e.g. medical supplies and food) ends up at contra camps. These groups also have conceded that their "humanitarian" aid to refugees (which include families of the contras) may indirectly aid the contras by freeing up the contra accounts to purchase weapons and pay combatants.[103]

Some of the aid, such as the "Shoeboxes for Liberty" shipped to Honduras by FOA, had more to do with propaganda than fueling the war effort, as did the aerobics instructor one group sent to "cheer the wretched in their squalid camps."[104] Nevertheless, Leslie Cockburn estimates that these groups shipped over $5 million in "humanitarian" aid to the contras between April 1984 and March 1985 alone,[105] a significant contribution to the economy of war, if only through diversifying sources of support to the contras and permitting contra finances to concentrate on purely military expenses.

[101] Sklar, *Washington's War on Nicaragua,* p. 235.
[102] For a description of these groups see ibid., pp. 233–242.
[103] *Who Are the Contras? An Analysis of the Makeup of the Military Leadership of the Rebel Forces and of the Nature of the Private American Groups Providing Them Financial and Material Support,* Congressional Arms Control and Foreign Policy Caucus, Washington, D.C., 18 April 1985, pp. 13–14, as cited in ibid., p. 237.
[104] Cockburn, *Out of Control,* p. 16.
[105] Ibid.

The pervasiveness of U.S. government influence in Honduras, with its categorization of Salvadoran refugees as "guerrillas" and Nicaraguan refugees as "freedom fighters," rendered the construction of humanitarian space difficult. But this difficulty was exacerbated by the political and ideological allegiances displayed by aid organizations themselves, which undermined their supposedly impartial and neutral character.

The perspectives and motivations of the various aid organizations followed three general tendencies: political, adhering to Cold War doctrine; ideological, following notions of a just war; and technocratic, focusing on practical concerns. Deviations from these tendencies, of course, occurred, particularly within NGOs which, as a collection of private individuals professing a self-imposed mandate, were prone to divergent opinions and motivations among their members. According to Bataillon, the perspectives of some aid organizations shifted in Central America during this period from what could be termed a politically based to a rights-based approach to humanitarian assistance.

POLITICAL ORIENTATION

Most of the European NGOs were driven by a strong political motivation, almost exclusively to the left. In the early 1980s the Salvadoran guerrillas were a particularly strong symbol for the left in Europe, and financial support and volunteers were readily available to NGOs that were seen to be assisting the victims of right-wing oppression. As mentioned earlier, many NGOs were "infiltrated" by hard-line volunteers, some of whom used the organizations for the plane ticket and Honduran visa, but disappeared upon arrival to join the FMLN. In spite of the general political leaning of the organizations, however, they were generally established NGOs which, at least at the organizational level, tried to adhere to humanitarian standards and modes of operation, unlike the private groups maneuvering outside the parameters of the aid operation on the other side of the country.

It is surprising that the use of the term "humanitarian" to describe the conservative U.S. groups which emerged in response to the postponement of government aid to the contras in 1984 did not cause more consternation among the established NGO community in the United States. The open espousal of partisan support for the contras by these groups, and their association with paramilitary organizations while operating under a humanitarian banner, compromised the reputations of the genuine humanitarian agencies. Furthermore, the new groups potentially absorbed a share of private and public funds. But opinion within and among mainstream NGOs was divided over the provision of aid to the contras. From a meeting in the United States organized in 1985 to review the "first principles" of humanitarian assistance, Larry Minear reported that "while PVO [private voluntary organization] alarm over the politicization of aid in Central America helped provide a place on the crowded InterAction agenda for the issue of humanitarian assistance, the process did not, as some PVOs had feared and other PVOs had hoped, line up the PVO community in opposition to Contra aid."[106]

Several U.S. aid organizations did, however, unite in opposition to the U.S. government's misuse of the term "humanitarian" to describe aid to a military force. Eleven NGOs issued a joint communiqué to this effect;[107] senior NGO executives wrote letters to Congress; and another coalition of NGOs published a full-page advertisement in the *New York Times*, stating that there was "nothing humanitarian about providing direct aid to the combatants in this tragic conflict."[108] Oxfam America followed this with further lobbying, unfazed by the government's consequent refusal to issue the agency an export license for aid to Nicaragua. However, rather than criticizing the abuse of the notion of humanitarian action, its lobbying took the inverse political stand, advocating an end to aid for the contras and renewed aid to the Sandinistas. The adoption of an equally partisan stance by a recognized aid agency further undermined traditional humanitarian doctrine.[109]

The aid organizations engaged in the public debate to counter views like that of a *Washington Post* editorial: "Anyone who examines the historical record of communism must conclude that any aid directed at overthrowing communism is humanitarian aid."[110] But Bruce Nichols says that they were unable to generate serious public discussion over the misuse of the term.[111]

[106] Minear, *Helping People in an Age of Conflict*, p. 11.

[107] "A Statement on the Nature of Humanitarian Assistance by U.S. Private and Voluntary Organizations" (Washington, D.C.: Church World Service, 1985), as cited in Sklar, *Washington's War on Nicaragua*, pp. 268–269.

[108] "U.S. Aid to the Contras: Humanitarian? Logistical? Defensive?" advertisement in the *New York Times*, 7 April 1986, p. 9, as cited in Bruce Nichols, "Rubberband Humanitarianism," *Ethics and International Affairs* 1 (1987): 191–210 at p. 204.

[109] Nichols, "Rubberband Humanitarianism," p. 205.

[110] "Editorial," *Washington Post*, 10 May 1985, as cited in Minear, *Helping People in an Age of Conflict*, p. 36.

[111] Nichols, "Rubberband Humanitarianism," p. 209.

The second type of aid organizations working in Honduras were those for whom motivation stemmed from an ideological belief in a "just war" against tyranny, regardless of the political doctrine espoused by the victims or the tyrants. Particularly for those working in the Salvadoran camps, the brutality of the Salvadoran armed forces and death squads shown in the deliberate bombing of civilians, the perpetration of human rights violations, and the use of napalm, white phosphorous, and chemical weapons[112] generated deep sympathy for the victims and support for the guerrilla forces. Influential segments of the Catholic Church were adherents of this perspective, advocating the right to insurrection within the Christian theological tradition. The message of the murdered Salvadoran archbishop Oscar Arnulfo Romero y Galdames was highly influential: "When a dictator seriously violates human rights and attacks the common good of the nation, when it becomes unbearable and closes all channels to dialogue, of understanding, of rationality—when this happens, the church speaks of the legitimate right to insurrectional violence."[113]

Thus through a conviction that it was essential to assist the poor and promote social change, a blend of radical Christian, Marxist, and nationalist currents permeated the opposition to the Salvadoran government. More conservative Christian groups, however, opposed any concession to communism, and tensions among the religious NGOs were clearly apparent in the camps. World Vision was accused by other NGOs of collaborating with the Honduran and Salvadoran forces against the refugees, espousing anticommunist beliefs, and pressuring the refugees to adopt fundamentalist religious beliefs as a precondition for receiving food and medicine.[114] Nichols writes:

> By early 1982, the church relief societies had become strongly polarized along lines determined by support or rejection of U.S. and Honduran refugee policies. Supporters of the government's refugee policies—evangelical agencies such as the California-based World Vision or conservative churches represented within CEDEN [National Evangelical Committee for Emergencies and Development]—were judged by Catholic and main-

[112] See the testimony of Richard Alan White, "The Use of Napalm, White Phosphorous and Other Anti-personnel Weapons: Reprisals against the Civilian Population," in Ramshaw and Steers (eds.), *Intervention on Trial*, pp. 17–23.

[113] Quoted in North and CAPA (eds.), *Between War and Peace in Central America*, p. 75.

[114] See Ferris, *Central American Refugees*, p. 101; Fagen and Aguayo, *Fleeing the Maelstrom*, n. 9, p. 90, and Schooley, *Conflict in Central America*, p. 209.

line Protestant groups to be naïve accomplices in governmental plans, trading their compliance with military authorities for government approbation.[115]

The controversy forced World Vision to leave Colomoncagua in 1981 and Mesa Grande in 1982.

Experiences like that of MSF in the Salvadoran camps, confronting the coercive domination and exploitation of the refugees by the camp committees, tempered the political opinion of some organizations over time. Bataillon argues that it was the experience of the French NGOs in Central America which shifted the basis for intervention from one of political motivation to one of solidarity with victims, recognizing that they could be found on both sides. He suggests that one of the imperatives these NGOs faced during this period was to convince their base of support, mainly progressive and leftist, that the Nicaraguan refugees fleeing the Sandinista revolution and the Salvadoran peasants fleeing the Salvadoran army had the same right to receive aid and the protection of UNHCR.[116] The NGOs also needed to convince their volunteers: Bernard Pécoul faced a strike by members of MSF when he deployed a doctor to assist with an influx of Nicaraguan refugees into the camps near Danlí, since the strikers were opposed to aiding any group that could have been associated with the contras. Individual convictions were difficult to moderate, and Bataillon notes that MSF staff increased their acts of friendship to the Salvadorans when the organization commenced work with the Nicaraguans, lending their vehicles to the health authorities during the weekends and financing activities more associated with political indoctrination than medical efficiency.[117]

TECHNOCRATIC ORIENTATION

The third type of response identifiable among the aid community was a technocratic approach, in which the practical concerns of providing relief to the refugees took precedence over considerations of the political or ethical ramifications of the assistance program. A technocratic approach can serve to justify an acceptance of the status quo which in reality is favoring a political or ideological cause, but is more often associated with a perceived inability to influence the political context, and hence a focus on the

115 J. Bruce Nichols, *The Uneasy Alliance: Religion, Refugee Work, and U.S. Foreign Policy* (New York: Oxford University Press, 1988), p. 125.
116 Bataillon, "L'action humanitaire des ONG françaises," p. 68.
117 Ibid.

technical aspects of relief delivery. This is characterized by adherence to performance indicators associated with, for example, income-generation projects, refugee self-sustainability, and adequate services in the camps while ignoring the "political" issues associated with security and protection. The remark of the CRS country director, Patrick Ahern, quoted earlier typifies this approach: for the benefits of perceived social cohesion and an efficient relief distribution system, Ahern accepted the domination of the refugee population by the camp committees and the diversion of relief supplies.

The technocratic perspective is also common among those NGOs for which the development of the organization is more important than the task of assisting vulnerable populations. The delivery of aid becomes the end in itself, and the drive to professionalize and compete with other NGOs to be bigger and better supersedes other considerations. This was well illustrated by the reaction of U.S. NGOs to an offer of collaboration from the U.S. Department of Defense in 1987. The director of the department's Office of Humanitarian Assistance, Dr. Robert Wolthuis, explained to an audience of NGOs that the Department of Defense was authorized to provide aid organizations with excess U.S. government property and transport for relief supplies on a space-available basis. Despite his disclosure that most of the first-year shipments had been for FOA, and that NGO eligibility was not restricted to those registered with USAID, the ensuing discussion generated as many questions pertaining to procedural and availability issues as to concerns about the appropriateness of the Defense Department's involvement in "humanitarian assistance."[118] A group of interested NGOs was formed to "explore improved and expanded cooperative arrangements with DoD,"[119] apparently indifferent to the likelihood that their relief supplies would be transported in U.S. government aircraft beside military equipment and supplies.

UNHCR

Dependent on discretionary funding from UN member states, UNHCR was intrinsically tied to the political context and, as such, does not fit well into any of the three categories. Throughout the conflict in Central America, the organization was constrained in the fulfillment of its mandate by its financial dependence on the United States, which contributed about one-third of UNHCR's regional budget.[120] The United States used this fi-

[118] See Minear, *Helping People in an Age of Conflict*, pp. 38–40.
[119] Ibid., p. 39.
[120] Comptroller General, *Report to the Congress of the United States*, p. 2.

nancial leverage to improve conditions for Nicaraguans in Honduras and to pressure UNHCR over issues concerning the relocation or repatriation of Salvadoran refugees.[121]

The UNHCR position was further weakened by the failure of Honduras to become a party to the 1951 Refugee Convention and 1967 Protocol. Although the principle of *non-refoulement* was included in domestic law, UNHCR's effectiveness in providing protection was compromised by the limitations imposed by the local authorities, who in turn were strongly influenced by the United States. Although the Honduran government depended upon UNHCR to meet the humanitarian needs of the refugees, the relief program was undertaken at the discretion of the Honduran authorities. The fragility of the relationship curbed UNHCR protests to the government about military infractions into the camps.

UNHCR was vulnerable to criticism for any action it undertook to improve protection of the refugees on both sides of Honduras. Further attempts to relocate the Salvadoran border camps would have resulted in the likely injury and death of refugees and would have been strongly denounced by the aid community, human rights organizations, church groups, and the refugees. Moreover, the refugee leadership may have compelled many of the refugees to return to El Salvador rather than move further inland, where their safety was far from ensured. In the east of the country, UNHCR's attempts to keep refugees a safe distance from the border were undermined by the policies of its principal donor. UNHCR had to weave a prudent path between ensuring protection for refugees and respecting the political imperatives of the U.S. government. The agency also had to consider the impact that its actions in Honduras would have on operations elsewhere and in the future. The Central American refugee crisis clearly illustrated the contradiction implicit in upholding a humanitarian mandate while dependent upon funding from politically interested states.

Conclusion: Serving Political Agendas

Several significant points emerge from the Central American refugee context. First and most important, this case illustrates that conceptions of what constituted a just cause among most humanitarian actors were highly subjective. Rather than applying humanitarian principles of impartiality and neutrality to the refugees on both sides of Honduras, aid agencies

---

[121] Loescher, "Humanitarianism and Politics in Central America," p. 181.

tended to work with the refugees with whom they sympathized. Although preference given to the Nicaraguan refugees by the Honduran authorities provided some justification for agencies to focus on the Salvadoran camps according to the proportionality precept of impartiality, few argued in terms of humanitarian principles in the highly politicized context.

Second, as aid agencies discovered in the Afghan context, espousing a "just" political cause was no guarantee of responsible leadership by the refugee-warriors, or concern for the welfare of the civilian population. Organizations working with both Salvadoran and Nicaraguan refugees permitted aid to serve the political agenda of the refugee leaders, despite its use as a coercive tool of refugee control. Some aid organizations considered that the political ends justified the means, and tolerated the practices in the refugee camps. Others, however, refused to accept that aid was manipulated in this way.

Third, circumstantial evidence from the Salvadoran refugee camps casts doubt on the claim that refugee-warriors can exist only on the territory of a host state sympathetic to their cause. An international presence in the camps, even when on hostile territory, provides some protection in a similar fashion to "safe areas" inside countries in conflict in the 1990s. Furthermore, although not significant in quantity, the elevated levels of aid in the camps permitted materials to be siphoned off to the guerrillas, and the camps' structures facilitated influence over the refugee population. The attitudes of the refugee leadership to camp relocation and refugee repatriation bear witness to the value of the camps to the guerrillas.

In fact in many respects, the Salvadoran camps played a more important role for refugee-warriors than the Nicaraguan camps. In comparison with the extent and nature of direct military support to the contras, the latter played a relatively minor role in the insurgency. The most significant contribution of the Nicaraguan refugees to the conflict was in a propaganda role to influence U.S. public opinion in favor of the contra cause. This in turn generated assistance from right-wing private aid groups and U.S. government programs to the border region, which brought economic benefits to the guerrilla forces. But the refugee camps and border settlements were not significant in the conflict; most of the literature on the contra war does not even mention the Nicaraguan refugees.

Finally, this case illustrates that the United States subjugated humanitarian concerns to foreign policy interests, hence highlighting the conflict for aid agencies between accepting government funds and undertaking independent, impartial humanitarian activity. This was nowhere more apparent than with UNHCR, and demonstrates the difficulty of reconciling a mandate to protect refugees with the role of providing assistance. Operational independence is a prerequisite for providing real protection, but UNHCR was dependent on governments for the funds needed to operate camps and provide aid. This contradiction, still apparent in UNHCR operations today, undermines the organization's effectiveness at carrying out its principal mandate: protection.

4

The Cambodian Refugee Camps in Thailand

The Cambodian refugee crisis along the Thai-Cambodian border, which unfolded in 1979, arguably posed the greatest challenge to the international humanitarian system of the Cold War period. Victims and oppressors, at the outset indistinguishable in their needs, became bound together in a symbiotic relationship by the relief operation and the politics that determined its path. Seemingly powerless to change the political context in which their work was embedded, aid agencies had to confront the probability that their aid was reviving one of the most brutal regimes in modern history, the Khmer Rouge.[1]

Unlike those in the situations described earlier, the Cambodian refugee camps were widely recognized by aid organizations, academics, and the press to be fueling one side of the conflict.[2] Critical works about the politicization of the aid program appeared from the early 1980s, and the media openly questioned the role of the camps. An article in the *New York Times Magazine* stated: "If the camps in Thailand are closed, the Khmer Rouge will be denied its prime source of sanctuary and supplies."[3]

Thailand played a vital role in supporting the resistance forces on Thai territory, but managed to blend its roles as a military and a humanitarian sanctuary more closely than did Pakistan or Honduras. Thailand officially proclaimed neutrality in the conflict between the Vietnamese-installed government in Cambodia and the Khmer resistance groups opposing it, but it used the latter and the hundreds of thousands of refugees under their control as a buffer against the Vietnamese forces. Restricting the Cambodian refugees to the border area to use their presence to provide a human-

---

[1] A note on names: The Khmer Rouge adopted the Khmer phonetic rendition for Cambodia, Kampuchea, in 1975 ("Khmer Rouge" was the nickname for the Communist Party of Kampuchea). The United Nations decided in 1984, however, to revert to the name "Cambodia" as the accepted common-usage designation for the country and its people.

[2] The Thai government did not confer refugee status on inhabitants of the border camps and referred to the structures as "displaced persons camps." Nevertheless, I use the term "refugee camp" interchangeably with "border camp" and "holding center" throughout this chapter.

[3] Steven Erlanger, "The Endless War," *New York Times Magazine*, 5 March 1989, p. 52.

itarian sanctuary for the resistance forces, the Thai government facilitated the transfer of arms and finance to the guerrilla factions. Rather than being unintended consequences of the relief effort, the paradoxes of aid were carefully orchestrated by the donor nations and the Thai government to pursue foreign policy goals.

Thailand as a Military Sanctuary

From the outset, the Cambodian refugees were an integral part of the shifting political alliances and conflict that had enveloped the Indochinese region since the 1950s. As in Central America, the region was the scene of intense superpower rivalry, not only between capitalist and communist camps, but also between China and the Soviet Union once these former allies became enemies. The Cambodian crisis was not the result of the classic Cold War bipolar conflict but of a tripartite power struggle, and socialist forces were involved on either side.

Never having been colonized, Thailand escaped the turmoil of nationalist-communist independence struggles in Indochina and retained a firm footing in the Western camp throughout the Cold War. It became an ally of the United States from the time of the Korean War (1950–53) and provided military bases, as well as combat troops, for American forces during the war in Vietnam (1965–75). The U.S. military also assisted the Thai government in suppressing internal communist movements by providing economic and technical assistance in counterinsurgency.

By contrast, Cambodia, declared a neutral state upon independence in 1954, vacillated in its Cold War loyalties, courting all three major powers at various times. Both right-wing and left-wing movements formed in opposition to Prince Sihanouk's regime, the Khmer Serei (Free Khmer) in 1956 representing the former, and the Khmer Rouge during the same period the latter. The United States provided economic and military aid until Sihanouk initiated ties with the Soviet Union and China in 1965. American support then shifted to the conservative Khmer Serei guerrillas. Relations between the two governments resumed in 1969, but Sihanouk continued to court both sides of the Cold War divide, permitting North Vietnamese forces to establish supply lines inside Cambodia and turning a blind eye to U.S. bombing of these routes. His overthrow in 1970 in a military coup led by his conservative prime minister, Lon Nol, permitted an intensification of U.S. bombing of the communist supply lines for the next three years. Nearly half of the 540,000 tons of bombs fell in the last six months.[4]

The indiscriminate bombing of the Cambodian countryside generated considerable opposition to the Lon Nol regime, and thousands of peasants joined one of the resistance groups, whether pro-Sihanouk, pro-Vietnamese communist, moderate, or hard-line Khmer Rouge. According to Ben Kiernan, U.S. bombing particularly contributed to the Khmer Rouge's rise to power, providing Pol Pot's forces with "an excuse for its brutal, radical policies and its purge of moderate communists and Sihanoukists."[5] Having decimated other opposition groups or forced them into exile, the Khmer Rouge marched on Phnom Penh and secured the surrender of the Lon Nol government on 17 April 1975. Thereafter ensued one of the most brutal periods in modern history, a period of violent socialist rule which, through policies of radical reforms and terror, resulted in the death of more than one million people by starvation, disease, and execution.[6]

Thailand joined other members of the Association of South-East Asian Nations (ASEAN) in recognizing the Khmer Rouge government, and, despite their ideological differences, closure of their common border, and numerous violent border incidents, the two governments maintained cordial diplomatic relations. The Vietnamese government, however, was less tolerant of Khmer Rouge border incursions, and tension escalated into open conflict following a Khmer Rouge attack against a Vietnamese provincial town in April 1977. Vietnamese forces invaded Cambodia in early 1978, and by December some 100,000 Vietnamese troops and 20,000 Cambodian guerrillas conducted an assault on the capital, which fell on 7 January 1979. The Vietnamese forces installed a government headed by a former Khmer Rouge official, Heng Samrin.

Very few countries recognized the new Vietnamese-backed government. Superpower politics and regional realignments overshadowed the removal of a regime responsible for widespread and massive human rights abuses and crimes against humanity. Following the Sino-Soviet split,

[4] Ben Kiernan, "Roots of Genocide: New Evidence on the U.S. Bombardment of Cambodia," *Cultural Survival Quarterly* 14, no. 3 (1990): 20–22 at p. 20.

[5] Ibid.

[6] Estimates of the number of deaths caused by the Khmer Rouge regime range from several hundred thousand to several million. Mass graves discovered by the Yale University Genocide Program, under the directorship of Ben Kiernan, in Cambodia in 1996 suggest that the death toll may have been closer to two million than one million. See Seth Mydans, "Cambodian Killers' Careful Records Used against Them," *New York Times*, 7 June 1996, p. A1 and p. A8.

China developed closer links with ASEAN nations, and although support-ing the North Vietnamese during the U.S.-Vietnam War, began to with-draw aid to Vietnam in 1975. Vietnam strengthened ties with China's principal foe, the Soviet Union, and China increased support to the Khmer Rouge and began to thaw relations with the United States. The ASEAN nations, toward which Vietnam's policy had been hostile since 1975, were strongly in opposition to Vietnam's invasion of Cambodia—particularly Thailand, which claimed that Vietnam posed a direct threat on account of having troops in both Laos and Cambodia.[7] Thus despite the record of the Khmer Rouge, political deals were struck among regional nations, largely on the basis that "the enemy of my enemy is my friend." Opposition to Vietnam and the USSR united former adversaries; the most remarkable rapprochement was that of Prince Sihanouk and the Khmer Rouge, an alliance brokered by China. The Chinese government was to have increasing influence in the ensuing years in sustaining the anti-Viet-namese resistance through diplomatic and military means.

Compromising moral standards in the pursuit of political expediency, the governments of the United States, Australia, Malaysia, Singapore, Japan, and the European Economic Community pledged financial backing for China's attempts to forge a united front among all opposition move-ments in Thailand, including the Khmer Rouge.[8] The Coalition Govern-ment of Democratic Kampuchea (CGDK), discussed further below, was formed in 1982 from a tripartite agreement between the Khmer Rouge, the Khmer People's National Liberation Front (KPNLF), and Prince Si-hanouk's United National Front for an Independent, Neutral, Peaceful and Cooperative Cambodia (Front Uni National pour un Cambodge In-dépendent, Neutre, Pacifique et Coopératif—FUNCINPEC). The al-liance served to dilute the visibility of the Khmer Rouge, thereby provid-ing Western nations with a façade behind which any means could be pursued to oppose the Vietnamese occupation of Cambodia.

Thailand's role as a military sanctuary for Cambodian resistance move-ments was limited before China became involved in creating opposition to the Vietnamese-backed regime in Phnom Penh. The border region north of Aranyaprathet had since the 1950s been the site of several resistance

---

[7] Tony Jackson points out that there is a dearth of evidence to substantiate claims that Viet-nam had expansionist aims. He suggests that these fears were exaggerated to justify the high levels of military spending by the West. Personal communication, 28 May 1999.

[8] Craig Etcheson, "The Khmer Way of Exile: Lessons from Three Indochinese Wars," in Yossi Shain (ed.), *Governments-in-Exile in Contemporary World Politics* (New York: Routledge, 1991), pp. 92–116 at p. 106.

camps run by right-wing guerrillas opposing Sihanouk, but these bases facilitated smuggling as much as military activities.[9] During the 1970s, many former officers and soldiers in Lon Nol's army also held bases in this region, but again these were predominantly used for black market trade in teak, gems, gold, and silver.[10] The Vietnamese invasion of Cambodia and the presence of Vietnamese forces in Laos, however, were perceived as direct threats to Thai security, and Thailand's role in the conflict grew from one of initially granting temporary refuge to Khmer Rouge troops to that of serving as a base for the resistance forces.

Thailand fulfilled several functions of a classic military sanctuary for the Cambodian resistance. First, safe passage through Thai territory was granted to Khmer Rouge soldiers retreating from Vietnamese army advances. Herding civilians with them, combatants passed through Thai territory to avoid Vietnamese attack; some 50,000–80,000 soldiers and civilians traversed the region near Aranyaprathet in April 1979 en route to rejoining Khmer Rouge units inside Cambodia.[11] When facing defeat, the Khmer Rouge retreated to the Cardamom Mountains in the southwest of Cambodia, from which they had access to sanctuary in Thailand. But although Thai authorities permitted safe passage to Khmer Rouge troops and civilians, they were initially reluctant to allow these groups to remain on Thai territory. In late April many Cambodians fled to the border as starvation and a severe outbreak of malaria began to decimate the Khmer Rouge base populations. The Thai authorities blocked their entry and forced those who had crossed the border to return to Cambodian territory. By October, however, the Thai prime minister had softened his stance, driven by a combination of the media images of dying Cambodians along the border and a warning from the Thai military that the collapse of the Khmer Rouge as a fighting force would leave no opposition to the Vietnamese in Cambodia.[12] The military recommended that the Khmer Rouge be permitted sanctuary in Thailand to escape annihilation and to regain troop strength. Hence Thailand became host to the remnants of the fighting force and its civilian entourage. The government announced an "open door" policy to Cambodian "refugees" following Western pledges of humanitarian aid and refugee resettlement opportunities.

[9] Josephine Reynell, *Political Pawns: Refugees on the Thai-Kampuchean Border* (Oxford: Refugee Studies Programme, 1989), p. 32.

[10] Judy A. Mayotte, *Disposable People? The Plight of Refugees* (Maryknoll, N.Y.: Orbis, 1992), p. 43.

[11] William Shawcross, *The Quality of Mercy: Cambodia, Holocaust, and Modern Conscience* (New York: Simon and Schuster, 1984), p. 85.

[12] Ibid., p. 172.

The government's mixture of security and humanitarian concerns about the Cambodian conflict permeated every aspect of Thai response in the ensuing years. Under the open door policy, the early refugees and Khmer Rouge soldiers were transported to holding centers inside Thailand, one at Sa Kaeo, sixty kilometers from the border, and the other at Khao I Dang, twelve kilometers from the border. But by February 1980, security considerations came to the fore, and the open door policy came to an abrupt halt. The strategic value of the refugees as a buffer along the border and as a source of support for the reemerging resistance movement determined refugee policy thereafter. The Thai military began to transfer refugees forcibly from the holding centers to the border during the night. Henceforth Cambodian asylum seekers were relegated to makeshift border camps that became a humanitarian sanctuary par excellence for the resistance forces (see Map 3).

The second classic role Thailand played as a military sanctuary was as host to a network of secret military camps, the majority of which were operated by the Khmer Rouge, in addition to the "refugee" camps, which were assisted by the aid community. The network of military camps traversed both sides of the Thai-Cambodian border, and most housed civilians as well as soldiers since the Khmer Rouge ideology did not differentiate between combatants and noncombatants. There were several types of camps: "remote camps," which were militarized but to which aid organizations had limited access; "hidden border camps," which contained civilians but to which no international access was permitted; and "satellite camps," which included front-line camps, military training camps, and rudimentary hospital camps, to which aid organizations also had no access.[13] Up to 100,000 Cambodians are estimated to have lived under Khmer Rouge control in the inaccessible satellite camps.[14] From these bases the Khmer Rouge was able to launch attacks into the interior of Cambodia, engaging Vietnamese troops and destroying infrastructure. The Khmer Rouge also operated bases inside Cambodia (see Map 3), which were supplied from Thailand. Sihanouk suggested that the Vietnamese tolerated the presence of these camps because the visible threat of the Khmer Rouge in Cambodia helped to justify the presence of Vietnamese troops.[15]

[13] Norah Niland, "The Politics of Suffering: The Thai-Cambodian Border: A Case Study on the Use and Abuse of Humanitarian Assistance" (master's thesis, University of Dublin, 1991), p. 101.

[14] *Violations of the Rules of War by the Khmer Rouge* (New York: Asia Watch, 1990), p. 3.

[15] Norodom Sihanouk, *Chroniques de guerre . . . et d'espoir* (Paris: Hachette/Stock, 1979), as cited in Joseph Zasloff, *Kampuchea: A Question of Survival*, part II: *The Political Dimensions*, report no. 47 ([New York]: American Universities Field Staff, 1980), p. 4.

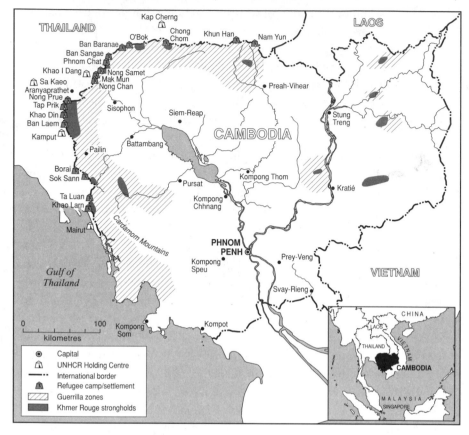

Map 3. Cambodian refugee camps and Khmer Rouge strongholds, 1980. From W. Courtland Robinson, *Double Vision: A History of Cambodian Refugees in Thailand* (Bangkok: Institute of Asian Studies, Chulalongkorn University, 1996), p. 75, and Claude Malhuret, *Les réfugiés d'Asie du sud-est en Thaïlande (1975–1980)* (Paris: Médecins sans Frontières, 1980), p. 29, as modified by author.

The scant information available about the Khmer Rouge military camps renders an assessment of the relative importance of humanitarian aid vis-à-vis military aid to the resistance difficult. Direct Chinese government support to the Khmer Rouge has been widely acknowledged, although the full extent of it is hard to determine. With the assistance of Thai authorities and institutions, the Chinese allegedly provided finance, medical supplies, food, and small arms to the bases,[16] and operated hospitals in some of the military camps.[17] One American observer remarked that

[16] Zasloff, *Kampuchea: A Question of Survival*, p. 9.
[17] See Reynell, *Political Pawns*, p. 129.

the Khmer Rouge bases were "amply armed by China with basic infantry weapons, rocket propelled grenades, and mortars . . . in excess of [their] needs,"[18] and Tony Jackson claims that an estimated 300–500 tonnes of Chinese military supplies were sent to the border through Thailand each month.[19] The Thai military provided logistical support for the transfer of arms supplies and even transport for soldiers to and from the civilian refugee camps for family visits.[20] Furthermore, Thai banks facilitated the transfer of funds. The Thai government benefited considerably from the use of Thai territory for Khmer Rouge resupply. William Shawcross states that, in exchange, the Chinese government pledged to decrease support for communist insurgents operating in Thailand, to guarantee Thailand's security in case of Vietnamese attack, and to sell the Thai government oil at subsidized prices.[21]

The United States also allegedly provided significant funds to the Khmer Rouge arsenal, although the U.S. government denies such support. However, a document produced by the U.S. Congressional Research Service in 1986 showed the transfer of $85 million from the U.S. government to the Khmer Rouge between 1980 and 1986, $73 million of which was granted in 1980 and 1981.[22] If these figures are accurate, such support would have constituted a major contribution to the Khmer Rouge's revival. By comparison, one U.S. estimate of the annual financial needs of the two non–Khmer Rouge resistance forces suggested that $15 to $20 million would "significantly increase the size of their order of battle."[23] U.S. National Security Adviser Zbigniew Brzezinski also admitted that the U.S. government had assisted the Khmer Rouge in 1979: "I encouraged the Chinese to support Pol Pot. I encouraged the Thai to help the D.K. [Democratic Kampuchea]."[24] Yet while pursuing this covert support, the United States publicly espoused anti–Khmer Rouge rhetoric, couching

[18] Statement by Karl D. Jackson, Deputy Assistant Secretary of Defense (East Asia and Pacific Affairs) in *Hope for Cambodia: Preventing the Return of the Khmer Rouge and Aiding the Refugees*, Hearings before the U.S. House of Representatives, 30 June 1988 and 28 July 1988 (Washington, D.C.: U.S. Government Printing Office), p. 50.

[19] Tony Jackson, *Just Waiting to Die? Cambodian Refugees in Thailand* (Oxford: Research and Evaluation Unit, Oxfam, July 1987), p. 18.

[20] Reynell, *Political Pawns*, p. 57.

[21] Shawcross, *Quality of Mercy*, p. 126.

[22] These figures come from a letter sent to Senator John Kerry's office from the U.S. Congressional Research Service in October 1986. See Reynell, *Political Pawns*, p. 41 n. 5.

[23] Senator Robert Kaster, Opening Remarks at *U.S. Policy toward Anti-Communist Insurgencies*, Hearing before a Subcommittee of the Committee on Appropriations, United States Senate, 8 May 1985 (Washington, D.C.: U.S. Government Printing Office, 1985), p. 7.

[24] Elizabeth Becker, *When the War Was Over* (New York: Simon and Schuster, 1986), p. 440, as cited in Etcheson, "The Khmer Way of Exile," p. 105.

justifications for increased financial support to the noncommunist forces in terms of preventing a Khmer Rouge return to power in Phnom Penh in the event of a Vietnamese withdrawal.[25] Thus whether from China alone or with additional funds and supplies from the United States, the Khmer Rouge were rehabilitated as a strong fighting force within two years of their defeat by the Vietnamese army.

Many of the Khmer Rouge military camps to which aid organizations had little or no access also derived some indirect assistance from the humanitarian relief effort through their location in the vicinity of a UN-assisted refugee camp. Asia Watch, by interviewing escapees from the camps, was able to piece together an outline of four main "clusters" of Khmer Rouge camps along the border in 1990 (see Table 2).

Several aid agencies made efforts to gain access to the military camps, since they were aware that many camp inhabitants were Cambodian peasants, confined there against their will and forced to perform military functions. But access was rarely granted. Instead of freeing the civilians from their captors, the proximity of the military camps to the UN-assisted camps put the latter squarely under the influence of the former, and refugees were forcibly transferred to the military camps whenever the Khmer Rouge leadership required.[26] In 1987, for example, over 1,000 men, women, and children were forcibly moved from the UN-assisted Site 8 to one of the closed Khmer Rouge camps on the northern border with Cambodia, despite protests from international agencies.[27]

The Khmer Rouge allegedly treated the military camp inhabitants in much the same way as they had treated the population of Cambodia during their reign. All camp residents were expected to contribute to the war against the Vietnamese and Heng Samrin forces. Able-bodied men were coerced into becoming fighters, and women and men were engaged as porters carrying war matériel to the front lines. Young children and the elderly were forced to work around the camps in support functions such as maintenance, wood collection, road clearance, and food production, and children as young as ten were deployed as porters. Many combatants and porters succumbed to enemy attack, malaria, or injuries inflicted by antipersonnel mines, which littered the areas through which they were forced to march. Carrying heavy loads of military hardware, medicine, and supplies, the porters would undertake trips into Cambodia which could last up to a month, and risked being killed if they refused such tasks.

[25] Kaster, Opening Remarks at *U.S. Policy toward Anti-Communist Insurgencies*, pp. 7–8.
[26] Mayotte, *Disposable People*, p. 99.
[27] Reynell, *Political Pawns*, p. 67.

Table 2. Khmer Rouge camp clusters in 1990

UN camp	No. of satellite camps	Civilian population assisted	Civilian population unassisted	Military population
O'Trao[a]	7	16,000	24,000	9,000
Site 8	3	40,000	20,000	7–8,000
Borai	2	4,400	15,000	7,000
Site K[b]	6	12,000	13,000	8–9,000

Source: Violations of the Rules of War by the Khmer Rouge (New York: Asia Watch, 1990), pp. 4–8.

[a] O'Trao camp was formed in 1988 from the amalgamation of Huay Chan and Natrao camps shown on Map 5.

[b] Thai authorites established Site K in 1989 for the inhabitants of Ta Luan, Borai, and their satellite camps. The Khmer Rouge in Borai resisted the move, however, and forced many camp residents across the border in 1990.

The Khmer Rouge employed various techniques to enforce the camp population's compliance with these demands, including disinformation and propaganda sessions, fear, retribution, and the denial of essential services. Food and medical assistance were not granted but earned; food rations were allocated according to the task performed. A fighter received the highest ration, porters received less, and camp laborers received less than half the ration of porters, which was inadequate to survive.[28] In this way the Khmer Rouge insured that there would be people willing to undertake the more dangerous tasks, and complete denial of food was used to punish insubordination.

Some of the Khmer Serei factions also had satellite military camps, part of the revenue for which came from taxes levied on black marketeers who came to the border to buy gold and gems from smugglers or to set up markets to sell goods to refugees. But the largest resource at the disposal of the non–Khmer Rouge leaders was provided by the aid program. Similarly, although China is known to have sent food and medical supplies to many of the Khmer Rouge military camps, a significant amount of food came from the humanitarian relief effort, through the Thai military. The World Food Programme (WFP) had discreetly agreed to deliver food to Thai army warehouses for onward delivery to "various populations of Khmer refugees and displaced Thai villagers."[29] Shawcross states that internal

[28] For the testimonies of former Khmer Rouge captives, see *Violations of the Rules of War by the Khmer Rouge.*

[29] Linda Mason and Roger Brown, *Rice, Rivalry, and Politics: Managing Cambodian Relief* (Notre Dame: University of Notre Dame Press, 1983), p. 165.

WFP documents show that officials were aware that this food went to feed the Khmer Rouge and other resistance groups.[30] While no one doubted the existence of Thai villagers displaced by the refugees, a census was never conducted of the number of affected Thais; however, daily rations for 85,000 people were, on average, supplied between 1979 and 1983.[31]

Thailand's role as a military sanctuary also extended into the political domain, permitting the establishment of a "government-in-exile" on Thai territory. As mentioned earlier, China brokered the formation of the anti-Vietnamese alliance among the factions opposed to the Heng Samrin regime: Prince Sihanouk's FUNCINPEC, Son Sann's[32] KPNLF, and the Khmer Rouge. Such an alliance was crucial for the international image of the Cambodian resistance, particularly once evidence of the Khmer Rouge regime's brutality began to circulate. Despite public statements of abhorrence at the behavior of the Khmer Rouge, Western nations considered it to be an integral component of the resistance forces, having a troop strength of 40,000 with a militia of another 10,000–15,000, compared with KPNLF's 12,000 troops and the Sihanoukist National Army's 3,000–5,000 combatants.[33] Hence the notion of a government-in-exile presided over by Prince Sihanouk was a way of reducing Khmer Rouge visibility to make the Cambodian resistance palatable to international opinion. Neither Son Sann nor Prince Sihanouk was comfortable with the alliance, however, resisting its formation until 1982, and then limiting the arrangement to that of a coalition instead of the united force that the Chinese proposed.[34] An image of unity was further enhanced when Thailand pressured the various Khmer Serei guerrilla groups to align under the banner of the KPNLF.

Thailand thus played an important role as a military sanctuary for the

[30] Shawcross, *Quality of Mercy*, p. 229. Also see Mason and Brown, *Rice, Rivalry, and Politics*, pp. 140–142.

[31] Shawcross, *Quality of Mercy*, p. 229. A UN document covering the period 1979–91 mentions relief and rehabilitation assistance delivered to 200,000 affected Thai villagers, "in cooperation with the Thai government and Army." *Cambodian Humanitarian Assistance and the United Nations (1979–1991)* (Bangkok: Office of the Special Representative of the Secretary General of the United Nations for Coordination of Cambodian Humanitarian Assistance Programmes [OSRSG], 1992), p. 28.

[32] Son Sann was a former prime minister during the time of Sihanouk, but the two men were not allies.

[33] *Washington Post*, 22 November 1983, as cited in W. Courtland Robinson, *Double Vision: A History of Cambodian Refugees in Thailand* (Bangkok: Institute of Asian Studies, Chulalongkorn University, 1996), p. 113. By 1989, American intelligence estimates put troop strength at between 28,000 and 60,000 for the Khmer Rouge, compared with 16,000 soldiers under Sihanouk and 11,000 under the KPNLF. Erlanger, "The Endless War," p. 27.

[34] Shawcross, *Quality of Mercy*, p. 340.

forces opposing the Vietnamese-installed regime in Phnom Penh, providing territory on which the factions could construct bases, facilitating the flows of finance and arms to the guerrilla groups, and enhancing the diplomatic legitimacy of the resistance through hosting a "government-in-exile." The performance of these functions, however, was markedly enhanced by the large humanitarian sanctuary that the refugees and the aid organizations assisting them provided. Unlike the Afghan refugee camps in Pakistan and the Salvadoran and Nicaraguan camps in Honduras, which played important but not crucial roles in support of resistance movements, the Thai-Cambodian border refugee camps were an integral component of the insurgency against Phnom Penh.

Thailand as a Humanitarian Sanctuary

PROTECTION

The confinement of Cambodian refugees to the border area between Cambodia and Thailand was intended to fulfill three principal objectives: to provide a buffer of humanity between the Vietnamese-affiliated forces and Thailand, to constitute a base of support for the resistance forces along the border, and to minimize the destabilizing effects that hundreds of thousands of refugees could have produced inside Thailand. Hence the notion that the refugees would provide an element of protection from the Vietnamese forces for both Thailand and the resistance factions was implicit in this strategy. The presence of civilians alongside combatants did not, however, deter the launching of attacks against the border camps, although whether such attacks would have been more severe had the refugees not been present is impossible to know. As Rufin pointed out, the protective function of a humanitarian sanctuary is mainly a result of the international condemnation that an attack against a refugee community might incur. But when the aggressor is already condemned internationally, as was the case in Cambodia and South Africa, the importance of international respectability diminishes. Phnom Penh was already deprived of the seat at the UN and was internationally isolated: what more could the West have done? Furthermore, the authorities in Phnom Penh would have been aware of the lack of distinction between civilians and combatants under the control of the Khmer Rouge, and thus may have considered all Cambodians along the border to be legitimate targets.

The first attack was launched against the refugee camps in June 1980 in response to the repatriation of refugees from Sa Kaeo and Khao I Dang to the border area, in which the United Nations High Commissioner for

Refugees had participated in an attempt to halt the forced night transfers by the Thai army. Phnom Penh saw the repatriation for what it was, a way of strengthening the resistance along the border. Hun Sen, Heng Samrin's foreign minister, sent a letter to the UN High Commissioner for Refugees, Poul Hartling, in which he labeled the move "an attempt to introduce into Kampuchean territory armed bands of the Pol Pot–Ieng Sary and Sereika clique, supplied and trained in Thailand by the Peking expansionists in collusion with the American imperialists."[35] The artillery attack and Thai counterattack killed some 400 refugees and wounded 900 others.

Each dry season an offensive was launched against the border camps which drove the camp population into temporary sites inside Thailand. The UN agency established to coordinate activities along the border, the UN Border Relief Operation (UNBRO), supervised eighty-five such camp evacuations between 1982 and 1984, sixty-five of them under fire.[36] At the end of 1984, the Vietnamese launched a particularly devastating offensive against the camps, but one that ultimately improved conditions for the refugee population. Following the attack and subsequent evacuation, the Vietnamese and Heng Samrin forces occupied the camps and sealed the border, preventing the refugees from returning. As a result, the Thai government was obliged to give UNBRO permission to construct new camps inside Thailand (see Maps 4 and 5), providing the opportunity to reorganize the camp populations to separate the military from civilians. As noted in the previous section, however, the resistance forces were still able to benefit from the presence of the refugees because each camp was officially affiliated with one of the CGDK factions and remained in close proximity to the military camps. Furthermore, civilian camps were located between one and six kilometers from the border and were thus within shelling range of the Vietnamese guns. So although security did improve and annual evacuations were no longer necessary, both military and civilian camps were still vulnerable to sporadic shelling, and refugees continued to be injured and to die as a result of mortar fire over the next four years.

The refugee population suffered attacks not only by the Vietnamese-backed forces in Cambodia, but also from the CGDK factions under whose control they were forced to live. They endured a lack of physical protection against the factions' organized violence, against the criminal activities associated with any large concentration of dispossessed and under-

[35] As cited in ibid., p. 318.
[36] Jackson, *Just Waiting to Die?* p. 4.

Map 4. Cambodian refugee camps on the Thai-Cambodian border, 1984. From W. Courtland Robinson, *Double Vision: A History of Cambodian Refugees in Thailand* (Bangkok: Institute of Asian Studies, Chulalongkorn University, 1996), p. 110, as modified by author.

employed people, and against violence and disciplinary measures that Thai military and paramilitary forces inflicted upon them.[37] Furthermore, most refugees were denied any form of legal protection as Thailand accorded refugee status only to a few thousand refugees in the Khao I Dang holding center who were eligible for resettlement in a third country.[38] Interna-

[37] The Thai government deployed a combined paramilitary and intelligence unit called Task Force 80, supposedly to protect the Cambodian population, but in reality to enforce the closed nature of the camps to prevent the refugee population from seeking sanctuary further in Thailand. See Reynell, *Political Pawns*, p. 143.

[38] Khao I Dang, which was managed by UNHCR and the Thai Ministry of the Interior and Supreme Command, was the holding camp for refugees scheduled to be resettled in a third country. It was officially closed to new arrivals in 1980, but Cambodians continued to enter by bribing officials or smuggling themselves in. Any unregistered camp occupants pres-

Map 5. Cambodian refugee camps on the Thai-Cambodian border, 1986. From Tony Jackson, *Just Waiting to Die? Cambodian Refugees in Thailand* (Oxford: Research and Evaluation Unit, Oxfam, July 1987), p. 5, as modified by author.

tional agency personnel were forbidden access to the hidden border camps and other military camps of the various factions except on rare occasions, so they had no possibility of providing security or legal protection to civilians retained therein.

WAR ECONOMY

From the outset of the relief program, humanitarian aid made a substantial contribution to the war economy of the various Khmer factions along the border. For the factions affiliated with the KPNLF, the revenue gained

---

ent after 1985 were considered to be "illegal immigrants" and were transferred back to the border. Robinson, *Double Vision*, p. 119, and Reynell, *Political Pawns*, pp. 136–138.

from the relief program and the refugees, together with smuggling and extortion activities, constituted the bulk of their resources, at least before the formation of the CGDK. The Khmer Rouge, in addition to covert military support, received supplies through the humanitarian relief program which did not have to be cunningly misappropriated, unlike those of the KPNLF groups. Similarly it seems that Prince Sihanouk's faction did not need to divert resources from the refugees to finance the war economy. The prestige and personal influence of the former royal ruler of Cambodia facilitated successful fundraising trips abroad, which enabled him to supplement resources in the Greenhill refugee camp, which he controlled.[39] Nevertheless, a survey of the occupation of camp inhabitants conducted in 1986 found that 50 percent of the men in Greenhill considered themselves to be soldiers.[40] Thus aid played a fungible role, releasing resources for military activities that would have otherwise been used to feed soldiers.

Camp leaders' diversion of food aid was a particularly grave problem in the Khmer Serei camps during the first years of the humanitarian relief effort. By inflating beneficiary numbers and distributing rations smaller than those calculated by the aid organizations, the camp leaders were able to amass considerable quantities of rice, oil, and other items to resell or transfer to military camps hidden along the border. Linda Mason and Roger Brown document two camps in which this process is clearly visible: Mak Mun, which was controlled by Van Seren, a rogue anti–Khmer Rouge military leader, and Nong Samet, controlled by In-Sakhan, leader of one of the bands of Khmer Serei guerrillas.[41] Food distributions to both camps commenced in late 1979 and were conducted by the "Joint Mission" of UNICEF and ICRC, which was the first arrangement established to coordinate relief along the border. In both sites, camp leaders offered their services to facilitate distributions to camp residents, suggesting that food be delivered to a central location from which camp administrative staff would ensure its distribution at the household level. The initial confidence in these leaders diminished when, after three months, the Joint Mission discovered that the population of Mak Mun was closer to 50,000 than the 300,000 that Van Saren had specified. Similarly, the Joint Mission revised its delivery figures from 180,000 to 60,000 rations in Nong Samet once re-

[39] Reynell, *Political Pawns*, p. 60.

[40] Survey results from Site 2 indicated that 37 percent of men were soldiers, compared with only 2 percent of men in the Khmer Rouge Site 8, although 13 percent in the latter camp described themselves as ammunition porters. See ibid., pp. 102–103.

[41] The Mak Mun case is described on pp. 47–59 and the Nong Samet case on pp. 65–74 of Mason and Brown, *Rice, Rivalry, and Politics*.

ports that the camp administration was selling relief goods reached aid organizations. The diversion of aid supplies through inflated beneficiary numbers continued throughout the ensuing decade; a census conducted in Site 2 in July 1989 reduced the population from 180,000 to 140,000.[42]

Even more food was diverted from the camp population through the reduction of ration entitlements. A survey conducted in Nong Samet in December 1979 revealed that 49 percent of all rice delivered to the camp was taken to the military section, and that 46 percent of all water delivered was used by the military and privileged classes even though these comprised only 16 percent of the population.[43] Another monitoring report in February 1980 disclosed that 64 percent of the rice delivered to the camp never reached the household level, as persistently high levels of malnutrition in Nong Samet testified. Similarly in Mak Mun, despite the efforts of aid officials to bypass the central distribution level and deliver supplies directly to camp quarters, monitoring in February 1980 revealed that 89 percent of the rice and 80 percent of the oil delivered to the quarter-level distribution committee never reached the households.[44] Not all relief diverted in these camps went to support the war economy; as was common among the undisciplined elements of the Khmer Serei guerrillas, both Van Seren and In-Sakhan were concerned as much with enriching themselves as with fighting Vietnamese communists. The same cannot be said of Khmer Rouge guerrillas, however; their discipline and organization were so apparent in comparison with the corrupt system in Khmer Serei camps that the Joint Mission was impressed with their efficiency,[45] in spite of the historical implications of such discipline.

Whereas efforts to monitor distribution of supplies and restrict diversion to the military were attempted in Khmer Serei camps, very little monitoring of Khmer Rouge camps was undertaken. At the beginning of the relief operation, considerations of the nature of the Khmer Rouge leadership were superseded by concerns to address the desperate needs of the population under their control. Since the Khmer Rouge camps were situated in dangerous terrain on the Cambodian side of the border, food was delivered to points on the Thai side from which Khmer Rouge porters would collect it and distribute it to the cooperatives around which the camps were organized. Aid personnel had only occasional access to moni-

[42] Niland, "Politics of Suffering," p. 137.
[43] Mason and Brown, *Rice, Rivalry, and Politics*, p. 67.
[44] UNICEF Monitoring Report, 22 February 1980, as cited in ibid., p. 55.
[45] Mason and Brown, *Rice, Rivalry, and Politics*, pp. 138–139.

tor the way food was distributed,[46] but the few times they made visits, they found the system highly organized and efficient, with record-keeping systems and a relatively equitable distribution of goods. UNICEF personnel were particularly impressed in the early months of the border program, asserting at a food coordination meeting in March 1980 in Bangkok that the Khmer Rouge operation was a success and should be continued or even augmented, despite recognizing that food went to the Khmer Rouge military. A monitoring report of Khao Din on 5 February 1980 stated that "of the food delivered to Khao Din, 30 percent goes directly to the Khmer Rouge soldiers nearby."[47] ICRC, by contrast, was concerned by the prospect of feeding Khmer Rouge military, and in an internal document an official wrote: "despite our incessant efforts to make these people understand that this food is not for the Khmer Rouge army, we can state once again that our distribution criteria are not respected. I believe that here also, we must soon take more severe measures."[48] By April, as the health of Khmer Rouge camp inhabitants improved and the military agenda of the guerrilla group became clearer, UNICEF began to share the ICRC concerns, and the Joint Mission started to search for ways to end their involvement in feeding Khmer Rouge camps.

The same concerns were not apparently shared by WFP, which, as mentioned earlier, provided food to the Thai army for Khmer Rouge camps that were not serviced by the Joint Mission, and for Thai displaced villagers. Such food was delivered to Thai military warehouses, and the only monitoring mechanism was monthly warehouse inventories and distribution records completed by the Thais. This food also arrived at night in the Joint Mission–administered camps, which undermined UNICEF's efforts to distribute food only to women and children. ICRC withdrew from the feeding program in mid-1980 and from the Joint Mission at the end of that year, but UNICEF continued food deliveries to Khmer Rouge camps for another twelve months, with ad hoc distributions also made by two American NGOs, Catholic Relief Services (CRS) and World Relief, both of which had offered to undertake all Khmer Rouge camp distributions. UNICEF, however, was pressured into continuing its role feeding the Khmer Rouge camps, for reasons that will be discussed below.

[46] Reynell states that even after the 1985 camp move, four out of five Khmer Rouge camps were closed to relief officials. *Political Pawns*, p. 59.

[47] UNICEF Monitoring Report, 5 February 1980, as cited in Mason and Brown, *Rice, Rivalry, and Politics*, p. 139.

[48] ICRC internal document, 7–13 January 1980, translated from French, as cited in Mason and Brown, *Rice, Rivalry, and Politics*, p. 140.

The distribution of food and nonfood items to Khmer Rouge camps was the main way in which humanitarian aid contributed to the Khmer Rouge war economy. In the Khmer Serei camps, however, revenue gained through the diversion of food aid was supplemented by systems of taxation and extortion levied on refugees. Refugees interviewed by the Lawyers Committee for Human Rights reported, for example, that KPNLF officials charged asylum seekers 400 baht ($16) to cross the border area under their control, and a further 1000 baht ($40) to hire a KPNLF "guide" who would escort the refugees to Site 2.[49] Cambodians unable to pay this sum were forced to stay in the hidden border camps until the fee was forthcoming from relatives at Site 2 or from abroad. KPNLF-affiliated groups and Thai-Cambodian syndicates also ran a kidnapping racket, with ransoms of up to $10,000 demanded of relatives living in the United States.[50] Unlike Sihanouk's troops, who were regularly paid, the KPNLF soldiers only occasionally received 30–40 baht from their commanders; hence, robbery and extortion were important sources of revenue.[51]

Taxation of refugees and the many traders and merchants who established a black market in the camps was another source of revenue for the guerrilla factions and for Thai Task Force 80, the paramilitary/intelligence unit supposedly deployed to protect the refugees. The camp economy, conducted around the sale and trading of relief items, was supplemented by remittances that some of the refugees received from relatives in Thailand, Cambodia, or abroad; some 2 million baht ($150,000) were alleged to enter Site 2 each month.[52] Traders were charged a toll on goods brought in and out of the camps, and severe punishments were inflicted on traders who tried to smuggle goods past the guards. Camp administrators also levied taxes on Cambodian staff of aid agencies; Josephine Reynell's study found that in Site 2, Greenhill, and Site 8, all workers were required to pay two tins of fish from the dozen they earned as their weekly payment.[53] In Site 2 North, ordinary refugees were also taxed one tin of fish and one tin measure of rice per week from their general ration. Refugees stated that the food was taken for the military; in Greenhill and Site 2, soldiers visiting their families were provided with rice and fish during their stay, and in Site 2 each soldier was given two kilos of rice and two cans of

[49] *Refuge Denied: Problems in the Protection of Vietnamese and Cambodians in Thailand and the Admission of Indochinese Refugees into the United States* (New York: Lawyers Committee for Human Rights, 1989), p. 36.

[50] Ibid., p. 37.

[51] Reynell, *Political Pawns*, p. 103.

[52] Ibid., p. 85.

[53] Ibid., p. 66.

fish when he returned to the front. A portion of food grown in the camps was also sent to the military camps.

The camps' medical and training facilities also performed valuable support functions for the military. From February to November 1986, for example, 121 of 187 patients applying for prostheses in the Site 8 workshop were soldiers. Such injuries did not render these combatants *hors de combat*; many were reengaged as ammunition porters once they had been fitted with prostheses.[54] Medical supplies were stolen from camp dispensaries for use by the military, and even sewing machines given to the Greenhill camp were used to make clothing for the soldiers.[55] The military also co-opted graduates of medical training courses: CRS, for instance, lost fifteen of thirty-two trained medics upon completion of their studies in Greenhill in 1986.[56] Thus the humanitarian aid program greatly contributed to the economy of war of the Cambodian resistance factions. This was not, however, the most important role of the humanitarian sanctuary, since financial and military aid was also forthcoming from China and the United States, and could probably have been increased to cover the economic aspects of the guerrilla war, had it been necessary. Such military support could never, however, have fulfilled the most crucial functions the humanitarian sanctuary provided: the legitimacy that the presence of 250,000–300,000 refugees along the border bestowed upon the self-proclaimed government-in-exile after its formation in 1982, and the mechanisms with which to control the refugee population to ensure that such "legitimacy" was retained.

LEGITIMACY

As I mentioned earlier, the CGDK itself was formed in order to lend some legitimacy to the Khmer Rouge and to create an image of unity among opponents of the Vietnamese-installed regime. An identifiable population under the authority of the CGDK promoted the image of a government-in-exile: as Yossi Shain writes of all self-proclaimed governments-in-exile, "the support of their alleged constituencies may be the most critical factor in determining the validity of their claim and the attitude of foreign pa-

[54] Filip Werbrouck, "The Site 8 Artificial Limb Workshop: A Humanitarian or Military Programme?—A Study of Aid to a Khmer Rouge Camp on the Thai-Kampuchean border," April 1987, as cited in Jackson, *Just Waiting to Die?* p. 13.

[55] *Information Bulletin* (n.p.: FUNCINPEC/ANS, October 1986), p. 36, as cited in Jackson, *Just Waiting to Die?* p. 14.

[56] Catholic Relief Services letter to J. Lefevre, Deputy Director of UNBRO, 21 November 1986, as cited in Jackson, *Just Waiting to Die?* p. 13, and Reynell, *Political Pawns*, p. 66.

trons toward their struggles."[57] These claims to legitimacy in turn permitted the Cambodian seat at the UN to be passed from the Khmer Rouge, which had held it between 1979 and 1982 despite its human rights record and defeat, to the CGDK.

The way Western states dealt with the issue of the UN seat exemplifies the political compromises and tradeoffs that permeated the entire response to the Cambodian crisis, and the lack of regard for the welfare of the Cambodian refugees. In September 1979, the UN Credentials Committee recommended to the General Assembly that the delegation of "Democratic Kampuchea" be accepted as the recognized representative of Cambodia, and the recommendation was adopted by a vote of 71 to 35 with 34 abstentions. No Western-bloc country voted against acceptance of these credentials, and only Austria, Finland, France, Ireland, and Sweden abstained throughout the four years that the credentials were accepted. Hence until 1982 the Khmer Rouge held this seat, after which it was transferred to the CGDK, with the UN conveniently conceding that it was reprehensible for a genocidal regime to be the sole and legitimate representative of the Cambodian people.

The notion that the CGDK had any more legitimacy than the Khmer Rouge, however, was farcical. As Ramesh Thakur observed: "The CGDK is a total misnomer: it is not a coalition (Pol Pot's Khmer Rouge is the real power); it is not a government, having neither people, territory nor other attributes of government; it is decidedly not democratic; and it is not in Kampuchea, being located rather on the Thai side of the border."[58]

To take each point in turn: First, the Khmer Rouge held the dominant position in the coalition by virtue of its military strength and shrewd negotiation of the formal agreement. Khieu Samphan, one of Pol Pot's top officials, had insisted on the inclusion of a priority clause which stipulated that the sovereignty of Democratic Kampuchea be preserved in the event of a coalition split: "in the event that an impasse has developed which renders the coalition government of Democratic Kampuchea inoperative . . . the current state of DK led by Mr. Khieu Samphan will have the right to resume its activities as the sole legal and legitimate state of Kampuchea."[59] The important diplomatic post of permanent representative to the UN

[57] Yossi Shain, "Introduction: Governments-in-Exile and the Age of Democratic Transitions," in Shain (ed.), *Governments-in-Exile in Contemporary World Politics*, pp. 1–17 at p. 5.
[58] Ramesh Thakur, "The Afghan Road to Kampuchea?" *Asian Defence Journal*, August 1988, p. 58.
[59] See Colin Campbell, "3 Cambodian Groups Forming Coalition," *New York Times*, 21 June 1982, and Colin Campbell, "3 Cambodian Groups Form Exile Regime," *New York Times*, 23 June 1982, as cited in Etcheson, "The Khmer Way of Exile," p. 106.

was also held by a Khmer Rouge nominee, Ambassador Thiounn Prasith, who had been a top aide in the Ministry of Foreign Affairs during the Khmer Rouge rule of Cambodia.[60] Second, the CGDK "governed" only 300,000 of the 7 million Cambodian population and exercised control over these people in camps surrounded by barbed wire and policed by Thai paramilitary forces. Had the refugees been given the choice of transferring to a camp in the interior of Thailand, moving to a neutral camp, or even repatriating to Cambodia, the majority of them undoubtedly would have done so.[61]

Third, the CGDK held no territory in Cambodia, something which invalidated any claims to independent sovereign status, and was unable to maintain law and order in the border area, a role that the Thai government filled by placing the region under martial law. And fourth, the "government" was dependent upon donors and aid organizations to feed the population it was supposed to represent. Thus the Cambodian population along the border was held hostage in order to create the fiction that there was a legitimate government representing an exiled state of citizens. As Reynell writes, "without this population, continued recognition of the CGDK as a government would be virtually impossible."[62] UN member states opposed to the Vietnamese invasion of Cambodia did not need to vote in favor of the Khmer Rouge or CGDK to deprive Phnom Penh of recognition; they could have voted to leave the seat vacant.

The repercussions of this method of isolating Phnom Penh and its Vietnamese backers were felt not only by the Cambodians consigned to a decade of life in refugee camps along the border, but also by the inhabitants of Cambodia. The bestowal of the UN seat on the CGDK deprived Cambodia of all but "humanitarian" assistance. UN development assistance was not permitted to flow to countries in which the de facto government was not the government formally recognized by the UN.[63] Furthermore, the UN imposed a trade embargo on the country and in early 1982 declared the emergency period over, forcing the withdrawal of UN development agencies and a drastic reduction in assistance to the country from

[60] Tony Jackson, "How Pol Pot Dominates the Coalition Government of Democratic Kampuchea," Staff Briefing Paper (Oxford: Oxfam, 1988), p. 5.

[61] Approximately 200,000 Cambodians chose to return from the border to their homes in Cambodia in 1981 following economic improvements in Cambodia. But once the border camps moved permanently into Thailand, such a choice was no longer possible. Charlotte Benson, *The Changing Role of NGOs in the Provision of Relief and Rehabilitation Assistance: Case Study 2 — Cambodia/Thailand*, Working Paper 75 (London: Overseas Development Institute, 1993), p. 17.

[62] Reynell, *Political Pawns*, p. 38.

[63] *Cambodian Humanitarian Assistance and the United Nations*, p. 16.

Western-bloc nations.[64] The Eastern bloc continued its support, but until the Vietnamese troop withdrawal in 1989, the government in Phnom Penh remained an international pariah and Cambodia continued to be one of the poorest countries in the world.

The legitimacy the international relief effort conferred on the resistance factions was further exemplified by UNICEF's unsuccessful attempt to transfer the responsibility for feeding the Khmer Rouge camps to another aid organization. As discussed above, toward the end of April 1980, UNICEF began to share the doubts of ICRC regarding the implications of feeding the Khmer Rouge, and the Joint Mission announced that continuing to supply the armed elements in the camps would be in violation of the mandates of each organization. The Joint Mission suggested that either WFP and the Thai army extend the distributions they were already making, or that an NGO assume such a role, as CRS and World Relief had proposed. The issue, however, became hotly contested when Thai officials insisted that they wanted the Joint Mission to continue, even threatening to forbid UNICEF and ICRC involvement in the rest of the border program if they did not proceed. Thai authorities were not content to allow WFP and the Thai army to accept full responsibility for feeding the Khmer Rouge camps since this could create the perception that Thailand was aiding the guerrilla forces. In Mason and Brown's words, "The Thais wanted an international organization specifically to distribute in these camps to lend credibility to the relief effort . . . [and they] preferred the Joint Mission's international reputation and status to that of the volags [voluntary agencies or NGOs]."[65] U.S. government officials were also in favor of the Joint Mission's continuing to supply Khmer Rouge camps as a way to give a neutral and respectable hue to such activities. "We wanted ICRC and UNICEF to do the feeding because we did not want it to be a U.S. effort," explained a State Department official in Washington.[66] After several months of negotiations and the first Vietnamese attack on the border camps, ICRC withdrew from the food distributions, but UNICEF continued, insisting upon considerably reduced rations to the camp and distributions to women only. The Thai government agreed to this compromise since it still fulfilled the primary aim of having UNICEF's name associated with the feeding, and it was able to supplement the food distri-

[64] See Eva Mysliwiec, *Punishing the Poor: The International Isolation of Kampuchea* (Oxford: Oxfam, 1988), pp. 73–74.

[65] Mason and Brown, *Rice, Rivalry, and Politics*, p. 146 and p. 149.

[66] As cited in ibid., p. 159.

buted with the Thai army deliveries and the compliance of CRS and World Relief.

The humanitarian relief effort also inadvertently conferred legitimacy on individual Cambodian leaders and "middle-managers." The camp presidents and heads of relief departments established to oversee the distribution of various goods tended to be from former middle-class, educated backgrounds and able to speak French or English.[67] Many of these camp leaders cited customary expectations that leaders should be materially richer than the population to show their prowess as leaders, in order to justify keeping extra relief goods for themselves. As Reynell described the situation, "The appropriations both emphasize and consolidate the status and power differentials between the two groups. This practice has a long tradition in Kampuchea and therefore provides a model of action for those now in authority."[68] The offices of camp president and department head bestowed legitimacy and prowess on their incumbents, but it was their authority over the distribution of relief supplies which enabled these individuals to retain almost complete control over the refugee population.

POPULATION CONTROL

Controlling the lives of the Cambodian border population was crucial to the containment function of the refugee camps, and such control was maintained in a variety of ways. Externally, the imposition of martial law and the deployment of Thai Task Force 80 officers restricted the movement of refugees beyond the camps' perimeters, which were fenced with barbed wire.[69] The widely documented brutality of the Task Force 80 personnel dissuaded camp residents from violating regulations[70] and served to quash any refugee notions of permanent settlement in Thailand.[71]

The proximity of military camps to the civilian camps added another physical element of external control, and an even stronger control mechanism was the military appointment of all levels of civilian camp leadership. Reynell's study, in fact, found that in Site 8, Greenhill, and Site 2, top officials in the civilian administration were also officials in the military hierar-

[67] Reynell, *Political Pawns*, p. 70.

[68] Ibid.

[69] The only camp which was not surrounded by barbed wire was Greenhill, administered by Sihanouk's FUNCINPEC. See Jackson, *Just Waiting to Die?* p. 9.

[70] Complaints about the behavior of Task Force 80 personnel eventually led to its replacement with a specially trained security force, the Displaced Persons' Protection Unit (DPPU), in August 1988. See *Refuge Denied*, pp. 55–58, for testimonies of Task Force 80 brutality.

[71] Reynell, *Political Pawns*, p. 143.

chy.[72] Camp presidents were generally appointed by a political-military elite living outside the camps and in turn appointed officials to head the various camp departments, such as health, education, and security. These department heads chose their administrative team, the prerequisite for which was attendance at and a certificate from one of the camps' political education schools, known as "civic schools" or "psychological warfare schools."[73] The camp administrators also controlled the nomination of local staff to work with the aid organizations in the camps.[74] Hence conformity to CGDK political ideology was entrenched in the camps' administrative structure and enforced through the control that loyal supporters exercised over the aid distribution system.

Giving refugees autonomy to undertake as many functions as possible in a camp setting is a commonly held principle in refugee relief programs, and UNBRO and other aid agencies working in the camps delegated considerable responsibility to the refugees to run the camps and conduct distributions. Camp administrators were even given the responsibility of determining the quantity of rice each person was to receive when a direct system of distribution was introduced into Greenhill in 1986.[75] In addition, the refugee leadership selected civilian police to enforce camp rules and control internal security. However, these measures, while sound in theory, inadvertently assisted in institutionalizing and legitimizing the control of the CGDK-appointed personnel. Moreover, attempts to improve the day-to-day physical safety of the refugees, although important, were only cosmetic: the root of the problems lay in the very nature and raison d'être of the camps.

The aid structures in the refugee camps therefore assisted in establishing and maintaining control over the refugee population by physically restricting refugee movements and permitting the refugee leadership to hold authority over the food and nonfood items necessary to sustain life and over the camp judicial system. These forms of control were supplemented by the use of fear, intimidation, and violence against the refugee population, particularly in the Khmer Rouge camps. Executions of civilians and army deserters were reported from the closed camps, and in Site 8, the UN-assisted Khmer Rouge camp, rule infractions were punished with "reeducation," jail terms, or "disappearance."[76] Forced population trans-

---

[72] Ibid., p. 65.
[73] Ibid., p. 69.
[74] Ibid., p. 82, and Mason and Brown, *Rice, Rivalry, and Politics*, pp. 61–62.
[75] Reynell, *Political Pawns*, p. 75.
[76] *Refuge Denied*, pp. 47–50.

fers from civilian camps to military camps occurred on numerous occasions: the Lawyers Committee for Human Rights estimated that by December 1988 some 15,000 Cambodians under Khmer Rouge control had been moved to closed camps near the border, where they were subjected to shelling.[77] Reports of many refugee casualties reached aid organizations, but the Khmer Rouge leadership refused to let aid officials in to evacuate the wounded. ICRC consistently requested medical access to Khmer Rouge camps to no avail and only rarely received patients transferred to medical facilities in the Khao I Dang holding center. Invariably the patients were in such a critical state by the time they arrived that they died. The Khmer Rouge then used this as an excuse to forbid further transfers or access for aid organizations, attributing the deaths to Western medical techniques.[78]

Political intimidation was also common in the non–Khmer Rouge camps, with jail terms and "disappearances" inflicted on refugees expressing views contrary to those of the leadership. Reynell reports that even complaints about camp conditions or expressions of concern for the future were construed as disloyal and were thus punishable.[79] Conscription also occurred in all the camps, but UNBRO managed to curb this to a certain extent in Site 2 by threatening to cut off food supplies. This tactic did not work in the Khmer Rouge camps, however: in order to pressure for greater access, UNBRO terminated aid to the Huay Chan camp in May 1988. In response, the Khmer Rouge leadership dismantled the camp and moved the occupants to other Khmer Rouge camps in the region.[80]

Controlling the refugee population to maintain the image of a support base for the factions became equally, if not more, important when prospects of a peace agreement and a Vietnamese troop withdrawal began to surface in 1988. The stakes had suddenly altered from unity to competition among the factions, and the civilian populations constituted an important card in future political negotiations for power in Phnom Penh. Hence once again the refugees became a tool in the political process, and many were moved toward "repatriation camps" nearer the border in late 1988. The Khmer Rouge, with logistical support from the Thai army, virtually emptied many camps. The inhabitants were moved into "liberated" zones of Cambodia to provide a foothold and base of support for the fac-

[77] Ibid., p. 47.
[78] Ibid., p. 43.
[79] Reynell, *Political Pawns*, p. 129.
[80] *Refuge Denied*, p. 43.

tion following the withdrawal of Vietnamese troops.[81] In a letter sent to the Thai newspaper *The Nation*, a Khmer Rouge official denied that the refugees were forcibly relocated, stating: "whenever the National Army of Democratic Kampuchea succeeds in liberating wholly or partially any area of our territory which provides relative security, our people are bent on returning home. As Kampuchean citizens, this is not only their right but also their duty to participate in the war of liberation against the Vietnamese aggressors."[82]

Asia Watch reported that 20,000 people were moved into Cambodia by the various factions in the first three months of 1990,[83] and between 60,000 and 100,000 inhabitants of the Khmer Rouge "hidden camps" were also thought to have crossed that year.[84] The forced repatriation generated concern among aid agencies: the refugees' lack of choice was compounded by harsh conditions in Cambodia, and large numbers of refugees returned to the UN camps, many with malaria, malnutrition, and land mine injuries. Moreover, the partitioning of the country among the factions seemed likely to lead to a continuation of the war. "The resistance wants to populate the liberated areas with the refugees, not only to control the areas but also to keep their hold on these people," reported the head of ICRC in Thailand, Jean-Jacques Fresard. "This seems to lead to a Lebanonization of Cambodia."[85]

The issue of repatriation galvanized aid organizations, which had effectively remained silent over the preceding decade, into campaigning for the formation of a neutral camp in Thailand or neutral reception centers inside Cambodia, through which refugees could be channeled to their region of choice. Although Thailand officially agreed to the establishment of such a camp in March 1990, the factions opposed the idea as it was obviously not in their interests to "neutralize" their populations. The U.S. government was also against the initiative, claiming that "the closing of Site 2 would be a disaster" for the KPNLF.[86] In February 1991, a coup d'état in Thailand effectively ended Thai support for the establishment of neutral camps, and none were ever established.

[81] Murray Hiebert, "The Khmer Rouge Regroups," *Far East Economic Review*, 1 December 1988, p. 34.

[82] As cited in ibid.

[83] *Violations of the Rules of War by the Khmer Rouge*, p. 3.

[84] Peter Eng, "Cambodian Refugees Continue to Be Used as Pawns," Associated Press, 14 January 1991.

[85] As cited in ibid.

[86] Steven Erlanger, "Thai Wants Cambodia Refugees in Neutral Camps," *New York Times*, 25 March 1990, as cited in Niland, "Politics of Suffering," p. 146.

The NGO solidarity that characterized the campaign for a neutral camp at the end of the 1980s was, however, a significant reversal from the antagonisms which had permeated the border relief operation and aid to the interior of Cambodia a decade earlier. The political environment had polarized the aid community, and the majority of aid organizations were forced to choose whether they would work along the border or inside Cambodia.

The Relief Response: The Humanitarian Impasse

Why was it only in the mid-to late 1980s that aid agencies publicly lobbied for the creation of humanitarian space in the form of a neutral camp, when no such space had existed since the outset of the aid program, or inside Cambodia? Aid organizations were not permitted unhindered access to populations in need; they were unable to assess independently the needs of vulnerable groups; they were prevented from adequately controlling the distribution of relief supplies; and they were accused of political bias by both sides of the conflict. Furthermore, aid agencies did not have sufficient security guarantees to work freely in the border region, to stay overnight in the refugee camps, or to travel to many regions inside Cambodia. The organizations reached an impasse: the only "neutrality" possible in the provision of humanitarian assistance was ensuring that humanitarian aid benefited both sides equally. It was impossible to avoid contributing to the war effort. Given that it was the camps themselves and the aid which sustained them that compromised the safety of the refugees, why was there so little public condemnation of the system to which aid agencies were unwilling accomplices? Several interrelated factors help to explain the organizations' reluctance to challenge openly the misuse of aid by all parties.

THE PRICE OF ACCESS

Geopolitical strategic and ideological interests dominated humanitarian concerns, restricting the room for aid organizations to maneuver vis-à-vis the host governments and the conditions they imposed. The Thai government and Western donors dictated the terms of the border aid program by imposing strict regulations and controlling the financial arrangements that underwrote the relief system. From the outset Thai authorities clearly showed that they would not tolerate criticism, no matter how diplomatic. The ICRC head of delegation in Bangkok, Francis Amar, was told to leave Thailand after he appealed to the Thai government to halt the *refoulement* of some 42,000 Cambodians who were forced into mine-infested areas below Preah-Vihear. Amar's statement, that the people were pushed back against their will and might either lose their lives or again face the same situation which had forced them to seek refuge in Thailand, was angrily dismissed by Prime Minister Kriangsak as Thailand's business, "done to protect the national interest."[87]

Thai authorities also had no compunction in stopping humanitarian activities if aid agencies did not comply with their wishes, as is illustrated by the threat to prohibit the participation of ICRC and UNICEF in the entire relief program unless they resumed feeding the Khmer Rouge. Thailand also used the withholding of humanitarian aid as a way of punishing the Vietnamese-backed regime in Cambodia, suspending authorization of relief flights from Bangkok to Phnom Penh in response to the first offensive launched against the border refugee camps. The imposition of martial law enforced further restrictions on the activities and statements of aid personnel along the border. Authorization to enter the border area could be granted only by the military wing of the government.

The cautious attitude exhibited by aid organizations operating in Thailand was exemplified by UNHCR, which failed to honor its own mandate in order to avoid jeopardizing its presence in the country. Responsible for hundreds of thousands of Indochinese refugees in a country that had not signed the 1951 Refugee Convention or 1967 Protocol, UNHCR relinquished its protection responsibilities for Cambodians along the border in favor of concentrating on resettlement opportunities for refugees in the holding centers away from the border. Some 200,000 Cambodian refugees were resettled in the West, but the price for this success was silence. UNHCR did not even protest the refoulement at Preah-Vihear which, at the time, was the largest single case of forced repatriation since the agency's founding in 1951. Dennis McNamara, former head of the UNHCR Protection Unit in Geneva, later admitted that the lack of UNHCR protest "must be seen as one of the low points of its protection history."[88] The absence of UNHCR along the border deprived the refugees of legal protection since UNBRO did not possess such responsibility.

Donor pressure further suppressed the autonomy and independence of aid organizations. The purse strings of the border operation were firmly held by Western governments with an interest in sustaining the resistance movement through the humanitarian relief effort. The United States, in

---

[87] *Bangkok Post*, 12 June 1979, as cited in Robinson, *Double Vision*, pp. 55–56.

[88] Dennis McNamara, "The Politics of Humanitarianism: A Study of Some Aspects of the International Response to the Indochinese Refugee Influx (1975–1985)," unpublished manuscript, p. 47, Section V, p. 21, as cited in Robinson, *Double Vision*, p. 56.

particular, had significant leverage over the Thai government by virtue of its economic and military aid to Thailand and had direct influence over the border relief program as the largest single donor, meeting about one-third of the total cost.[89] Supporting the Khmer resistance movements through the aid program was an overt objective of the U.S. embassy in Bangkok,[90] and its funding commitments gave the United States a strong say over where and how the money would be spent. The monopoly of U.S. financial control was consolidated when UNBRO assumed coordination of the border program in early 1982 because between 90 and 100 percent of NGO programs, with the exception of Christian Outreach and Handicap International, were funded through UNBRO.[91] Itself dependent on voluntary contributions from states, UNBRO was obliged to explain and justify its program and expenditure to donors in pledging meetings held two or three times per year. This funding system and the requirement that NGOs obtain UNBRO permission to commence operations along the border effectively guaranteed that donor states retained full control of the aid operation. Aid agencies were reluctant to challenge the hand that fed them. As Jackson remarked: "Where the voluntary agencies have fallen down is . . . in serving as a voice for the people for whom they are working. . . . the agencies have been effectively muzzled by their close association with UNBRO. Being almost totally dependent on it for funding appears to have made the agencies unwilling to look into the implications of their work."[92]

The regime in Phnom Penh was no less influential in determining the direction of the interior aid effort. Aware that aid to the border region nourished forces opposing Phnom Penh, the Heng Samrin regime made cessation of aid to the border a condition of operating inside Cambodia, granting only rare exceptions.[93] Thus aid agencies were forced to choose

[89] Some $36 million per year was channeled to the border programs, of which the United States met 33 percent, Japan met 28 percent, the EEC 8 percent, and Australia 2 percent. Reynell, *Political Pawns*, p. 57.

[90] The U.S. embassy's stated objectives along the border were to feed and protect the Cambodian refugees, support the Khmer resistance movements, and resettle Cambodians in the United States. See Mason and Brown, *Rice, Rivalry, and Politics*, p. 101.

[91] Benson, *Changing Role of NGOs*, p. 32.

[92] Jackson, *Just Waiting to Die?* p. 21.

[93] The Joint Mission of ICRC and UNICEF successfully negotiated a presence in both regions during the emergency period of 1979–81, due to the legitimacy their presence accorded to the regime in Phnom Penh. World Vision was also an exception during this period, which Benson suggests was a result of the large financial resources the organization offered Cambodia, including a $3 million project to rehabilitate the pediatric hospital in Phnom Penh. After the emergency period and until 1987, only two NGOs, Handicap International and the Japan Volunteer Centre, were permitted to work in both places. See Benson, *Changing Role of NGOs*, p. 87.

on which side they would work. A litany of other government controls followed. Agencies had to submit detailed lists and schedules of relief supplies and to consign all relief to the government for distribution, thereby relinquishing control over where and to whom the aid would be distributed.[94] Western medical personnel were not permitted to work in the country for the first two years, and no personnel could obtain visas if the authorities deemed the quantity of material destined for technical projects insufficient. In fact, the number of visas issued to staff of aid organizations was directly proportional to the budgets of agencies. Hence UNICEF and World Vision with budgets of $5 million each could obtain about twelve visas, but agencies with small budgets were threatened with nonrenewal of visas if their planned expenditure was not augmented.[95]

The Vietnamese determination to impose a compliant regime in Cambodia made all other issues subservient. Policies to consolidate the regime prioritized food distributions to the army and government bureaucrats over those to the general population, and the political indoctrination of the Cambodian people took precedence over technical training. Political education sessions interrupted the work of all Cambodians, with detrimental consequences for the rehabilitation of infrastructure and services. The priority given to strategic and ideological interests over humanitarian concerns was starkly illustrated by the decision to construct a bamboo wall along the western border of Cambodia, allegedly to prevent guerrilla incursions into the country and the exodus of Cambodians. Commencing in early 1984 and codenamed "K5," the project engaged a fixed number of "voluntary workers" from each province for 3–6 months to clear land in the malaria-and mine-infested jungle. Exacerbated by lack of food and physical exhaustion, malaria was estimated to have killed 5 percent or 50,000 of the one million peasants who were forced to participate in the first two years.[96] Lacking any real strategic value, the project succeeded in keeping the population in a permanent state of mobilization and under tight government control.

The price of humanitarian access to Cambodia was compromise and silence; the aid agencies rarely protested against the unacceptable conditions of operation[97] and never mentioned human rights abuses or forced labor. In fact the only time they broke their silence was to issue a statement in fa-

[94] See Shawcross, *Quality of Mercy*, pp. 365–370, for a detailed discussion of the inability of aid agencies to monitor the distributions of relief.

[95] Esmeralda Luciolli, *Le mur de bambou: Le Cambodge après Pol Pot* (Paris: Éditions Régine Deforges, 1988), p. 280.

[96] Ibid., p. 128.

[97] In 1979 and early 1980, ICRC and UNICEF did complain to the Phnom Penh authorities about food diversions, inadequate logistics, and a lack of monitoring, but these com-

vor of the regime in Phnom Penh. In April 1985, for example, a report appeared in the *Bangkok Post* detailing some of the forced labor involved in the construction of the bamboo wall, in which aid organizations were cited as the source of the information. In response, the UNICEF representative in Phnom Penh prepared a declaration for the newspaper on behalf of all agencies in Cambodia which was copied to the Cambodian Ministry of Foreign Affairs, denying the medical consequences of the "agricultural clearance." Only one NGO representative refused to sign the statement.[98]

Humanitarian principles were compromised along the border and inside Cambodia, and room for aid organizations to maneuver to claim humanitarian space was extremely limited. To complain about the imposed conditions risked expulsion from Thailand and Cambodia. Weighing that against the dubious potential gains such complaints could achieve, most agencies judged that it was better to remain silent in order to continue to participate in the relief program. These limitations were compounded by the propaganda war in which the prospect of famine and the response to it were the major weapons.

THE CRISIS OF WESTERN CONSCIENCE

The use of famine as a propaganda tool by both sides of the conflict exacerbated many of the problems the aid agencies experienced in negotiating humanitarian access to Cambodia and in publicizing the true extent of the difficulties of providing humanitarian assistance. After months of denying aid organizations authorization to conduct an assessment inside Cambodia, Phnom Penh permitted a short visit in July 1979, during which the administration proclaimed that a famine threatened the lives of two million Cambodians. Access to the rural areas was refused, but what the aid officials saw around Phnom Penh left them with little reason to question the validity of the claim. They proposed to mount an immediate emergency response, but protracted negotiations with Phnom Penh over the conditions of operations slowed the process, with UNICEF and ICRC reluctant to accept the limitations imposed.

The media frenzy sparked by images of the aftermath of the Khmer Rouge regime, however, forced the hand of the aid agencies. By September 1979, increasingly dramatic analogies were being drawn between Pol Pot and Adolf Hitler, and stories of a Cambodian holocaust flashed around

---

plaints were rarely made public since they jeopardized funding for the Cambodia programs, as I discuss further below.

[98] Luciolli, *Le mur de bambou*, p. 296.

the world. The specter of famine killing "two million more before Christmas" was added to the fray, with the fundraising campaigns conducted by aid agencies propelling the imperative to "do something." "If we don't act by Tuesday—come Friday they won't be starving—they'll be dead," declared a World Vision advertisement. The British Red Cross pictured an emaciated child with the caption, "Some children in Kampuchea look like this . . . the rest are dead."[99] Journalists such as John Pilger added fuel to the fire, vehemently criticizing the United States for its lack of aid to Cambodia, claiming that the Vietnamese were placing no obstacles to the implementation of an aid program, and blaming the aid organizations for the slow response.[100] Pilger added further pressure on UNICEF and ICRC by suggesting that the public donate to Oxfam rather than other agencies. Oxfam had recently entered Cambodia and accepted all the government demands including providing no aid to the border, an act which threatened to undermine the stance of UNICEF and ICRC. Before long the pressure of public opinion led the Joint Mission and the Heng Samrin regime to make concessions: the former relaxed their normal monitoring requirements and the latter softened its insistence that ICRC and UNICEF stop their operations along the border. According to Shawcross, "there was no single moment in Phnom Penh in which such compromises were openly made and agreement was explicitly reached."[101]

Each side used the issue of famine to attack the other. Having invited Western aid to Cambodia in July to alleviate famine, Phnom Penh claimed in late October that the problem had been solved: starvation had been averted through aid from socialist countries. Moreover the regime charged that fears of famine were a plot hatched to discredit the regime and to supply food and equipment to Pol Pot's forces. Aid personnel were granted access to rural areas of Cambodia in mid-November and indeed found no evidence of famine, only pockets of hunger. The United States, its allies, and Western journalists, however, refused to believe that this could be so, instead viewing the denial as part of a policy to orchestrate famine and eliminate internal resistance to Vietnamese rule. The Vietnamese obstruction of aid efforts then became the focus of attack, and donors became reluctant to provide more aid in the absence of monitoring reports. Thus the issue of famine had benefited Phnom Penh by attracting international agencies and the legitimacy they bestowed on the country. The famine also benefited the West, which, exploiting public guilt at having forsaken

[99] Shawcross, *Quality of Mercy*, p. 204.
[100] Ibid., pp. 140–141.
[101] Ibid., p. 161.

the Cambodian people during the Pol Pot years, could demonize the Vietnamese regime for allowing the population to suffer again and could justify its support to the opposition movement. As Rufin points out, "our way of envisaging socialist countries oscillates constantly between an ironic criticism of their inefficiency, and suspicion that they can orchestrate diabolical plots in fine detail."[102]

The polarization of the aid issue left humanitarian organizations in a quandary. Although there was no famine, the needs of the population were still immense, and the increasing reluctance of donors to provide funding jeopardized aid programs. Any public statements issued by aid organizations played into the hands of either side. An ICRC official, for example, lamented the problems of food distribution in Cambodia and warned that the aid flow could not continue indefinitely unless distribution was improved. In response, a *New York Times* editorial stated that "whatever one calls it, the lack of food has killed many people, food remains in short supply, and Phnom Penh and Hanoi refuse to give full support to those most able to help. . . . Phnom Penh, Hanoi and Moscow are making any civilized arrangement more difficult with their cynical tolerance of starvation when there is food at hand. They must be doing something very, very wrong when they drive professional feeders of the hungry to start talking about withholding food."[103] The acrimonious context made it impossible to raise an honest and detached debate about the true extent of the humanitarian needs in Cambodia and the most appropriate response to them. It was futile to appeal to donors or diplomatic parties to assist in negotiating conditions of operation.

TAKING SIDES

The ban imposed by Phnom Penh on agencies working along the border denied the possibility of asserting a neutral position in the conflict for all but the few agencies which were granted exemptions. Each aid organization was forced to choose the side on which it would operate. Reflecting on the options available, Rony Brauman explained that "the choice was . . . not between a political position and a neutral position, but between two political positions: one active and the other by default."[104] Either aid or-

---

[102] Jean-Christophe Rufin, *Le piège humanitaire, suivi de Humanitaire et politique depuis la chute du Mur*, revised and updated edition (Paris: Jean-Claude Lattès, 1993), p. 209.

[103] As cited in Shawcross, *Quality of Mercy*, p. 216.

[104] Rony Brauman, "Refugees Camps, Population Transfers, and NGOs," in Jonathan Moore (ed.), *Hard Choices: Moral Dilemmas in Humanitarian Intervention* (Oxford: Rowman and Littlefield, 1998), pp. 177–193 at p. 181.

ganizations consciously determined which side or faction they would work with, or they assumed a political position by virtue of their presence.

The choice was not easy. Other Cold War contexts had presented identifiable "good" and "bad" sides: in Afghanistan, the disproportionate force used by the Soviet regime clearly delineated the "victims" from the "oppressors," and in Central America, "victims" and "oppressors" were defined according to right-wing or left-wing ideology. But in Cambodia, both sides contained "oppressors." The Khmer Rouge had annihilated part of the Cambodian population and espoused a radical socialist ideology. And the Vietnamese, although initially liberating the country, remained as an army of occupation. Instead of allowing people to choose their future path, they had imposed communism, and brutal policies of forced labor and reform cast dark shadows over the regime for all but the staunchest communists and Vietnamese sympathizers.

In the absence of a clearly "good" side, most aid agencies decided to assist the side for which they felt the least aversion, rather than the most affinity. There were some exceptions to this pattern of choice, such as the Comité d'Aide Sanitaire à la Population Cambodgienne, a French NGO run by communist doctors. Its support of the regime in Cambodia extended to screening potential organizations and personnel offering assistance and backing Phnom Penh's claims that no medical personnel, only equipment, was needed in Cambodia.[105] But for most agencies, the decision about whom to support was based on a strong aversion either to communism and Vietnamese expansionism or to the Khmer Rouge. The so-called crisis of Western conscience played a role on each side. Oxfam, for example, readily agreed to provide no aid to the border in order to assist Cambodians who had been neglected by the West throughout the Pol Pot years. According to Shawcross, Oxfam and ICRC officials believed that an even more important contribution than humanitarian aid "lay simply in being in Cambodia, considerate ambassadors from the world against which the Khmer Rouge had raised the barricades, a testament to some form of humanitarian victory over foul revolution and impoverished diplomacy."[106] Aid organizations like CRS and the International Rescue Committee (IRC), by contrast, were strongly anticommunist and looked to the "boat people" fleeing Vietnam to dispel doubts about the threat of Vietnamese tyranny.

A few aid agencies such as MSF had a strong aversion to both the

---

[105] See Rufin, *Le piège humanitaire*, p. 216. Of 450 doctors in Cambodia in 1975, only 45 remained after 1979.

[106] Shawcross, *Quality of Mercy*, p. 379.

Khmer Rouge and the Vietnamese regime in Phnom Penh. MSF withdrew support from the Khmer Rouge camps as soon as the emergency period subsided, and restricted its assistance to the non–Khmer Rouge refugee camps.[107] The organization also refused to work inside Cambodia following a visit there in 1979, judging that aid was not reaching the civilian population, but remaining in the hands of the government. Furthermore, MSF refused to submit to the system of payment for access to Cambodia and to the obligatory accompaniment of government officials when assessing the needs of the population. In one of the only public advocacy campaigns undertaken by aid organizations during the Cambodian crisis, MSF, Action Internationale Contre la Faim, and IRC organized a "March for the Survival of Cambodia" along the Thai-Cambodian border in 1980. Although fairly successful in publicizing the lack of access to the Cambodian population, the march abetted the propaganda war of political powers and further polarized the aid community.

Such agencies as CRS and World Relief also openly assumed a political position, having little compunction in offering to replace UNICEF and ICRC in supporting Khmer Rouge camps. For other agencies, however, a mixture of naïveté and the "culture of justification" helped to sustain their positions. Shawcross comments on the naïveté and ignorance he encountered when talking with some aid workers who had no idea of the history of the Khmer Rouge and the atrocities they committed.[108] The "well-organized" nature of Khmer Rouge camps impressed many aid personnel, in contrast to the rather chaotic nature of non–Khmer Rouge camps. Other aid workers believed that the relief agencies' contact with the Khmer Rouge would "tame" individuals and change their behavior. "To a certain extent," Norah Niland suggests, "this perspective became both motivation and rationale to work alongside the Khmer Rouge however disquieting their record or disturbing their practices."[109] Most aid personnel also adopted sanitized language to diminish the discomfort caused by the obvious misuse of aid. The Khmer Rouge feeding program was referred to as "feeding in the south," stealing was called "leakage," and soldiers who arrived for treatment at medical clinics were referred to as "people from outside the camp."[110]

Concentrating on the technical aspects of aid delivery was another way

---

[107] See Claude Malhuret, *Les réfugiés d'Asie du sud-est en Thaïlande (1975–1980)* (Paris: Médecins sans Frontières, 1980), pp. 20–21 for elaboration of MSF's position.

[108] Shawcross, *Quality of Mercy*, pp. 308–309.

[109] Niland, "Politics of Suffering," p. 110.

[110] Mason and Brown, *Rice, Rivalry, and Politics*, pp. 60–61.

aid organizations pushed aside the dilemmas inherent in working in the Cambodian crisis. The provision of aid along the border was a large operation and logistically challenging. By narrowing the operational focus to satisfying the physical needs of the refugee population, aid organizations could deem the program a success. This attitude is epitomized in the foreword to *Rice, Rivalry, and Politics*, one of the earliest books to expose the stark dilemmas confronting the aid organizations in the Cambodian refugee camps. Using the absence of famine and starvation as the benchmarks for success, Rudy von Bernuth, at that time the director of CARE Bangladesh, dismisses the political arena as "mundane" and therefore inconsequential:

> In the face of the often conflicting and sometimes petty interests they describe, perhaps one must conclude that the miracle of the Cambodian refugee operation was that the success of the whole somehow transcended the sum of its parts. . . . Brown and Mason are fortunate enough to write about an effort which accomplished its fundamental objectives of averting famine and starvation. If by the end of 1980 the dimension of human tragedy that captured the world's attention in 1979 has been replaced by a return to mundane coldwar political rivalries, this transition was a tribute to the collective efforts and policies of the relief community which Mason and Brown so effectively analyze.[111]

Agencies working inside Cambodia also used technical successes to justify the continued provision of humanitarian assistance after the emergency period of 1979–81. They dismissed the conditions of work and constant surveillance as details and rarely acknowledged the difficulties of operating in the country.[112] The "culture of justification" was exacerbated by the need to convince donors to continue supporting programs in Cambodia when funding was jeopardized by the propaganda surrounding the issue of famine. In contrast to ICRC, which publicly acknowledged difficulties, Oxfam withheld information about the absence of famine and issued statements in support of the honesty and dedication of officials in the Heng Samrin regime.[113] The standards and mandates to which aid organizations usually adhered were also relaxed in Cambodia to avoid jeopardizing their status in Phnom Penh. Organizations usually professing support for "grassroots organizations" and "proximity to the victims" found themselves working exclusively with members of the government from their of-

---

[111] Rudy von Bernuth, foreword to ibid., p. xv.
[112] Luciolli, *Le mur de bambou*, p. 262.
[113] Shawcross, *Quality of Mercy*, pp. 215–216.

fices in hotels reserved for foreigners. Cambodians were forbidden to speak to the "imperialist spies," and aid organizations allocated finance to construction projects with little human dimension. The truth was suppressed or altered, even in reports appearing a decade later. Charlotte Benson, for example, cites a 1990 United Nations Development Programme report which characterized the relationship with the Heng Samrin regime as "open and collaborative" during the emergency period, and Benson adds that "the Cambodian government controlled the relief efforts centrally, but was relatively flexible, accepting all offers of assistance."[114]

Esmeralda Luciolli, who worked in Cambodia in 1984–86, however, suggests that it was precisely the limitations placed on the number of aid organizations permitted in Cambodia that exacerbated the NGO compromises and undermined the solidarity among agencies.[115] A queue of organizations had requested permission to work in Cambodia, but the ceiling imposed meant that one had to leave before another was permitted to enter. The organizations' bargaining power was curtailed under such conditions, and one agency was unlikely to back another with the risk of expulsion so close at hand. Luciolli cites the experience of the Swiss Red Cross to illustrate this point. After working in the hospital in Kampong Cham since 1981, the team was expelled in 1985 after one of the surgeons asked a Vietnamese military officer who was smoking to leave the operating room. Subjected to a trial, the team members were accused of being enemies of the people and CIA agents, and were told to leave. The issue was allegedly not even discussed in the scheduled coordination meeting of the agencies in Cambodia, but instead dismissed as an affair of the Swiss team.

The lack of solidarity within the aid community, the justification of inappropriate policies and regulations, and the sanitized hue given to operations in Cambodia and along the border all undermined the capacity of the aid community to uphold their responsibilities to the people they professed to assist and to improve the conditions under which aid was provided. Rather than fighting to claim humanitarian space and trying to remain as independent as possible of the political agendas steering the aid program, the aid organizations became part of the conflict and contributed to the arsenals of both sides. The dominance of Cold War political stakes and the use of humanitarian concerns for propaganda purposes limited the extent to which aid organizations could influence the course of the aid

---

[114] *NGO Assistance to Cambodia, 1979–90: Lessons for the United Nations Development System,* Report of a United Nations Development Mission to Cambodia (New York: United Nations Development Programme, 1990), in Benson, *Changing Role of NGOs,* p. 74.

[115] See Luciolli, *Le mur de bambou,* pp. 263–266.

program. But the acquiescence in the status quo and the excuses aid agencies made for accepting the unacceptable also contributed markedly to the absence of efforts to address the real needs of the refugee and internal Cambodian populations.

Conclusion: Accepting the Unacceptable?

Humanitarian aid played an integral role in a vicious circular process that enveloped the Cambodian refugee program in Thailand. Cambodian refugees fled to the Thai border in search of sustenance and protection, but in the ubiquitous political environment the provision of the former compromised the latter. The camp structures became mechanisms for controlling the refugees, whose presence was crucial to the existence and legitimacy of the coalition government. The formation of this government-in-exile and the presence of its forces in turn jeopardized the physical safety of the refugees, subjecting them to attack from Vietnamese troops in Cambodia and the Khmer Rouge coalition partner. Hence humanitarian action sustained the refugees, whose presence sustained the CGDK, whose activities against the Cambodian regime provoked attacks against the camps which housed the refugees.

The negative consequences of humanitarian action in the Cambodian crisis, unintended by aid organizations, were deliberately orchestrated by the host and donor governments. The absence of humanitarian space in the refugee camps rendered apolitical humanitarian assistance impossible; to be present was to contribute to the political objectives of the border relief operation. Similarly in Cambodia, it rapidly became apparent that humanitarian aid destined for the survivors of the Khmer Rouge regime would assist in sustaining the Vietnamese-installed government in power. Aid agencies were caught between the duty to meet the needs of the refugees and interior Cambodian population, and the repercussions of strengthening both sides of the conflict. A combination of public pressure and the burden of Western conscience drove many agencies to work in Cambodia or along the border at any cost. The Cambodian crisis raises the question, At what point should aid organizations refuse to accept the unacceptable? Professing to alleviate suffering, they were at best ineffective and at worst accomplices in a situation which led to greater suffering for the populations held hostage along the border and subjected to human rights abuses.

Aid organizations were aware of the dilemmas the circumstances provoked. There was a flow of reports from advocacy and human rights

groups illuminating the problems and recommending various improvements, such as moving the camps away from the border.[116] Operational
agencies also engaged in advocacy on specific issues, such as proposed
cuts in aid budgets; human rights abuses, particularly the forced population movements of the Khmer Rouge; the lack of access to the hidden
border camps; and the Khmer Rouge occupancy of the Cambodian seat
at the UN.[117] However, no unified approach to the broader issues was
tackled until the issue of a neutral camp arose in response to repatriation concerns. NGOs operating in Cambodia were also vocal, even
forming an NGO Forum on Kampuchea in 1986, based in Brussels.
Their advocacy, however, was also less about obtaining humanitarian
space in their operations than challenging the international isolation of
Cambodia.

The humanitarian aid organizations faced many obstacles to more concerted attempts to improve the plight of the refugees. They were largely left
with the choice of complying with the conditions imposed or not participating in the relief program. A few agencies took a stance and refused to provide
aid to the Khmer Rouge or Vietnamese-backed government. The participation of the Khmer Rouge in the coalition, however, made association with the
faction only one step removed: the difference was only whether aid directly or
indirectly assisted their resuscitation. Sukhumbhand Paribatra, former director of Security Studies Program at Chulalongkorn University, was convinced
that had the CGDK won a military victory against the Vietnamese forces the
Khmer Rouge would have dominated the postwar government, in spite of
Western assurances that they opposed a Khmer Rouge return to power:

> Despite the much-touted improvements made by the non-communists, the
> facts are clear: while the Khmer People's National Liberation Front
> (KPNLF) has considerable assets in terms of its population base and a num-
> ber of troops but little or no unity or political will, the Armée Nationale Si-
> hanoukiste (ANS) seems to have both the unity and the will, but not the
> numbers, and the Khmer Rouge remain by a long way the most coherent,
> organized, determined, well-armed and numerous of the three factions.[118]

Twenty years after the beginning of the refugee influx into Thailand,
the last remnants of the Khmer Rouge are finally emerging from the jun-

[116] See, for example, *Cambodians in Thailand: People on the Edge* (Washington, D.C.: United
States Committee for Refugees, 1985), p. 20.

[117] See Benson, *Changing Role of NGOs*, pp. 64–65.

[118] Sukhumbhand Paribatra, *Kampuchea without Delusion* (Malaysia: Institute of Strategic
and International Studies, 1986), p. 14, as cited in Jackson, *Just Waiting to Die?* p. 19.

gles. Humanitarian aid, ostensibly given to people in need because they are members of humanity, helped to revive and sustain a military force which showed the least regard for humanity. Aid organizations incur responsibilities to the recipients of their assistance when they choose to intervene in a crisis. Just as their presence can confer legitimacy on regimes or authorities, so it imparts a sense of solidarity with the "victims" and an element of trust. Operating through administrative structures which controlled and dominated the refugee population violated that trust. The refugees were deprived of their rights as asylum seekers and suffered human rights abuses on a regular basis. The aid organizations were indirect accomplices in this system, but through their acquiescence in the status quo and their acceptance of funds from donors implicated in the abuse of the refugee population, aid organizations were partly responsible for its continuation.

5

The Rwandan Refugee Camps in Zaire

ifteen years after the first Cambodian peasants were marched across the Thai border by the Khmer Rouge, the same scenario was replayed with different actors on a different continent. In a small country in central Africa, the governing regime ordered the annihilation of a segment of the population, and was ousted from power by an invading force. To avoid defeat, the regime directed the exodus of two million of its compatriots to neighboring countries and settled among them, evading justice and rearming for future conflict. The analogy with the Khmer Rouge was immediately drawn: "Hurry to Prevent a Cambodian Epilogue in Rwanda" was the title of an article contributed to the *International Herald Tribune* by Alain Destexhe.[1] Yet for all the prior warning, and live media coverage of the genocide and refugee exodus, the refugee camps became sanctuaries for another genocidal regime.

The Rwandan genocide, which claimed up to one million lives in less than one hundred days, was orchestrated by hard-liners in the Rwandan government intent on preventing the implementation of a power-sharing agreement with the minority Tutsi ethnic group. A planned campaign to exterminate anyone perceived to support the Tutsi-dominated Rwandan Patriotic Front (RPF) commenced on 6 April 1994 and ended with the defeat of the government by the RPF three months later. State directives drove the slaughter of Tutsi, and state directives encouraged the Hutu population to flee the country when the Rwandan Armed Forces (Forces Armées Rwandaises—FAR) faced imminent defeat. Two million Hutu sought asylum in Zaire, Tanzania, and Burundi until the majority were forced to return to Rwanda in late 1996.

[1] Alain Destexhe, "Hurry to Prevent a Cambodian Epilogue in Rwanda," *International Herald Tribune*, 11 August 1994, p. 6.

Zaire as a Military Sanctuary

Zairean authorities played a pivotal role in facilitating the rearming and training of the former Rwandan government forces (ex-FAR) and militias in Zaire. The host nation provided the ex-FAR with the territorial base on which the army could reorganize, permitted the army and government officials free movement, and ignored international calls for the arrest of war criminals. The ex-FAR established military bases, and Zaire became a conduit for weapons and supplies to the force. Furthermore, the ex-FAR was able to create a highly organized military structure while in exile in Zaire and launched frequent attacks on Rwandan officials and infrastructure. Documents found in the camps after they were attacked in late 1996 provide a rare insight into the way in which the former army and government reorganized after their defeat, and how humanitarian aid became integrated into their planning and operations.[2]

The Rwandan army fled into Zaire virtually intact, having faced a rapid defeat at the hands of the RPF. As soon as the genocide began, signaled by the shooting down of President Juvénal Habyarimana's plane on 6 April 1994, the RPF began their offensive from the demilitarized zone in the north of the country, and from Kigali where a 600-strong battalion was stationed under the Arusha Accords.[3] The RPF rapidly gained territory against the larger and better-equipped army, taking control of Kigali on 4 July. The report of a meeting of the high command of the ex-FAR held in Goma, Zaire, in early September 1994 blamed a combination of external and internal factors for the defeat.[4] Externally, the ex-FAR accused the United Nations Assistance Mission for Rwanda (UNAMIR) of complicity with the RPF; implicated Uganda, Belgium, the United States, and Burundi in the RPF victory; and cited their sudden abandonment by France, formerly their principal and only reliable military partner. In addition, the

[2] I am grateful to Sam Kiley of the London *Times*, Massimo Alberizzi of the Italian newspaper *Corriere della Sera*, Christian Jennings of Reuters, and Chris Tomlinson of the Associated Press for these documents. The documents were left behind after the ex-FAR fled the attack against the Goma camps in late 1996. Many of them were contained in a filing cabinet belonging to Major-General Augustin Bizimungu, chief of staff of the ex-FAR. Documents from this source are hereafter marked with the letters (c.d.), for "camp document."

[3] The Arusha Accords were the peace and power-sharing agreements between the Rwandan government and the RPF, signed on 4 August 1993. The Accords included provision for the integration of the RPF into the FAR.

[4] "Rapport de la Réunion du Haut Commandement des Forces Armées Rwandaises et des Membres des Commissions tenue à Goma du 02 au 08 Septembre 1994" (Goma: mimeo, 1994), pp. 32–33 (c.d.).

report laments the failure of the Rwandan regime to organize "parallel supply circuits to by-pass the [arms] embargo"[5] which the UN Security Council had imposed on the Rwandan government in Resolution 918 of 17 May 1994. Internal factors included the lack of unity between the politicians and the military; poor training, management, and planning; power struggles within the military after 6 April 1994; an erosion of discipline at all levels; and the presence of RPF allies at the heart of government and in the FAR.

President Mobutu's close alliance with Habyarimana ensured a secure sanctuary for the defeated army and government officials in Zaire.[6] They arrived en masse with hundreds of thousands of civilians, encouraged and sometimes forced to leave with the retreating troops. Crossing the border into North Kivu in mid-July 1994, senior officials initially resided in tourist hotels along Lake Kivu before becoming better organized and regrouping militarily. "Regroupment is our number one priority," proclaimed the chief of staff, Major General Augustin Bizimungu, in an interview with Le Monde in late July.[7] Senior officers in Goma moved to "the Bananeraie" near the Lac Vert refugee camp, while the soldiers lived in the large refugee camps, particularly Mugunga (see Map 6). In South Kivu, where the exodus to Zaire was slightly later due to the protection provided by the French Opération turquoise, the military were organized into two principal camps, Panzi for those accompanied by families, and Bulonge for single men. Another military camp was based on Idjwi Island in Lake Kivu.

The armed forces restructured in the first few months in exile, fusing with the National Gendarmerie under a single authority called the "Rwandan Armed Forces Command."[8] This was initially placed under the auspices of the minister of defense, Colonel Athanase Gasake. Four commissions were established: Social Affairs, Information and Documentation, Planning and Operations, and Capital and Finance. The meeting of the high command held in September 1994 also mentions a fifth commission, Politics and External Relations. The armed forces were consolidated into two divisions, the first containing 7,680 men and the second 10,240 men. Separate support units were also established, which consisted of an addi-

---

[5] Ibid., p. 32.

[6] Mobutu deployed several hundred members of his Division Spéciale Présidentielle to Rwanda in October 1990 in response to an RPF invasion from Uganda.

[7] Jean-Baptiste Naudet, "L'ex-armée gouvernementale entre les mains du Zaïre," Le Monde, 27 July 1994, p. 6.

[8] Major-Général Augustin Bizimungu, "Restructuration des Forces Armées Rwandaises" (n.p.: mimeo, n.d.) (c.d.).

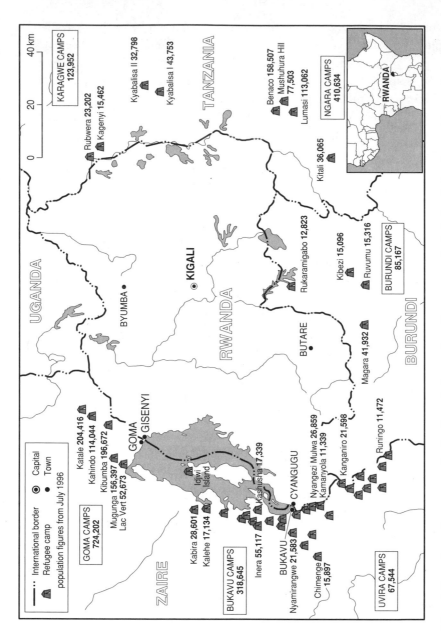

Map 6. Rwandan refugee camps in the Great Lakes region. Camp names included only for those with populations over 10,000. From UNHCR, as modified by author.

tional 4,000 men, to make a total of approximately 22,000 soldiers.[9] This figure is slightly lower than most external estimates of troop strength, which suggested that between 30,000 and 50,000 ex-FAR resided in Zaire.[10] The military documents offer little clarification on the number of Interahamwe and Impuzamugambi militia[11] living in the camps, the estimates for which vary between 10,000 and 50,000. References to the militias in the military documents are limited to complaints about the liability caused by their lack of discipline, and a decision to forbid their presence in the military camps unless they underwent proper military training.[12]

The self-proclaimed government-in-exile also restructured following a meeting of the political parties held in Bukavu on 2 and 3 September 1994, when it reduced the number of ministries to seven. Théodore Sindikubwabo and Jean Kambanda remained as president and prime minister respectively, and Callixte Kalimanzira, formerly of the Interior Ministry, became minister of social affairs and refugees.[13]

[9] Gratien Kabiligi, "Projet: Libération du Rwanda" (n.p.: mimeo, n.d.) (c.d.).

[10] *Refugee Camp Security in the Great Lakes Region*, EVAL/01/97, Inspection and Evaluation Service (Geneva: UNHCR, April 1997), p. 9, estimated that 30,000 of the 40,000 Rwandan Armed Forces fled to Zaire, and numbered the Interahamwe militias at 10,000–15,000. The Joint Evaluation of Emergency Assistance to Rwanda estimated "30,000 government soldiers, militia members, local officials and former national leaders": Howard Adelman and Astri Suhrke, "Early Warning and Conflict Management," Study 2 of *The International Response to Conflict and Genocide: Lessons from the Rwanda Experience* (Copenhagen: Steering Committee of the Joint Evaluation of Emergency Assistance to Rwanda, 1996), p. 58. William Cyrus Reed estimated that the combined ex-FAR and militias in Zaire numbered 50,000: Reed, *Refugees and Rebels: The Former Government of Rwanda and the ADFL Movement in Eastern Zaire* (Washington, D.C.: U.S. Committee for Refugees, 1997), p. 7. A UN Secretary-General's report to the Security Council estimated that 50,000 ex-FAR and their dependents resided in Zaire, and at least 10,000 militia members: *Report of the Secretary-General on Security in the Rwandese Refugee Camps*, S/1994/1308, 18 November 1994, p. 3.

[11] The militia known as the Interahamwe ("those who work together") was created in 1992 as the "youth movement" of the ruling party of Habyarimana, the Mouvement Révolutionnaire National pour le Développement et la Démocratie (MRND). The Impuzamugambi ("those who have the same goal") was the militia of MRND's coalition partner, the Coalition pour la défense de la République. These militias were among the main perpetrators of the genocide. Gérard Prunier, *The Rwanda Crisis, 1959–1994: History of a Genocide* (London: Hurst, 1995), pp. 367–368.

[12] "Rapport de la Réunion," p. 20.

[13] The other "portfolios" were filled as follows: Joseph Kalinganire was minister of information; Jérôme Bicamumpaka remained minister of foreign affairs and cooperation; Stanislas Mbonampeka who had been minister of justice before the genocide was reinstated; Innocent Habamenshi was minister of capital and equipment; Frédéric Kayogora was minister of mobilisation and youth, and Athanase Gasake was minister of defense. This list was published in *Amizero—L'Espoir* no. 0 (7–14 November 1994), pp. 9–10, as summarized in ASBL Dialogue (ed.), *Revue de la presse rwandaise* (Brussels), available on a CD-ROM produced by the International Documentation Network on the Great African Lakes Region, Geneva, no. 5, 1998, vol. 1.

The ex-FAR and former government had considerable financial and military resources at their disposal: cash and assets requisitioned from Rwanda before they retreated, private and government foreign bank accounts, and arms sold by states willing to breach the UN arms embargo. All movable assets were requisitioned by the army or senior officials during their retreat to Zaire, and the banks, in which Tutsi accounts had been frozen at the beginning of the genocide, were emptied of cash. Gérard Prunier estimates that some $30–40 million worth of local currency (Rwandan francs) and another $30–40 million of foreign currency were taken into Zaire.[14] In addition to cash, hundreds of vehicles, buses, trucks, and machinery worth millions of dollars left Rwanda. "We have money, we left Rwanda with everything except the houses," claimed Colonel Anselme Nkuliyekubona.[15] Not all of this cash and property remained at the disposal of the government or military, however: the sale of state property for individual profit was so prevalent that it became the target of the notorious extremist publication *Kangura*.[16] The paper stated that goods sold for personal profit included 610 trucks, 1,380 cars, coffee to the value of $300,000, minerals, and property from the country's biggest oil company, Petro-Rwanda.[17] It also accused the former director of a tea enterprise of the theft of $520,000; the former defense minister, Augustin Bizimana, of the theft of $640,000; and the former minister of public works of the misappropriation of $1,000,000 and 13 trucks from the ministry.[18] Nevertheless, many assets did remain at the disposal of the ex-FAR for military use and to earn revenue from the refugees and aid organizations, which is discussed further below.

The ex-FAR also managed to enter Zaire with considerable quantities of military hardware. Although the Zairean authorities confiscated many weapons at the border, personnel from Human Rights Watch Arms Project state that these were kept in military bases near Goma and were maintained by ex-FAR soldiers.[19] One inventory of Rwandan military hardware

[14] Personal communication, 5 May 1999.

[15] Naudet, "L'ex-armée gouvernementale entre les mains du Zaïre."

[16] For a description of the role of *Kangura* as the "mouthpiece of the most fanatical of extremists" since its establishment in 1990, see *Rwanda: Death, Despair, and Defiance*, revised edition (London: African Rights, 1995), pp. 70–75.

[17] "Quels sont les politiciens qui se sont montrés cupides depuis notre exil?" *Kangura* no. 62 (1–15 November 1994), p. 14, as summarized in ASBL Dialogue, *Revue de la presse rwandaise*.

[18] "Gens recherchés pour vol," *Kangura* no. 65 (1 January 1995), p. 11, as summarized in ABSL Dialogue, *Revue de la presse rwandaise*.

[19] *Rwanda/Zaire. Rearming with Impunity: International Support for the Perpetrators of the Rwandan Genocide*, Human Rights Watch Arms Project vol. 7, no. 4 (New York: Human Rights Watch, May 1995), p. 12.

in the possession of the Zairean army listed six helicopters, over 1,000 artillery pieces, some 35,000 light weapons, and several armored vehicles.[20] Amnesty International reported that some weapons were sold back to the ex-FAR.[21] Certain pieces of equipment, such as the helicopters, were useless in the absence of spare parts and maintenance, and some equipment including three of the helicopters was reported to have been returned to Kigali by the Zairean government in February and April 1996 (see Appendix A).[22] But these supplies were augmented by new shipments of arms to the camps, either directly facilitated by Zaire or tacitly permitted entry to Zairean territory.

Rumors of arms flights landing at Goma airport at night resounded in the aid community and the press. Proof of such flights, however, was more difficult to obtain, as a report of the UN Commission of Inquiry established to investigate breaches of the arms embargo attests.[23] The inquiry, which investigated allegations made by Human Rights Watch Arms Project, Amnesty International, television documentaries,[24] and the press, did manage to verify two of the arms shipments cited which were sold by the government of the Seychelles to Colonel Théoneste Bagosora, in the belief that the purchase was on behalf of the Zairean government. The two shipments, which landed in Goma in mid-June 1994, contained AK-47 rifles, mortar shells, and ammunition, and were flown on Air Zaire aircraft.[25] The cost of the two shipments was $330,000.

Invoices and air waybills found in the camps also document the arrival of weapons in Goma. Many of these arrived before the imposition of the UN arms embargo on 17 May 1994, but after the genocide had commenced, while at least two showed shipments after the embargo had been imposed. Most of the invoices were from a British firm, Mil-Tec Corporation, which operates from the Isle of Man. Addressed to the minister of defense in Bukavu, Zaire, one statement of invoices and payments shows eight flights between 18 April 1994 and 18 July 1994 at a cost of

[20] "Situation Armement Remis aux FAZ" (n.p.: mimeo, n.d.) (c.d.).

[21] *Rwanda: Arming the Perpetrators of the Genocide*, AFR 02/14/95 (London: Amnesty International, June 1995), p. 2 and p. 4.

[22] "Armement Dont Dispose le FPR" (n.p.: mimeo, 26 September 1996) (c.d.). (FPR is the French acronym for RPF.)

[23] *Report of the International Commission of Inquiry (Rwanda)*. Annex to *Letter dated 13 March 1996 from the Secretary-General addressed to the President of the Security Council* (S/1996/195, 14 March 1996). The UN Security Council established the International Commission of Inquiry in UN Resolution 1013 of 7 September 1995.

[24] *Rwanda/Zaire. Rearming with Impunity; Rwanda: Arming the Perpetrators of the Genocide; The Big Story*, Twenty-Twenty Television, 17 November 1994; and "Merchants of Death," Carlton Television, 13 June 1995.

[25] *Report of the International Commission of Inquiry (Rwanda)*, p. 15.

$6,515,313. Payments made were shown to total $4,807,000, indicating an outstanding balance of $1,708,313. A letter dated 7 December 1994 requests payment of the outstanding balance, stating that funds paid for the last flight of 18 July had been blocked in Cairo by the U.S. government "due to the situation in Rwanda at that time." The letter reminds the minister of defense of the service rendered by Mil-Tec over the past five years, particularly the rapidity of the response to the minister's urgent request for arms on 10 April 1994 (see Appendix B). A waybill dated 18 May 1994 indicates that Mil-Tec shipped arms from Tirana, Albania, to Goma on Okada Air, and the accompanying invoice lists the cargo as 2,500 AK-47 rifles, 10,000 30-round magazines with 2,500 vests with magazine and grenade pouches, 2,000 60mm mortars, 255,360 rounds of 7.62 × 39 ammunition, 6 155mm mortars, and 102 RPG7 rockets. The total cost of the cargo, freight, handling, and insurance was $1,074,549. Another invoice dated 13 July lists ammunition and RPG7 rockets as cargo, with a destination of Kinshasa. Since this invoice was in the possession of the ex-FAR, it can reasonably be assumed that the shipment was destined for the former Rwandan army. Recording Kinshasa as the destination reduced suspicions that the arms shipments were circumventing the UN embargo.

Other allegations of arms deliveries to Goma implicate South African, Israeli, Albanian, and Chinese officials. Habyarimana's wife, Agathe Kanziga, and her brother, Séraphim Rwabukumba, for example, allegedly purchased $5 million worth of rifles and grenade launchers while on a trip to China in October 1994.[26] The French government was also deeply implicated in supporting the FAR.[27] In addition to the well-documented military assistance given to Rwanda before and during the genocide,[28] troops

[26] "Bears Guard Honey," *Africa Confidential* no. 288 (20 February 1995) as cited in *Rwanda/Zaire. Rearming with Impunity*, p. 15.

[27] Some of the accusations levied at the French government by the Human Rights Watch Arms Project, however, seem to have a tenuous factual base. Claims made of French involvement in arms deliveries to Goma and in training the ex-FAR at French military bases in the Central African Republic were investigated by *Libération* journalist Stephen Smith, who challenged the evidence on which the allegations were based: "Livraisons d'armes au Rwanda: Retour sur un rapport contestable," *Libération*, 31 July 1995, p. 8. He found that the primary source of the information, Jean-Claude Urbano, was inaccurately described as a French government official. Urbano also denies making the statements attributed to him. Furthermore, Smith could find no evidence of Rwandan soldiers trained at French military bases in the Central African Republic.

[28] See Prunier, *The Rwanda Crisis*, pp. 100–114, 227–311, and 336–345; *Leave None to Tell the Story: Genocide in Rwanda* (New York: Human Rights Watch, 1999), pp. 116–125 and 654–668; and Jean-François Bayart and Gustave Massiah, "La France au Rwanda: Entretien," *Les Temps Modernes* 583 (July–August 1995): 217–227.

deployed for Opération turquoise facilitated the protection and retreat of the army and interim government from the "safe humanitarian zone" in the southwest of Rwanda. French Lieutenant-Colonel Jean-Claude Perruchot acknowledged that the Rwandan interim president, Théodore Sindikubwabo, and three of his ministers were present in the safe zone.[29] The French government issued contradictory statements about its intentions to arrest those responsible for genocide, but ultimately French authorities deemed this beyond their mandate. "Our mandate does not authorize us to arrest them on our own authority. Such a task could undermine our neutrality, the best guarantee of our effectiveness," the French Foreign Ministry declared on 16 July.[30] On 17 July the French military "initiated and organized" the evacuation of the interim government to Zaire.[31] Human Rights Watch documented reports of the French refueling army trucks loaded with looted goods and delivering ten tonnes of food to the army in Goma on 21 July.[32]

The hard currency required to purchase weapons came from embassy and private bank accounts abroad in addition to the looted Rwandan banks and sale of stolen property. Prunier claims that Rwabukumba had control of bank accounts in Belgium containing approximately $50 million.[33] Delays by some foreign governments in recognizing the new regime in Kigali also permitted the former government to continue to draw on embassy accounts for up to ten months after the government's demise. In Kenya, the Netherlands, Tanzania, Egypt, and Zaire, diplomats of the former regime continued to occupy diplomatic property and removed all assets before they left.[34] The former regime also sought to recoup any funds remaining on Defense Ministry contracts which had not been fulfilled. A report of the Commission du Patrimoine, Finances et Accroissement des Ressources (Commission for Capital, Finance, and Resource Growth) listed several million dollars worth of deposits and payments made for contracts that were never fulfilled. These included a deposit of $1 million with a company named OMI in Nairobi for which no delivery had been

[29] "Rwandan Officials Escape to Safe Zone," *International Herald Tribune*, 16–17 July 1994, p. 5.

[30] Assemblée Nationale, Mission d'information commune, *Enquête sur la tragédie rwandaise (1990–1994)*, vol. 1, Rapport, p. 325 as cited in *Leave None to Tell the Story*, p. 686.

[31] Patrick de Saint-Exupéry, "Rwanda: Les 'trous noirs' d'une enquête," *Le Figaro*, 17 December 1998, as cited in *Leave None to Tell the Story*, p. 687.

[32] *Leave None to Tell the Story*, p. 688. Also see Adelman and Suhrke, "Early Warning and Conflict Management," pp. 54–57, for a discussion of the ambiguous nature of Opération turquoise.

[33] Prunier, personal communication, 5 May 1999.

[34] Reed, *Refugees and Rebels*, p. 7, and *Rwanda/Zaire. Rearming with Impunity*, p. 4.

received, and half of a $4.6 million contract with a Monsieur Lemonier which was suspended due to the imposition of the arms embargo. A $4.5 million contract with a private South African arms dealer was also unfulfilled, and $1.7 million was to be reimbursed from Captain Paul Barril since Opération turquoise reportedly restricted Barril's ability to fulfill his training contract with the FAR.[35] The report mentions that debts with regular arms suppliers had to be settled before new orders could be placed, and also emphasizes the need to unblock funds still held in the Rwandan National Bank before the new Rwandan regime could claim them. Whether or not the government was successful in recovering any of these funds is unclear.

The $30–40 million worth of Rwandan francs taken to Zaire was used to conduct a profitable smuggling operation between Kigali and Goma, where the exchange rates to the U.S. dollar were 200 and 700 respectively.[36] This prompted Kigali to issue new tender of the 500, 1,000 and 5,000 Rwandan franc notes in January 1995 to invalidate this source of revenue for the former regime. The ex-FAR was also able to pay its soldiers in Zaire from this fund and to reward the loyalty of infiltrators and "partisans" inside Rwanda. The budget for a military operation into Rwanda, for instance, mentions the payment of daily allowances in Rwandan francs: 500 Frw per soldier, 500 Frw per guide, 2,500 Frw per partisan, and 10,000 Frw per "*agent passeur*" (smuggler or courier).[37] The operation was aimed at "sowing maximum insecurity" in the western regions of Rwanda. Targets suggested in the plan included bridges on principal roads, power lines, small units of Rwandan Patriotic Army (RPA—successor of the RPF) soldiers from which military equipment could be seized, lightly defended detention centers, political leaders and RPA personnel, populated communities (*colonies de peuplement*), and town water supplies in Gisenyi, Ruhengeri, and Kibuye. Mention was also made of urban terrorism, and the document states that "for propaganda purposes, the accent should be put on influential persons such as business people, teachers and health personnel."

The cross-border raids into Rwanda, which commenced soon after the exodus to Zaire, served several purposes. First, the creation of a climate of

---

[35] Human Rights Watch also mentions Captain Paul Barril's contract with the Rwandan Ministry of Defense to conduct training at the Bigogwe military camp in the northwest of Rwanda. See *None Left to Tell the Story*, pp. 665–668. Barril and his private security company, "Secrets, Inc." is also discussed by Prunier, *The Rwanda Crisis*, n. 4, p. 128, and pp. 216–219.

[36] Gérard Prunier, *Rwanda: Update to End of March 1995* (U.K.: Writenet, May 1995), p. 3.

[37] Annex 2, "Plan Ops 1 Div," and Annex 3, "Plan Ops 2 Div," of an unknown document (c.d.).

insecurity in Rwanda helped to dissuade the refugees from returning home. The attacks added weight to the constant repetitions of the military leaders that they would reinvade Rwanda and reclaim power by force. The specific targeting of returnees such as Dr. Anatole Bucyendore, a Hutu regional medical officer who returned to Gisenyi from Goma and was shot dead in February 1995, increased the reluctance of refugees to return.[38] Second, the guerrilla attacks provoked harsh reprisals by the RPA against civilian populations suspected of sympathizing with Hutu rebels. These reprisals renewed fears in the Hutu population of arbitrary justice and victimization, and damaged the image of the RPA and the Rwandan government internationally. Third, the continuing costs associated with the destruction of property placed an additional burden on the Kigali government. The financial problems imposed by the looting of the country, and the long delays experienced by Kigali in accessing international sources of finance, were exacerbated by the further destruction these raids caused. Fourth, by showing that the war was not over between the RPA and the ex-FAR, the latter hoped to generate pressure on Kigali to negotiate with the former regime. And fifth, cattle looted and equipment seized in Rwanda helped to maintain the strength of the forces in Zaire.

The target of guerrilla incursions during 1996 increasingly became genocide survivors and witnesses to the genocide, presumably to eliminate potential sources of testimony in national genocide trials, which began later that year. The UN Human Rights Field Operation in Rwanda reported that at least 98 cases of attack against genocide survivors or witnesses were recorded between January and June 1996, 85 of which resulted in death.[39] Evidence collected suggested that members of the ex-FAR perpetrated 90 of these 98 cases. Many of the victims' names allegedly appeared on death lists, indicating the organized nature of the killings. In one example, a group of 40–50 infiltrators from Idjwi Island in Lake Kivu attacked a small village in the south of Kibuye Préfecture on the night of 18 June 1996. Some ten or twelve genocide survivors and their relatives were killed.[40]

The guerrilla strategies and tactics employed in the raids into Rwanda constituted a major part of the training curriculum of the ex-FAR in Zaire. Because they were largely unaccustomed to fighting in this way, numerous

---

[38] See *Rwanda: Arming the Perpetrators of the Genocide*, p. 5.

[39] *Attacks on Genocide Survivors and Witnesses to the Genocide Update*, HRFOR/STRPT/20/2/5 July 1996/E (Kigali: UN Human Rights Field Operation in Rwanda, 5 July 1996), p. 1.

[40] Ibid., p. 3.

courses were held for all echelons of the military. Training manuals covering subjects like leadership, the history of guerrilla warfare, Rwanda's military history, and propaganda were found among Bizimungu's papers. One course conducted in early 1996 for the police in the Kibumba refugee camp included sessions on guerrilla—*maquis;* special operations and military tradition; clandestine life and survival techniques; individual and section tactics; ideology; raids, ambushes, and infiltration; and orientation, map reading, and communication. In a letter on official Rwandan Defense Ministry letterhead from Colonel Tharcisse Renzaho to the ex-FAR command, Renzaho discussed the organization of a military course to be held at the Katale and Mugunga refugee camps (see Appendix C). He requested that 200 exercise books be made available, and food and accommodation at Bulengo between 22 and 30 October 1995. He also requested use of a minibus to facilitate travel.

More important than technical training, however, was the promulgation of propaganda designed to ensure the continued loyalty of soldiers and the general population to the extremist agenda. The importance of adhering to a common discourse was clearly expressed by the Commission for Information and Documentation in the meeting of the high command in September 1994, and plans were made to reinstate Radio Rwanda and Radio-Télévision Libre des Mille Collines (RTLM) and to establish a printing plant to "facilitate the birth of favourable newspapers in the region."[41] The propaganda produced by the military and former government was shrewdly adapted to specific audiences and events, yet constantly reiterated a central theme: that the Hutu were the victims of the Rwandan crisis. This victim discourse subscribed to the following logic: The Hutu have always been oppressed by the Tutsi, but have suffered increased atrocities at the hands of the Tutsi since the RPF invasion of 1 October 1990. The Hutu are demonized by the propaganda of the RPF and the partiality of the UN, international media, and certain states, which falsely claim that they perpetrated a genocide against the Tutsi. As the majority, the Hutu should be in power, but the RPF refuses to negotiate with the Hutu, wanting to retain complete power in Rwanda. The insecurity in Rwanda and the reluctance of the refugees to return is evidence of the brutal oppression and lack of legitimacy of the new government. The political stalemate leaves the former government, army, and the refugees with no other option than to return to Rwanda by force.

A document titled "Our Liberation Struggle" is exemplary:

[41] "Rapport de la Réunion," p. 24.

All Hutu people, whether in the interior or in exile, are demonized. They are held globally responsible for the misfortune which they did not cause or provoke in the least. "The genocide" has become a commercial fund for the RPF which uses it as a pretext for refusing dialogue between Rwandans aimed at definitively resolving the ethnic conflict which has ravaged Rwanda since 01 October 1990.[42]

Claims of genocide against the Hutu were an important component of the victim discourse. In a letter to the Zairean Ministry of Defense, the second in command of the ex-FAR, Gratien Kabiligi, claimed that the killings perpetrated by the RPA in Rwanda constituted proof of the continuing genocide of the Hutu by the Tutsi:

> The hypothesis according to which the RPF kill the Hutu "in revenge" is simply unacceptable by the principles of human rights, and fallacious since this extremist Tutsi organization has selectively massacred Hutu since October 1990. . . . The massacre of these Hutu constitutes one of the elements (among others) which shows that the Tutsi army aimed and planned the reduction, or even methodical elimination of Hutu populations in the region, and that it is, as a consequence, responsible for the genocide.[43]

The propaganda was generally based on actual events or issues discussed in the media, with the interpretation manipulated to fit the extremist agenda. Widespread criticism of the failure of the UN forces to stop the genocide in Rwanda, for example, was repeated in the camp literature, but with the emphasis changed to the failure of UNAMIR to halt the RPF invasion. Events like the massacre of some 4,000 internally displaced Hutu at the Kibeho camp in southwestern Rwanda by the RPA in April 1995 fed into the existing propaganda of Tutsi repression of the Hutu, and the failure of the UN troops present to stop the massacre again "proved" the partiality of the UN force. Accusations of UN partiality were not restricted to internal consumption; Augustin Bizimungu also blamed the international community for the former government's defeat in an interview with the French newspaper Le Figaro.[44] By adhering closely to real events reported by human rights organizations and the international media, the leadership in Zaire appeared reliable and justified in their calls for the Rwandan pop-

---

[42] "Notre Lutte de Libération," Annex 6 of unknown document (n.p.: mimeo, n.d.), p. 1 (c.d.).

[43] Letter from Gratien Kabiligi to the Defense Minister of Zaire, "Memorandum Relatif au Drame Rwandais" (Goma, 25 June 1995), p. 5 (c.d.).

[44] Patrick de Saint-Exupéry, "Jamais nous ne baisserons les bras," Le Figaro, 28 July 1994, p. 2.

ulation to remain "in exile." New recruits were also encouraged by slogans exaggerating many of the real problems of justice in Rwanda such as:

A Hutu kills a Tutsi = Genocide! We hang him
A Tutsi kills some Hutu = Legitimate Defense Reflex[45]

In denying the genocide and blaming the RPF for violating the peace agreement by invading Rwanda, the former government and military sought to justify a return to the power-sharing agreements made under the Arusha Accords. The Commission of Politics and Exterior Relations considered that:

the path of negotiations is the least costly, the most simple and the fastest way to facilitate the return of the Rwandan population to their country and that it is necessary, by consequence, to encourage all initiatives to support direct negotiations between the RPF and the government-in-exile. The base of negotiations should be the Arusha Peace Accords. The Commission thinks that all possible means should be used to apply pressure on the RPF to accept to negotiate (interior sabotage, the media, the deployment of emissaries to foreign countries, etc).[46]

Thus the commission recommended that the military remain subordinate to the former government's authority since it was a party to the Arusha Accords and, "in spite of everything, remained credible and popular with the population."[47] However, the military expressed serious misgivings about the loss of the government's international legitimacy and absence of official recognition as the "government-in-exile," and recommended the formation of a politico-military structure of its own in case the government-in-exile proved a failure. By early 1995, this premonition threatened to become a reality as Kigali refused categorically to engage in dialogue with the former regime. This refusal helped the propaganda cause, "justifying" the call for a return to Rwanda by force, which, as mentioned above, kept

---

[45] "Le FPR Se Confirme Comme un Front Tribaliste Anti-Hutu" (n.p.: mimeo, n.d.), p. 3 (c.d.).

[46] "Rapport de la Réunion," p. 9. The UN Secretary-General's report of 18 November 1994 (S/1994/1308, p. 4) noted that some of the demands made by the former political and military leaders in discussions with UNAMIR included negotiations with the new government; involvement of the UN in facilitating negotiations with the new government; revival of acceptable elements of the Arusha Accords; power-sharing; the establishment of an international tribunal to address massacres committed since 1990; and the organization of early elections, and guarantees of security and the return of property in Rwanda.

[47] "Rapport de la Réunion," p. 5.

the military mobilized and the refugees in constant fear of returning. But on the political front, the deadlock necessitated a new strategy and the establishment of a more "legitimate" negotiating partner for the RPF. In April 1995 Le Rassemblement pour le Retour et la Démocratie au Rwanda (Rally for the Return and Democracy in Rwanda—RDR) was formed, the legitimacy for which derived, as the name suggests, from the refugees. Having failed to regain international support, the military sought to dissociate itself from the tarnished image of the former government and looked to the most important resource the defeated regime had at its disposal— the population. The limits of the military sanctuary provided by Zaire were reached; it was in the humanitarian domain that the conditions necessary to mount a return to Rwanda were sought. The military high command issued a declaration published in *Kangura* in May, stating that the relationship between the FAR and the government-in-exile ceased on 29 April 1995, and threw its weight behind the RDR.[48]

Thus during two and a half years in Zaire the defeated government and military pursued parallel strategies on the diplomatic and military front to regain power in Rwanda. But while there were several indications that the military became increasingly organized in Zaire between 1994 and 1996,[49] it is unlikely that the ex-FAR had the capacity to realize its numerous threats of a full-scale invasion of Rwanda. Evidence of the ex-FAR's military inferiority vis-à-vis the RPA was clear in late 1996 when they were chased from the refugee camps and military bases in eastern Zaire by the Alliance forces. Their organization on paper and in the minds of international observers was not matched by realities on the ground. But the perception of an imminent invasion sowed fear in the minds of the refugees and aimed to complement diplomatic attempts to bring Kigali to the negotiating table. Prunier suggests, furthermore, that the new Rwandan government also exaggerated the ex-FAR's level of military preparedness in order to legitimize its own future actions against the camps by convincing international public opinion that the ex-FAR constituted a formidable

[48] "Déclaration du Haut Commandement des FAR réuni à Bukavu les 28 et 29 avril 1995," *Kangura* no. 70 (May 1995), pp. 8–9 as summarized in ABSL Dialogue, *Revue de la presse rwandaise.*

[49] In addition to suggestions contained in the ex-FAR's own documents, international observers noticed a greater professionalism among the military. In an internal memo dated 12 July 1996, the head of sub-office of UNHCR in Goma, Joël Boutroue, remarked that the activities of the ex-FAR had become less numerous but were of better quality: more targeted and focused, and more destabilizing. He also noted that improvement in military organization had led to a decreased number of soldiers in the refugee camps. Memo from J. Boutroue to A. Akodjenou, "Re: E-mail from J. van Drunen of 12 July," 12 July 1996.

threat.[50] Rather than a military solution, the ex-FAR and former government depended upon a diplomatic solution, based primarily on the return of the two million refugees under their control. It was the Rwandan population and the humanitarian aid they attracted that constituted the most important resource at the hands of the former regime.

Zaire as a Humanitarian Sanctuary

Media images, first of genocide, and later of hundreds of thousands of people streaming across Rwanda's borders, were beamed into living rooms across the globe. While hand-wringing and denial were the hallmarks of the international response to the genocide, the massive population exodus and looming public health catastrophe galvanized the major powers into action. But the action was of a humanitarian rather than political nature, and despite widespread knowledge of the composition of the population flow, the focus for the next two years remained on the provision of humanitarian assistance. Echoes and warnings from the past were to no avail. Within days of the exodus, Prunier predicted that if the former leaders retained their power in the camps they would divert aid supplies, deter the refugees from returning, and conduct military operations into Rwanda, thereby sprouting "the roots of the next crisis."[51] Destexhe cautioned that "in no circumstances should the humanitarian agencies use the former administration of Rwanda to help them channel distributions of aid."[52] The warnings went unheeded: ignorance could not be blamed for the predicament that ensued.

THE POPULATION EXODUS AND INTERNATIONAL RESPONSE
The exodus of two million Rwandans to neighboring territories was propelled both by fear of the RPF advance and by orders given by the Rwandan state apparatus. The instigators of the genocide had sought to inculpate the entire Hutu population in the killing; leaving few with clean hands minimized the risk of finger pointing and accusations once the extermination was complete. Thousands participated in the massacres, many because of hatred or for financial gain, and the rest reluctantly, from fear or because they were ordered to do so. As the RPF gained ground, gov-

[50] Prunier, personal communication, 5 May 1999.
[51] Gérard Prunier, "Rwanda: La crise rwandaise: structures et déroulement" (U.K.: Writenet, July 1994), also reprinted in *Refugee Survey Quarterly* 13, nos. 2 and 3 (1994): 13–46, cited in *Refugee Camp Security in the Great Lakes Region*, pp. 19–20.
[52] Destexhe, "Hurry to Prevent a Cambodian Epilogue."

ernment officials encouraged the population to flee, and whole villages headed toward Rwanda's borders.

The first massive exodus occurred into the Ngara district of Tanzania in late April 1994 when approximately 170,000 Rwandans crossed in one twenty-four-hour period. Thousands more crossed in the ensuing months and were settled in several camps, the largest of which was Benaco. The main exodus into Zaire was even more rapid; between 500,000 and 800,000 Rwandans crossed into North Kivu between 14 and 17 July 1994.[53] The scale of the influx overwhelmed the capacity of aid organizations to respond adequately, and the lack of sanitation facilities and presence of large polluted water sources provoked an epidemic of cholera and dysentery. The epidemics killed at least 50,000 refugees in the month after their arrival, between 6 and 10 percent of the total population.[54]

The public health disaster provided UN member states with the perfect scenario to elicit a large-scale response from the "international community": a dramatic, well-publicized show of human suffering in which the enemy was a virus and the savior was humanitarian aid. Paralyzed during the political crisis, military forces were suddenly mobilized for the "humanitarian" disaster, transforming the genocide into a "complex emergency" in which there was no good or bad side, only victims. The U.S. government, which warned its officials to avoid using the word "genocide" because of the legal and moral obligations the term invokes,[55] did nothing to halt the bloodshed in Rwanda but deployed a military force 3,000 strong to Goma to fight the ravages of cholera. "The United States is determined to lead a worldwide humanitarian response, working with the United Nations to mobilize the international community," declared the

---

[53] Initial population estimates were as high as 1.2 million, but by early August cluster-sample surveys, mapping exercises, and aerial photographs suggested lower numbers. Goma Epidemiological Group, "Public Health Impact of Rwandan Refugee Crisis: What Happened in Goma, Zaire, in July, 1994?" *Lancet* 345 (February 1995): 339–344 at p. 340.

[54] Ibid., p. 342.

[55] The State Department and the National Security Council issued instructions to administration spokespersons to say that "acts of genocide have occurred." The *New York Times* reported: "American officials say that so stark a label [as genocide] could inflame public calls for action the Administration is unwilling to take. . . . without oil or other resources as a rationale, the case for intervention would have to be based on whether ending the killing is worth the cost in American lives and dollars." Douglas Jehl, "Officials Told to Avoid Calling Rwanda Killings 'Genocide,' " *New York Times*, 10 June 1994, p. A8. Secretary of State Warren Christopher defined responsibility for stopping the genocide in strictly legal terms: "The international community as a whole has a general obligation to do what they can to avoid genocide, but it does not impose on the United States or any other country a specific obligation to go into that country and to prevent the genocide, either by the use of force, or otherwise." Elaine Sciolino, "Secretary Reframes U.S. Obligation in Rwanda," *International Herald Tribune*, 23–24 July 1994, p. 4.

head of the U.S. Agency for International Development (USAID), J. Brian Atwood.[56] "The U.S. government response so far has been massive, aggressive, and immediate as possible . . . ours is the only response that could have handled this problem."[57] A more modest contribution from the United States three months earlier might have saved hundreds of thousands of lives.[58]

Atwood characterized the genocide and its aftermath as "chaos," the obvious remedy for which was "humanitarian assistance" and "stability": "the United Nations must be on the front lines in the war against chaos. . . . the desperate people in Goma, make no mistake about it, are the victims of this chaos. . . . we simply can not let the cancer of chaos spread."[59] He called upon the international community to join the United States as "it develops the machinery for effective crisis prevention." Adding insult to injury, Atwood called upon the new Rwandan government to "embrace the call for meaningful power-sharing"[60] and ensure that war criminals are "tried under a fair judicial process," while offering scant resources to the government to undertake these noble tasks.[61] Moreover, the U.S. military foray into Goma, Operation Support Hope, was established as a strictly "humanitarian" operation and was not, therefore, given the mandate to arrest the war criminals that Atwood insisted must receive a fair trial. While claiming to be developing machinery to prevent crises, the military forces

[56] J. Brian Atwood, "Relief Immediately, Then Crisis Prevention Quickly," *International Herald Tribune*, 25 July 1994, p. 4.

[57] J. Brian Atwood, prepared statement for "Crisis in Central Africa," Hearing before the Subcommittee on African Affairs of the Committee on Foreign Relations, U.S. Senate, 26 July 1994, pp. 9 and 10.

[58] The former Force Commander of UNAMIR, General Roméo Dallaire, considered that a total force of 5,000 troops and a peace enforcement mandate could have prevented most of the killing in Rwanda. UNAMIR's mandate extended to 2,500 troops, thus necessitating only an additional 2,500 if Dallaire's assessment was accurate. See Scott R. Feil, *Preventing Genocide: How the Early Use of Force Might Have Succeeded in Rwanda* (New York: Carnegie Commission on Deadly Conflict, 1998).

[59] Atwood, "Relief Immediately."

[60] Ibid.

[61] The U.S. government was slow to recognize the new Rwandan government and was influential in stalling earmarked funds from the World Bank, which insisted that the Rwandan government repay $10 million in arrears in order to unblock the $250 million allocation. When the United States did allocate funds to Rwanda, the amount was significantly less than that for the neighboring refugee camps: $231.9 million in humanitarian assistance for the regional Rwandan crisis compared with $73.3 million to Rwanda in fiscal year 1994; $242.4 million compared with $46.2 million in 1995; and $177.9 million compared to $13.2 million in 1996. *Chronology of U.S. Government (USG) Humanitarian Assistance to Rwanda and Eastern Democratic Republic of Congo (DROC) (since April 6, 1994)* (Washington, D.C.: USAID/Bureau for Humanitarian Response Office of U.S. Foreign Disaster Assistance, 1997), pp. 10, 13 and 17.

on the ground permitted war criminals and an entire army to mingle with the refugees and set up camp in Zaire. The military logistics helped establish a humanitarian sanctuary in which the war criminals and army received protection, sustenance, and legitimacy, and continued to control the population which they had shepherded into Zaire for that purpose.

It is important to state that the refugee camp inhabitants were a mixture of bona fide refugees, Rwandans who had been ordered to flee, and people evading revenge or prosecution for crimes they committed during the genocide. The last group should have been excluded from refugee status under international conventions that are discussed further below, but in the absence of mechanisms for removing suspected war criminals, they resided in the camps and benefited from the international rights accorded to refugees. Some authors, notably Alex de Waal, refer to the refugees as Externally Displaced Persons to reflect the illegitimacy of refugee status for such individuals.[62] However, such a term denies the existence of real refugees among the population which fled, and implies that they did not warrant international protection.

Generalizations like de Waal's abound in the literature in support of arguments to either assist or abandon the camp population. The fact that half the camp inhabitants were women and children and thus "innocent" was frequently invoked, yet being female does not preclude participation in genocide. The notion that the refugees were "hostages" of the former regime was also regularly espoused, yet this denied individual agency and any responsibility of the refugees themselves for the status quo. While generalizations are often necessary, it is important to bear in mind that the camp inhabitants were not a homogeneous population, and that many fled Rwanda owing to a well-founded fear of persecution. This fact, in particular, was concealed and remains overlooked for reasons of political expediency. Thus a brief digression here is warranted to explain the justified fear of returning that many refugees harbored.

Evidence that the RPF committed atrocities during their march on Kigali surfaced in August 1994 during an inquiry into conditions for repatriation commissioned by UNHCR. The investigating team, headed by a highly experienced and respected U.S. government consultant, Robert Gersony, found that the RPF had killed between 25,000 and 45,000 persons between April and late August 1994. But UN Secretary-General

[62] Alex de Waal, *Famine Crimes: Politics and the Disaster Relief Industry in Africa* (Oxford and Bloomington: African Rights and the International African Institute in association with James Currey and Indiana University Press, 1997), p. 204.

Boutros Boutros-Ghali suppressed the Gersony Report following U.S. pressure to do so, and Gersony's findings either were discredited as having a weak factual base[63] or were said to "not exist,"[64] although officials of UN-HCR had already presented them to members of the Rwandan government.[65] A combination of guilt at the lack of international initiatives to halt the genocide, the political expediency of having the refugees return, and a desire to delineate clearly a "good side" from a "bad side" made international observers reluctant to raise issues of human rights abuses by members of the new regime. Gérard Prunier, testifying at the Belgian Senate Inquiry into the genocide, had the courage to revisit his earlier skepticism about Gersony's findings,[66] saying "je crois aujourd'hui que ce chiffre est une sous-estimation."[67] He admitted that at the time of Gersony's inquiry, he considered the results to be an overestimate because he did not want to believe that the people to whom he felt ideologically close could commit massacres. After conducting interviews of his own, however, he reached a conclusion similar to Gersony's.[68] Although incommensurate with the extent of the killings carried out by the former Rwandan regime, the exactions committed by members of the RPF gave Rwandans a genuine reason to flee—a state of affairs contradicting the generalized notion that all the camp inhabitants were brainwashed "hostages" of the deposed government forces.

[63] A spokesperson for the UN Rwanda Emergency Office said that the report gave no physical or forensic evidence of its claims: "These are sensitive allegations made without proof." "Two UN Agencies at Odds on Report of Rwanda Killing," *International Herald Tribune*, 26 September 1994, p. 4. See also John Borton, Emery Brusset, and Alistair Hallam, "Humanitarian Aid and Effects," Study 3 of *The International Response to Conflict and Genocide: Lessons from the Rwanda Experience* (Copenhagen: Steering Committee of the Joint Evaluation of Emergency Assistance to Rwanda, 1996), p. 49 n. 49.

[64] A letter from the UNHCR branch office in Kigali to the representative of the special rapporteur for Rwanda states that the Gersony Report "does not exist." A copy of the letter is included in *Leave None to Tell the Story*, p. 726. According to sources close to the investigation, the discussion of the Gersony Report in *Leave None to Tell the Story* (pp. 726–735) is the most accurate and authoritative available.

[65] Senior UNHCR official, personal interview, March 1998. Gersony's notes were allegedly kept in the safe of the High Commissioner for Refugees, Sadako Ogata.

[66] In *Rwanda Crisis*, pp. 323–324, Prunier cast doubt on the credibility of the contents of the Gersony Report, suggesting that killing 250–300 persons per day without attracting attention would have been very difficult. He suggested that the Gersony Report "tended to obscure rather than clarify the problem."

[67] "I believe today that this number is an underestimate." *Commission d'enquête parlementaire concernant les événements du Rwanda* (Brussels: Compte Rendu Analytique des Auditions, Senat de Belgique, 11 June 1997), p. 717.

[68] Ibid. Also see *Témoignages de nouveaux réfugiés sur les violations des droits de l'homme perpétrées par le FPR* (Bukavu: Ligue des Réfugiés Rwandais pour les Droits de l'Homme, December 1994) for testimonies of refugees who fled Rwanda after October 1994.

Although many Rwandans fled to neighboring countries of their own volition, the evacuation of the population was also a calculated military strategy aimed at undermining the credibility of the new Rwandan government and providing the ousted regime with a strong asset with which to claim legitimacy and attract international sympathy. RTLM, the station that had been instrumental in inciting people to genocide, warned the "Hutu Nation" to take refuge in Zaire.[69] A member of the Foreign Ministry in the former government said, "even if they [the RPF] have won a military victory they will not have the power. We have the population. They only have the bullets."[70]

Retaining the population in exile became imperative to the prospects of the former regime, and the military was directed to "continue to play their role of *avant-garde* in all initiatives aimed at a return to Rwanda, to warn of any uncoordinated returns and, above all, to discourage them by creating a climate of insecurity in Rwanda."[71] The leadership adopted a multifaceted approach to dissuade the refugees from repatriating, combining intimidation, violence, and propaganda with the creation of control mechanisms at every administrative level within the camps. As the latter became entrenched, the need for the former diminished, and events taking place in Rwanda also militated against enthusiasm among the refugees for a return home.

During the first few months, violence was rife in the Zaire camps and was the primary tool used to control the refugee population. A retrospective survey undertaken in one camp suggested that 4,000 refugees died as a result of violence perpetrated by the militia, undisciplined Zairean soldiers, and other refugees.[72] Individuals or families who expressed the desire or tried to return to Rwanda were accused of sympathizing with "the enemy" and threatened or killed. Others were beaten along the road to Rwanda and told that the beating saved their lives because, according to an anonymous pamphlet which circulated in Mugunga, "of all those made to return by UNHCR, not one has survived."[73] Rumors of infiltrators in the

[69] Linda R. Melvern, *A People Betrayed: The Role of the West in Rwanda's Genocide* (London: Zed Books, 2000), p. 217.

[70] Jean Bosco Barayagwiza, former director of political affairs in the Foreign Ministry, as quoted in *Rwanda: Death, Despair, and Defiance*, p. 1094.

[71] "Rapport de la Réunion," p. 12.

[72] John Eriksson, "Synthesis Report" of *The International Response to Conflict and Genocide: Lessons from the Rwanda Experience*, p. 29.

[73] Cited in *Rwanda and Burundi. The Return Home: Rumours and Realities*, AFR 02/01/96 (London: Amnesty International, 1996), p. 36.

camp generated an atmosphere of fear and violence and resulted in the death of hundreds of refugees suspected of being "RPF agents," often without any provocation. Allegations of poisoning were particularly prevalent, and food vendors often came under attack if something was awry or if a client became ill. Names of "bandits" and enemy networks appeared on lists in the camps together with the locations of the *blindés* (refugee shelters) in which they lived.

Security conditions for the staff of international aid agencies were also precarious, and attempts to direct aid to the most vulnerable refugees rather than the most powerful provoked threats and intimidation of local and international staff. An observer returning from Goma in late 1994 predicted that it was "only a matter of time before one or more international relief workers are assassinated in the Goma camps."[74] The Canadian branch of CARE decided to withdraw from Goma after a serious incident in the Katale refugee camp. CARE had established a security structure separate from that run by the political and military leadership and had hired a Rwandan "Scout" organization to help control access to the camp and direct traffic. In September, a group of militia blamed the death of a bandit in the camp on the Scouts, went searching for them, and issued death threats to several CARE staff members. The international staff evacuated the camp but upon their return found that thirty-five of the Scouts had been murdered and replaced at the camp entrance by armed militia members.[75] CARE Canada announced its withdrawal in October.

By early 1995 several events contributed to the reduction in the level of conspicuous insecurity in the camps and the adoption of more subtle methods of population control. First, a contingent of 1,500 Zairean military personnel (Contingent Zaïrois de Sécurité dans les Camps—CZSC) was deployed in the camps under an agreement with the UN. Unsuccessful attempts to solicit troops from UN member states (discussed below) had left few other options than accepting the Zairean government's offer, and an *aide-mémoire* was signed on 27 January 1995. The force was charged with improving public order in the camps, preventing intimidation and violence aimed at deterring the voluntary repatriation of refugees, protecting humanitarian facilities and personnel, and escorting refugee

---

[74] Jeff Drumtra, *Site Visit to Rwanda, Zaire, and Burundi* (Washington, D.C.: U.S. Committee for Refugees, 20 October to 17 November 1994), p. 15.

[75] See Bruce D. Jones, *Rwanda Report: International NGOs in the Response to the Rwandan Emergency* (London and Toronto: "NGOs in Complex Emergencies" Project, a Collaborative Project of CARE Canada, the Harrowston Project on Conflict Management, University of Toronto, and the Conflict Analysis and Development Unit, London School of Economics, July 1997), section 2.3.2.

convoys to the Rwandan border. The first contingent, which was recruited from the Special Presidential Division of the Zairean armed forces, had some success in improving the conditions in the camps, but the second contingent engaged in exploitative activities, "extorting money, levying taxes on refugees illegally carrying on economic activities, and allegedly using refugees for sex or for prostitution."[76] According to Marie-Béatrice Umutesi, a former refugee who lived near Bukavu, the CZSC "became the principal source of insecurity" for the refugees.[77] The CZSC never managed to prevent intimidation against refugees opting for repatriation[78] but did produce some sort of *rapport de force* with the camp leadership.

The second and more important reason for the decline in violence was the leadership's need for international recognition and sympathy once a return to Rwanda by force became increasingly unlikely. The threatened withdrawal of fifteen NGOs from the camps in Goma unless security improved coincided in November 1994 with the reorganization of the former government and army and a review of their strategy of return to Rwanda. It was strongly in the interests of the former regime to quell the violence in the camps, to avoid jeopardizing the presence of the aid organizations and precipitating a deterioration of camp services. Furthermore, the withdrawal of NGOs would have further reduced international sympathy for the refugees and compromised the efforts of the former regime to improve its international image in the hope of opening dialogue with Kigali.

The third reason for the reduction in overt violence was the consolidation of more subtle forms of control in the camps. The placement of loyal supporters in strategic administrative posts and the revival of the propaganda machine—much of the material for which was based on real events in Rwanda—superseded the controlling role of direct violence and intimidation. Within a few months of their formation, the organizational structures of the camps functioned to control the refugee population almost completely. Several observers have remarked that the same administrative structures that existed in Rwanda were re-created in the Rwandan camps in Tanzania and Zaire: *préfectures, communes, secteurs,* and *cellules.*[79] But in many camps, in fact, several organizational structures were superimposed on one another to monitor and control refugee activities even more assiduously.

[76] *Refugee Camp Security in the Great Lakes Region,* p. 24.

[77] Marie-Béatrice Umutesi, *Fuir ou mourir au Zaïre: Le vécu d'une réfugiée rwandaise* (Paris: L'Harmattan, 2000), p. 94.

[78] *Refugee Camp Security in the Great Lakes Region,* p. 13.

[79] See, for example, *Rwanda and Burundi. The Return Home,* p. 32; Prunier, *The Rwanda Crisis,* pp. 313–314; and Borton, Brusset, and Hallam, "Humanitarian Aid and Effects," pp. 96–97.

The "cellule to préfecture" system was retained as one level of administrative organization, even though the refugees in the Zairean camps were more scattered than in Tanzania, where communes of origin had been geographically maintained. Only in Kahindo in Zaire were the refugees physically grouped according to their regions and villages of origin.[80] A semblance of democracy was introduced in the camps in 1994, with refugees electing leaders at the commune level. International organizations were invited to attend the election to "verify" the democratic nature of the vote, although the process by which candidates were nominated was not clear. Speeches generally ensued and refugees formed a line behind the candidate of choice. The elected commune representatives then elected a *préfet* (although they dropped these political titles in favor of "representative").

After the former government and military reorganized in September 1994, they imposed another level of authority on the refugee camps. One of the recommendations made at the meeting of the high command was that "the government must make every effort to supervise this population, especially as the refugees have elected their leaders at the camp level."[81] Hence, in early November, members of the newly formed political commissions, mentioned in the previous section, were placed in the camps. In Goma, the Social Commission of Rwandan Refugees of North Kivu, which had fifteen members, established four main subcommissions: security, social, capital and finance, and communication and information. They appointed four persons in each préfecture to represent these commissions, with the exception of "capital and finance," which was replaced at the camp level by a distribution commission. The four commission appointees elected one representative to sit on the camp council (*conseil du camp*), which was the liaison committee that met with UNHCR, the Zairean authorities, and the NGOs.

The commission then replicated in the camps the type of "*auto-défense*" neighborhood security system that had been so effective in locating and killing Tutsi during the genocide for "self-defense." The camps were geographically delineated into *quartiers*, *sous-quartiers*, and then into cells of ten or so blindés. A security officer was elected in each cell by his neighbors; these officers then elected sous-quartier officials, who in turn elected a head of each quartier. All *chefs de quartier* were represented on the camp council. UNHCR had geographical zones for distribution, but these did

---

[80] Report from Eleanor Bedford to MSF Amsterdam and Brussels, "Update weeks 6–7 (January 15–February 1)" (Goma: mimeo, 7 February 1995), p. 2.
[81] "Rapport de la Réunion," p. 12.

not necessarily match those of the quartiers, so three levels of organization effectively existed.

UNHCR refused to meet with the government-in-exile in Zaire specifically to avoid according legitimacy to these individuals as a negotiating partner of the UN. Meeting with other war criminals was sometimes unavoidable, however, if they held positions in the camps that entitled them to sit on the camp councils. The social commissions also contained extremists, the most notorious of whom, François Karera, was best known for his justification of the genocide because "the Tutsi are originally bad."[82] Living in Zaire with impunity, he oversaw many of the refugee camp functions, including presiding over the local elections in "Ruhengeri préfecture" in early December 1994.[83] He was the former préfet of Greater Kigali and number 43 on the Rwandan government's list of principal génocidaires, wanted for trial.

Again in accordance with the proposals made in the meeting of the high command, a final layer of control was placed over the refugee camp population. The meeting recommended that

> The military leaders must ask Rwandan intellectuals to assist the politico-administrative authorities in raising awareness and supervising the refugees. They should be asked to take initiatives to create reflection groups on subjects of patriotism and the return to our country. Ask them to approach foreign organizations to make them understand our cause and to request their assistance for the population. . . . The Rwandan intellectuals should seek employment in the international realm to get close to the foreigners.[84]

Such "reflection groups" were established in most camps and served as an important medium through which to transmit the revised Rwandan history and messages of Hutu victimization that I discussed earlier. Attended by refugees, these meetings were held regularly to discuss politics, security, developments in Rwanda, and constraints faced by the refugees in returning there. In addition, the Social Commission urged the refugees to create a variety of associations in the camps including women's associations, associations of handicapped persons, and intellectual associations. A Rwandan NGO collective was also formed, although Umutesi, who was an active member, says that its objective was to provide an alternative message from

[82] Jane Perlez, "A Hutu Justifies Genocide," *International Herald Tribune*, 16 August 1994, p. 1.
[83] Report from Eleanor Bedford to MSF Amsterdam and Brussels, "Elections" (Goma: mimeo, 5 February 1995), p. 2.
[84] "Rapport de la Réunion," p. 6.

that of sources close to Kigali or to the former regime. Nevertheless, she admits that the collective's attempts to be "as objective as possible" about "the Rwanda problem" were misunderstood as being complicit either with the génocidaires or with the Kigali regime, underlining the effectiveness of the camp propaganda.

The formation of the RDR, mentioned above, was also an attempt to gain increased legitimacy for the Rwandan leaders, who claimed through it to represent the refugee population. Evidence suggests that the RDR was formed as an alternative to the government-in-exile and was specifically led by people not directly associated with the genocide. The director was François Nzabahimana, the former minister of commerce, and the executive secretary was Innocent Butare, who was out of the country when the genocide commenced. Espousing rhetoric of justice, tolerance, respect for human rights, and the end of ethnic cleavages, the RDR sought to open negotiations with Kigali as a first step in the dignified repatriation of the refugees. The aid organizations in the camp initially welcomed the RDR and bestowed considerable kudos on it as an organization until they came to think it had been undermined by extremists.[85] The heavily edited manifestos of the RDR and its embryonic predecessor, the Front Démocratique Rwandais (FDR), found in Bizimungu's files suggest, however, that extremists always ran it. In one version of the FDR statutes (see Appendix D), Article 1 has been amended by hand from a "politico-military movement" to a "socio-political organization." It is also interesting to note how the terminology of UNHCR has been adopted: to the first objective of the FDR, the organization of refugee repatriation, has been added "in dignity and security to Rwanda."

Finally, as illustrated in the previous section, the production and widespread distribution of propaganda in the camps contributed to maintaining psychological control over the refugee population. The extremist newspaper *Kangura*, responsible for espousing ethnic hatred before and during the genocide, continued to be produced under the editorship of indicted war criminal Hassan Ngeze and distributed in the camps. Another extremist publication, *Amizero*, began in November 1994 and was published by the Association des Journalistes Rwandais en Exil, with the former editor-in-chief of RTLM, Gaspard Gahigi, as editor. Articles in these publications often tried to reflect the concerns of the refugees. In *Kangura* in early 1995, Ngeze wrote:

[85] Joël Boutroue, UNHCR team leader, Goma, personal interview, 8 August 1997. Members of the media were not so naïve, questioning the credibility of the RDR from the outset. See "You're Saying We Did It?" *Economist*, 3–9 June 1995, p. 44.

There are questions that everyone asks. When we will return? How will we return? Where are the preparations? No one is resolving these questions. To be able to return, the refugees must win 3 wars: a war of arms, of politics, and of information. Everyone must examine their conscience to determine their contribution. *"What should I do to make our problem known to the international community," "Can I financially support a newspaper? Can I give a donation to buy arms? Can I analyze the current situation and propose solutions?"* It is regrettable that the intellectuals and former authorities are conspicuous by their lack of thought and their indifference. It is time for the refugees to collaborate, from the peasant to the businessman, from the military to the religious. The young and the old must be ready: the time to enter by force is close since the RPF have refused all negotiation.[86]

Clandestine radio also periodically broadcast in the camps, and a variety of other forms of dissemination were used to spread messages aimed at dissuading the refugees from returning to Rwanda. Some of the clergy produced the most inflammatory literature, including a pamphlet which used passages from the Bible to justify genocide.[87]

Thus the former politicians and military retained strong control over the refugees through the use of violence, coercion, authority, propaganda, and social networks. The need for open intimidation and violence to prevent the refugees returning to Rwanda lessened as a web of subcommittees, neighborhood security units, and associations embracing almost all segments of society was cast over the camps. The growing insecurity in Rwanda, partly provoked by cross-border military raids, but also due to the rising power of hard-liners within the Kigali regime, added weight to the discourse promulgated in the camps, and discouraged refugee returns. As the special envoy of UNHCR, Carol Faubert, said in an interview with *Le Monde* in July 1995: "The violence has disappeared in the camps, but it could recur. For the moment, three months after the Kibeho massacre, the camp extremists have no need to discourage the refugees from returning."[88] The organizational structures of the refugee camps facilitated the mechanisms of control, but the paramount problem from which all other

---

[86] Hassan Ngeze, "Editorial: Apprenons à parler et à poser des questions. Sachons découvrir la vérité et soyons clairvoyants," *Kangura* no. 65 (1 January 1995), pp. 1–2, as summarized in ABSL Dialogue, *Revue de la presse rwandaise.*

[87] Report from Eleanor Bedford to MSF Amsterdam and Brussels, "March 6–19" (Goma: mimeo, 27 March 1995), p. 12. Even in a letter to the pope dated August 1994 a group of priests in Goma justified the killings and claimed that "the number of Hutu civilians killed by the army of the RPF exceeds by far the Tutsi victims of the ethnic troubles." See *Rwanda: Death, Despair, and Defiance*, pp. 906–907.

[88] Jean Hélène, "Des organisations humanitaires reprochent aux autorités rwandaises de ne pas favoriser le retour des exilés," *Le Monde*, 30–31 July 1995, p. 4.

paradoxes of humanitarian assistance in the camps stemmed was the presence of the former army and government.

The defeated government and its supporters gained two types of protection by seeking asylum in Zaire: legal protection through recognition as refugees, and physical protection since the RPA did not, for the most part, pursue them across the border. They acquired legal protection because under the provisions of Article 1.2 of the 1969 OAU Convention Governing Specific Aspects of Refugee Problems in Africa, prima facie refugee status was accorded to all asylum seekers who fled Rwanda. This convention grants status to "every person who, owing to external aggression, occupation, foreign domination or events seriously disturbing public order in either part or the whole of his country of origin or nationality is compelled to leave."

As I mentioned in chapter 1, exclusions clauses contained in the 1951 and 1969 Refugee Conventions disqualify from refugee status persons suspected of committing war crimes and crimes against humanity, but the blanket bestowal of refugee status precludes individual status determination. Central to the protection tenet of international refugee law is the principle of *non-refoulement*, the guarantee that states will refrain from forcing refugees to return to their country of origin. Recognizing that refugee status in the Rwandan case protected criminals, the Bujumbura Conference on Assistance to Refugees, Returnees and Displaced Persons in the Great Lakes Region in 1995 noted that the principle of non-refoulement did not apply to those suspected of genocide. Its Plan of Action noted: "If it is determined that certain individuals do not deserve international refugee protection, in which case the principle of non-refoulement does not apply, such persons may be subjected to extradition procedures, under conditions of due process of law."[89] But these legal prescriptions presupposed a capacity to identify individuals implicated in the genocide and, once they were identified, to have them removed from the refugee camps and extradited to Rwanda or to the International Criminal Tribunal for Rwanda (ICTR) in Arusha, Tanzania. The Exclusion Clause was applied to twenty Rwandans once the ICTR indicted them in September

[89] *Plan of Action*, 1995/BUJCONF.3, Regional Conference on Assistance to Refugees, Returnees and Displaced Persons in the Great Lakes Region, 12–17 February 1995, Bujumbura Item 11.

182   CONDEMNED TO REPEAT?

1996,[90] but thousands of others remained in Zaire benefiting from protection against prosecution rather than persecution.[91]

Under international law it is the host nation that is responsible for ensuring that refugee camps have an "exclusively civilian and humanitarian character."[92] As an ally of the former Rwandan regime, the Zairean government was, on the one hand, reluctant to arrest war criminals or jeopardize the prospects of the regime's return to power in Rwanda. But on the other hand, Zaire was in need of the international prestige conferred upon states hosting refugees. Whether by design or by default, the Zairean authorities managed to weave a path through the conflicting loyalties, compromising one for another when necessary. Uncertainty about Zaire's reliability is reflected in several of the ex-FAR's military documents—a suspicion well founded in light of Zaire's return of military equipment to Rwanda in early 1996. From the UN perspective too, Zairean authorities proved to be unpredictable negotiating partners. In the initial months of the relief operation, the Zairean government indicated to the UN Department of Peacekeeping Operations (DPKO) its readiness to separate the military and former government officials from the rest of the refugees, to bring the latter to Kinshasa for movement to a third country, and to allocate sites away from the border to which the military could move.[93] None of these actions was ever carried through, however, and the *aide-mémoire* signed for the CZSC deployment made no mention of separating or arresting the former government authorities. The Zairean government also violated the principle of non-refoulement in August 1995, expelling some 14,000 Rwandans and 2,000 Burundian refugees from Zaire. This move came in response to the UN Security Council's decision to lift the arms

[90] *UNHCR Excludes 20 Indicted Rwandans* (Geneva: Public Information Section, UNHCR, 24 September 1996).

[91] The synthesis report of the Joint Evaluation of Emergency Assistance to Rwanda suggested that 10–15 percent of the camp population was directly implicated in the mass killing, although no explanation of the basis for this calculation was provided. See Eriksson, "Synthesis Report," p. 39. Claudine Vidal argues that it is impossible to estimate the number of people who participated in the killings. She shows that many studies of the genocide make unfounded assertions about the nature of Rwandan peasants and their supposedly blind adherence to authority. Vidal, "Questions sur le rôle des paysans durant le génocide des Rwandais tutsi," *Cahiers d'études africaines* 38, nos. 2–4 (150–152) (1998): 331–345.

[92] In accordance with EXCOM Conclusion 48 of 1987, "no. 48 (XXXVIII) Military or Armed Attacks on Refugee Camps and Settlements," 1987 Executive Committee—38th Session, in *Conclusions on the International Protection of Refugees adopted by the Executive Committee of the UNHCR Programme* (Geneva: UNHCR, 1991), pp. 109–111 at p. 110.

[93] "United Nations Mission on Security in the Rwandese Refugee Camps. Terms of Reference" (New York: Department of Peace Keeping Operations, mimeo, 1 September 1994).

embargo on Rwanda.[94] Invoking national security concerns, the government of Zaire reminded the UN member states of the importance of Zairean hospitality toward the refugees.[95]

In addition to the legal protection that the body of refugees obtained for those responsible for genocide, the presence of hundreds of thousands of refugees provided a human shield against attack until late 1996. The proximity of the refugee camps to Rwanda permitted the launching of cross-border raids without provoking harsh reprisals for over two years.

Yet the protection they provided eventually made the camps targets, and the attacks on them provoked only muted reactions from the rest of the world. As illustrated in earlier chapters, the physical protective function of refugee camps is usually derived from the international condemnation that an attack on the refugee population would provoke. But in the case of the camps in Zaire, the stage was set during two years of shrewd analysis and careful planning by the Rwandan government to minimize the diplomatic repercussions of the assault on, and destruction of, the camps. First, although RPA involvement in the offensive was widely assumed, the Rwandan government consistently denied any involvement in the offensive against the camps until July 1997, thus attracting public denunciation only from one of Zaire's allies, Gabon.[96] When Vice President and Minister of Defense Paul Kagame did admit Rwanda's role, he justified the action by stating that the UN had failed to resolve the security threat the camps posed to Rwanda. "We told them clearly: Either you do something about the camps or you face the consequences."[97] Kagame had, in fact, issued repeated warnings of Rwanda's intention to attack this source of re-

[94] See Boutros Boutros-Ghali, "Introduction," in *The United Nations and Rwanda, 1993–1996* (New York: UN Department of Public Information, 1996), pp. 3–111 at pp. 89–90.

[95] The refoulement also reflected the political relationship between President Mobutu, who was in favor of hosting the refugees, and Prime Minister Kengo wa Dondo, who wanted the refugees to leave Zaire. Both sought to capitalize on the presence of the refugees in this traditionally antigovernment region of Zaire: Mobutu by permitting the refugees, dependent upon his good will, to remain in the region, and Kengo by promising the local inhabitants, resentful of the refugee presence, that the refugees must return to Rwanda. William Cyrus Reed, "Contested Government, State Decay, and Public Policy: The Role of Zaire in the Great Lakes Crisis," second draft of a paper presented to the International Studies Association Convention, Washington, D.C., February 1999.

[96] Peter Smerdon, "Rwandan Links with Zaire Rebels Hard to Disguise," Reuters, 22 November 1996.

[97] John Pomfret, "Rwanda Admits It Led Drive to Topple Mobutu," *International Herald Tribune*, 10 July 1997, p. 7.

gional instability since March 1995,[98] and it came as no surprise to most informed observers.

Second and most important, the dismantling of the camps and the return of the refugees to Rwanda was the outcome that the UN and donor governments wanted but had failed to accomplish themselves. The U.S. government, in particular, had sanctioned a tougher approach to the refugee problem, stating at the Rwandan Roundtable meeting in June 1996 that "while voluntary repatriation remains the preferred option of the U.S. government, the on-the-ground reality in the camps dictates that this option becomes less and less viable over time. . . . It is time to look at other options to maintaining the current status of the refugee camps no matter how difficult it is to reconcile those options with refugee conventions."[99]

There is little doubt that individuals in the U.S. government approved of the offensive against the camps: Kagame even publicly commended the United States for "taking the right decision to let it proceed."[100] The camps were expensive to maintain and created regional destabilization, and attempts to encourage the voluntary repatriation of the refugees had been largely unsuccessful over the preceding two years. The situation had reached an impasse because UN member states had failed to support initiatives aimed at breaking the hold of the political and military leaders over the refugees. Boutros-Ghali recognized in November 1994 that "the most effective way of ensuring the safety of the refugees and their freedom to return to Rwanda would be the separation of political leaders, former Rwandese government forces and militia from the rest of the refugee population."[101] He proposed several options involving the deployment of UN troops to undertake tasks ranging from progressively establishing security in the camps for refugees and aid personnel, to the separation of the military and political elements from the refugees under Chapter VII of the UN Charter. Noting the difficulty of obtaining the necessary number of troops for UNAMIR in Rwanda, Boutros-Ghali recommended the option

[98] Kagame stated in March 1995 that his government would pursue any criminals who attacked Rwanda by attacking the country in which they were found. See *Question of the Violation of Human Rights and Fundamental Freedoms in Any Part of the World, with Particular Reference to Colonial and Other Dependent Countries and Territories*, UN General Assembly Report A/51/942, Human Rights Questions: Human Rights Situations and Reports of Special Rapporteurs and Representatives, July 1997, pp. 17–18.

[99] U.S. Statement delivered by Richard McCall, chief of staff, USAID, to the Rwandan Roundtable Conference, Geneva, 20–21 June 1996, p. 4 and p. 6.

[100] Pomfret, "Rwanda Admits It Led Drive."

[101] *Report of the UN Secretary-General on Security in the Rwandese Refugee Camps* (S/1994/1308), p. 1.

which required fewer soldiers. But even this proposal proved unpopular with UN member states, and only one country of the sixty approached agreed to provide personnel. The opportunity to avert a deadlock in the crisis and work toward a resolution was relinquished.

Thus in providing legal and physical protection to the former government and army for over two years, the Rwandan refugee camps in Zaire became a "legitimate" target of attack for the Rwandan army and allied Zairean rebels. States were unwilling to commit the necessary resources to Zaire to address problems impeding a resolution of the refugee crisis and welcomed an initiative directed toward an outcome desired by the "international community." The fact that Rwanda had warned of such an outcome for eighteen months, had gained tacit American approval, was discreet about its involvement, and directed the bulk of refugees back to Rwanda averted international condemnation of the attack. The camps' protective functions had been short-lived, not only for those undeserving of such protection but also for the genuine refugees.

WAR ECONOMY

The political and military leadership in the Rwandan refugee camps employed diverse initiatives to generate revenue for their activities in exile. They derived some income directly from the humanitarian relief effort by inflating population numbers, stealing aid supplies, and taxing local employees of humanitarian organizations. Other income was indirectly gained from the refugees as consumers, a source of substantial profits. Brothels, cinemas, bars, restaurants, health centers, import/export offices, money-changers, transport services, and commercial shops of all description were established in the camps with the extensive haul of equipment, vehicles, and capital taken from Rwanda. Many refugees also had assets at their disposal, having fled with household goods, money, and other belongings. This was fed into the booming camp economy controlled by the camp leadership.

The extent of the revenue directly sourced from the humanitarian relief program varied according to the camp and region. Inflated beneficiary numbers, for example, was a bigger problem in Bukavu and in the Tanzanian camps in Ngara than in the refugee settlements around Goma. The first official registration of refugees in Ngara in July 1994 produced a figure of 230,000, which was significantly lower than the 350,000 names appearing on lists provided by the camp leadership.[102] Hence for ten weeks

[102] *Lessons Learnt from the Rwanda Emergency*, EC/1995/SC.2/CRP.21 (Geneva: Sub-committee on Administrative and Financial Matters, Executive Committee of the High Commissioner's Programme, 7 June 1995), in Annex C of *Lessons Learned from the Burundi and Rwanda*

humanitarian aid for 120,000 people was misappropriated by those in charge of the distribution process. In Bukavu, a refugee count undertaken in late February 1995 reduced the beneficiary population from 350,000 to 300,000 refugees, indicating that aid for 50,000 refugees for six months had "disappeared." In Goma, by contrast, the original planning figure of 1.2 million was revised to 850,000 by August 1994 on the basis of aerial surveys taken by the U.S. and French military, and the number requiring food was further reduced to 740,000 at the end of September.[103] The census of late January 1995 registered a total of 722,000 refugees, which, according to a UNHCR evaluation, "tallies well . . . if departures are taken into account." The report asserts that "at no time during the emergency was food either delivered or distributed in excess of these requirements."[104] The assumption that aid was not wasted is accurate, however, only if the 71,395 spontaneous returns to Rwanda that UNHCR recorded between October 1994 and the end of January 1995 (of a total 201,702 since July)[105] were among refugees already excluded from the food distribution. The Goma representative of the World Food Programme (WFP), Robert Hauser, was quoted in *Libération* disputing the September estimate. Commenting on the high malnutrition rates in the camps he stated that they were even more unacceptable given that "we deliver daily in all camps sufficient food to meet the needs of 740,000 refugees when we know that there are approximately 600,000."[106]

The debate about refugee numbers reemerged as an intensely political issue following the 1996 attack on the camps and the disappearance of an unknown number of Rwandans. Other methods of verification, such as medical data and statistics derived from nutritional and vaccination surveys, however, indicated that UNHCR's figures were fairly accurate before the destruction of the camps.[107]

The establishment of accurate beneficiary numbers ran counter to the

---

Emergencies, Eval/04/96/Rev.1, Inspection and Evaluation Service (Geneva: UNHCR, 1996), p. 7.

[103] "Situation Report no. 10" (Goma: UNHCR mimeo, 25 September 1994) and Borton, Brusset, and Hallam, "Humanitarian Aid and Effects," p. 106.

[104] *Lessons Learnt from the Rwanda Emergency: Further Reflections*, EC/46/SC/CRP.28 (Geneva: Standing Committee, Executive Committee of the High Commissioner's Programme, 28 May 1996), in Annex D of *Lessons Learned from the Burundi and Rwanda Emergencies*, p. 4.

[105] Situation Report no. 19, 15 January–15 February 1995 (Goma: UNHCR mimeo, February 1995).

[106] Alain Frilet, "Le tranquille exil des chefs de guerre hutus," *Libération*, 23 November 1994, p. 15.

[107] See Jean-Hervé Bradol and Anne Guibert, "Le temps des assassins et l'espace humanitaire, Rwanda, Kivu, 1994–1997," *Hérodote* no. 86/87 (1997): 116–149 at p. 137.

interests of the political and military leadership, and attempts to conduct refugee registrations faced sabotage. In addition to economic gains, exaggerating the number of refugees outside Rwanda vis-à-vis the number in the interior was central to attempts to discredit the new Rwandan regime and challenge its right to power. The government-in-exile claimed that 4,050,000 refugees resided in Zaire, with 500,000, 300,000, and 50,000 refugees in Tanzania, Burundi, and other countries respectively.[108] Thus the first attempt at conducting a census in October 1994 was plagued by insecurity, and the registration was postponed until January. The January registration encountered attempts of fraud, and in some communes ration card verification had to be repeated up to five times. Eventually UNHCR arrived at a satisfactory figure, having uncovered many fictitious cellules, secteurs, and even communes. However, a renewed attempt at registration in August 1996 failed after the 700,000 refugees boycotted the count. Rumors had circulated in the camps that the ink used for registration caused sterility and death, and would identify refugees if they were forced to return to Rwanda. Since a joint communiqué announcing the start of repatriation had been issued by the prime ministers of Zaire and Rwanda on 22 August, the latter rumor fed into the real fears of the refugee population.

Registration exercises, in any case, did not stop the theft of aid supplies. The high malnutrition rates mentioned by the WFP representative in Goma in 1994 were largely a reflection of the uneven distribution of rations within the camps. Relying on the commune heads to prepare lists of beneficiaries and assist in the distribution left the system open to manipulation. One estimate suggested that a quarter of the 10,000 tonnes of food destined for distribution was diverted to the camp leadership.[109] A food basket monitoring survey undertaken in the Goma camps in October 1994 revealed the disparities of rations: 40 percent of households in Kibumba received less than the 2,000 Kcal ration to which they were entitled, with 29 percent receiving less than 1,000 Kcal, and 13 percent receiving more than 10,000 Kcal rations. Rations containing less than 1,000 Kcal were found among 32 percent of the population in Kahindo, 19 percent in Mugunga, and 9 percent in Katale.[110] Rates of severe malnutrition in Mugunga increased from 3.3 percent of children under five years of age in August to 8.2 percent in October 1994. Increases in rates of severe malnutrition were also experienced in the Kibumba and Kahindo camps.

---

[108] Thacien Hahozayezu, "Les vrai statistiques des réfugiés," *Amizero—L'Espoir* no. 0 (7–14 November 1994), pp. 6–7, as summarized in ABSL Dialogue, *Revue de la presse rwandaise.*
[109] Frilet, "Le tranquille exil," p. 15.
[110] Borton, Brusset, and Hallam, "Humanitarian Aid and Effects," p. 96.

Katale had a small decrease, but the rate remained high at 5.9 percent in October.[111]

The defeated forces also directly looted warehouses containing food and other aid supplies; in November 1994, for example, WFP officials discovered 200 tonnes of food from their warehouse being loaded on a barge for Bukavu, headquarters of the former government.[112] But toward the end of 1994 much of the overt theft and diversion of food aid had diminished, and the camp malnutrition rates began to decline, reflecting the change in strategy and increased professionalization of the military and political leadership outlined in the previous section. While a considerable amount of food was probably stockpiled in the earlier months, a combination of the threat of withdrawal from the camps made by the NGOs in November and the redefinition of the military and political structures led to a decrease in the pillage of aid supplies. Images of massive theft portrayed in the international media compromised the new objectives of gaining international legitimacy and sympathy for the refugees.

Other, more discreet forms of income generation from the humanitarian aid operation continued. The taxation of tens of thousands of refugees employed by international agencies provided the camp leaders with a steady income, although the amount is impossible to quantify. Interviews with former refugees indicated that the tax varied from site to site: in Benaco in Tanzania the refugees were apparently taxed 2 days' pay per month, plus 100 Tanzanian shillings per person over eighteen years of age, whereas in Goma a 20–30 percent levy was imposed on all employed refugees. The salaries paid to local staff in Goma until March–April 1995[113] ranged from $270 per month for a doctor to $2 per day for a casual laborer. Engineers and administrators earned $210 per month; drivers, $180; nurses $120–180; auxiliary health staff and cooks, $95; and cleaners, $75. The difficulty of calculating an average wage across all casual and permanent employees is compounded by variations in the numbers of refugees employed between the periods of intense activity and those of consolidation and stability—some 100 international NGOs were present in Goma at the peak of the cholera epidemic.[114] But although the full ex-

[111] Situation Report no. 6, 1–31 July 1994 (Goma: UNHCR mimeo, July 1994).

[112] Frilet, "Le tranquille exil," p. 15.

[113] As discussed further below, several NGOs in Goma reduced salaries to the equivalent rates in Rwanda and reverted from payment in dollars to the Zairean currency to reduce the sum taxed by the camp leadership.

[114] See Borton, Brusset, and Hallam, "Humanitarian Aid and Effects," p. 38. By the end of 1994 there were 45 NGOs in Goma, 44 in South Kivu, and 31 in Tanzania working as implementing partners of UNHCR. *Impact of Military Personnel and the Militia Presence in Rwan-*

tent of revenue earned from taxation can never be accurately determined, a rough indication of the scale can be extrapolated by considering one NGO program during the nonemergency period. In July 1995 the Belgian section of MSF was employing 550 local staff in its health program in Kahindo, which housed 108,000 refugees. The program included running a 230-bed hospital, a 24-hour nutritional center, 3 dispensaries, 4 health posts, and a community health care program. Given that the number of casual laborers employed at this time would have been minimal, an average wage could be expected to have been at least $100 per month. If 550 employees paid one fifth in tax each month, then the camp leadership collected $11,000 per month from the local staff of one NGO in one camp alone. Multiplied by the number of local staff employed in food and nonfood distributions, water and sanitation activities, camp management, warehousing and shelter, social programs for orphans and the handicapped, family tracing, education, agriculture, and vocational training, the revenue would have been considerable. Moreover, salaries were paid in U.S. dollars until mid-1995 since sourcing an adequate quantity of Zairean currency was problematic.

The camp leadership often charged refugees for supplies to which they were freely entitled from UNHCR. One former refugee reported that when she and her family arrived in the Inera camp near Bukavu they were obliged to purchase the land on which to build a shelter.[115] She said that the price of land varied according to the location, with the highest prices paid for the sites closest to camp facilities. Her family paid $100 for a whole package of land, plastic sheeting, a blanket, a cooking set, and their first ration. Items were also individually sold; plastic sheeting cost $20 per piece. She also purchased a place on a distribution list, claiming it was a faster way to receive food than via the official UNHCR system. Having bought beer for the *chef de quartier*, she said that over time he replaced a false name on his list with her real name.

The vehicles looted from Rwanda became another source of revenue for the camp leadership. Several bus and taxi services were established around and between the various camps and Goma town. A report of the activities of Bus A9240 dated 14 October 1995 indicated that $3,018 was made in a five-month period from servicing the Mugunga-Katale-Mu-

dese Refugee Camps and Settlements, 1995/BUJCONF.3, Regional Conference on Assistance to Refugees, Returnees and Displaced Persons in the Great Lakes Region, 12–17 February 1995, Bujumbura, p. 3.

[115] Personal interview with Marie-Rose Mukamudenge, Kigali, 4 January 1997.

gunga route. The report also shows that $2,875 of this was spent on construction costs for the 2nd Division of the ex-FAR, reconnaissance missions, and the purchase of technical materials.[116] Some revenue also came directly from aid organizations to which vehicles were rented. An accounting sheet of the Capital Commission in North Kivu (see Appendix E), for instance, showed bus rental to the Irish NGO Goal among its revenue details for the period April to September 1995. According to the report, Goal paid $6,680 between April and June for the rental of Bus A9225.[117]

The Rwandan refugee camps in Zaire thus provided an effective humanitarian sanctuary to members of the former Rwandan government and army. Protected from prosecution, they resided in the camps with impunity and manipulated the aid structures to increase their military and political power. The sanctuary Zaire provided enabled them to resume the killing they had started in April 1994 and to sabotage reconstruction and reconciliation attempts in Rwanda. The camp leadership prevented the refugees from returning to Rwanda and injected them with hatred and genocidal rhetoric for over two years. After repeated warnings by the Rwandan government, the camps were attacked and destroyed by the Rwandan army and Zairean rebel forces.

The offensive began against the Uvira camps in South Kivu in October 1996, ostensibly led by Zairean Banyamulenge rebels of the Alliance des Forces Démocratiques pour la Libération du Congo-Zaïre (Alliance of Democratic Forces for Liberation of Congo-Zaire—AFDL). Persecution of Tutsi members of the Banyarwanda[118] population living in North Kivu had risen dramatically since the influx of predominantly Rwandan Hutu refugees, and this, together with an expulsion order for the Banyamulenge issued on 7 October 1996 by the deputy governor of South Kivu, was given as rationale for the assault.[119] The speed and precision with which the offensive occurred rapidly overcame opposition, and refugees fled the camps. By early November the AFDL coalition reached the camps in the

[116] Joël Bararwerekana, "Rapport d'activities du Bus A9240" au Comd 2 Div (Mugunga: handwritten mimeo, 14 October 1995) (c.d.).

[117] Gaston Iyamuremye, "Rapport de Gestion Financière de la Commission du Patrimoine de la Communauté Rwandaise en Exil au Nord-Kivu" (Mugunga: mimeo, 30 September 1995) (c.d.).

[118] The Banyarwanda of North Kivu and the Banyamulenge of South Kivu are speakers of Kinyarwanda, the language also spoken in Rwanda. Many lived in Kivu before the colonial boundaries were drawn, and others moved into the region during colonial times and since.

[119] For a report on the persecution of Tutsi in the Masisi region of eastern Zaire see *Ethnic Cleansing Rears Its Head in Zaire: Population in Masisi Suffers Untold Hardship* (Amsterdam: Médecins sans Frontières, 1996).

Goma region.[120] The refugees initially fled west, but their path was blocked by the advancing troops, and most were routed back to Rwanda. Those from Bukavu and Uvira, however, were pursued west and were attacked on numerous occasions as aid organizations attempted to assist them.[121] Hundreds of thousands died or disappeared.

Paul Kagame, the mastermind behind the destruction, blamed the organizations which maintained the camps for their violent demise: "I think we should start accusing these people who actually supported these camps—spent one million dollars per day in these camps, gave support to these groups to rebuild themselves into a force, militarized refugees, and when, in the end, they are caught up in the fighting and they die I think it has more do with these people than Rwanda, than Congo, than the Alliance. Why shouldn't we accuse them?"[122]

While deflecting personal responsibility for unsavory events in the region has become a trademark of Kagame, his question is valid, although not to the extent he suggests. Primary responsibility for the attack on the camps resides with the authorities who ordered, organized, and participated in efforts to destroy them and kill the remnants of the refugee camp population. Secondary responsibility lies with those actors who provided the means of destruction, and whose tacit approval, silence, or denial of events as they occurred made them accessories to such acts. But how much responsibility rests with the UN, donor governments, and private aid agencies which sustained the refugee camps in the knowledge of their role in the conflict, and of the probability that the camps would attract such an assault? To what extent did their acquiescence in the status quo inculpate them in the ensuing crisis?

The Relief Response: Imperatives Versus Consequences

Two factors, in particular, in the international response to the Rwandan exodus exacerbated the negative consequences of humanitarian action in the refugee camps. First, in the rush to meet the material needs of the mas-

[120] For refugee accounts of the attacks on the camps see *Zaire: "Attacked by All Sides": Civilians and the War in Eastern Zaire*, Human Rights Watch Africa, vol. 9, no. 1 (A) (New York: Human Rights Watch, 1997).

[121] For a personal refugee account of the violence encountered in Zaire, see Umutesi, *Fuir ou mourir au Zaïre*. See also *Forced Flight: A Brutal Strategy of Elimination in Eastern Zaire* (Paris: Médecins sans Frontières, May 1997); excerpts presented in Stephen Smith, "MSF Accuse: 190,000 réfugiés hutus disparus au Zaïre," *Libération*, 20 May 1997, pp. 1–2.

[122] As cited in Philip Gourevitch, "Continental Shift," *New Yorker*, 4 August 1997, 42–55 at p. 55.

sive population flowing into Tanzania, analyses of the history and the nature of the refugee caseload were delayed. The entire refugee program in Tanzania was constructed on a false premise, and local leaders, many of whom were implicated in the genocide and exodus, were appointed to act as liaisons between the refugees and the aid agencies. By June 1994, however, any enduring doubts within the aid community of the true nature of the refugee leadership were dispelled when an attempt to remove a known génocidaire, Jean-Baptiste Gatete, from the Benaco refugee camp almost caused a riot when his followers, brandishing machetes, sticks, and rocks, surrounded the UNHCR compound.

Nevertheless, the same mistakes were made in Goma and Bukavu one month later, but this time it was the humanitarian imperative to save lives which prevailed over all other concerns. The difficulty of responding to the refugee influx into Goma cannot be overstated. The sheer volume of refugees was compounded by environmental constraints imposed by the hard volcanic rock and problems of access to clean water supplies, which continued at Kibumba long after they were resolved at the other sites.[123] In addition to the devastating cholera and dysentery epidemics, malnutrition rates were high, and a meningitis epidemic surfaced in late July, necessitating a mass vaccination campaign against meningitis in addition to the routine measles vaccination program.

The second factor that exacerbated the negative consequences of aid in the camps concerned the role of powerful states. But in a reversal of the situation in the past, where aid had been used in pursuit of foreign policy objectives, in the Rwandan case it was used to avoid foreign policy engagement. The humanitarian response was a substitute for political action in a region deemed to be outside the foreign policy interests of the wealthier nations. By engaging the military in a war against cholera, the governments of the United States, Israel, Japan, and the Netherlands demonstrated their concern for the "chaos" in which the Rwandan population was embroiled, without committing themselves to the potentially dangerous task of dealing with the génocidaires.[124] They were opting for the "apolitical" domain of humanitarian assistance even though the absence of any military initiative to remove the political leaders or at least the uni-

[123] Trucking water to the Kibumba camp cost $1 million per month. Drumtra, *Site Visit to Rwanda, Zaire, and Burundi*, p. 14.

[124] The French military were active in the war against cholera, but are excluded here because they also engaged in a political response in Opération turquoise, albeit under a humanitarian mandate. Since the French had political interests in the region, they followed the previous pattern of professing "humanitarian" intent to pursue foreign policy objectives.

formed soldiers from the camps permitted them to remain in the humanitarian sanctuaries. Once reorganized and having reestablished control in the wake of the epidemics, the political and military leadership was much harder to remove. The lack of an appropriate political mandate for the international forces led to greater problems in the long term.

The constraints on effective action imposed by limited mandates were recognized in an official inquiry into lessons learned from the UNAMIR mission in Rwanda.[125] But reflecting the pusillanimous concerns of states to remain aloof from political or military engagement, the report did not suggest a more robust mandate, but recommended increased measures to publicize the limits of the military role to reduce future expectations:

> Many Rwandese believed that the United Nations was there to stop the genocide and were bitterly disappointed when this was not the case. . . . UNAMIR should have done much more to inform the public about its limited role and mandate early on, particularly for the protection of civilians at risk, so as not to give the people a false sense of security. This might have also averted disasters such as the Kibeho massacre, where internally displaced people in the Kibeho camp believed that UNAMIR soldiers would protect them from the RPA.[126]

It is beyond the scope of this chapter to analyze the purpose of military deployment if it is not to prevent civilians from being massacred. Suffice it to say that the emergence of a new normative paradigm in the post–Cold War world, in which humanitarian action becomes an alibi for politicians driven to "do something" by domestic constituents, gives humanitarian assistance an additional paradoxical consequence. Furthermore, in the Rwandan camps the purely humanitarian response of powerful nations was accompanied by a discourse that assisted in the transformation of the genocide into a "complex emergency." Former UN Secretary-General Boutros-Ghali called upon the international community to address the " 'genocide' of hunger, thirst and disease"[127] among the refugees in Zaire.

[125] Astri Suhrke, by contrast, shows that UNAMIR did have various mandates to protect Rwandan civilians, including the rules of engagement drafted by Dallaire, number 17 of which specifically stated that "UNAMIR will take the necessary action to prevent any crime against humanity." Suhrke, "Dilemmas of Protection: The Log of the Kigali Battalion," in Howard Adelman and Astri Suhrke (eds.), *The Path of a Genocide: The Rwandan Crisis from Uganda to Zaire* (New Brunswick, N.J.: Transaction, 1999), pp. 253–270 at pp. 264–265.

[126] *Comprehensive Report on Lessons Learned from United Nations Assistance Mission for Rwanda (UNAMIR), October 1993–April 1996* (New York: Lessons Learned Unit, UN Department of Peacekeeping Operations, 1996), p. 42.

[127] *Report of the Secretary-General to the General Assembly on Emergency Assistance for the Socio-economic Rehabilitation of Rwanda* (A/49/516, 14 October 1994), paragraph 26.

Trivializing the significance of the Rwandan genocide in this way served to put all the victims on an equal footing and avoided the need to apportion blame. Rony Brauman suggests that it is tantamount to calling rape a "gynacological crisis."[128]

By the end of 1994, it was clear that neither an international military nor a civilian police force was going to be deployed to the camps to address the problems of the camp leadership or to protect the refugees. It was also clear that the presence of the former political and military leaders in the camps would at best constitute an enormous obstacle to a resolution of the crisis by blocking refugee repatriation, and at worst would reignite the Rwandan conflict and possibly lead to a broader one. Thus for the aid agencies present in the camps, the humanitarian imperative to give aid wherever it was needed clashed with the responsibility to ensure that their aid was not used against those for whom it was intended. Privileging the humanitarian imperative meant remaining in the camps and providing assistance, regardless of the broader consequences of that action. Privileging concern for the consequences of providing assistance under such conditions meant withdrawing from the camps. A few aid organizations decided to withdraw. The majority decided to remain.

WEIGHING THE CONSEQUENCES

Two NGOs withdrew from the Rwandan refugee camps on ethical grounds once the emergency phase of the relief operation subsided. The French section of Médecins sans Frontières and the International Rescue Committee (IRC) weighed the potential consequences of continued support to the camps against the imperative to remain, and decided to leave.[129] This decision was determined by several interrelated factors. First, while it was impossible to predict precisely what consequences the militarized refugee camps might have for the future of the refugees and the region, the agencies drew analogies from past experience, particularly the revival of the Khmer Rouge. Alain Destexhe, who was secretary-general of MSF at the time, wrote in the *International Herald Tribune* in August 1994:

---

[128] Rony Brauman, "Genocide in Rwanda: We Can't Say We Didn't Know," in François Jean (ed.), *Populations in Danger 1995: A Médecins sans Frontières Report* (London: La Découverte, 1995), pp. 85–90 at p. 89.

[129] This analysis more fully reflects the position of MSF than that of IRC since I am better acquainted with the arguments of the former. However, an interview with Roy Williams, formerly of IRC, confirmed that the organization debated whether to leave or remain in the camps, and withdrew for moral reasons. It was the first time in sixty-four years that the IRC board had made such a decision. Personal interview, 2 October 1997.

The situation in Rwanda is beginning to have a dangerously close resemblance to Cambodia in the 1980s, when humanitarian aid provided by the international community revived and boosted the Khmer Rouge war effort. . . . If the United Nations does not act immediately to ensure safe conditions for the return of the Rwandan refugees, it will be too late to prevent the authors of the genocide from asserting control over the refugees.[130]

As I highlighted in the introduction, MSF engaged in rigorous internal debate over the dilemmas posed by working in the refugee camps and framed the question in terms of the ultimate purpose and use of humanitarian aid and MSF's responsibility for this. Some staff members strongly predicted that the camps would create greater problems in the future. A special newsletter written to explain MSF's position to supporters noted: "Far from participating in the resolution of the conflict, international aid perpetuates the situation and, worse still, prepares the crisis of tomorrow. . . . when they refuse to take into account the context in which they operate, in the name of a misunderstood neutrality, the international organizations prepare . . . the worst for tomorrow."[131]

The lack of international support for initiatives proposed by UNHCR and others to demilitarize the camps, and the probability that the overall status quo would remain unchanged, heightened the second consideration in arguments for withdrawing. Should a humanitarian aid organization professing to alleviate suffering be an accomplice of a system which so obviously violates this fundamental principle? NGOs do not have a mandate to react to every situation in which there are humanitarian needs; they choose between those they respond to and those they do not. The question of complicity in strengthening a regime responsible for committing genocide was particularly strong, since it was the aid mechanisms themselves in the camps which permitted the former government to retain control over the refugee population. As this book illustrates, it is not unusual for aid to have unavoidable side effects. But in the case of the Rwandan camps it was nothing *but* the aid which was sustaining the viability of the old regime, and it was actually being used against the refugees through distribution mechanisms, health structures, refugee administration, and policing initiatives. MSF drew the line when aid was turned

[130] Destexhe, "Hurry to Prevent a Cambodian Epilogue."
[131] Médecins sans Frontières, *Pourquoi nous quittons les camps de réfugiés rwandais* (Paris: MSF, December 1994), p. 1.

against the very people it was trying to assist, and withdrew from the camps.

The prospect of withdrawing inevitably raised the question of the fate of the bona fide refugees in the camps. This was the point on which advocates of a withdrawal found their staunchest critics. The arguments espoused by the United Nations High Commissioner for Refugees, Sadako Ogata, were indicative of the prevailing discourse. Asked why UNHCR did not withdraw, she replied: "there were also innocent refugees in the camps; more than half were women and children. Should we have said: you are related to murderers, so you are guilty, too?"[132] But MSF viewed it as a systemic problem, not as a question of whether individual refugees deserved food or not. "It is not the aid given to children which must be questioned," wrote Dominique Martin, one of the MSF directors in Paris, "but the logic of the system where the populations are used by their 'shepherds' for political ends. They serve as hostages, bait for international aid which permits the refugee leaders to build up their political strength."[133]

Other aid agencies grappled with the moral dilemmas, and divergences of opinion were common. The emergency operations manager for CARE UK, James Fennell, for example, recommended that CARE continue assistance to the camps only on the proviso that the international community bring the génocidaires to justice. CARE UK's former chief executive, Charles Tapp, however, publicly distanced himself from Fennell's comments. He acknowledged that "we are going to be feeding people who have been perpetrating genocide," but considered that "our remit is to provide humanitarian assistance. That is what we have to do."[134] UNHCR also faced calls for its withdrawal from the Rwandan refugee camps from internal staff and external advisers. Internally, calls for the deployment of an international military presence resounded, and one position paper suggested that if no such assistance eventuates, "UNHCR should seriously consider and be prepared to pull out."[135] The paper suggested that a United Nations Border Relief Operation (UNBRO)–style organization

[132] Cited in Ray Wilkinson, "The Heart of Darkness," *Refugees*, no. 110 (Winter 1997): 5–13 at p. 9.

[133] Dominique Martin, "Face à l'inacceptable dans les camps de réfugiés ruandais" (Paris: MSF mimeo, n.d.), pp. 2–3.

[134] Mark Huband, "Aid or Justice for Rwanda?" *Observer*, 31 July 1994, as cited in *Rwanda: Death, Despair, and Defiance*, p. 1091.

[135] S. Lombardo and K. Paul, *Position Paper on International Protection Issues in Eastern Zaire*, 20 October 1994, as cited in *Lessons Learned from the Burundi and Rwanda Emergencies*, p. 15.

could take the place of UNHCR, having no protection role but only relief functions.

Externally, Guy Goodwin-Gill, professor of international refugee law at Oxford University and a former senior legal research officer with UN-HCR, also questioned the logic of UNHCR's continued presence in the camps of Zaire. Pointing out that the UNHCR mandate is not to provide material assistance but is to protect refugees, he suggested that, after the initial emergency was over, some serious reanalysis should have been undertaken. "At that point, and in the face of the international community's unwillingness to take the necessary supportive steps, UNHCR's inability to fulfill its primary responsibility *to provide international protection* to refugees, let alone promote its declared objective of facilitating return, might well have conditioned a response to withdraw."[136]

The International Protection department of UNHCR, however, determined that "the mandatory function entrusted to UNHCR by the international community in assisting host countries to cope with refugee influxes . . . justifies our continued presence even under the most trying circumstances."[137] The high commissioner agreed. "My mandate—unlike those of private aid agencies—obliges me to help."[138] The clear censure Ogata received from Boutros-Ghali over her outspokenness during the Yugoslav crisis may also have influenced her decision not to defy the wishes of the UN leadership or UNHCR's main donor governments. Moreover, there were fears inside UNHCR that a withdrawal could make the organization irrelevant in refugee contexts of the future, particularly in light of the growing aversion to refugee asylum and erosion of the central tenets of refugee protection.[139] Such a fear was not unfounded: the dominant role of NATO in providing for the Kosovar refugees in 1999 shows how easily UNHCR can be marginalized. Thus UNHCR remained present in the camps.

THE IMPERATIVE TO REMAIN

UNHCR played an unenviable role in the Rwandan refugee crisis as intermediary between the various stakeholders. The organization was required

[136] Guy Goodwin-Gill, "Rwanda-Zaire: Refugee Camps and the Protection of Refugees," *International Journal of Refugee Law* 8, no. 4 (1996): 630–639 at p. 632.

[137] A paper presented to the High Commissioner by the Director of International Protection on 18 November 1994, cited in *Lessons Learned from the Burundi and Rwanda Emergencies*, p. 16.

[138] Cited in Wilkinson, "The Heart of Darkness," p. 9.

[139] Jean-François Durieux, UNHCR Geneva, personal communication, 8 August 1997.

to contend constantly with the conflicting demands of the Zairean authorities, the refugees, the camp leadership, the Rwandan government, the NGOs, and the institutional donors while trying to uphold its own mandate to provide protection to refugees. The UN explored several options to alleviate the problems in the camps, including moving the camps farther from the border and hiring a private security firm to police them, but these were rejected on financial and logistical grounds.[140] The lack of alternatives placed the onus on UNHCR to find a "durable solution" to the crisis, the obvious being repatriation to Rwanda. But the challenge was to reconcile the principles embedded in refugee law, particularly with regard to the voluntary nature of repatriation and security guarantees for returnees, with the competing demands of the donors and the Rwandan government to resolve the refugee problem and of the refugees to remain in exile.

In the latter half of 1994, UNHCR withstood considerable pressures from other UN agencies and donors and suspended its role in repatriation because of concerns raised in the Gersony Report about the safety of returnees. By December repatriation resumed, but the number of returnees dropped from 800 per day in February to none following the Kibeho massacre in April 1995.[141] The refugee refoulement from Zaire in August shifted UNHCR's priority from facilitating repatriation to promoting it,[142] and initiatives such as cross-border visits and information campaigns were launched to counter the extremist propaganda in the camps. The limited success of these endeavors led to increased pressure from the donors, particularly the United States, to compromise some of the principles of refugee asylum for a resolution to the refugee problem. The attack on the camps preempted such a move toward the refugees in Zaire, but UNHCR became less averse to forced repatriation from Tanzania in December

---

[140] In September and October 1994 a joint UNHCR/UNAMIR team inspected sites proposed by the government of Zaire on which to construct military camps. Even had the military been willing to move, the option was still judged to be too costly and logistically difficult. See *Impact of Military Personnel and the Military Presence*, p. 9. The UN Secretariat also explored the possibility of contracting a private security organization for the camps, but the $60 million per year price tag "undoubtedly contributed to the option being discarded": *Refugee Camp Security in the Great Lakes Region*, p. 11. UNHCR has also been reluctant to engage private security firms for reasons of principle and accountability, and because such a measure would detract from the responsibility of host states to ensure the security and the humanitarian and civilian character of refugee camps. See *The Security, and Civilian and Humanitarian Character of Refugee Camps and Settlements*, EC/49/SC/INF.2, Executive Committee of the High Commissioner's Programme, Geneva, 14 January 1999, paragraph 16.

[141] UNHCR, *State of the World's Refugees 1995: In Search of Solutions* (Oxford: Oxford University Press, 1995), p. 33.

[142] See *Rwanda and Burundi. The Return Home*, p. 49.

1996, which drew sharp criticism from many organizations.[143] Throughout the period UNHCR shifted its approach to the refugee issue in accordance with the latest priority, determined by the actions of the multiple stakeholders in the crisis. UNHCR invoked the obligations contained in its mandate as a rationale for remaining in the refugee camps, but ultimately failed to ensure either the legal or the physical protection of the Rwandan refugees.

NGOs remaining in the Rwandan refugee camps had no such mandate requirements, adhering instead to self-imposed regulations and objectives. The importance aid organizations placed on the ethical issues raised by the Rwandan crisis varied greatly. Of those that considered their presence within an ethical framework, the majority prioritized the humanitarian imperative to give assistance wherever it is needed, and relegated responsibility for the outcomes to the political domain. Five main, though overlapping, areas of argument and approach can be identified among the NGOs who continued to work in the camps: adherence to the humanitarian imperative in itself, the belief in a possibility of change, a pragmatic focus on technical service delivery, a business or institutional logic, and an ideological commitment to amend the "victimization" of the Hutu people. Most approaches contained elements of each.

The imperative to assist members of humanity regardless of who they are or what they have done was invoked by many organizations. Indeed, neutrality for some meant refraining from making judgments about who did and who did not warrant assistance. All in need were entitled to aid, the purpose of which was not to solve the crisis or address the causes, but to treat the symptoms. The rest was inherently political and thus not compatible with the neutral and impartial nature of aid. Peter Walker of the International Federation of Red Cross and Red Crescent Societies (IFRCRC), a staunch defender of the humanitarian imperative, considered that leaving the camps was analogous to refusing to treat an injured drunk driver in order to prevent the driver from repeating the act.[144]

Considerations of the potential longer-term consequences of the camps, including their possible role in the prolongation of conflict, caused consternation among many agencies but was ultimately deemed to be the

[143] Raymond Bonner, "Refugee Agency's Rwanda Policy Is Assailed," *International Herald Tribune*, 23 December 1996, p. 7.

[144] Peter Walker, Director of Disaster and Refugee Policy, IFRCRC, interview, 5 August 1997. IFRCRC is not an NGO but worked in the Rwandan camps by choice rather than by mandate.

responsibility of the political actors who had failed to meet their responsibilities to ensure the civilian nature of the camps. Some agencies also disputed that the outcome would inevitably be pernicious and argued that the short-term consequences could be more accurately predicted than those of the future. Nick Stockton of Oxfam, for example, argued that the removal of water distribution services from the camps was more certain to provoke a large loss of life than the future of the refugee camps per se.[145] Oxfam frequently debated withdrawing but decided to remain, judging that the rights of the refugees to receive aid superseded the problems derived from supplying it. It was considered to be morally and legally unacceptable to achieve a punishment by withdrawing rights.[146] One set of rights, it was argued, cannot be sacrificed to achieve another.

While debating many of these issues, some NGOs were swayed in their decision to stay by a commitment to try to influence the way the camps were administered to minimize the perverse effects of humanitarian assistance. Some, such as the Dutch and Belgian sections of MSF, felt that their ability to continue to lobby for change in the camps would be jeopardized by leaving.[147] Organizations have far greater access to information and stronger legitimacy when operational than on the sidelines, and continued operations could be used to engage donors more in the process they were financing. Hence some NGOs worked together to pressure for changes in the camps and, through conducting a *"résistance humanitaire,"*[148] managed to reduce the quantity of aid resources that were diverted to the military. As mentioned earlier, a coalition of NGOs lobbied for change and threatened to withdraw from the camps in Zaire unless security conditions and access to the vulnerable improved.[149] They also advocated for and assisted in conducting censuses to reduce inflated population figures, and together reduced the number and salaries of local employees, previously higher than for equivalent positions in Rwanda, to limit the tax imposed by the military. Furthermore, the payment of local salaries was changed from

[145] Nick Stockton, Emergencies Director, Oxfam, personal interview, 22 August 1997.
[146] Ibid.
[147] MSF produced two reports aimed at lobbying for change, *Breaking the Cycle* (Amsterdam: MSF, November 1994) and *Deadlock in the Rwandan Refugee Crisis: Virtual Standstill on Repatriation* (Brussels: MSF International, July 1995). The remaining MSF sections withdrew from the camps in late 1995.
[148] Alex Parisel, General Director of MSF in Brussels (formerly the head of MSF-B in Goma), personal communication, 7 January 1999.
[149] The NGOs which signed the petition were: MSF (3 sections), CARE (6 sections), IRC, American Refugee Committee, Farmacenticos sin Fronteras, Centre Canadien d'Étude et de la Coopération Internationale, Oxfam, and Médecins du Monde.

U.S. dollars to local currency among the larger NGOs. Implementing these changes was dangerous in the insecure context of Zaire,[150] and personnel of aid organizations received death threats and were menaced. Nevertheless, some of the lobbying had a positive effect, and security in the camps improved.

The third and most prevalent approach adopted by NGOs was a pragmatic focus on the technical provision of relief. As the earlier case studies illustrated, this technocratic focus tends to judge the success and failure of programs by the achievement of practical standards such as the number of liters of water available per person, the malnutrition rates in the camps, the vaccination coverage achieved, or the numbers of children attending school. The Joint Evaluation of Emergency Assistance to Rwanda exemplified this perspective, assessing the performance of NGOs according to professional standards. It ignored the ethical issues. The only reference made to the withdrawal of MSF from the camps was in relation to service delivery: "This withdrawal meant that other agencies, in some cases less experienced than MSF-France, had to take-over the services provided by the agency. The [Joint Evaluation] Team were unable to assess the extent to which this had a negative impact on the quality of services provided to the refugees in those camps where MSF-France had worked."[151]

By ignoring the ethical issues and emphasizing technical standards, some of the NGOs undermined efforts of agencies that were striving to minimize the abuse of aid. The levels of assistance provided to the camps was disproportionate to that given to local Zairean and Tanzanian populations and to the interior of Rwanda. Of the total emergency assistance provided by donors from April to December 1994, only one-third was spent inside Rwanda,[152] and much of that was allocated to the internally displaced Hutu populations. The Rwandan government resented the disparities in aid. Relatively sophisticated vocational training and psychosocial programs were being conducted in the camps while funding requests to enable rudimentary improvements to the justice system in Rwanda were

[150] In Tanzania threats were also made against staff, but fewer agencies actively challenged the misuse of aid. Concern was the only agency responsible for food distributions that attempted to change the system to minimize diversions. The attempt in the Lumasi camp was successful. See Johan Pottier, "Why Aid Agencies Need Better Understanding of the Communities They Assist: The Experience of Food Aid in Rwandan Refugee Camps," *Disasters* 20, no. 4 (1996): 324–337.

[151] Borton, Brusset, and Hallam, "Humanitarian Aid and Its Effects," p. 48 n. 36.

[152] Tor Sellström and Lennart Wohlgemuth, "Historical Perspective: Some Explanatory Factors," Study 1 of *The International Response to Conflict and Genocide: Lessons from the Rwanda Experience*, p. 5. See n. 61 above for the disparities in U.S. allocations to the regional humanitarian crisis vis-à-vis Rwanda, which exemplifies this larger trend.

ignored, in spite of the widespread acknowledgment that justice was a prerequisite to breaking the cycle of impunity that plagued the country.

While rejecting the idea that refugees anywhere prefer to remain in camps due to the services provided than return to their homes, UNHCR and the NGO coalition considered that the special nature of the Rwandan camps warranted reduction of services to a minimum to curb aid abuses by the former regime and encourage repatriation. They implemented changes and encouraged other agencies to do likewise, but some NGOs continued to make camp improvements and to increase the number of refugees employed.[153] Moreover, some NGOs ignored the ethical implications of having génocidaires on their payrolls and did not screen either existing or new recruits.[154]

An element of institutional logic influenced the way many NGOs working in the camps reacted to the crisis. There can be a thin line between lobbying for action to prevent or stem a crisis and raising the funds necessary to react to it. NGOs are dependent on securing finance to mount an operation through contracts with the UN, project funding from donor agencies, and contributions from the general public or private corporations. Advertising is expensive, so when the media cover a disaster, the free publicity for organizations interviewed or filmed is of immeasurable worth. For many, the intense media coverage of the refugee exodus and cholera epidemic in Goma meant that they could not afford not to be present.[155] Thus the necessity to find a niche and become operational took precedence for many over analyzing the context. And once lucrative contracts were obtained from UN and donor agencies, the prospect of leaving became even more remote since it could jeopardize all future relationships with the donors.[156]

The compulsion to be visible generated competition among aid organizations, particularly in Goma. Flags, stickers, and T-shirts bearing the logos of organizations, once a protective measure to alert belligerent parties

[153] See Jeff Drumtra, *Rwandan Refugees: Updated Findings and Recommendations* (Washington, D.C.: U.S. Committee for Refugees, October 1995), p. 4.

[154] Ibid.

[155] Save the Children–UK did not intervene in Goma owing to a lack of available resources, thereby forgoing considerable fundraising revenue, a decision which some members of the organization such as the future representative of SCF in Rwanda, David Shearer, thought was foolish. John Seaman, one of the senior directors in London, however, believes that the delay provided "the luxury of a period of thought." SCF avoided the moral turmoil by working only on reconstruction in Rwanda. Personal communications, August 1997.

[156] The relationship between UNHCR and the French section of MSF deteriorated markedly as a result of the withdrawal. UNHCR asked how they could rely upon MSF in the future.

to a humanitarian presence, became turf markers in the battle to secure a niche. In an article titled "Did you see me in Goma? War of Logos in the Supermarket of NGOs," Richard Dowden remarked that the atmosphere in Goma gave the impression that an election was under way, with the agencies "exhibiting their name and their logo in the manner of soft-drink manufacturers."[157] The stiffest competition revolved around media-friendly tasks such as managing orphanages and organizing family re-unions. Constructing latrines and spraying for vector control rarely sparks the imagination of journalists the way that orphan babies do. Thus for many aid organizations operating in Zaire, the priority was to mount a high-profile program, raise the organization's level of exposure at home, and replenish bank accounts to ensure the continued viability of the organization as a whole.

Finally, there were some aid agencies present in the Rwandan refugee camps which sympathized with the cause espoused by the Hutu hard-liners and assisted the refugee leaders to this end. Most aid workers were influenced by the context in which they worked and their relationships with the local population, and expressed compassion for the predicament of the refugees. But for a few agencies, particularly those attached to the Catholic church, support went beyond this. Caritas provided food to the Panzi and Bulonge military camps near Bukavu and defended their decision to the Human Rights Watch Arms Project, saying that Caritas had "no choice" because no other organization was prepared to feed them and that "they have to eat, they are not all murderers."[158] The decision was further justified in the Caritas Information Report No. 7 of September 1995 as a preventive measure to stop camp inhabitants stealing food from other refugees: "The starving refugees of Bulonge will not let the WFP trucks pass to distribute goods to their neighbors in Cimanga, and those of Panzi will probably try to stop and to pillage the trucks destined for Nyangezi."[159] Such an image of destitute and starving military personnel is at odds with evidence I reviewed earlier, but if this were true, a case could

[157] Richard Dowden, "M'as-tu vu à Goma? Guerre des logos au supermarché des ONG," *Courier International* no. 202 (15–21 September 1994): 33 (reprinted from the *Independent on Sunday*).

[158] *Rwanda/Zaire: Rearming with Impunity*, p. 16 n. 67.

[159] Abbé Pierre Cibambo, "Caritas—Info no. 7" (Bukavu, September 1995) in Philippe de Dorlodot (ed.), *Les réfugiés rwandais à Bukavu au Zaïre: De nouveaux Palestiniens?* (Paris: Groupe Jérémie and L'Harmattan, 1996), pp. 225–232 at p. 232. This book contains a collection of articles, speeches, information reports, and letters written by Catholic groups in Bukavu.

perhaps be made for such a pragmatic approach. Other messages emanating from Caritas and its associate organizations under the church umbrella, however, indicate that their sympathies were biased against the new Rwandan regime. Claims of a double genocide permeate articles written by Caritas staff[160] and documents produced by religious reflection groups in Bukavu.[161] Furthermore, François Nzabahimana, director of the RDR, was formerly the president of the executive committee of the White Father missionary society's periodical *Dialogue* and had strong links with the Bukavu groups. His material received endorsement through publication in the collection of works by the Groupe Jérémie, a religious association for the promotion of peace, democracy, and human rights, including the RDR declaration and a report citing the presence of 4 million refugees in Zaire.[162] The work was published in 1996, long after the RDR was known to follow a hard-line agenda.

The question remains, then, of the extent to which aid organizations that supported the camps share responsibility for the consequences. The death of 4,000 camp inhabitants owing to violence in the camps, mentioned earlier, is significant in itself. But the destruction of the camps and massacres that followed claimed many more victims. Had the AFDL not routed the refugees back to Rwanda—the timing of which suggests that its aim was to quash the rationale for an international military intervention that might otherwise have interfered with the push for Kinshasa—the consequences might have been worse. As it is, the total cost in human lives is still not known: by July 1997, UNHCR recorded a return to Rwanda of 834,000 refugees, and another 52,000 were located in Zaire and its neighboring countries, leaving some 213,000 unaccounted for.[163] Thousands of

[160] See, for example, Alphonse Ngamije, Agent de la Caritas à Goma, "Réfugiés rwandais: Quel avenir?" *Dialogue*, no. 181 (March 1995): 27–32 at p. 31.

[161] A piece written on 26 July 1994 by Philippe de Dorlodot, the editor of the collection of texts from the Catholic church, discusses the treasonous betrayal that the Hutu felt at the loss of their country to the minority Tutsi. He states that an objective view of Rwandan history is indispensable to understanding the stakes, particularly "the will of the minority Tutsi to reconquer the power." He claimed that the West was manipulated and ill informed about facts concerning the Hutu-Tutsi problem. "There are *two genocides in Rwanda*." "Quelques vérités sur l'enfer rwandais," in Dorlodot (ed.), *Les réfugiés rwandais à Bukavu au Zaïre*, pp. 88–89 at p. 88.

[162] François Nzabahimana, "La situation dans les camps," and François Nzabahimana, "Rassemblement pour le Retour et la Démocratie au Rwanda (RDR)," in Dorlodot (ed.), *Les réfugiés rwandais à Bukavu au Zaïre*, pp. 134–136 and pp. 179–181 respectively.

[163] UNHCR, *The State of the World's Refugees: A Humanitarian Agenda* (Oxford: Oxford University Press, 1997), p. 23. The number of refugees who fled west was the subject of acrimonious debate in the wake of the offensive, and diverted attention from the crucial issue of how to assist these people.

these are known to have been killed.[164] Thus the aid regime established to protect the refugees actually endangered them.

In chapter 1 I noted two important factors to be considered in apportioning liability: the knowledge on which aid organizations based their decisions, and their capacity to have acted differently. If we look briefly at each in turn, it is interesting how few agencies referred to past experience gained when working in militarized refugee camps. The previous chapters demonstrated the similarity of problems faced by aid agencies in other refugee contexts, particularly Cambodia, yet few in the aid community reflected on the parallels. Aid organizations also had forewarning of the possible destruction of the camps, as Kagame repeated his threat on several occasions. Doubts about the Rwandan government's determination to resolve problems of this kind should have been dispelled by the massacre at Kibeho in April 1995. Thus aid organizations could not claim ignorance of the manipulation of humanitarian action in the camps, the threats made to close them, or the consequences of the militarization of refugee camps in the past for the welfare of the refugees and future stability of the country.

Their capacity to change the situation, however, was more limited. Not having the capability to remove the former regime from the refugee camps, aid agencies could only choose between remaining or withdrawing. Most rejected the option of withdrawal; Hugo Slim says that to have withheld aid meant working on the principle of "doing evil that good may come"—a principle that he says would make an absurdity of the humanitarian mandate of relief agencies.[165] But the idea that withholding aid is doing evil presumes that external aid is indispensable to the survival of the refugees. This assumption warrants challenging; even a cursory glance at results of the Rwandan refugee return suggests that aid organizations may exaggerate their importance to the survival of vulnerable populations.

Once forced back from Zaire, the refugees were required by the Rwandan government to return immediately to their home communes. The establishment of transit or internally displaced person (IDP) camps was prohibited to avoid problems like those of Kibeho resurfacing, and aid activities were restricted to the provision of dry food, water, and emer-

---

[164] See Bradol and Guibert, "Le temps des assassins," pp. 144–148.

[165] Hugo Slim, *Doing the Right Thing—Relief Agencies, Moral Dilemmas, and Moral Responsibility in Political Emergencies and War,* Report no. 6, Studies on Emergencies and Disaster Relief (Uppsala: Nordiska Afrikainstitutet, 1997), pp. 12–13.

gency medical care at way-stations along the road. The aid organizations were indignant about their restricted role, which was further reduced during the refugee repatriation from Tanzania in which only two aid organizations, the Rwandan Red Cross and IFRCRC, were authorized to assist. The result, however, was that road congestion was minimized and the refugees returned to their home communes with few problems that the presence of aid personnel could have averted.[166] This was not the first time that successful relief operations were mounted with minimal or no assistance from international agencies: relief programs for Sahrawi refugees in Algeria in the 1970s and Afghan refugees in Iran in the 1980s were undertaken without international aid. In Iran, over 2 million refugees were integrated into the local community without the establishment of parallel services as occurred for the Afghan refugees in Pakistan. And when UNHCR personnel gained access to the Sahrawi refugee camps in the Algerian desert in the 1980s, they found the camps to be so well organized that no further intervention was necessary.[167] The assumption that the withdrawal of assistance necessarily condemns refugees to an unacceptable fate does not withstand scrutiny.

A further point to consider in any assessment of the responsibility of aid organizations for the consequences of the camps is that the choice they faced between remaining or withdrawing arose because others had already failed to uphold their responsibilities. The belligerents on both sides failed to respect international humanitarian law obliging a distinction between combatants and noncombatants, and governments failed in their responsibility to uphold and enforce such laws in refugee camps. Aid organizations do not inherit the responsibilities that others have failed to meet, but to be absolved of fault, is it enough for them to decry the "humanitarian alibi" and blame the international community for its lack of political courage? After all, if Ambassador Aldo Ajello, special envoy of the European Union to the Great Lakes Region, blames the "international community" for the

---

[166] It should be mentioned, however, that the absence of a major cholera outbreak among refugees returning from Zaire was probably due to enduring partial immunity to the disease, since the entire population of Goma was infected with the cholera bacterium in 1994 (only a small percentage of cholera infections result in severe symptoms). No one is sure how long such immunity lasts, but the low incidence in 1996 suggests that it could be for two or more years. Of those who did contract the infectious disease, the case-fatality rates were low owing to the preparation and skill of aid workers. I am grateful to Dr. Ron Waldman of the Program on Health Consequences of Forced Migration at Columbia University for a discussion of this point (11 January 1999).

[167] Peter Hakewill, former UNHCR medical coordinator, personal communication, January 1999.

Great Lakes crisis,[168] as does Bill Richardson, U.S. ambassador to the United Nations,[169] who or what is the "international community"? It seems to be a nebulous entity to which all blame can be apportioned with no responsibility assumed.

There has to be a point at which aid organizations acknowledge that by choosing to intervene and professing to alleviate suffering they undertake certain responsibilities to the people whose expectations they raise. Furthermore, they should acknowledge that they are part and parcel of the system they lament. While criticizing the humanitarian alibi, aid organizations are accepting the government funds that create the façade. In a sense, by fulfilling the duty to aid and appeasing public consciences aroused by the sight of suffering, aid agencies are inadvertently permitting states to abrogate their higher-order responsibilities of prevention and protection.

Exploring some of the broader policies pursued by donor governments with respect to the Rwandan crisis raises further questions about how aid organizations can reconcile their duty to vulnerable populations with the often conflicting concerns of the institutions that finance their activities. The attainment of stability, however superficial, was the principal policy pursued by donors in Rwanda in the aftermath of the genocide, superseding all other issues, including human rights and justice. It is ironic that the same donor community that funded the largest source of insecurity to Rwanda sought stability inside the country to such an extent that it suppressed the Gersony Report, which alleged serious human rights abuses by members of the new regime.[170] Although donors were justifiably embarrassed to censure human rights abuses of the Rwandan government after having done nothing to stop the genocide and permitting génocidaires to live with impunity in UN-sponsored refugee camps, the dismissal of excesses as "normal" after such a tragedy aided the rise of hard-liners in the government at the expense of the moderates.[171] Donors had leverage with

---

[168] Aldo Ajello, Opening Statement at the Second International Berlin Workshop, *Improving African and International Capabilities for Preventing and Resolving Violent Conflict: The Great Lakes Region Crisis*, 3–5 July 1997 (Berlin: Stiftung Wissenschaft und Politik), pp. 35–39.

[169] Bill Richardson was quoted in Gourevitch, "Continental Shift," p. 52, saying: "The failure of the international community to respond adequately to both the genocide and the subsequent mixing of genocidal killers with the legitimate refugee population in the former eastern Zaire only served to prolong the crisis."

[170] The Joint Evaluation of Emergency Assistance to Rwanda remarked that the Gersony Report was suppressed because "had it been officially released at the time it would have reduced the legitimacy of the new government and severely jeopardized efforts by UN agencies and many of the donor organizations to assist the new government to establish an effective administration." Borton, Brusset, and Hallam, "Humanitarian Aid and Effects,", p. 49 n. 49.

[171] Three senior Hutu members of the government were sacked in August 1995: the prime minister, Faustin Twagiramungu, the minister of the interior, Seth Sendashonga, and the

the new government; when cautionary representations were made in the wake of the Gersony Report and prior to the donor conference of January 1995 in Geneva, the killings dropped markedly.[172] But once the $587 million was pledged, "the killing spree started again," according to former Interior Minister Seth Sendashonga,[173] culminating in the Kibeho massacre of April 1995.

The international reaction to the Kibeho massacre and its aftermath exemplified the political expediency dominating donor policies toward Rwanda. Although several donors suspended nonhumanitarian aid to Rwanda following the massacre to show their concern at the human rights violations,[174] aid was resumed within one month upon the publication of the report of an International Independent Commission of Inquiry into the massacre,[175] despite the flagrant sham the commission created. Four features of the commission and its findings are particularly salient. First, the legitimacy and independence of the commission were highly questionable. It was proposed by and answerable to the accused party, the Rwandan government, and the appointed Rwandan representative was Christine Umutoni, a former Director of Cabinet and part of the Ugandan inner circle (*Akazu*) of the RPF.[176] Created as an ad hoc body, the commission was

---

minister of justice, Alphonse-Marie Nkubito. Twagiramungu, in particular, had been publicly critical of the "parallel government" which had formed its own army and a "ministry of walkie-talkies" from the diverse secret service organizations. See Stephen Smith, "Twagiramungu, martyr de la réconciliation," *Libération*, 30 August 1995, p. 6. See also Prunier, *Rwanda: Update to End July 1995*, for a discussion of the rise of hard-liners to power within the government.

[172] *Leave None to Tell the Story*, p. 14.

[173] Seth Sendashonga's outspoken criticism of the Rwandan government after his departure led to an attempt on his life in Nairobi in February 1996. The would-be assassin, Francis Mugabo, was in charge of visas at the Rwandan embassy in Nairobi. Since he held diplomatic immunity, he was deported to Rwanda. Sendashonga was murdered in May 1998, shot in his car on his way home from a meeting. Gérard Prunier, personal communication, 17 November 1999.

[174] The United States suspended nonhumanitarian assistance; Belgium suspended part of its bilateral aid; and the Netherlands and the European Union froze their assistance. The British, by contrast, took no punitive action. Anton Barré, David Shearer, and Peter Uvin, with contributions from Christian Scherrer, *The Limits and Scope for the Use of Development Assistance and Disincentives for Influencing Conflict Situations, Case Study: Rwanda* (Paris: Informal Task Force on Conflict, Peace and Development Co-operation, Development Assistance Committee, OECD, 1999), p. 18.

[175] The commission, officially established on 27 April 1995, consisted of ten members, representing France, Belgium, Canada, the United States, the United Kingdom, the Netherlands, Rwanda, the Organisation of African Unity, and the UN. It submitted its report to the Rwandan government on 18 May 1995.

[176] See Jean-Pierre Mugabe, "The Killings Resume: Preparing for the Next Rwandan War," *Strategic Policy*, no. 4, 1999, http://www.strategicstudies.org/crisis/rwanda.htm. Umutoni was probably the only Kinyarwanda speaker among the commission members, giving

not accountable to an established institution, a situation making for minimum potential follow-up.

Second, and indicative of its lack of independence, the commission failed to determine even a range of the number of deaths at Kibeho. The Rwandan government alleged 334 fatalities, and the UN counted 4,000, although it revised the official figure to 2,000. The commission avoided comment, suggesting on the one hand that "the numbers are more than those formally counted in the Kibeho camp," and on the other noting "the unusual discrepancy between the various initial counts and estimates of fatalities and the actual number of non-fatal casualties, suggesting over-estimation in the initial fatality counts and estimates."[177] Even if one puts aside the obvious alternative—that all the injured were killed—it is surprising that an estimate could not be made considering the presence of a forensic specialist on the investigative team and the testimony of UN peacekeepers who physically counted 4,000 dead and 650 wounded with a pace counter before they were halted by an RPA patrol.[178]

Third, because of the omission or glazing over of important facts, the report was biased in favor of the government position. For example, despite mentioning that of the 70,000 IDPs who had returned home from Kibeho by March 1995, 60 percent had subsequently stayed in their communes (hence 40 percent had not),[179] the commission failed to acknowledge the legitimate fears that the IDPs had of conditions at home. These included widespread incidents of violence and insecurity throughout the country; the growing number of arrests of genocide suspects, many of whom even the government admitted were innocent;[180] and the illegal occupation of houses by returnees from the Tutsi diaspora, complaints against whom could result in false accusations of guilt and hence imprisonment. Instead, the commission emphasized the Rwandan government rationale for wanting the camps closed, primarily strong suspicions that the camps sheltered

---

her privileged access to interviewees. It would be interesting to know whether the government provided the translators for the commission members.

[177] *Report of the Independent International Commission of Inquiry on the Events at Kibeho, April 1995*, submitted to the Government of Rwanda, 18 May 1995, Kigali, p. 10.

[178] Colonel Peter Warfe, "Recent Examples of the Application of International Humanitarian Law in Conflict Situations," address to the Australian Red Cross National Conference, International Humanitarian Law: The Challenge of Effective Implementation, 22–23 July 1999, Hobart. Colonel Warfe was the force medical officer of the Australian contingent in UNAMIR II in April 1995. In spite of the number of dead counted by the Australians, the official UNAMIR death figure was put at 2,000. Warfe says that this figure was a compromise between numbers submitted by the force provost marshall, the Zambian Battalion, and the Australian troops. Military observers also reported seeing the RPA exhuming bodies in the camp and transporting them elsewhere.

[179] *Report of the Independent International Commission of Inquiry*, p. 6.

[180] Adelman and Suhrke, "Early Warning and Conflict Management," p. 94 n. 132.

génocidaires who were responsible for continuing instability in the south. The commission found that the action of the RPA was "disproportionate and, therefore, violative of international law," but offered five factors as explanations, bordering on justifications, for the slaughter, including deficiencies in communication, equipment, training, and experience. These findings partly explain the reluctance of the commission to verify the number of deaths: at some point the argument in favor of the "accidental" nature of the killings would have been hard to sustain.

The fourth feature and *pièce de résistance* of the report is that it apportions responsibility for the deaths at Kibeho among the RPA, NGOs, UNAMIR, and the unidentified armed elements among the IDPs. In other words, the report concludes that the failure of UNAMIR and the aid agencies to persuade or coerce the internally displaced to leave the camp carried the same weight as opening fire with machine guns on a crowd of detained men, women, and children. Having effectively excused the Rwandan authorities of wrongdoing and paved the way for the resumption of aid, the report closes with the recommendation to the international community "to continue encouraging and assisting the Rwandan Republic in its efforts to achieve justice, national reconciliation and reconstruction."[181] It was only a small step from "resolving" the IDP problem at Kibeho to "resolving" the refugee problem in Zaire, and all in tune with the donors' objectives.

In many respects it is not the commission's report in itself that is most tragic; inaccurate or biased reports are nothing new. It is the acceptance of such an overtly flawed report by donor governments, journalists, the UN, and NGOs alike. Rather than challenging the validity of the findings and uniting to denounce the violation of human rights and reassert humanitarian principles, international agencies blamed each other and further deflected responsibility from the people who undertook the killing. Philip Gourevitch, one of the apologists for the Kibeho massacre, cites the deputy chief of the UN Human Rights Mission in Rwanda, Mark Frohardt, as saying:

> I have no intention of trying to justify the manner in which Kibeho was closed . . . but I do believe that it is important to understand that the inability of the relief organizations to coordinate a successful operation set the stage for the tragedy that followed. Once the army saw that the efforts of relief agencies to move people out of the camps were ineffective, they knew

---

[181] *Report of the Independent International Commission of Inquiry*, p. 13.

they were the only institution, or force, in the country capable of closing the camps.[182]

In spite of his role as a human rights official, he seems to suggest that aid organizations should have transported people home against their will and with no guarantee of safety, in order to avoid a massacre he intimates was otherwise inevitable. Yet to blame NGOs for the massacre is absurd. The men who ordered and carried out the killings are to blame for the massacre. Aid agencies had stopped providing assistance to the camp and had no access to the population. After that, the refusal to participate in such a process is a legitimate ethical choice. As Rony Brauman has written in reference to other situations, "deciding to act means knowing, at least approximately, why action is preferable to abstention."[183] Had international personnel been aware that the RPA would open fire on the displaced population if they did not leave the camps, then they were obliged to pressure the Rwandan government to prevent human rights abuses, rather than participate in the violation of one set of rights to achieve another.

The DPKO "lessons-learned" report absolves the Rwandan regime of responsibility even more thoroughly, not even mentioning the bullets, but blaming a lack of coordination for the massacre:

> One instance when the coordination mechanism of the integrated operations center failed was in the Kibeho camp for internally displaced people in late April, 1995. The government's decision to close the camp, by force if necessary, resulted in a stampede in which many people lost their lives. Some of those interviewed stated that if the government, UNAMIR and the humanitarian community had coordinated well with each other by providing transportation and allowing sufficient time to those who were willing to return to their home communes, some lives could have been saved.[184]

Even a recent Organisation for Economic Co-operation and Development study analyzing the role of official development assistance in producing incentives and disincentives for conflict failed to question any aspect of the commission's report despite the weight that it carried in the resumption of donor funding. Although it constitutes an important finding in itself, the

---

[182] Philip Gourevitch, *We Wish to Inform You That Tomorrow We Will Be Killed with Our Families: Stories from Rwanda* (New York: Farrar, Straus and Giroux, 1998), p. 205.

[183] Rony Brauman, "Refugee Camps, Population Transfers, and NGOs," in Jonathan Moore (ed.), *Hard Choices: Moral Dilemmas in Humanitarian Intervention* (Oxford: Rowman and Littlefield, 1998), p. 192.

[184] *Comprehensive Report on Lessons Learned from United Nations Assistance Mission for Rwanda (UNAMIR), October 1993–April 1996*, p. 35.

report notes only with relation to the Kibeho incident that the policies pursued by individual donor nations and the European Union were "if not directly conflicting, at least inconsistent."[185] The Rwandan regime had skillfully deflected attention away from its strong-arm tactics and laid the blame on the aid community for supporting the structure. It was a dress rehearsal for the refugee camps in Zaire eighteen months later.

Conclusion: Shedding Responsibility

Some significant points arise from the Rwandan case. First, the refugee camps played a vital role in the insurgency against the Rwandan regime. Although the former Rwandan government and army fled to Zaire with considerable financial and material assets, it was the humanitarian sanctuary that permitted their continued survival as an entity until late 1996. Despite the professionalism of the ex-FAR and government-in-exile on paper, benefit of hindsight illustrates that the former government and army never had the capacity to reinvade Rwanda successfully. The refugees were the crucial bargaining chips in the former regime's plan to start negotiations with Kigali, and the camp structures helped to keep the population in exile. In addition, the guerrilla attacks launched from Zaire helped to keep loyal supporters mobilized, sabotaged reconstruction and reconciliation efforts inside Rwanda, and generated reprisals against the Hutu population which added weight to the hard-liner discourse promulgated in the camps. Thus rather than playing a complementary role to a military strategy supported by external patrons, the Rwandan refugee camps and the humanitarian aid therein guaranteed the survival of the genocidal force.

Second, in spite of the knowledge acquired by aid organizations in the past about the negative consequences of humanitarian action, these recurred and were more insidious than on previous occasions. Yet unlike in the Afghan, Cambodian, Salvadoran, or Nicaraguan refugee camps, for all but the pro-Hutu agencies working in the Rwandan camps the humanitarian aid was not misused in the name of a "just" cause. The vast majority of aid organizations did not justify their tolerance of the abuse of aid by appealing to a greater good that would be served by permitting the revival of the former Rwandan regime, and government donor funds were not channeled to the camps to serve this end. The paradoxes of humanitarian action were genuinely unintended.

[185] Barré, Shearer, and Uvin, *The Limits and Scope for the Use of Development Assistance and Disincentives for Influencing Conflict Situations*, p. 18.

Aid organizations share responsibility for some of the tragedies in the Great Lakes region since 1994 because by accepting the priorities and agendas of the government donors whose money they accept, they permit governments to abrogate their political responsibilities to address the more profound issues at the root of the crisis. Through half-hearted political engagement in the Rwandan crisis, donor governments assisted in the reemergence of extremists on both sides of the political and ethnic divide, with the resultant attack on the refugee camps and the erosion of norms of refugee protection. In the end, it is the people that aid organizations are trying to help and the principles protecting future populations that fall victim to the politically expedient policies of powerful states.

Moreover, by permitting humanitarian action to be manipulated, and dismissing an ethic of refusal, aid agencies risk seeing humanitarian action become a scapegoat for the failure of others to uphold their obligations and responsibilities. Senior U.S. officials like Brian Atwood and Leonard Rogers used their "revelation" in March 1997 about the perverse effects of humanitarian action to call for a future policy linking humanitarian aid more closely to U.S. foreign policy. In the *International Herald Tribune* they wrote:

> It now seems clear that in those camps more than a million people were controlled against their will by the perpetrators of genocide in Rwanda. . . . Shocking but true, the provision of humanitarian assistance by the United States, the European Union and others helped those who committed genocide to control these people for more than two years. . . . The future course seems clear: Humanitarian aid must be linked more closely to our foreign policy.[186]

Feigning ignorance of the militarized nature of the refugee camps and blaming aid for the problem was a shameless attempt to shed responsibility for the failures of political leaders to address all but the humanitarian consequences of the crisis from the outset. After all, this book has shown that the United States is one of the nations best acquainted with the role that refugee camps can play in war, yet the lessons of history are selectively applied. When U.S. officials raised the Khmer Rouge analogy, it was not to argue for a tougher stand against those responsible for genocide, but to

[186] J. Brian Atwood and Leonard Rogers, "Rethinking Humanitarian Aid in the New Era," *International Herald Tribune*, 12 March 1997, p. 10. At the time of writing, the authors were the administrator of the U.S. Agency for International Development and the acting administrator of its Bureau for Humanitarian Response, respectively.

advocate a less voluntary policy of repatriation. Richard McCall, chief of staff, USAID, ended his speech at the 1996 donor meeting with these words:

> I am still haunted by the role that humanitarian assistance and humanitarian sanctuary in Thailand played in guaranteeing the survival of the Khmer Rouge. We all tried to do the right thing, but we accomplished the wrong result. Nearly twenty years later, the people of Cambodia are still paying the price. The situation in the refugee camps, particularly in Zaire, is not unlike the choices we faced 20 years ago on Cambodia. And I very much hope that we do not repeat the same errors.[187]

For the aid organizations, operating in the Rwandan refugee camps involved difficult tradeoffs between competing moral principles. Most agencies decided to stay to meet the immediate needs of the population at the possible expense of future needs. Others decided that if they could not achieve what was just, they should at least not participate in what was obviously unjust. Weighing the pros and cons of each position is a difficult exercise, particularly when future events cannot be foretold. But there are few scenarios in humanitarian aid operations which had more relevant precedents and could be as accurately predicted as the Rwandan refugee context. The Rwandan crisis raises serious questions about honoring the humanitarian imperative above all else.

[187] U.S. statement delivered by Richard McCall to the Rwandan Roundtable Conference, Geneva, 20–21 June 1996, p. 6.

6

Humanitarian Action in a Second-Best World

As Narcisse and hundreds of thousands of his compatriots watched the international staff of aid organizations depart from Uvira, Bukavu, and Goma, they realized that they were alone to face the consequences of the misuse of the refugee camps. In spite of the millions of dollars pumped into the camps and the impressive technical achievements of the hundreds of aid organizations in providing adequate shelter, water, food, and sanitation in the hostile terrain of eastern Zaire, the refugees lacked the one element they needed most to survive: protection. With the best intentions, aid organizations had come to their assistance, and, with the gravest concerns for their future, the aid organizations withdrew. At that point aid agencies had realized the limits of humanitarian action, but it was too late. The limits has been exceeded long before, but they had continued to play along as if meeting the material needs of the refugees translated into a humanitarian act. Limiting their focus to the number of liters of water available per day and the vaccination coverage of children blinded them to the context in which the refugees were embroiled.

Fortunately, the sight of suffering in one part of the world generates a strong impulse in another to do something to alleviate that suffering. It mobilizes thousands of individuals from every nationality to dedicate their time, their resources, and sometimes their lives to uphold an ideal that people should not suffer. But, as we have seen, this noble gesture of solidarity can incur terrible paradoxes that vitiate efforts to improve conditions for those who suffer. Good intentions are not enough; humanitarian actors must recognize that their action and their inaction have important consequences for the people in whose name they intervene. By their presence, aid organizations convey a message to those who suffer that help is at hand, that the world is aware of their plight and will come to their rescue. It is a heavy responsibility to bear, but it is a responsibility that aid organizations need to assume if they genuinely want to work in the interest of victims. We can never construct the best world in which our compassion can immediately translate into an end to suffering, but we can try to build a second-best world based on hard-headed assessments of needs and options.

Rather than accepting the instrumentalization of humanitarian action to disguise overt political ends or a lack of political interest, humanitarian actors need to reclaim an activist role, reminding states that failure to meet their higher responsibilities is what allows crises to unfold in the first place. Humanitarian action no longer represents the ultimate expression of deontological reasoning, but incurs consequences that, whether intended or not, can undermine the very logic on which such action is based. Claims that potential consequences of relief operations cannot be predicted are flawed; the preceding chapters have shown the similarities of the paradoxes of humanitarian action in several cases. Realizing that past experience— even experience during the Cold War period—is relevant to the contemporary problems facing aid agencies is the first step to addressing them.

Some of the reasons for the persistence of the paradoxes of aid have been alluded to in the course of the book. This final chapter draws these together by exploring some of the institutional constraints aid organizations face in preventing the recurrence of negative effects, and some of the implications of these constraints for future humanitarian action. But first I review the main findings that emerged from the situations examined.

Refugee-Warriors and Humanitarian Action

THE RELATIONSHIP BETWEEN AID AND CONFLICT

How important was humanitarian action to the war efforts of belligerents? Table 3 presents a summary of the "performance" of each sanctuary, ranked from low to high. The judgment is based on the relative value of aspects of the humanitarian and military sanctuaries to each guerrilla movement; it is not a comparison between cases. Hence although the financial aid provided by the United States to the Nicaraguan contras in 1979–89 ($400 million) was less than one third of that provided to the Afghan mujahideen in 1980–87 ($1.5 billion), in both cases it eclipsed the relative contribution of aid to the war economy and thus both instances of financial aid are given a "high" rating.

The most prominent conclusion observable in the table supports Jean-Christophe Rufin's initial idea regarding the relative benefits of humanitarian sanctuaries: the legitimacy derived from refugees and the control mechanisms provided by refugee camp structures were the most consistently advantageous aspects of refugee camps to combatants. Insurgents who enjoyed strong support from host states and external patrons had less need of

Table 3. Relative benefits of military and humanitarian sanctuaries to guerrilla movements

| | PAKISTAN | HONDURAS | | THAILAND | ZAIRE |
| | Afghan | Nicaraguan | Salvadoran | Cambodian | Rwandan |
	mujahadeen	contras	FMLN	CGDK	Ex-FAR
Military sanctuary					
Protection	Med–High	High	Low	Medium	Medium
Military aid	High	High	Low	High	Low
Financial aid	High	High	Low	Med–High	Low
Political aid	High	High	Low	High	Low–Med
Humanitarian sanctuary					
Protection	Med–High	Low	Low–Med	Low	High/none[a]
War economy	Low	Low–Med	Low–Med	Med–High	High
Population control	Medium	Low	High	High	High
Legitimacy	High	Medium	Low–Med	High	High

[a] The camps provided a high level of protection until they were attacked and destroyed.

the protective functions of refugee camps, or of humanitarian aid to supply the war economy, than did those without such benefits. The Nicaraguan situation is largely the inverse of the Rwandan. External backers had little influence over relations between the guerrilla movement and the civilian population, so it was in facilitating this influence through controlling and legitimizing functions that refugee camps were most important.

This finding, although not astonishing in itself, has two implications. It provides weight to arguments that the end of superpower patronage of guerrilla factions is likely to increase the importance of other resources available to support war economies, one of which is humanitarian aid. The importance of humanitarian aid to the war economy is likely to be proportional to the resource base of the warring parties. In areas bereft of easily accessible and salable natural resources, such as Somalia, humanitarian aid will have a greater impact on the conflict than in resource-rich areas such as Sierra Leone, Liberia, and Angola. This has implications for the deliberations of aid organizations concerning the relative good and harm of humanitarian action in each context.

Yet the findings also show that, although the diversion of aid commodities to warring parties is the most visible paradox of humanitarian action and hence the most common basis of claims that aid prolongs conflict, this is not necessarily the most significant contribution of humanitarian action to war. The legitimacy and control mechanisms provided to belligerents are more important in certain conflicts. Hence although they are less easily measured than contributions to the war economy, these side effects of humanitarian assistance must be included in deliberations on overall impact.

The histories I have examined illustrate the difficulty of determining whether humanitarian action can be said to have prolonged a given conflict. In the Afghan and Nicaraguan cases, the level of military support lent to the mujahideen and contras suggests that aid played a complementary but not essential role in their respective conflicts. In both cases the refugees had strong symbolic value and helped to justify Western support to the resistance. In the Cambodian conflict, the ultimate importance of humanitarian assistance is harder to assess: on the one hand, the humanitarian sanctuary resuscitated the Khmer Rouge forces after their defeat and empowered and legitimized the Coalition Government of Democratic Kampuchea (CGDK). On the other hand, strategic imperatives would no doubt have prompted allies to supply food and other goods in addition to military equipment to the anti-Vietnamese forces even without the humanitarian façade provided by the relief program. The Khmer Rouge kept up to 100,000 civilians in hidden border camps, and with backing from the Chinese government would doubtless have continued to wage the guerrilla war against Phnom Penh regardless of the border aid operation. Again, the refugees held a primarily symbolic value to sanction policies pursued by Western governments.

In the Rwandan refugee case, by contrast, evidence suggests that humanitarian action prolonged the conflict. It certainly increased its intensity. Although the defeated regime and army had considerable assets at their disposal in Zaire, it is doubtful that they could have survived as more than roving guerrilla groups without the protection and sustenance provided by the refugee camps. The contemporary Armée de Libération du Rwanda (ALIR), which consists of ex-FAR and Interahamwe members, provides an indication of how the defeated force might have organized without the refugee camps. Yet this new force received backing from Laurent Kabila's government in the context of the regional conflict in the Democratic Republic of Congo. Given that in 1994 Mobutu's government did not pay its own soldiers, it is unlikely that the génocidaires would have received the kind of support from Mobutu that the ALIR received from Kinshasa. Moreover, without the large number of refugees to disrupt the ethnic balances in North Kivu, the ex-FAR and Interahamwe might have found hostile hosts in the Tutsi Banyarwanda living in the Masisi region.

The international response to the Rwandan crisis followed a trend seen in Kurdistan and Bosnia, which suggests that humanitarian action in the post–Cold War period has been transformed from a tool with which governments pursue foreign policy objectives to a tool with which to avoid foreign policy engagement. During the Cold War battle for ideological supremacy, refugees were a potent symbol of the tyranny of the opposing side and helped to justify and legitimize support for refugee-warriors in accordance with tenets of the Reagan Doctrine. Humanitarian action was deployed and manipulated to serve this end, and aid organizations faced obstacles when applying humanitarian principles and influencing the policies of actors in the omnipresent political environment. The ending of the Cold War eased the domination of political imperatives over humanitarian concerns, but rather than empowering humanitarian organizations to reassert respect for humanitarian values, political disengagement left humanitarian action in a vacuum. Without the power or mandate to address the causes of crises, yet deployed as the primary response, humanitarian action is reduced to a palliative to assuage the domestic public conscience in industrialized nations. Ironically, the paradoxes of humanitarian action were worse when unintended, as in the Rwandan refugee camps, than when they were deliberately orchestrated in other contexts by donor governments to advance foreign policy goals.

THE KNOWLEDGE AND ATTITUDES OF AID AGENCIES

Four main points emerge from the examples examined regarding the attitudes and approaches of aid organizations to the paradoxes of humanitarian action. First, it seems that the extent to which the side effects of aid were acknowledged and debated depended largely upon the perceived justness of the cause that humanitarian action was inadvertently assisting. Afghan self-determination was widely supported, and aiding the resistance generated little debate, whereas the camps in Central America and Cambodia polarized the aid community around contending images of the "good" side. Rwanda generated the most consternation among humanitarian actors since, for the first time, the side effects of aid were not serving some perceived greater good.

Second, the prevalence of technical approaches to humanitarian action in each case partly explains the widespread tolerance of the misuse of aid. For aid agencies that focused first and foremost on meeting the material needs of refugees, issues of a political or ethical nature were suppressed. For some, the neutrality of humanitarian action necessitated an apolitical focus, a refusal to engage in any form of political debate or controversy. For others, a perceived inability to influence the situation provoked a pragmatic response to the crisis. Successes and failures could be judged in terms of technical standards of aid delivery; recall that the efficiency and organization of the Khmer Rouge camps impressed several aid workers. As all the cases illustrate, however, by the fact of their participation aid organizations were necessarily implicated in the larger political picture, particularly when in receipt of funds from governments pursuing a political agenda. Whether they acknowledged it or not, unless they intervened equally on both sides of a conflict or ensured that their aid accrued no benefit to a warring party—something impossible—aid organizations were supporting one side by default.

Third, when humanitarian principles clashed, aid organizations differed in the priority they accorded to each. The ethical evaluations implicit in the tradeoffs were guided by different factors. Of paramount concern to ICRC was the application of strict neutrality to its operations, which facilitated access to the heart of conflicts in some instances and restricted access altogether if permission was not forthcoming. In the Cambodian crisis, ICRC's insistence on a presence on both sides of the conflict successfully overcame Phnom Penh's prohibition of other agencies, whereas in Afghanistan ICRC was not permitted to work in resistance areas until 1988.

MSF and Oxfam, by contrast, privileged principles of proportionality over concerns of neutrality, judging that the needs on one side were often greater than on the other, or that the nature of the regime precluded aid effectively reaching the people in need. Thus Oxfam's abhorrence of the Khmer Rouge and concerns about justice for the Cambodian people directed its decision to work inside Cambodia and not with the refugees along the Thai-Cambodian border. MSF similarly chose not to work with the Khmer Rouge, but because it considered that the nature of the Vietnamese-backed regime in Phnom Penh obviated the possibility of aiding civilians inside Cambodia, it limited assistance to non–Khmer Rouge camps. In the Afghan conflict, MSF worked inside Afghanistan with the mujahideen, judging that the indiscriminate and disproportionate force employed by Soviet troops warranted aiding the victims of atrocities regardless of the violation of neutrality and state sovereignty. In Honduras, MSF made a concerted effort to assist refugees fleeing the right-wing government in El Salvador and the left-wing government of Nicaragua, recognizing that there were victims of atrocities on both sides.

Finally, perceptions of a just cause often guided aid organizations in choosing sides and shaped their attitudes toward the abuse of humanitarian assistance by guerrilla movements. Yet in each case the "justness" of the cause was no guarantee that the guerrilla leadership was concerned for the welfare of the civilians under their control. Although helping to free people from the tyranny of oppression may be a humanitarian act, the use of humanitarian action to pursue such ends is problematic. As I indicated in chapter 2, while leaders like General Massoud showed genuine concern for the welfare of civilians, others, like Gulbuddin Hekmatyar, did not. Once the Soviets withdrew and the factions turned their guns on one another, as far as the West was concerned the idealized "freedom fighters" became "warlords" as the humanitarian aid they were accustomed to diverting was no longer being given in the name of a "just" cause. The subjectivity of the judgments made by aid organizations was most starkly illustrated in Honduras, where groups chose to work with refugees according to ideological interpretations of what was just. Again, although the Salvadorans were fighting to overthrow a regime responsible for terror and widespread human rights abuses and as such gained the support of many aid agencies, the means employed in the refugee camps violated the safety and freedom of the refugees.

Cambodia most clearly illustrated the limits of invoking claims of a just war to defend the manipulation of aid by one party to a conflict: oppressors were found on both sides. Aid organizations had to turn a blind eye to many abuses in order to defend the compromises made in operating along the border or inside Cambodia. The inclusion and dominance of the Khmer Rouge in the CGDK discredited claims that working in non–Khmer Rouge camps entailed no ethical compromises, and although the regime in Phnom Penh faced harsh treatment from the "international community," this did not justify the behavior of the Vietnamese-backed regime toward Cambodian civilians or aid organizations. One wonders whether the Cambodian peasants appreciated the gesture of solidarity shown by the aid agencies based in Phnom Penh as they were marched to the border to construct the bamboo wall.

These cases illustrate the pitfalls of a "solidarity" approach to humanitarian action and the repercussions of permitting humanitarian action to be manipulated for a "good" cause. In each case it was the people to whom the aid organizations had primary responsibility who suffered as a consequence of the lack of humanitarian space. The fight against tyranny and totalitarianism may have been just, but did this end justify all means to achieve it? This raises broader questions about the labeling of victims and the basis on which aid organizations judge the side they consider is right. It is interesting to note that the Kosovo Liberation Army, "freedom fighters" opposing the tyranny of former Serbian President Slobodan Milosovic, took steps to "cleanse" the territory of Serbian residents after its NATO-assisted victory in much the same way that Milosovic had attempted to do with Albanian residents a few months earlier. The victims of today are potentially the aggressors of tomorrow.

Institutional Constraints to Learning

The preceding chapters highlighted external constraints that confront aid organizations in applying humanitarian principles to their operations and mitigating the negative consequences of humanitarian action. In addition to these external factors, over which aid organizations have little control, there are many endogenous determinants of the international relief system that help to explain why the paradoxes of humanitarian action recur and persist. Several institutional factors impede the ability of aid organizations to learn from past experience and to change their behavior accordingly. But it is important to reiterate the inevitability of the occurrence of negative consequences: humanitarian action is imbued with an inherent and inescapable paradox.

The humanitarian constraints imposed on the conduct of war are broadly concerned with two areas: discriminating legitimate from illegitimate targets, especially combatants from noncombatants; and the principle of proportionality to limit unnecessary suffering and destruction. But any rules constraining the means of warfare are likely to slow the speed of victory, hence lengthening the duration of conflict. Military leaders throughout history have debated whether it is less cruel to have a swift, decisive victory ignoring humanitarian restraints, or a conflict drawn out by respect for humanitarian laws. Thus the idea at the heart of restraining the means of conflict potentially prolongs it.

At another level, provisions of humanitarian action and the requisites of war lead to the inevitable use of the former in pursuit of the latter. The granting of immunity to medical installations and wounded combatants permits military personnel to be resuscitated and returned to combat. Protected spaces in war are liable to be infiltrated when one party to the conflict is facing defeat and possible annihilation, thereby violating the sanctity of the protected space and jeopardizing its raison d'être. Guerrilla warfare blurs the distinction between combatants and noncombatants, raising ethical issues about the level of complicity—and hence legitimacy as targets—of individuals undertaking vital, yet unarmed, combat support functions. And the provision of essential goods and services is crucial to generate real or perceived civilian allegiance necessary to claims of power and legitimacy. Humanitarian aid enters regions lacking essential provisions, and aid becomes a stake in power struggles. Thus at an intrinsic and practical level, the paradoxes of humanitarian action will persist.

In chapter 1 I noted Mary Anderson's assertion that aid organizations should "do no harm." This assumes that they can indeed contrive to do no harm, yet such an idea is an illusion. Recognizing it as such is essential to deliberations over the most ethically sound approach to a given situation: doing no harm is not possible because humanitarian action will always generate winners and losers. The best that aid organizations can hope to do is *minimize* the negative effects of their action. Applying knowledge gained from past experience is an important prerequisite for achieving this, but as this book has shown, few of the lessons of the past are heeded. I noted earlier that the status of knowledge and ignorance is an important determinant in judging culpability for a given outcome; thus it is important to explore some of the constraints that aid organizations face in applying lessons of the past. After analyzing factors that influence learning at the individual level, the following section examines aspects of the international aid regime that impede the process by which individual learning can be transformed into positive changes in the provision of humanitarian relief.

INTERPRETATION OF EXPERIENCE

At the most rudimentary level, the way individuals interpret experience is shaped by the conceptual and analytical framework they apply to observations—in other words, the lens through which they view the context. Every aid worker enters the field with his or her own history, assumptions, beliefs, motivation, and expectations of what one can hope to achieve. As the case studies illustrate, the ways that aid personnel interpreted events differed according to individual political and ideological views. Only in the Rwandan crisis was there widespread consensus about the nature of the problem. But opinions were still divided over the most appropriate course of action to follow.

Individuals are also influenced by the organizational culture of the agency with which they are affiliated. Most aid organizations have moments in their history or certain personalities that define the essence of the organization and become part of its identity. Individuals shape the organizational culture as their experiences and behavior become integrated into the structure of the agency, and this in turn influences the way that members of the organization interpret experience.

The ways that individuals cope with the stress of relief operations is also significant in shaping perceptions of experience. As the case studies illustrate, individuals must reconcile the competing needs and demands of refugees, refugee leaders, host authorities, donor governments, head office staff, international and national team members, and personnel of other organizations. The magnitude of the problem is often larger than can be met with a humanitarian response, and aid personnel are expected to be adaptable and proficient in undertaking a multiplicity of tasks.[1] Dealing with suffering and death is emotionally stressful, particularly if insufficient means are available to meet the needs of the population, necessitating choices about who will receive assistance and who will not. Even when this is not the case, the utilitarian public health approach applied to aid operations means that refugees in need of "specialized" care might not receive it. These causes of stress are compounded when insecurity and concerns about the misuse of aid generate questions about the viability and side effects of the aid program.[2]

In an insightful study, Mark Walkup examines some of the psychological coping strategies that aid personnel adopt in response to the stress of their environment, and how these become part of the organizational culture of aid agencies. The four stages through which he suggests such coping strategies develop—overwork, detachment, transference, and reality distortion—help to shed light on some of the phenomena I noted in earlier chapters.

Walkup suggests that, in the first stage, aid personnel often try to overcome the distress of their environment and the relative limits of their effectiveness by overworking. In the process, colleagues and refugee representatives are often excluded from participation in decision-making and implementation since including them is perceived to slow progress. Overworking commonly produces "burnout," which impairs a worker's effectiveness and lucidity, reducing analytical potential and capacity for change. To Walkup's observations could be added a tendency at this stage to focus on the immediate and microlevel dimensions of the problem, rather than the overall context and potential repercussions of decisions and actions undertaken.

A second phase is one in which aid workers become detached from the people they are trying to assist. Such detachment eases the guilt and frustration of not being able to resolve all the problems with which refugees

[1] Hugo Slim, "The Continuing Metamorphosis of the Humanitarian Practitioner: Some New Colours for an Endangered Chameleon," *Disasters* 19, no. 2 (1995): 110–126.

[2] For a more detailed discussion of the stress experienced by emergency workers see Ruth A. Barron, "Psychological Trauma and Relief Workers," in Jennifer Leaning, Susan M. Briggs, and Lincoln C. Chen (eds.), *Humanitarian Crises: The Medical and Public Health Response* (Cambridge: Harvard University Press, 1999), pp. 143–175.

are confronted, and manifests itself both mentally and physically. Less contact with the refugees reduces the burden of requests or complaints, and aid personnel spend more time isolated in the vehicle or office. As was evident in many of the situations described, adopting a technical focus and concentrating on concrete, measurable tasks helps deflect attention from emotionally or ethically disturbing areas. Walkup also looks at the tendency of humanitarian personnel to isolate themselves with other expatriates in compounds and engage in black humor as a way of coping.

When aid workers can no longer detach themselves, they begin to rationalize behavior by transferring guilt away from themselves toward other factors, like "politics," "donors," the "host government," and even the "victims." In the Rwanda crisis, it was the "international community" which was to blame. By professing to have no control or power over the system, aid workers can rationalize inaction, or, as the Honduran and Cambodian examples show, acceptance of the status quo. Using terms like "complex emergency" and reiterating how much more complicated, dangerous, and ubiquitous disasters are today than they were in the past also help to excuse by transferring blame to the nature of crises themselves.

Walkup recognizes that there are many external constraints confronting aid personnel but argues that they are reluctant to admit that their policies or actions may contribute to the problem. This tendency is due in part to a sense that benevolence should somehow be above critical scrutiny, that acts undertaken with good intentions can be excused from judgment. Aid personnel are often indignant that their good will and hard work are subject to review, an attitude that they manifest in sentiments from "at least we tried" to "you can't put a price on life." Complaints from the recipients of aid tend to generate the worst form of indignation among aid workers, and the rights of refugees as individuals become lost among claims of self-sacrifice by aid workers and accusations of ingratitude toward the refugee population. Yet in spite of this aversion to criticism, Walkup notes that "most personnel are quick to point out errors of other organizations, while maintaining that 'our organization is different.' "[3]

The final stage Walkup identifies is reality distortion: "when reassigning the blame no longer satisfies and protects the ego, or when it is no longer possible to conceal the inadequacies, aid workers create false illusions of success to enable them to feel a sense of self-worth and accom-

[3] Mark Walkup, "Policy Dysfunction in Humanitarian Organizations: The Role of Coping Strategies, Institutions, and Organizational Culture," *Journal of Refugee Studies* 10, no. 1 (1997): 37–60 at p. 46.

plishment in the midst of institutional inadequacy or failure."[4] One of the most common manifestations of this distortion, he suggests, is the perception Barbara Harrell-Bond noted among aid personnel, that people of other cultures do not suffer to the same extent as people in the West; that their greater exposure to pain and suffering somehow makes them immune.[5] Kurt Jansson, the first director of the UN Emergency Office in Ethiopia during the famine of 1984–85, engaged in this type of cultural relativism when criticizing MSF's public denunciation of the Ethiopian government's resettlement program. He conceded that "no doubt there were casualties in the very hasty and badly organized transport of people . . . and conditions in many resettlement areas were bad," but dismissed the concerns as emanating from a young and inexperienced team who were "highly excitable, reacting emotionally to any events that they with their Western standards did not think appropriate."

To be sure, they had seen people in poor health leaving relief camps for transport to a transit camp or to a settlement area, and had seen the often harsh way local officials dealt with these people. This was nothing new to those relief workers aware of the marks that centuries of feudalism and oppression had left on the mentality of the peasant population, but it was quite understandable that some MSF staff, young and inexperienced as they were, should have been upset at what they saw. Ethiopia is not France.[6]

Jansson also characterized Colonel Mengistu as a man of "intelligence, quiet dignity, reserve and great courtesy" who held "a deep concern for the fate of his own people,"[7] illustrating the extent to which reality can be distorted. It is interesting to note that it was Jansson who headed UNICEF in the Joint Mission in Phnom Penh from June 1980. William Shawcross remarked that relations between the Heng Samrin regime and the Joint Mission improved after Jansson's appointment "not because the program in Cambodia started to work smoothly; it was rather that Jansson considered that complaint was now counterproductive."[8] This demonstrates how im-

---

[4] Ibid.

[5] Barbara E. Harrell-Bond, *Imposing Aid: Emergency Assistance to Refugees* (Oxford: Oxford University Press, 1986), p. 206, as noted in ibid., p. 47.

[6] Kurt Jansson, Michael Harris, and Angela Penrose, *The Ethiopian Famine* (London: Zed Books, 1990), pp. 24–25.

[7] Ibid., p. 29 and p. 31.

[8] William Shawcross, *The Quality of Mercy: Cambodia, Holocaust, and Modern Conscience* (New York: Simon and Schuster, 1984), p. 178.

portant individual agency and perception can be in determining the ethical and practical parameters of an aid operation.

The use of sanitized language, as was evident in the Khmer Rouge camps in Thailand, is another example of reality distortion, this time a conscious form to insulate individuals from the implications of their task. An even more significant form of self-delusion was expressed by aid workers who claimed that through engaging with Khmer Rouge officials they could influence their behavior. Perceptions of the nature of the Vietnamese-backed regime were also distorted to accord with the image of a responsible regime, necessary to secure funding for humanitarian activities.

These psychological coping strategies impact upon the way that experience is interpreted, particularly in generating a defensiveness toward criticism that impedes the ability of individuals to admit to, and learn from, mistakes. Not all of these tendencies among aid workers can be attributed to coping strategies alone, however; there are other equally important factors to consider. The necessity, for example, of choosing between two equally undesirable courses of action and defending such a choice may involve strong moral arguments that are not determined by psychological stress. Furthermore, criticisms of one aid agency by personnel of another do not necessarily indicate a transference of blame but may be generated by competition between agencies for media exposure and recognition, or may really be in response to incompetence and bad practices. The contemporary discourse emphasizing the increased complexity of crises and the dichotomy between the Cold War and post–Cold War environments also influences the interpretation of experience, imbuing aid workers with the idea that there are no relevant precedents from past, that the complexity is new and requires novel solutions and approaches. Experiences are interpreted on the basis of this premise.

The individual interpretation of events may then be assimilated into the organizational beliefs of each agency, and analyses of the same aid operation can differ markedly from one agency to the next even when hindsight has afforded greater scrutiny of facts and interpretations. The Cambodian operation, for example, is still perceived very differently by members of MSF and those of Oxfam, illustrating how different views have permeated each organizational culture. Responding to a 1997 MSF publication reflecting on the past that characterized the Heng Samrin regime as a "pitiless and predatory dictatorship," a member of the Oxfam affiliate in Australia (Community Aid Abroad) wrote: "this comes as somewhat of a surprise given that the Heng Samrin regime did its best in international isolation and not only rebuilt a country shattered by the most brutal geno-cide in recent memory but did it with little external assistance."[9] The au-thor then states that "this type of attack which is all too frequent in the book highlights both an ideological agenda and a self-righteous tone which only diminish the complex issues raised," illustrating the strength with which different opinions can endure. The lack of common analysis among agencies has strong implications for the ability of the aid system as a whole to adjust its behavior to diminish the negative consequences of hu-manitarian action.

But even assuming that there was a "correct" analysis to be made of a given situation, the assimilation of this knowledge into a change in policies or prac-tice can be blocked at several stages along the way. There are two phenom-ena, in particular, that impede the ability of aid organizations to learn from the past: a culture of justification that is manifested externally to protect pub-lic confidence in humanitarian action; and a logic of institutional self-preser-vation that determines much of the interagency dynamic that occurs within the aid system. These are not mutually exclusive, and each contains many tendencies that might just as easily be associated with the other explanation.

THE CULTURE OF JUSTIFICATION

Part of the culture of justification stems from individual defensiveness in the face of criticism that becomes assimilated into organizational behavior, as Walkup suggests. But the refusal of criticism has a more important sys-temic rationale that is intrinsic to the way that aid organizations—NGOs in particular—function.

In contrast to business, where it is the satisfaction of the client that en-sures financial viability, in humanitarian action it is the satisfaction of the donor. To exist and have the financial resources necessary to respond to emergency situations, aid organizations depend upon the generosity of the public in industrialized nations, either directly through fundraising activi-ties or indirectly through aid allocations in government budgets. Thus aid agencies have a strong institutional incentive to portray humanitarian ac-tion as an indispensable remedy for human suffering. For the most part, accountability to donors takes precedence over ensuring that target popu-lations receive timely and appropriate humanitarian assistance, and the negative consequences of humanitarian action are downplayed.

It seems that in Western industrialized nations, a sense of duty and re-

[9] Patrick Kilby, "Review of Médecins sans Frontières, *World in Crisis: The Politics of Survival at the End of the Twentieth Century,*" *African Studies Review and Newsletter* 19, no. 1 (June 1997): 39–41.

sponsibility to assist distant members of humanity arises only when they are perceived to suffer extreme hardship. Even then there are apparent limits to empathy (discussed below). The perceived need to justify foreign aid to domestic audiences and highlight its positive attributes is demonstrated by the Australian Agency for International Development (AusAID) on its official website. Rather than explaining its foreign aid budget in terms of Australia's responsibilities to the world community, AusAID justifies it by downplaying the cost of aid. It shows that of $100 of government expenditure, only $1.20 is spent on aid compared with $36 for social security and welfare, and $8 for defense. It justifies the allocation further by saying that most of the $1.20 is spent inside Australia.[10] The majority of Americans are also averse to their current level of aid expenditure, with three-quarters considering that the amount is too large and two-thirds advocating a reduction.[11] Thus it is not only the voluntary sector that must appeal to the public's sense of common humanity; governments must justify spending taxpayers' money in this way.

The fragility of the base of public interest and support in humanitarian action creates two related tendencies among aid organizations. The first is the perceived need to amplify the gravity of a situation or selectively report the worst aspects of it in order to arouse sufficient awareness and action to raise a response. The media play a vital role in this process, and a symbiotic relationship exists between aid organizations and journalists: the former rely on coverage and the latter benefit from subject matter, insights, and logistical assistance in the field.[12] Both aid organizations and journalists benefit from presenting images that shock Western audiences, often giving rein to what has been described as "disaster pornography."[13] The "CNN factor" has become notorious in contemporary international

[10] http://www.ausaid.gov.au/australianaid/ozaido1.htm (1997), as noted in Fiona Terry, "The Paradoxes of Humanitarian Aid," *Agenda: A Journal of Policy Analysis and Reform* 5, no. 2 (1998): 135–146 at p. 136.

[11] Carol Lancaster, *Aid to Africa: So Much to Do, So Little Done* (Chicago: University of Chicago Press, 1999), pp. 105–106.

[12] This relationship suffered a major setback during the Rwandan crisis, however, with several journalists complaining that they had been lied to and manipulated by aid organizations in connection with fears about the safety of refugees dispersed by the attacks on the Rwandan camps. The return en masse of the majority without significant incident was taken as proof that the aid organizations had lied for fundraising purposes. The fact that 200,000 refugees were missing was overlooked in the outrage generated by the sight of healthy refugees returning. For a detailed discussion of the dispute between journalists and aid organizations at this time see Nik Gowing, "New Challenges and Problems for Information Management in Complex Emergencies: Ominous Lessons from the Great Lakes and Eastern Zaire in Late 1996 and Early 1997," conference paper for "Dispatches from Disaster Zones: The Reporting of Humanitarian Emergencies," London, 27–28 May 1998.

[13] David Rieff, "The Humanitarian Trap," *World Policy Journal* 12, no. 4 (1995–96): 1–11 at p. 7.

affairs, on the one hand raising awareness of problems across the globe as they occur, but on the other desensitizing audiences by allowing graphic pictures rather than in-depth reporting to convey the story. Although the "CNN factor" is widely believed to be another of the post–Cold World changes with which the aid community must contend, this effect of media reporting was noted earlier. Shawcross remarked in 1984: "The flood of instant information in the world today—at least in the western industrialized world—sometimes seems not to further but to retard education; not to excite but to dampen curiosity; not to enlighten, but to dismay. The poet Archibald MacLeish once noted 'We are deluged with facts but we have lost or are losing our human ability to feel them.' "[14] The lack of public interest in distant disasters then generates a greater need to dramatize problems to arouse concern, and the situation spirals.

The Rwanda case shows the magnet effect of media coverage to aid agencies, and the perception among many that they could not afford to be absent from Goma. The opportunity for free publicity at a time of heightened public awareness generated competition for visibility and the resultant ubiquitous display of agency logos and quest for media-friendly projects. This media-and donor-driven context is not conducive to generating the sound political analysis and considered response necessary to limit the potential for the misuse of aid. It also skews attention and resources to regions that are judged of interest to Western audiences. We only need to glance at the tins of chicken pate, foil-wrapped cheeses, and fresh fruit and milk provided to Kosovar refugees to see that budget allocations were greater there than in forgotten tragedies away from the media spotlight.

The second implication of the reliance of aid organizations on support by the general public is that it discourages open discussion among the organizations about the failures or negative consequences of humanitarian action. Most aid agencies paint their activities only in a positive light. A comment by an official of World Vision captures the prevailing view: "You can't confuse the public with complex issues. Starving babies and droughts are something that people can understand. But trying to explain corruption or aid abuses is not going to help our fundraising and will only hamper our work."[15]

Aid organizations depend upon an image of "doing good" for their

[14] William Shawcross, "The Numbing of Humanity: Have We Had One Atrocity Too Many?" *Washington Post National Weekly Edition*, September 1984, 23–24 at p. 23.

[15] As cited in Edward Girardet, "Public Opinion, the Media, and Humanitarianism," in Thomas G. Weiss and Larry Minear (eds.), *Humanitarianism across Borders: Sustaining Civilians in Times of War* (Boulder, Colo.: Lynne Rienner, 1993), pp. 39–55 at p. 46.

support and are reluctant to jeopardize this image by airing concerns that aid may not be serving the purposes for which it was intended. Similarly, agencies are quick to thwart any accusations of wrongdoing or failure. The aid industry has little regulation, and one of the purposes of the various codes of conduct is to improve self-regulation to enhance accountability. However, the repercussions of serious criticisms levied at one organization can reverberate throughout the industry as a whole, as allegations against CARE Australia illustrated to the Australian aid community in 1995.[16] Thus agencies are more likely to close ranks and stifle criticism of aid practices and operations than engage in honest public debate.

The increased criticism of humanitarian action that appeared in the wake of the Rwandan crisis provoked widespread reflection within the aid community and a greater commitment to evaluating aid programs. While a positive development, evaluations in themselves provide no guarantee of organizational learning: failures in the Rwandan operation were not due to a paucity of information. Evaluations must be read and acted upon. The danger with this sudden fad is the false sense of achievement and "accountability" that it creates. As Larry Minear points out:

> The swing of the pendulum from a dearth of thoughtful material to an abundance of it is welcome and overdue. Yet the latter extreme may be as unhelpful to the process of learning and change as was the former. Even the proliferation of so-called lessons learned units is not in and of itself a sign of progress. Since serious learning requires institutional change, such units might better be called "lessons-learning" or "lessons identified" units and viewed as means to an end rather than ends in themselves.[17]

The culture of justification may have dictated that a more responsible image of aid is required to avert criticism and a loss of public confidence, but whether greater recognition of the problems will lead to less abuse of aid remains to be seen.

THE LOGIC OF INSTITUTIONAL PRESERVATION

In contrast to the culture of justification, which is projected predominantly toward external audiences, a logic of institutional preservation

---

[16] A two-part exposé containing allegations of financial mismanagement and misleading advertising, among other issues, was aired on Australian commercial television in 1995. All Australian aid agencies experienced a loss of public confidence as a result.

[17] Larry Minear, "Learning to Learn," paper prepared for OCHA Seminar on Lessons Learned on Humanitarian Coordination, Stockholm, 3–4 April 1998, p. 9.

dominates much of the organizational response and behavior of aid agencies with respect to other actors within the aid regime. The culture of justification impedes organizational learning by limiting the extent to which individual knowledge is absorbed and assimilated into organizational culture, and the logic of institutional preservation hinders the application of knowledge to changes in policies and practice. This logic has three aspects that illuminate why the paradoxes of aid recur and persist in spite of knowledge acquired. The first two relate to the preservation of the aid industry as a whole—why it will prevail. The third concerns the logic of organizational preservation—how individual aid agencies respond to this. The logic of institutional preservation particularly militates against the likelihood that aid organizations will countenance an ethic of refusal in humanitarian action even when the harm of an operation appears to outweigh the good.

First, underpinning the logic of institutional preservation is the aid community's ingrained belief that humanitarian action is indispensable to the survival of refugees and other victims of disasters. Although studies of local coping mechanisms may contradict this assumption—Alex de Waal holds that "relief is generally merely a footnote to the story of how people survive famine"[18]—it remains the axiomatic starting point for humanitarian action. Moreover, it continues to be largely unquestioned despite increased reflection on humanitarian issues within the aid community, indicating that although aid organizations may be willing to reconsider changes in behavior and enhanced accountability, they are unwilling to question their raison d'être.

In fact, the very tools developed to increase the responsibility of aid organizations are built around the primacy of the humanitarian imperative. The principal code of conduct affirms the right to give and receive humanitarian assistance as the first principle of humanitarian action, and this frequently translates into a demand for humanitarian access in the field.[19] Emphasizing access to vulnerable populations shifts attention from protection for the people in need to the means with which to assist them. This

[18] Alex de Waal, *Famine Crimes: Politics and the Disaster Relief Industry in Africa* (Oxford and Bloomington: African Rights and the International African Institute in association with James Currey and Indiana University Press, 1997), p. 1.

[19] The press release issued by MSF upon winning the 1999 Nobel Peace Prize exemplifies the arrogance often associated with such demands: "MSF is independent and impartial in the name of medical ethics and demands that the right to humanitarian assistance be respected. MSF demands full and unhindered freedom to carry out its mandate." "MSF Welcomes Nobel Support for Peoples' Right to Humanitarian Assistance," MSF press release, Brussels, 15 October 1999.

aid-centricity is most apparent when peacekeepers are given the mandate to protect humanitarian convoys and personnel, not the local people for whom the aid is intended. This occurred in northern Iraq, Somalia, and Bosnia, "as if soap or milk powder could prevent bombs from falling on hospitals, or generosity could offer protection against murder and expulsion."[20] The provision of humanitarian aid is a means to an end, the end being the preservation of life and dignity. While insecurity or belligerent actions can prevent aid reaching vulnerable populations, the deployment of military forces to protect the means in isolation of the ends is a dangerous travesty. A full belly does not provide civilians with protection. What is the point of securing humanitarian access to people if it deters us from recognizing that they are in danger of losing their lives to violence?

Perhaps the most significant illustration of the overweening belief in the indispensability of humanitarian action is the growing consideration given to employing private security companies to enforce the right of humanitarian access. Subscribing to the discourse of greater chaos and complexity, and less respect for international law in the "new world disorder," such measures are deemed necessary in the context of declining state interest in intervening militarily.[21] According to an article in *Jane's Intelligence Review*, Defence Systems Limited (DSL) already counts the UN, CARE, and Goal among its clients, alongside Shell, Mobil, and De Beers.[22] The article notes that supporting "humanitarian" missions has gradually gained DSL respectability, even allowing it to shed its "mercenary tag."[23] The ethical and practical issues raised by the hiring of private security are too numerous to be dealt with in this book:[24] suffice it to suggest that if humanitarian action has been reduced to a logistical exercise,

[20] Françoise Bouchet-Saulnier, "Peacekeeping Operations above Humanitarian Law," in François Jean (ed.), *Life, Death, and Aid: The Médecins sans Frontières Report on World Crisis Intervention* (London: Routledge, 1993), pp. 125–130 at p. 128.

[21] For a excellent example of a dramatized account of problems in providing aid that leads to a proposal to engage private security, see Michael Bryans, Bruce D. Jones, and Janice Gross Stein, *Mean Times: Humanitarian Action in Complex Political Emergencies—Stark Choices, Cruel Dilemmas*, Report on the NGOs in Complex Emergencies Project, vol. 1, no. 3 (Toronto: Program on Conflict Management and Negotiation, Centre for International Studies, University of Toronto, 1999).

[22] Kevin O'Brien, "Freelance Forces: Exploiters of Old or New-Age Peacebrokers?" *Jane's Intelligence Review* (August 1998): 42–46 at p. 44.

[23] Ibid., p. 45.

[24] In addition to all the implications this issue raises concerning the responsibilities of states, the meaning of humanitarian action, the concept of "rescue," and the repercussions of creating a new market for private security forces, the idea of aid organizations protected by private security delivering humanitarian aid to Grozny in defiance of the Russian army is absurd.

better to contract a supermarket chain to deliver aid with the protection of DSL and at least avoid the humanitarian pretense.

The second aspect of the logic of institutional preservation is closely related to the first: the humanitarian enterprise *will* prevail owing to the nature of democratic governance in the West. Deploying a humanitarian response is a visibly effective way for politicians to respond to public calls to "do something," thereby satisfying their constituents. Demands for more concerted action will generally not be made given the prevalence among the public of what Rony Brauman calls the "politics of pity,"[25] rather than of compassion, empathy, or justice. Michael Ignatieff articulated the difference with reference to the Bosnian war:

> If the cause of Bosnia failed to arouse the universal outrage and anguish that the atrocity footage on our television screens led one to expect, it was not because those watching such images in the comfort of their living rooms lacked ordinary human pity. The charitable response was quite strong. The real impediment to sustained solidarity ran deeper: in some deeply ingrained feeling that "their" security and "ours" are indeed divisible; that their fate and ours are indeed severed, by history, fortune, and good luck; and that if we owe them our pity, we do not share their fate.[26]

In a unipolar world, it seems that "humanitarian" action will be the preferred tool of politicians because of its media appeal and public display of concern. The way that politicians react to early-warning signs versus emergencies in the international arena is much the same as in the domestic sphere: millions of dollars may be allocated to saving the life of a lone yachtsperson whose predicament is broadcast on the evening news, but the same sum is unlikely to go to an improved weather forecasting system that could prevent future tragedies for many more sailors. Moreover, although it is known that humanitarian action is not the answer to crises generated by conflict, public pressure will ensure its deployment; in the same way, prisons are known to be ineffective in reducing crime rates and reforming criminals, yet the public outcry in the face of serious crimes guarantees that prisons will prevail.

[25] See Rony Brauman, "L'assistance humanitaire internationale," in Monique Canto-Sperber (ed.), *Dictionnaire de philosophie morale et politique* (Paris: Presses Universitaires de France, 1996), pp. 96–101.

[26] Michael Ignatieff, *The Warrior's Honor: Ethnic War and the Modern Conscience* (London: Chatto & Windus, 1998), p. 108.

The third aspect of this logic concerns the way in which aid organizations position themselves vis-à-vis these realities and in relation to one another. The expansion of humanitarian activity at the end of the Cold War and the proliferation of NGOs has created a veritable "aid industry." Larger global budgets for humanitarian aid—$6 billion by 1995[27]—and the readiness of aid organizations to expand the notion of "humanitarian" activity beyond the provision of life-saving relief into areas of postconflict peace-building and reconstruction have opened up new markets for Western commercial interest, and aid is becoming an enterprise. Since 1996, for example, "WorldAid" conferences have brought together "all those with a stake in aid to voice their concerns, promote their ideas and debate aid's future"[28] around exhibits of the latest technological wares in water purification systems, communication equipment, high protein biscuits, plastic sheeting, prosthesis materials, and even mine detectors. Most aid organizations have embraced the expanded role, and the technocratic approach looks likely to flourish in the future. The former UN High Commissioner for Refugees, Sadako Ogata, fully supports the expanded domain, suggesting that "governments, business and humanitarians share a goal: meeting the needs of people, whether we look at them as citizens, as shareholders and customers, or as victims of war and persecution."[29]

This growth of the "aid industry" has been accompanied by attempts to consolidate and regulate it. Evaluations have consistently identified a lack of coordination among agencies as a major shortcoming of relief operations, and increased coordination has been embraced as a panacea for problems. This climate generates strong pressure to conform to the dominant views of government donors and UN agencies striving to forge a "coherent" response. The UN's Strategic Framework for Afghanistan exemplifies this trend, prohibiting partner agencies from voicing divergent views on issues of principle. In this atmosphere of coordination and conformity, aid organizations that prefer to retain independence or hold different views are increasingly regarded as recalcitrant. This trend militates against the likelihood that agencies will oppose the views of donor

[27] Randolph C. Kent, "The Battle for the Soul of Aid," in *WorldAid '96: A Special Supplement of the Crosslines Global Report on WorldAid '96* [30 September–4 October 1996, Geneva], http://www.worldaid.org/wa96/battle.htm.

[28] Randolph C. Kent, "WorldAid '98 Conference Examines Aid's Unprecedented Changes," 24 June 1997, http://www.worldaid.org/conf/htm.

[29] Sadako Ogata, "Let's Get Business and Humanitarians Together," *International Herald Tribune*, 25 November 1999, p. 4.

governments or withdraw from a context for other than security reasons. It goes against the logic of self-preservation.

This applies both to NGOs and to UN agencies. The Rwandan crisis showed how quickly one NGO was replaced by another, even when the first was withdrawing because of ethical concerns that all aid organizations professed to share,[30] and David Rieff has noted how competition for donor funds can determine an NGO's entire rationale for action.[31] As the Honduran and Rwandan histories showed, UNHCR is not immune from such pressure because it depends on voluntary financial support from UN member states. UNHCR faces a conflict between its protection and assistance tasks: the more effectively it undertakes the former, the less likely it is that it will receive funding to undertake the latter. The Rwandan context clearly illustrated this clash, and UNHCR's response to it was mixed. It privileged protection concerns when acting on the findings of the Gersony Report, opposing the wishes of donors and the opinions of other UN agencies. But UNHCR privileged its assistance function and future relevance overall in the Rwandan camps by choosing to remain in spite of its inability to protect refugees. The expansion of UNHCR's tasks has been undertaken at the expense of its traditional protection role.

Although there are irremediable constraints to escaping the negative side effects of humanitarian action, the different interpretation of matters by individual aid personnel, the way this influences and is influenced by the organizational culture, the culture of justification that permeates the entire aid community, and the logic of institutional preservation all weigh against diminishing the paradoxical consequences of humanitarian action. The mantra of "complex emergencies," "humanitarian crises," and the "new world disorder" distorts analysis of contemporary situations. As George Orwell said of the condition that clichés and stereotypes produce: "this reduced state of consciousness, if not indispensable, is at any rate favourable to political conformity."[32]

---

[30] John Prendergast noted the lack of solidarity between NGOs in Sudan in 1992 when the UN suspended convoys to an area because of the murder of three relief workers and a journalist, yet Norwegian People's Aid and Catholic Relief Services expanded their food deliveries to cover the area that the UN was boycotting. John Prendergast, *Frontline Diplomacy: Humanitarian Aid and Conflict in Africa* (Boulder, Colo.: Lynne Rienner, 1996), p. 23.

[31] Rieff cites a member of Action Internationale Contre la Faim in Sudan who said that the organization retained a presence in a region of the Sudan only to be visible to the European Community Humanitarian Office. Rieff, "Humanitarian Trap," pp. 4–5.

[32] George Orwell, "Politics and the English Language," in *Inside the Whale and Other Essays* (Markham, Ontario: Penguin, 1988, originally published in *Horizon* 76, April 1946), p. 153, as cited in Catherine Lu, "Cosmopolitanism and Humanitarian Intervention," paper pre-

The willingness of aid organizations to comply with the objectives and priorities of government donors and UN agencies even when these are obviously driven by political expediency, as in Rwanda, does not bode well for the values on which humanitarian action was founded. Rather than applying knowledge gained in the past to contemporary operations, donors, particularly members of the U.S. government, have used "lessons" instrumentally, to support policy preferences. Invoking memories of the Khmer Rouge to justify "less voluntary" repatriation from the Rwandan camps in 1996 and using "revelations" in 1997 of the abuse of refugee aid to call for tighter controls in the future were shameless abuses of history.

The continued ascendancy of technical responses to crises is liable to dominate moral and ethical issues and concerns. Harrell-Bond remarked more than a decade ago that "discussions of aid programmes conducted under the banner of humanitarianism concentrate . . . not on reasons for failures, but on competing claims to moral rectitude. The struggle for moral supremacy," she added, "can be fierce indeed."[33] Yet it is interesting to note that when an aid organization does make an ethical or moral stand, other agencies tend not to engage in debate on this plane, but attempt to discredit or undermine the position on technical grounds. Jansson's dismissal of MSF's credibility in Ethiopia was recounted above, and similarly de Waal, although agreeing with MSF's move out of Ethiopia, diminished it as arising from "political naïveté." He surmised that had MSF field staff been more aware of the implications of reporting what they had seen "they would have followed their colleagues in other agencies and remained silent."[34] This contrasts with MSF's own interpretation.[35]

In a similar way several aid organizations dismissed MSF's withdrawal from the Rwandan refugee camps. Caritas staff said that the rationale was "purely budgetary," but was justified on political grounds,[36] and Charles Tapp of CARE argued that MSF had run out of funding.[37] The most interesting to note, however, was Bruce Jones, who discussed MSF's depar-

sented to the International Studies Association Convention, Washington, D.C., 16–20 February 1999, p. 10.

[33] Harrell-Bond, *Imposing Aid*, p. 26.

[34] De Waal, *Famine Crimes*, p. 124.

[35] See Médecins sans Frontières, *Pourquoi nous avons été expulsés?* (Paris: MSF, December 1985).

[36] Alphonse Ngamije, "Réfugiés rwandais: Quel avenir?" *Dialogue* 181 (March 1995): 27–32 at p. 29, and Jean-Pierre Godding, "Les camps de réfugiés de Goma, mort et espérance," *Dialogue* 181 (March 1995): 19–26 at p. 25.

[37] Personal interview, 27 November 1997. This view is even more remarkable given that some NGOs considered that they could not afford to be absent from the Rwandan camps because of the revenue their presence generated from donors.

ture in ethical terms in an influential essay published in *Millennium* in 1995.[38] Yet in a report he produced for CARE Canada two years later, he wrote that MSF "had already pulled out of one camp, citing ethical issues, but MSF communications personnel privately will admit that MSF's role in the camp was in any case at an end, and that the ethical issue was not the one which determined the timing of the withdrawal."[39] Even after being sent MSF internal and external documentation to show the contrary,[40] Jones retained the remark—attributed to a confidential interview with an MSF staff member—in subsequent revisions of the report. It is ironic that a publication in the same series coauthored by Jones five years after MSF's withdrawal recommends that NGOs develop a new humanitarian ethic that includes the option of withdrawal or disengagement.[41]

Implications

Even if aid organizations did countenance the possibility of withdrawal, the basis of such a decision would no doubt differ greatly from one group to the next. There is no universal formula that can be applied to every aid organization or every context to determine the most ethical approach to a situation. Chapter 5 highlighted two conceptions of ethical evaluation: one that privileged the humanitarian imperative above all else, and one that privileged concern for the consequences of the camps. Most aid organizations subscribed to the former. As a senior official of UNHCR argued:

> We know we are often in a lose-lose situation. But if we leave, however we justify it to ourselves in terms of not collaborating with criminals, what it means on the ground is that we are abandoning the innocent civilian population to its fate. They are in no position to do anything to change their leaders, if they wanted to. It seems to me that what is truly unacceptable—I

[38] He cites an MSF statement that said: "In Bukavu the situation has deteriorated to such an extent that it is now ethically impossible for *Médecins sans Frontières* to continue aiding and abetting the perpetrators of the Rwandan genocide," which was quoted in the *Glasgow Herald*, 15 November 1994, p. 4. Bruce D. Jones, " 'Intervention without Borders': Humanitarian Intervention in Rwanda, 1990–94," *Millennium* 24, no. 2 (1995): 225–249 at p. 245 n. 60.

[39] Bruce D. Jones, *Rwanda Report: International NGOs in the Response to the Rwandan Emergency* (London and Toronto: NGOs in Complex Emergencies Project, a Collaborative Project of CARE Canada, the Harrowston Project on Conflict Management, University of Toronto, and the Conflict Analysis and Development Unit, London School of Economics, July 1997), section 2.3.3.

[40] I sent the documentation after reading the draft report and meeting with Jones in London.

[41] Bryans, Jones, and Stein, *Mean Times*, pp. 37–41.

mean for us, both within the U.N. system and the NGOs—is to abandon them. I believe that morally there is nothing for us to do *except* stay.[42]

But the decision to refuse to collaborate with criminals was not merely a self-justification but a positive ethical decision founded on an idea of what humanitarian action represents. After all, these were not just any criminals, but criminals who had initiated, and continue to pursue, a political project that ran counter to every idea underpinning humanitarian action. Furthermore, the notion of abandoning refugees to their fate denies their own responsibility for their predicament: to what extent did they try to oppose the power of these leaders? They were not behind bars or under the same duress as Cambodian civilians in Khmer Rouge camps along the Thai-Cambodian border or North Koreans today. Some 160,000 refugees voluntarily returned to Rwanda soon after the camps were established in 1994,[43] and representatives of Rwandan NGOs in the camps were able to travel to Nairobi and Belgium to participate in discussions on the refugee problem.[44] A stronger case for staying could have been made if aid were helping refugees oppose the control of their "leaders." But instead, humanitarian aid was strengthening the leaders and turned against the people it was intended to assist. The stronger ethical case for humanitarian organizations, I believe, was to refuse to participate in such a system.

How can we reconcile the humanitarian imperative with the need to consider the consequences of humanitarian action? Some indications can be found by looking beneath humanitarian principles to what humanitarian action represents in terms of intention, means and methods, and consequences. Bearing these parameters in mind can help focus on the act, guide the implementation, and take into account the context of humanitarian action.

INTENTION

Given that humanitarian action upholds a conviction that all people have equal rights to certain standards by virtue of their membership in humanity, any assistance, if it is to be humanitarian, must be motivated first and foremost by a concern for the welfare of people, regardless of who or where they are. Assistance directed toward a particular group on the basis

---

[42] As cited in Rieff, "Humanitarian Trap," p. 9.

[43] UNHCR, *The State of the World's Refugees 1997–98: A Humanitarian Agenda* (Oxford: Oxford University Press, 1997), p. 21.

[44] Marie-Béatrice Umutesi, *Fuir ou mourir au Zaïre: Le vécu d'une réfugiée rwandaise* (Paris: L'Harmattan, 2000).

of their religious, political, or other affiliation is not humanitarian aid, nor is any assistance given to induce political or religious compliance. The sole determinant in the allocation of humanitarian assistance should be the level of need of the target population, with priority accorded to the most vulnerable.

Second, in order to be humanitarian, assistance must be in response to a crisis that was not caused by the provider of the aid.[45] If the donor caused or had complicity in causing the disaster, then any aid offered is compensation for the harm wrought, rather than humanitarian assistance. American aid given to Iraqi Kurds fleeing oppression by Saddam Hussein, for example, should be considered compensation rather than humanitarian assistance, because U.S. forces share responsibility for the Kurds' predicament through having incited them to revolt during the Gulf War. Moreover, the aid operation was motivated less by concern for the welfare of the Kurds per se than by fear of the destabilizing effect that millions of Kurdish refugees would have on Turkey. The "humanitarian" operation returned the Kurds to their villages and supplied them with aid, while effectively denying their rights to asylum and ignoring the political roots of their predicament.

In a similar vein, humanitarian assistance must be freely given; the transfer of financial or material resources cannot be considered humanitarian if it was already "owed" to the recipients. If government A is ordered to pay government B one million dollars in reparations for an oil tanker spill off its coast, then the provision of a million dollars by government A to help feed families affected by the oil slick is not humanitarian aid.

Third, although it seems too obvious to state, humanitarian assistance must be intended for victims. As Henry Shue argues, "the question is not *what* one gives—it is to *whom* one gives it."[46] Food, water, and clothing intended for an army cannot be labeled humanitarian, as such assistance to the Nicaraguan contras was in the mid-1980s; it is logistical support for the military. But a rifle might constitute humanitarian assistance if provided to villagers who suffer from attack by wild animals. Shue notes that "if an army cannot afford both guns and food, giving it food is providing military assistance. . . . the question is: is the food preventing a victim of poverty from starving, or is it enabling an invasion force to move forward?"[47]

---

[45] Henry Shue, "Morality, Politics, and Humanitarian Assistance," in Bruce Nichols and Gil Loescher (eds.), *The Moral Nation: Humanitarianism and U.S. Foreign Policy Today* (Notre Dame: University of Notre Dame Press, 1989), pp. 12–40 at pp. 21–24.

[46] Ibid., p. 23.

[47] Ibid., p. 24.

In practice, the response to this question is often "both." In most situations of conflict it is impossible to reach those in need without providing some advantage to combatants, as this book has shown. However, the intention behind the provision of aid must be to alleviate the suffering of victims.

MEANS AND METHODS

A humanitarian end, such as easing the suffering of a population, cannot justify any means to achieve it. Means cannot be used that oppose the values underpinning humanitarian action. A "humanitarian war" is an oxymoron: it contradicts the fundamental rationale of humanitarian action to countenance killing in its name. Humanitarian action aims to minimize the harm caused by war; a humanitarian rationale cannot be invoked to justify the killing of one set of people in order to save another. This does not imply that some wars are not just: humanitarian organizations called for military intervention in Rwanda to stop the genocide because it was political, not humanitarian action that was required. Similarly, the bombing of Serbian targets by NATO forces in 1999 was a profoundly political act, not a humanitarian act as it was labeled.

There are certain methods of undertaking relief assistance that can help to ensure that it is given in accordance with its intention and not diverted or misappropriated for another purpose. The overriding condition that we need to ensure is that there is the possibility of creating a humanitarian space in which the spirit of humanitarian operations will be respected. Such a space entails the freedom to forge a relationship with the people we are there to help—to listen to their stories and discuss their predicament as the first step to really respecting their dignity. Without this connection, we reduce human beings to their biological state, defined and represented by what they lack to stay alive. The possibility of discussing their requirements independently of local authorities is also a precondition for ensuring that aid is in the interests of the victims and not an auxiliary to these same authorities, and that assistance is directed to the most vulnerable population and not toward one group at the expense of another. Finally, aid needs to be monitored and evaluated to ensure it is reaching and helping those most in need. If not, it may be strengthening the hand of the people responsible for the suffering.

What this means in practice is that the humanitarian imperative must always be privileged at the outset of an emergency, as it is only by being present and trying to forge decent conditions in which to work that aid organizations will know what are the possibilities and constraints of their action. If local authorities do not permit a free exchange and dialogue with the population in distress, then questions immediately arise concerning the power relationships that exist, and whose interests the aid will serve. Such analysis and negotiation are possible only when agencies are present in the field.

This process of negotiation guides analysis of the potential good versus harm of humanitarian action and provides more objective criteria than perceptions of a just cause. The aid operation assisting Ethiopian and Eritrean populations through the guerrilla fronts in the 1980s is viewed as a model approach to aid, not because of the justice of the fight against the Mengistu regime per se, but because of the responsibility and concern the guerrillas showed for the civilian populations under their control. Aid organizations knew that although aid fed soldiers, it also reached the civilian population for which it was intended. By the same token, the refusal of the regime in Phnom Penh to agree to any of these conditions in the early 1980s should have warned aid organizations of its indifference toward the Cambodian people. Similarly, none of the characteristics of humanitarian space exists in North Korea today, rendering it impossible to know whether food aid entering the country is helping to alleviate the slow-motion famine or is sustaining the political project of the last Stalinist dictatorship on earth. It is hard to defend the "humanitarian" nature of aid to North Korea either in its intention, which for major government donors is to prevent the sudden collapse of the regime to avoid destabilizing the region, or in its methods.

Of course not all conditions may be successfully negotiated in every context: local authorities may insist that "minders" accompany aid workers when they are conducting surveys and evaluations, and security concerns or logistical constraints may hinder the thorough monitoring of aid. Respect for some standards needs to be weighed against the nonrespect for others and decisions of the relative good or harm of aid judged accordingly, and in relation to the gravity of distress or danger of the vulnerable population. But a bottom line of acceptable compromise needs to be established to ensure that the negative effects of aid do not outweigh the good. The predominant view among aid agencies about the indispensability of aid has skewed the weight of the humanitarian imperative in considerations of the most appropriate action to pursue. Once this assumption is questioned, agencies can consider circumstances in which the best approach might be to withdraw.

CONSEQUENCES

The nature of any action, even with the best intentions and methods, cannot be separated from the context in which it is provided and from the consequences it incurs. Of course, the consequences of an action cannot always be predicted, but it is not enough to assume that certain acts are merely good in themselves. Take the medical act of saving a life, for instance. Few would contest that it is a profoundly good act. But place that act in the context of a torture chamber, where a doctor is keeping a patient alive in the knowledge that another round of torture will commence.[48] Is saving the life of the patient still an ethical act? Is the doctor not an accomplice to torture?

Humanitarian action is more than a technical exercise aimed at nourishing or healing a population defined as "in need"; it is a moral endeavor based on solidarity with other members of humanity. If reduced to a technical act it can be employed in the service of any kind of abuse. Thus the consequences of humanitarian action must be given equal weight with the intention if an ethic of responsibility is to be more than an ethic of response.

Humanitarian principles provide important guidance for humanitarian action and furnish the framework for consistent behavior, which is an important basis of any moral position: as Neil MacCormack argues: "whatever be the variations in possible moral positions which people may have, there are criteria of coherence and consistency of judgements and principles which can be and ought to be applied to anything which claims to be a 'moral position,' as distinct from mere gut reaction or knee-jerk prejudice."[49] But rather than constituting values that should be honored in themselves come what may, they may have to be called into question in extreme situations, or tempered by what Paul Ricoeur calls "practical wisdom": "inventing the conduct that most satisfies the exception requested by the victims and least betrays the rules."[50] Humanitarian principles need to be weighed against other values in determining which line of action promotes the best overall good. In exceptional circumstances—like those of the Rwandan refugee camps—in which it is humanitarian action itself that is harming those it aims to assist, refusing to subscribe to the humanitarian imperative may promote a better overall consequence for the population. To say "let humanitarianism prevail though the heavens fall" (fiat justitia ruant coeli)[51] is absurd.

Given the inescapable nature of the paradoxes of aid, humanitarian aid

[48] Paul Ricoeur, preface to Valérie Marange, *Médecins tortionnaires, médecins résistants: Les professions de santé face aux violations des droits de l'homme* (Paris: La Découverte, 1989).

[49] Neil MacCormack, *Legal Right and Social Democracy: Essays in Legal and Political Philosophy* (Oxford: Oxford University Press, 1982), p. 129.

[50] Paul Ricoeur, *Soi-même comme an autre* (Paris: Seuil, 1990), p. 312.

[51] Literally translated the phrase means "let justice prevail, though the heavens fall."

organizations should be aiming to minimize the negative consequences of their actions. Reflection and vigilance should be directed toward a form of "harm minimization" like that of some programs seeking to help drug addicts: the programs do not attempt to address the addiction, but try merely to avoid some of the deadly concomitants such as overdose or HIV infection. Humanitarian actors should ensure that the essential tasks—such as alleviating life-threatening suffering—are undertaken with minimal harm before considering expanding humanitarian action beyond them. If aid organizations pursue conflict resolution and peace-building activities, they are likely not only to increase the negative consequences of humanitarian action, but to further exonerate states of their responsibilities in these realms. Aid organizations cannot lament the humanitarian alibi while contributing to it by undertaking state functions. Furthermore, broadening the role and interpretation of humanitarian action is likely to increase its manipulation by political powers as the traditional values and principles on which it stands become eroded.

In all the self-examination in which the aid industry must engage, it is important to remember that aid organizations do not inherit responsibilities that others have failed to honor. It is not the humanitarian actors who pull triggers or launch grenades. The ultimate responsibility for human horror lies with those who do, and it is perhaps an important element of vigilance not to accept horror as a given with which humanitarian action must deal. The first response should be militancy against it rather than rescue from its consequences.

This book has shown that humanitarian action is imbued with inherent paradoxes that inevitably lead to some negative consequences, but that these are exacerbated by the behavior and culture of aid organizations. The paradoxes of humanitarian action will recur and persist, and the most that aid organizations can hope to do is minimize the negative consequences. This inevitability provides an ethical imperative for vigilance in humanitarian action. Humanitarian action will never attain perfection: rather than aiming for a first-best world, we must aim for a second-best world and adjust to that accordingly.

Appendix: Documents from the Rwandan Refugee Camps

A. List of RPF Armaments

Le 26 Sep 1996

G E N R E	P R O V E N A N C E
I. ARMES INDIVIDUELLES	
- KV AK 47	CHINE, URSS
- R4	R S A
- FAL	OTAN, 290 FAL ont été rétrocédés par le ZAIRE AU RWANDA le 13 Fév 1996 à GISENYI
- 14 X G3	Rétrocédés par le ZAIRE.
II. ARMES CP	
1) Mitrailleurses	
- Mi.50 (nombreuses)	U S A
- Mi 14.7	
- FM	
- MILO	27 ont été rétrocédées par le ZAIRE le 13 Fév 96
- SS 77	R S A, 36 ont été rétrocédées par le ZAIRE.
-MIAA 12.7	CHINE
- M A G	Belgique, 70 ont été rétrocédées par le ZAIRE.
- 292 BREN	Rétrocédées par le ZAIRE le 13 Fév 96.
2) Mortiers	
- Mor 60 mm	CHINE, RSA
- Mor 80 - 81 mm	
- Mor 82 mm	
- Mor 120 mm	dont 3 rétrocédés par le ZAIRE le 13/2/96
- Mor 122 mm	
3) Canons	
- CSR 75 mm	2 ont été rétrocédés par le ZAIRE
- Canon 105 mm	2 ont été rétrocédés par le ZAIRE
- Canon 106 mm	
- Canon 122 mm	2 ont été rétrocédés par le ZAIRE
4) -LR de différentes calibres	Laissées surtout par la MINUAR lors de sa fuite en Avril 1994.
-LRM (KATIOUSHA) 107 mm	Dont 1 rétrocédé par le ZAIRE
III. VEHICULES BLINDES	
- 2 X Véh Bl se trouvent à l'entrée de la forêt de NYUNGWE (Forte barrière)	Rétrocédés par le ZAIRE (?)
- 3 X AML 60 mm	Rétrocédés par le ZAIRE le 13 Fév 1996
	N.B: Un accord de vente de pièces de réchange vient d'être conclu entre la RSA et le Rwanda le 28 Sep 1996.

IV. Le FPR n'a pas d'UTK connue mais plusieurs CHARS ont été observés à la Base US de MULINDI près de KANOMBE.	U S A
V. AVIATION 3 aéronefs dont:	− 2 Héli rétrocédés par le ZAIRE le 13 Fév 96 à GIS à la délég RWANDAISE − 1 Héli rétrocédé par le ZAIRE le 3 Avr 96 à KINDU (MANIEMA) au Comd Avn Mil (Maj MUNYURANGABO), transporté à Kgl grâce à l'appui Log de la MINUAR.
VI. D C A (Défense contre les avions) L'APR dispose d'une petite Unité de Déf AA (Air Défense artillery) équipée de quelques missiles SAM 7; d'obus AA genre canon BITUBE 37 mm et des Mi QUADRUPLES 14.5 mm	4 canons BITUBES rétrocédés par le ZAIRE 1 X Mi QUADRUPLE rétrocédée par le ZAIRE.
VII. MARINE − Zodiacs équipés de MAG et de de Mi.50 (pat dans le lac KIVU) − 2 X Vedettes dotées de RADARS de SURVEILLANCE (Pat dans le lac KIVU)	CANADA (après les combats d'IWAHU)
VIII. ARMES TRADITIONNELLES − Arcs + flèches Des Trg au maniement de ces armes ont été remarqués dans le RUGEZI en Commune BUTARO (RUHENGERI)	Fabrication locale
IX. En plus de tout cet armt, le FPR dispose de 4 X DS 47.3 pour le déminage.	U S A

N.B: Chaque Bde dispose de son Unité d'appui feu direct (Direct Support) tandis que les armes d'appui général (general support) sont stockées à KANOMBE (KIGALI) et à MULINDI (BYUMBA, ancien QG du FPR).

B. Mil-Tec Corporation Documents

MTC   MIL-TEC CORPORATION LIMITED

RAGNAL HOUSE, 18 PEEL ROAD, DOUGLAS-ISLE-OF-MAN

7th DECEMBER 1994.

THE MINISTER OF DEFENSE,
REPUBLIC OF RWANDA,
BUKAVU.
ZAIRE.

YOUR EXCELLENCY,

RE:OUTSTANDING PAYMENT.

We refer to a meeting held in Nairobi on the 5th December
1994 at your Embassy, with His Excellency the Minister of
Finance His Excellency the Ambassador to Kenya and Col
Kayumba Cyprien.

The meeting was arranged by MIL_TEC, after months of
uncertainty and loss of contact due to the current situation
in Rwanda and most of all the lack of communication.

Your excellency, as you are well aware, we have been
suppliers to your Ministry for over 5 years, and were able
to assist you with supplies during your time of need.

We were asked to supply goods in April and May of 1993
(ANNEX 1 AND 2) for which we were promised payment
but never paid.

We were approached for very urgent supplies on the 10th
of April 94, after the tragic death of His Excellency the
President, we received this urgent request from Col
Kayumba, Major Tereraho and finally from the, then
Minister of Defense Augustin Bizimana, as you will see our
first shipment was delivered 8 days later at this time we
insisted to the then Minister for the outstanding payment
and we were assured these would be paid forthwith, the
schedule of our shipments amounts of our invoices and
payments received are reflected in our statement (ANNEX
3).

...ayments were made to us from Kigali,Belgium, France and Cairo, we also received 1 payment of 450.000 dollars from one of your suppliers (DYL INVESTMENTS) who was unable to fulfil his delivery commitments to you, but had been paid by your Ministry.

A transfer of U.S.Dollars 578.645.00 was effected from Cairo for our last shipment on 18/7/94, we however never received the payment, we reported this matter to Col Kayumba, Mr.Bizimana and Mr.Zikamabhari of your Cairo Embassy, who informed us that the funds had been blocked in the U.S. We believe the blockade was initiated by the U.S. due to the situation in Rwanda at that time.

It was suggested by some of your officials that the amount of U.S.S 578,645.00 was received by us, we enclose a confirmation from our Bank (ANNEX 7) we can assure you, that had we received this payment we would not be making any claims for it.

We spoke to Major Tereraho on various occasions, who confirmed to us the receipt of all the goods in good order.

We also believe that we were the only suppliers who successfully supplied your Government with goods, where as your other suppliers did not perform despite having been paid for the goods in question.

As you are aware that the credit given to you is against borrowing from Commercial Banks and as such we have to charge you interest at the rate of 1.25% per month, from the time the money has been outstanding.

You will realize that we have gone out of the way to assist your Ministry in times of need.

Our current and very difficult financial situation has been explained to His Excellency, the Minister of Finance, and we can not express our very serious problems with our Bankers because of this long outstanding of U.S.Dollars 1,708,313.09 as per (ANNEX 3) plus the interest as per (ANNEX 4-5 AND 6).totaling to U.S.Dollars 254,062.90 respectively, making a grand total outstanding of U.S.Dollars 1,962,375.90

Under the circumstance we will be obliged if you would kindly review the above situation urgently and we await your most urgent action and settlement.

May we also add that we are able to assist you in the future if you so require.

Yours sincerely,

FOR AND BEHALF OF:
MIL-TEC CORPORATION LTD.

c.c.   HIS EXCELLENCY THE PRIME MINISTER
HIS EXCELLENCY THE MINISTER OF FINANCE
HIS EXCELLENCY THE AMBASSADOR TO KENYA
COL KAYUMBA CYPRIEN
MAJOR TERERAHO CYPRIEN
MR.BIZIMANA AUGUSTIN (FOR INFORMATION)

ANNEX 1

MTC MIL-TEC CORPORATION LIMITED

RAGNAL HOUSE, 18 PEEL ROAD, DOUGLAS-ISLE-OF-MAN

28th MAY 1993.   INVOICE NO:0105.

MINISTRY OF DEFENSE.,
B.P. 23,
KIGALI.
RWANDA.

1.	1,000.000	CARTOUCHES X 5.56mm @ U.S.$ 210 PER 1000	=	210.000.00
2.	177.640	CARTOUCHES X 7.62mm LOOSE @ U.S.$ 310 PER 1000	=	55.068.00
3.	417.220	CARTOUCHES X 7.62mm LINK @ U.S.$ 390 PER 1000	=	162.715.00
4.	40.000	CARTOUCHES X 7.62mm LINK 4 BALL – 1 TRACER @ U.S.$ 390 PER 1000	=	15.600.00

TOTAL F.O.B.	U.S.$	=	443.383.00
FREIGHT	U.S.$	=	98.000.00
INSURANCE	U.S.$	=	8.120.00
TOTAL C.I.F. KIGALI	U.S.$	=	549.503.00

ORIGIN : ISRAEL

CONTRACT N°: 1626/06.1.9. DATED 11 MAY 1993. AND OUR
             PRO-FORMA INVOICE N°:MIL/MINADEF/05/93/05
             OF 10-05-1993.

FOR & ON BEHALF OF:-

MIL-TEC CORPORATION LTD.

MIL-TEC CORPORATION LTD

201 DITYK ROAD
HOVE
SUSSEX DELLA SERA
U.K.
Tel.(44)0273-732533
Fax.(44)0273-822614

28th APRIL 1993.

INVOICE NO: 0101

MINISTRY OF DEFENSE
B.P. 23
KIGALI
RWANDA

500 ONLY ACCUS CD N1 - 1,2V, 7Ah @ FF: 421 = 210.500.00

TOTAL C.I.F. KIGALI FRENCH FRANCS = 210.500.00

ORIGIN : E.E.C.

PAYMENT: UPON RECIEPT OF GOODS IN KIGALI.

FOR & ON BEHALF OF: -

MIL-TEC CORPORATION LTD.

ANNEX 3

MTC MIL-TEC CORPORATION LIMITED

RAGNAL HOUSE, 18 PEEL ROAD, DOUGLAS-ISLE-OF-MAN

THE HON.MINISTER.,
MINISTRY OF DEFENSE,
BUKAVU,
ZAIRE.

STATEMENT
U.S.DOLLARS

FLIGHT N°	FLIGHT DATE	TRANSACTION NUMBER	INVOICE AMOUNT U.S.$	PAYMENT RECEIVED US$	BALANCE U.S.DOLLARS.
1	18.04.94	INVOICE	853.731.00		
		PAYMENT		1.265.500.00	
2	25.04.94	INVOICE	681.200.00		
		INVOICE	56.000.00		
		PAYMENT		667.000.00	
		PAYMENT		596.000.00	
3	03.05.94	INVOICE	942.680.00		
		PAYMENT		450.000.00	
		PAYMENT		130.000.00.	
4	09.05.94	INVOICE	1023.840.00		
5	PREVIOUS	INVOICE	549.503.00		
6	PREVIOUS	INVOICE	511.415.09	(EQUIVALENT TO FF(2.710.500)	
7	20.05.94	INVOICE	1074.549.00		
		PAYMENT		500.000.00	
		PAYMENT		523.500.00	
		PAYMENT		500.000.00	
8	18.07.94	INVOICE	753.645.00		
		PAYMENT		175.000.00	
		INVOICE	68.750.00		
			6.515.313.09	4.807.000.00	1.708.313.09

U.S.DOLLARS   BALANCE DUE   1.708.313.09.

CORSERA

U.S. DOLLAR INTEREST CALCULATION
OUTSTANDING AMOUNT U.S. 549503.00
RATE OF INTEREST 1.25% PER MONTH.

	AMOUNT	INTEREST	TOTAL
28/MAY/1993-	549503.00	6868.79	556371.78
28/JUNE/1993	556371.78	6954.65	563326.42
28/JULY/1993	563326.42	7041.58	570368.00
28/AUG/1993	570368.00	7129.60	577497.60
28/SEPT/1993	577497.60	7218.72	584716.32
28/OCT/1993	584716.32	7308.95	592025.27
28/NOV/1993	592025.27	7400.32	599425.58
28/DEC/1993	599425.58	7492.82	606918.39
28/JAN/1994	606918.39	7586.48	614504.86
28/FEB/1994	614504.86	7681.31	622186.17
28/MAR/1994	622186.17	7777.33	629963.49
28/APR/1994	629963.49	7874.54	637838.03
28/MAY/1994	637838.03	7972.98	645811.00
28/JUNE/1994	645811.00	8072.64	653883.63
28/JUL/1994	653883.63	8173.55	662057.17
28/AUG/1994	662057.17	8275.71	670332.88
28/SEPT/1004	670332.88	8379.16	678712.04
28/OCT/1994	678712.04	8483.30	687195.94
28/NOV/1994	687195.94		

**TOTAL INTERST
OUTSTANDING
AS AT 28/NOV/1994 U.S. DOLLARS 137693.03**

ANNEX 5

U.S. DOLLAR INTEREST CALCULATION
PRICIPAL AMOUNT 2,710,500 FRENCH FRANCS
AT EXCHANGE RATE 5.3 OFF TO 1 U.S. DOLLAR
OUTSTANDING AMOUNT U.S. DOLLAR 511415.09
<u>**RATE OF INTEREST 1.25% PER MONTH.**</u>

	AMOUNT	INTEREST	TOTAL
1/12/93	511415.09	6392.69	517807.77
1/1/94	517807.77	6472.59	524280.36
1/2/94	524280.36	6553.51	530833.86
1/3/94	530833.86	6635.42	537469.28
1/4/94	537469.28	6718.37	544187.64
1/5/94	544187.64	6802.35	550989.98
1/6/94	550989.98	6887.38	557877.35
1/7/94	557877.35	6973.47	564850.81
1/8/94	564850.81	7060.64	571911.44
1/10/94	571911.44	7148.89	579060.33
1/11/94	579060.33	7238.25	586298.58
1/12/94	586298.58		

TOTAL INTERST AS AT 1/12/94
U.S. DOLLARS   74883.56

ANNEX 6

U.S. DOLLAR INTEREST CALCULATION
OUTSTANDING AMOUNT U.S. 647395.00
RATE OF INTEREST 1.25% PERMONTH.

	AMOUNT	INTEREST	TOTAL
18/07/94	647395.00	8092.44	655487.43
18/08/94	655487.43	8193.59	663681.02
18/09/94	663681.02	8296.01	671977.03
18/10/94	671977.03	8399.71	680376.74
18/11/94	680376.74	8504.71	688881.44
18/12/94	688881.44		

TOTAL INTEREST OUTSTANDING
AS AT 18/12/94   U.S.DOLLARS 41486.46

National Westminster Bank

Kilburn Branch
74 Kilburn High Road
London NW6 4HU

Telephone 071-624 4822
Facsimile 071-372 7663

Your ref:
039853/CSE001/MF/230

Our ref:

Date: 11 November 1994

Mil-Tec Corporation Limited
c/o Mr Rajpar
Ragnall House
18 Peel Road
DOUGLAS
Isle Of Man

Dear Sir

Re: Mil-tec Corporation Limited

Further to your meeting with Mr Pugh on the 7th November, I write
to confirm that we have not received the sum of $578,645.00 from
Cairo.

I trust this is satisfactory but if I can be of any further
assistance, please do not hesitate to contact me at this office.

Yours faithfully

MFranklin

Foreign Business Officer
Mrs M Franklin

RÉPUBLIQUE RWANDAISE   MUGUNGA, le 11 Octobre 1995

MINISTERE DE LA DEFENSE NATIONALE
ARMEE RWANDAISE
ETAT-MAJOR

                        Au Comd FAR

                 Info : Comd Bde 2 Div (Tous)

OBJET : C.C.C

1. La première période de cours C.C.C est programmée du ~~25~~ [23] au ~~31~~ [29] Oct 95 pour
   les 23-24 et 25 Bde.

2. Le nombre de candidats est ± 80 dont la ½ se trouve à KATALE-KAHINDO.
   Pour des raisons pratiques une classe sera organisée à KATALE et une autre
   à MUGUNGA. Les candidats de KIBUMBA feront partie de la classe de MUGUNGA.
   Pour MUGUNGA l'endroit du cours est BULENGO tandis que le Comd 24 Bde
   déterminera lui-même l'endroit convenable à KATALE.

3. Les matières suivantes seront dispensées :
   - La politique
   - Les causes de la défaite
   - L'idéologie
   - Le leadership *(psychologie du conflit)*
   - La guerilla (OPS guerilla - la vie dans la clandestinité)
   - OPS spéciales (Raid-embuscade-contrôle de zone
   - Recherche Rens
   - Utilisation du Gn

4. Nous demandons votre intervention pour disponibiliser le moyens suivants :
   - Les cahiers (± 200)
   - Logement à BULENGO pour 15 personnes de KIBUMBA du ~~24~~ [22] AU ~~31~~ [30] Octobre 1995
     ainsi que leur alimentation évaluée approximativement comme suit ;
     (2 x repas par jour et 3 repas de viande) 80 Kg de haricot - 56 Kg de Riz
     128 Kg de pomme de terre - 12 Kg de viande - ingrédients + légumes (non
     évalués)
   - Moyen de Tpt : 1 x MINIBUS pour assurer déplacement candidats de MUGUNGA
     à BULENGO chaque jour (aller-retour).

                         .../...

La 25 Bde fournira 1 x Ctte pour la même mission.

Les candidats de KIBUMBA se déplaceront par BUS 2 Div à l'aller comme au retour. (Arrivé à MUGUNGA le 24 Oct 95, départ le 04 Nov 95).

- Une bouteille par candidat à la clôture de la période soit 85 bouteilles.

5. Vous trouverez en annexe le CANEVAS des cours. Je vous demanderais de libérer les Maj NTILIKINA et RWAGAKIGA retenus pour donner respectivement le cours d'utilisation du Gn et le cours d'idéologie de guérilla.

RENZAHO Tharcisse
Col/i.G
Comd 2 Div

<u>C A N N V A S</u>

Date heure	Matières	Instructeurs clanse MUGUNGA	Classe KATALE
Lundi 23 Oct 0800-0900B	Ouverture	Offr EM 2 Div	Comd 2 Div
0920-1120B	Politique	Lt Col NKUNDIYE	Maj ~~BABUKA~~
1130-1300B	Cause de la défaite	Maj BARARWEREKANA	~~Maj SUBIRA~~ _Maj ANZABAHIRANA_
Mardi 24 Oct 0800-1300B	Idéologie	Maj HAGUMA	Maj NTAMAGEZO
Mercredi 25 Oct 0800-1300B	Leadership	Maj RUHUMULIZA	Lt Col ~~///////~~ RWARAKABIJE
Jeudi 26 Oct 0800-1300B	Guérilla	Lt Col BIVUGABAGABO	Maj NGENDAHIMANA
Vendredi 27 Oct 0800-1300B	OPS Spec	Maj KAREGEYA	Maj TULIKUHKIKO
Samedi 28 Oct 0800-1000B	Utilisation du Cn	Maj NTILIKINA	AC NKULIYINGOMA
1010-1300B	Recherche du Rens	Maj BARARWEREKANA	Maj NTAMAGEZO
Dimanche 29 Oct 0800-1100B	Test (1 x question par matière)	Comdt 25 Bde	Comdt 24 Bde
1100-1200B	Clôture	Comd 2 Div	Offr EM 2 Div

D. Statutes Proposed for the Rwandan Democratic Front

REPUBLIQUE RWANDAISE

PROJET : STATUTS DU FRONT DEMOCRATIQUE RWANDAIS

I. DU FRONT DEMOCRATIQUE RWANDAIS

Article 1

Il est créé une ~~Mouvement Politique Militaire~~ *organisation socio-politique* "Front Démocratique Rwandais" en abrégé : (FRODERWA).

Article 2

Les buts poursuivis par le FRODERWA sont :

a. organiser les réfugiés rwandais en vue de leur retour ~~au~~ *pays en dignité et la sécurité au Rwanda.*

b. lutter pour la Démocratie, le respect des Droits de l'Homme et la Justice Sociale au Rwanda.

c. Amener le peuple rwandais à prendre conscience de son rôle dans l'attribution et l'exercice du pouvoir.

d. Stimuler les efforts du peuple rwandais en vue de la *Réconciliation* ~~Reconstruction Nationale~~ et le progrès socio-économique au Rwanda.

Article 3

Le FRODERWA a pour Devise:
SOLIDARITE - ~~PAIX~~ *Justice* - DEMOCRATIE.

Article 4

Le Drapeau du FRODERWA est constitué de Gauche à Droite par les couleurs ROUGE et BLANC signifiant *vert* ~~lutte pour et~~ ~~Paix~~ *et espoir.*

Article 5

Le siège du FRODERWA est établi provisoirement au "ZAIRE". Il ~~peut être transféré~~ *décision* ~~ultérieurement en un lieu décidé par le Président après avis conforme du Congrès du FRONT.~~ *On par l'assemblée générale.*

Article 6

Les moyens d'action du FRODERWA sont notamment :
- L'organisation des réunions, conférences, séminaires et congrès.
- ~~La publication des revues, journaux et des dépliants de toutes sorte~~ *et l'utilisation des médias*
- La constitution d'un budget
- Le maintien de la cohésion des rwandais
- L'encadrement du peuple ~~éducative de~~
- ~~La formation de la jeunesse~~
- ~~l'organisation d'une force armée pour libérer le pays.~~

Article 7

Grâce à ses structures et cadres, le FRODERWA:
- Détermine, enseigne et interprète sa doctrine politique.
- Eduque, sensibilise et maintient la cohésion de ses membres.
- S'assure de cadres compétents jouissant de la confiance du peuple et ayant foi dans ses objectifs.

à Commission : (handwritten)

2

– Adapte ses méthodes d'actions ~~et~~ ses enseignements et sa
·doctrine à l'évolution.

II. DES MEMBRES DU FRODERWA

Article 8
Tout Rwandais est libre d'adhérer au FRODERWA. Les membres
doivent se conformer aux statuts et Règlements du FRODERWA.
At ;– (handwritten)

Article 9
Tout membre du FRODERWA a le droit d'élire et d'être élu aux
organes dirigeants dans les conditions déterminées par les
statuts, Règlements et Instructions du FRODERWA.

Article 10
Les étrangers peuvent être membres sympathisants. *est* (handwritten)
considéré comme membre sympathisant, tout étranger qui
soutient le FRODERWA et apporte une contribution
appréciable à la réalisation des objectifs du FRODERWA.
Les membres fondateurs ⊗ – Membres fondateur d'honneur – adhérants (handwritten)

III. DES ORGANES CENTRAUX DU FRODERWA
Article 11

Les Organes Centraux du FRODERWA sont :
1° ~~Le Président du FRODERWA~~ *Bureau exécutif* (handwritten)
2° ~~L'Assemblée Générale~~ *Comité Directeur* (handwritten)
3° ~~Le Comité Directeur.~~ *Assemblée générale* (handwritten)
Congrès (handwritten)

Article 12
Le ~~Président~~ *exécutif* FRODERWA ~~er~~ est l'organe ~~suprême~~ *exécutif* La (handwritten)
direction du ~~Président~~ du FRODERWA est assurée par une
Président qui représente le FRODERWA et qui en est
responsable devant ses membres. Il convoque ~~L'Assemblée~~ *Congrès* (handwritten)
~~Générale~~ et le Comité Directeur et préside leurs séances.
En cas d'absence ou d'empêchement, les réunions sont
présidées par le ~~1er Vice-général~~ du FRODERWA.
Le Président du FRODERWA oriente et contrôle tous les
Organes. Il ~~nomme et révoque le~~ Secrétaire Général et les
~~membres du Comité Directeur.~~ ~~Il se~~ choisit les Conseillers
à la Présidence.

* Prés (handwritten)
1er V (handwritten)
2e V (handwritten)
SECRET. exécutif (handwritten)
secr. ex.-adjt (handwritten)
Trésorier général (handwritten)
trésorier général adjt (handwritten)

~~Article 14~~ *Article 1* (handwritten)
Le Président du FRODERWA est élu par ~~L'Assemblée Générale~~ *le congrès* (handwritten)
pour un mandat de 4 ans ~~non~~ renouvelable à la majorité
absolue des membres ~~de l'Assemblée Générale~~ *du Congrès* (handwritten)
En cas de vacance du Président par décès, démission ou
pour tout autre cause de cessation de fonctions, les
fonctions de Président sont assumées provisoirement par le
~~Secrétaire général~~ qui convoque ~~l'Assemblée Générale~~ pour
les élections d'un autre Président dans un délais de 60
jours qui suivent l'ouverture de la vacance.
Lorsque le Président et le ~~Secrétaire général~~ se trouvent
simultanément dans l'un des cas prévus ci-dessus les
fonctions de Président sont provisoirement exercés par le

3

2° Vice président

~~TRÉSORIER~~ du ~~Comité Directeur~~. Le Nouveau Président est désigné suivant la procédure prévu dans le présent article.

Article 14

L'Assemblée ~~Générale~~ *du Congrès* est composé~~e~~ :
- 1° Des membres du Comité Directeur
- 2° Des ~~membres des~~ *de tous les* Comités de Secteurs

Article 15

le Congrès est l'organe suprême

L'Assemblée ~~Générale~~, se réunit une fois ~~tous les six mois~~ *par ans* en session ordinaire ~~par~~ *un* acte de convocation qui contient l'ordre du jour est communiqué aux membres de ~~l'Assemblée~~ ~~deux semaine~~ avant la date de la réunion et sous plis confidentiel.

Article 16

L'~~Assemblée Générale~~ se prononce sur tous les problèmes concernant le~~s~~ FRODERWA. Il a notamment pour rôle principale de :
- a. Adopter le Rapport du Comité Directeur
- b. Fixer au moyen des Manifeste le programme d'action du FRODERWA *pour une durée*
- c. Elire ~~le~~ *et* Président du FRODERWA *et les autres membres du Comité directeur*
- d. Arrêter ~~les~~ *ratifier* Statuts et Règlements du FRODERWA
- e. Dissoudre les ~~Organes des Secteurs centraux~~ *l'organisation à la*
- f. Prendre toutes résolutions ~~sur les questions d'ordre~~ *majorité* ~~politique~~ *dans tous les domaines*
  ~~8. Droi~~

Article 17

le Congrès

L'~~Assemblée Générale~~ peut être convoqué à tout moment en session extraordinaire par le Président ~~du~~ FRODERWA. Il examine uniquement les points inscrits à l'ordre du jour contenu dans l'acte de convocation.

Article 18

Congrès

L'~~Assemblée Générale~~ adopte ses résolutions à la majorité ~~des 2/3~~ *simple* des membres présents. *Le quorum pour ~~siéger~~ et délibérer valablement est de 2/3.*

Article 19

Le Comité DIRECTEUR est composé :
- a. Du ~~Président du FRODERWA~~
- b. ~~Du Secrétaire Général~~
- c. ~~Du Trésorier du FRODERWA~~
- d. Des ~~5~~ *présidents des Commissions*

Article 20

Tous les membres du Comité Directeur sont élus par l'~~Assemblée Générale~~. *le Congrès.*

Article 21

Sous la conduite du Président, le Comité Directeur dirige la Politique du FRODERWA et arrête ~~le~~ *son* budget du FRODERWA.

Article 22

Le Comité Directeur se réunit tous les Trois mois en session ordinaire. Il peut être convoqué en sessions

extraordinaires aussi souvent que les circonstances
l'exigent.

Article 23 : ~~Le Comité Directeur comprend~~ Les Commissions dont il et question à l'article 18.
Commissions:
- Commission Politique ~~Intérieure~~
- Commission Patrimoine et Finances
- Commission Sociale
- ~~Commission de Défense~~ des affaires juridiques
- Commission de ~~Relation aux~~ Extérieure - Commission Informat & Propagande
Les membres des ~~8~~ Commissions sont choisit par ~~le Président~~
~~du FRODERWA parmi les membres~~ Ide Comité Directeur.

Article 24

a. La Commission Politique traite des Affaires Politiques,
Administratives, ~~Judiciaires~~ et disciplinaires et des
questions relatives à L'idéologie. & la sécurité et à l'idéologie.

b. La Commission du Patrimoine et des Finances traite des
Affaires Financières, Economique et de Budget.

c. La Commission Sociale traite des affaires Sociales, du patrimoine
Jeunesse, et de la Santé.
Culturelle

d. La Commission ~~de Défense~~ juridiques traite des affaires ~~juridiques~~ et du
Contentieux

e. La Commission de ~~Relation~~ extérieures traite des
affaires de relation diplomatiques ~~et de la presse et de~~
et de la coopération
f. L'information traite des affaires travit des Médias - Renseignt.
des Relations avec la presse

Article 25 : DES ORGANES DE SECTEUR
Les Organes de Secteur sont :
1° ~~L'Assemblée~~ de Secteur
2° Le Comité de Secteur
3° LE

Article 26

Le ~~Comité~~ de Secteur examine toutes les questions lui
soumis par ses membres et se prononce sur le bilan des
réalisations et l'évolution du FRODERWA dans le Secteur sur
tout les plans politique, économique, social et culture.

Article 27

Le ~~Assemblée~~ de Secteur, composée des chef ~~tous les~~ membres du Comités
~~de Cellule~~ élit en son sein le Comité de Secteur de ~~5~~ membres.

Article 28 29

Le Comité de Secteur et composé d'un Président, du 25V
Secrétaire et d'un Trésorier ~~et du 2 membres~~.

Article 30

Le Comité de Secteur est l'organe exécutif ~~du~~ l'Assemblée
de Secteur. il veille à l'exécution des directives de
Comité de Secteur ~~l'Assemblée~~ il traite toutes les questions
intéressant ~~la l'organisation~~ membres du Secteur sur le plan
politique, ~~économique, social et culturel~~ et fait rapport
dans

5

~~Bureau exécutif~~

au ~~Comité Directeur~~ •

Il peut de sa propre initiative étudier toutes les questions qui se posent au FRODERWA sur tous les plans et proposer au ~~Comité Directeur~~ toute mesure de nature à améliorer le fonctionnement et l'efficacité ~~du FRODERWA~~ Il oriente et contrôle les activités ~~du FRODERWA~~ dans le Secteur

→ Les ~~congrès~~ Présidents des comités de secteur ~~de leur~~ d'une région

Article 30 se réunissent sous la présidence des FRODERWA pour élire en son sein : - un coordinat. et un coordination adjt. chargé d'assurer la coordination harmonisation des activités dans la région.

Art 33 Les Secteurs créés sont :

Art 32 Les régions

1. Au ZAIRE :   Secteurs   - GOMA   - ~~KATALE KIBURON~~ -Kayinzo activités dans
                               - BUKAVU   - ~~WALUNGU~~ Walungu
                               - UVIRA   - KINSHASA ×

2. Af de l'EST + Burundi ~~Au~~ KENYA   Secteur   NAIROBI - ~~Dar es Salam~~ - ~~BENACO~~ -Gisoro
                                                    BENACO - NGARA - NGOZI - GISORO

3. Europe + Asie ~~Au~~ CAMEROUN   Secteur   - YAOUNDE ~~~~~~

4. Af centrale ect.   Au RWANDA   Secteur   - KIGALI   - GITARAMA   - BUTARE
                                             - GIKONGORO - CYANGUGU   - KIBUYE
                                             - GISENYI   - RUHENGERI   - BYUMBA
                                             - KIBUNGO   - KIGALI-Ville

En TANZANIE   Secteurs :   - ~~BENACO~~   ~~DAR-ES-SALAM~~

Europe
En BELGIQUE   Secteur   - BRUXELLES - Paris - Bonn - Tokyo •

En FRANCE   ~~Secteur~~   - ~~PARIS~~

~~R F A~~ Europe   Secteurs   - ~~Cologne - Bonn~~
~~Amérique~~ ~~secteur~~   - WASHINGTON - ~~Ottawa~~ QUEBEC

Le Président du Comité de Secteur est automatiquement le Porte-Parole du FRODERWA dans le Secteur.

Article 34 Les camps de réfugiés là où ils existent constituent des cellules. Le comité de cellule est composé d'un président d'un responsable de camp, d'un vice président, d'un secrétaire et d'un Trésorier élu par les membres de la cellule•

IV. DES RELATIONS EXTERIEURES

Article 35

Le FRODERWA peut devenir membre d'un MOUVEMENT INTERNATIONAL ou ~~DECIDER d'une unité~~ de collaborer d'action avec des Mouvements étrangers.

Le Président du FRODERWA peut pour le compte et dans l'intérêt du FRODERWA établir toute relation avec les Mouvements étrangers ~~dans l'intérêt de l'organisation~~.

VI DU PATRIMOINE DU FRODERWA

Commission : { *Col BAGOSORA*
Projet de statut
Maj Kpriph +2 juristes de son choix

6

Article 32 *3/6*
Les avoirs du FRODERWA sont constitués par :
- Ses biens propres
- Les cotisations
- Le Produit de la vente du Matériel
- Les dons ~~et legs~~
- ~~Les biens du Gouvernement en Exil.~~

Article 33 *37*
La Perception, la gestion ~~et le contrôle~~ financiers sont *financière*
assurés par ~~une~~ Commission ~~désignée par le Président du~~
~~FRODERWA.~~ *du patrimoine et des finances*

Art 38 le contrôle / ~~budget~~ financier est assuré par
3 commissaire aux Comptes élus par le congrès
pour 1 mandat d'un an renouvelable.

VII. DE LA DISCIPLINE

Article 34 *3/*
Les fautes disciplinaires sont :
- Les préjudices portés aux intérêts ~~du Front~~ ainsi que la
  violation ou la déviation de ses principes tels que
  définis par les manifestes. ~~du Front~~

- Tous les actes contraires aux statuts et règlement.

Article 35
Un membre reconnu coupable fait l'objet de sanction dans
les conditions déterminées par le Règlement Intérieur.

~~(handwritten struck-through line)~~

Fait à GOMA, le

VII. Les dispositions finales

Les signataires

E. Financial Report of the Capital Commission

Mugunga, le 30 Septembre 1995

RAPPORT DE GESTION FINANCIERE DE LA COMMISSION DU PATRIMOINE DE LA COMMUNAUTE

RWANDAISE EN EXIL AU NORD-KIVU

1. QUELQUES CONSIDERATIONS UTILES

   a. Ce rapport concerne la période allant du 14 Avril au 30 Septembre 1995, période pour laquelle j'exerce la fonction de Trésorier de la Commission du Patrimoine.

   b. Il y a lieu de signaler qu'aucune remise-reprise n'a été effectuée entre Mr MUTEMBEREZI Pierre Claver, Trésorier sortant et moi-même en date du 14/4/95. D'ailleurs, Mr MUTEMBEREZI a disparu depuis cette date sans laisser de traces avec un détournement de 15.431 $US non encore récupérés jusqu'à présent. Mr HIGIRO Léonidas, actuel Président de la Commission du Patrimoine à partir du 14/04/95, doit également 165 $US envers la caisse, somme à sa charge durant la Présidence de la Commission du Patrimoine par Mr MUTEMBEREZI.

   c. Un cahier, sorte de livre de caisse à la disposition du Trésorier, sert à l'enregistrement des recettes et des dépenses et chaque opération effectuée porte un numéro d'ordre. Exemple: 001/D/95 pour les opérations de dépenses; 001/R/95 pour celles de recettes pour Exercice 1995.

   d. Ce rapport présente les opérations comptables par mensualité et un tableau synthétique est fourni à la fin.

   e. Il y a à déplorer l'absence de mécanisme de contrôle financier au sein de la Commission du Patrimoine. L'argent, c'est la confiance; mais jusqu'où peut aller cette confiance lorsque l'argent appartient à toute une Communauté?

2. RECETTES ET DEPENSES REALISEES DU 14/04/95 AU 30 SEPTEMBRE 1995

   a. Mois d'Avril 1995

   1. RECETTES

POSTE	DATES	LIBELLE	MONTANT ($)	SOMME CUMULEE ($)
001/R/95	26/4	Produit location Bus A9225 Chez GOAL	2.530	2.530

2. DEPENSES

POSTE	DATES	LIBELLE	MONTANT ($)	SOMME CUMULEE ($)
001/D/95	26/4	Frais Taxi à NSANZABAGANWA	120	120
002/D/95	26/4	Charges Bus A9225	600	720
003/D/95	"	F.R. à KIBUMBA	07	727
004/D/95	"	F.R. à KIBUMBA	10	737
005/D/95	"	F.R. à TWAGIRAYEZU Laurent	10	747
006/D/95	"	F.R. à KIBUMBA	25	772
007/D/95	"	Remboursement RWAJEKARE	64	836
008/D/95	"	Frais Taxi NSANZABAGANWA	20	856
009/D/95	28/4	Remboursement ONATRACOM	67	923
010/D/95	29/4	Prime chauffeur NSHIMIYIMANA	40	963
011/D/9R	"	Prime chauffeur MUGABO	40	1.003
013/D/95	26/4	Avance Perdiems	1.350	2.353
014/D/95	30/4	F.R. à KIBUMBA	11,5	2.364,5
015/D/95	"	Achat d'un cachet Commission P.	20	2.384,5
017/D/95	"	Rapport au Portier chez GOAL	10	2.394,5

   3. SOLDE: 2.530 $ - 2.394,50 $ = 135,50 $.

.../...

b. MOIS DE MAI 1995

1. RECETTES

002/R/95	16/5	Produit location Bus A9225 chez GOAL	1.200	1.200
003/R/95	29/5	" " " " " "	1.250	2.450

2. DEPENSES

012/D/95	01/5	Prime chauffeur RUMBEKI	40	40
016/D/95	"	Achat matériel de bureau	10	50
018/D/95	03/5	F.R. MUGUNGA	26	76
019/D/95	06/5	Prime MBAGOROZIKI L.	10	86
020/D/95	09/5	Achat d'un registre	10	96
021/D/95	13/5	F.R. à MUGUNGA	13	109
022/D/95	17/5	Achat cahier du Trésorier	05	114
023/D/95	"	Avance perdiems	575	689
024/D/95	05/5	F.R. Dossier MUTEMBEREZI	40	729
025/D/95	04/5	Investigations CAME 1513	05	734
026/D/95	25/5	F.R. Contact à la 4° REGION MILITAIRE	35	769
027/D/95	16/5	F.R. Dossier MUTEMBEREZI	21	790
028/D/95	23/5	Investigations sur véhicule CNFR par MBAGOROZIKI	50	840
029/D/95	16/5	Rapport Col KUSIKUSA	300	1.140
030/D/95	24/5	Achat d'un registre	10	1.150
031/D/95	18/5	F.R. à MUGUNGA	18,5	1.168,6
032/D/95	09/5	F.R. à MUGUNGA	11	1.179,5
033/D/95	24/5	F.R. à KIBUMBA	12	1.191,5
034/D/95	29/5	Rapport à la G.C. de GOMA	500	1.691,5
035/D/95	"	Frais négociation dossier Bus A9224	110	1.801,5
036/D/95	31/5	Achat matériel de bureau	20	1.821,5
037/D/95	"	Rapport Salle de réunion à KIBUMBA	05	1.826,5
039/D/95	"	F.R. à KIBUMBA	13	1.839,5

3. SOLDE : 2.450 $ - 1.839,50 $ = 610,50 $

c. MOIS DE JUIN 1995

1. RECETTES

004/R/95	27/6	Produit location Bus A9225 chez GOAL	1.700	1.700

2. DEPENSES

038/D/95	07/6	Prime de dactylographie	20	20
040/D/95	08/6/	Charges Bus A9225	124	144
041/D/95	09/6	Achat Pièces de rechange Bus A9225	312	456
042/D/95	09/6	Frais de photocopie	08	464
043/D/95	02/6	Frais d'essence CTTETS	10	474
044/D/95	14/6	Frais photocopie dossier pr KINSHASA	20	494
045/D/95	21/6	F.R. Visite C.Z.S.C.	28	522
046/D/95	23/6	Achat matériel de bureau	10	532
047/D/95	28/6	F.R. dans la recherche d'un local pour les travaux de la Commission du Patrimoine	08,5	540,5
048/D/95	28/6	F.R. à MUGUNGA	18,5	559,0
049/D/95	29/6	Rapport aux Autorités Zaïroises	500	1.059
050/D/95	"	Frais négociation pour la réduction de Taxe à la contribution	100	1.159
051/D/95	"	Charges Bus A9225	100	1.259

3. SOLDE : 1.700 $ - 1.259 $ = 441 $.

...../....

d. MOIS DE JUILLET 1995

1. RECETTES

005/R/95	21/7	Produit de location Bus A9225	1.211	1.211
006/R/95	29/7	Produit de vente d'une Jeep SUZUKI à KIBUMBA	1.800	3.011
007/R/95	31/7	Produit location Bus A9225	1.140	4.151
008/R/95	31/7	Produit de vente CAME1513,		
		- 1ère avance	3.000	7.151
		- 2ème avance *ca hiburishi*	495	7.646

2. DEPENSES

052/D/95	03/7	Expédition du Courrier à KINSHASA	20	20
053/D/95	04/7	F.R. à KATALE	10	30
054/D/95	05/7	F.R. à KIBUMBA	12	42
055/D/95	21/7	Frais de taxi	40	82
056/D/95	21/7	F.R. payés à SEKABUGA F.	20	102
057/D/95	"	Prime à un expert pour R.O.I./C.P.	66	168
058/D/95	"	Charges Bus A9225	30	198
059/D/95	"	Frais entretien Bus A9225	55	253
060/D/95	"	F.R. à MUGUNGA	08	261
061/D/95	22/7	F.R. à KIBUMBA	16,5	277,5
062/D/95	24/7	Versement à 1'EM.FAR	2.000	2.277,5
063/D/95	"	Prime de gardiennage Jeep SUZUKI vendue à KIBUMBA	500	2.777,5
064/D/95	06/7	Contact avec clients du CAME 1513	50	2.827,5
065/D/95	10/7	" " " "	40	2.867,5
066/D/95	11/7	Investigations sur CA.MITSU avec CZSC	75	2.942,5
067/D/95	12/7	" " " "	40	2.982,5
068/D/95	24/7	Visite famille feu MAKOMBE	50	3.032,5
069/D/95	"	Prime à un expert T.M.	50	3.082,5
070/D/95	"	F.R. à MUGUNGA	14	3.096,5
071/D/95	"	Frais entretien Bus A9225	100	3.196,5
072/D/95	26/7	Achat matériel de bureau	124	3.320,5
073/D/95	"	Frais d'essence CTTE TS	10	3.330,5
074/D/95	"	Frais de mission	15	3.345,5
075/D/95	"	F.R. à BULENGO-MUGUNGA	30	3.375,5
076/D/95	30/7	Avance perdiems	1.800	5.175,5
077/D/95	"	Payement perdiems	452,5	5.628,0
078/D/95	"	Payement perdiems	140	5.768
079/D/95	"	Prime de dactylographie	5	5.773
080/D/95	"	Prime à NDAGIJIMANA	75	5.848
081/D/95	"	F.R. contact à 1'EM/CZSC	15	5.863
082/D/95	"	Achat Pièces de rechange Bus CZSC	200	6.063
083/D/95	"	Frais mission à BUTEMBO	500	6.563
084/D/95	31/7	Location Taxi	40	6.603

3. SOLDE : 7.646 $ - 6.603 $ = 1.043 $.

e. MOIS D'AOUT 1995

1. RECETTES

009/R/95	16/8	Produit de vente CTTE TOYOTA DYNA Commune NKUMBA	800	800
010/R/95	"	Produit de vente CTTE T. HIAON D.C.	1.000	1.800

2. DEPENSES

085/D/95	02/8	Investigations sur un camion	40	40
086/D/95	05/8	Charges Bus A9225	186	226
087/D/95	06/8	Achat matériel de bureau	30	256

.../...

088/D/95	06/8	Rachat prison BAHEMBERA	300	556
089/D/95	08/8	Frais d'entretien Bus A9225	150	706
090/D/95	09/8	Frais de prison BAHEMBERA	100	806
091/D/95	10/8	Prime à un technicien	30	836
092/D/95	14/8	Versement à l'EM. FAR	804	1.640
093/D/95	16/8	Visite père KANYANKOROTE	40	1.680
094/D/95	16/8	Prime à un indicateur	20	1.700
095/D/95	23/8	Financement Comité de Crise Camp MUGUNGA	200	1.900
096/D/95	24/8	" " "	20	1.920
097/D/95	29/8	" " "	100	2.020

3. SOLDE : 1.800 $ - 2.020 $ = - 220 $

f. MOIS DE SEPTEMBRE 1995

1. RECETTES

011/R/95	14/9	Produit location Bus A9225	1.444	1.444
012/R/95	18/9	Produit de vente du CA.MITSU Benne - 1ère avance	5.000	6.444

2. DEPENSES

098/D/95	01/9	Financement Comité de crise Camp MUGUNGA	100	100
099/D/95	02/9	Contact avec Cdt CZSC Camp MUGUNGA	80	180
100/D/95	05/9	Financement C.C.C.MUGUNGA	100	280
101/D/95	07/9	Financement C.C.C.MUGUNGA	200	480
102/D/95	"	Achat matériel de bureau	35	515
103/D/95	"	" "	96	611
104/D/95	12/9	Frais de mission	50	661
105/D/95	"	Financement C.C.C.MUGUNGA	100	761
106/D/95	13/9	Rachat prison TERERAHO	300	1.061
107/D/95	15/9	Charges Bus A9225	266	1.327
108/D/95	"	Versement à l'EM.FAR	1.178	2.505
109/D/95	16/9	Frais Commission à GATSINZI	640	3.145
110/D/95	18/9	Faux billet remis à HIGIRO	100	3.245
111/D/95	18/9	Argent emporté par HIGIRO	120	3.365
112/D/95	22/9	Frais de mission à BUTEMBO-BENI	2.500	5.865
113/D/95	20/9	Frais de mission	50	5.915
114/D/95	27/9	Investigations/Pelle Chargeuse	100	6.015
115/D/95	27/9	" " "	20	6.035
116/D/95	28/9	Frais de Commission au Lt NZOLO	160	6.195
117/D/95	28/9	Filature CA.MITSU de MURWANASHYAKA	80	6.275
118/D/95	30/9	Filature pelle-chargeuse	05	6.280
119/D/95	30/9	Filature pelle-chargeuse	30	6.315

3. SOLDE: 6.444 $ - 6.315 = 129 $

3. TABLEAU SYNTHETIQUE DES RECETTES ET DEPENSES

MOIS	RECETTES ($)	DEPENSES ($)	SOLDES ($)
AVRIL 1995	2.530,00	2.394,50	+ 135,50
MAI 1995	2.450,00	1.839,50	+ 610,50
JUIN 1995	1.700,00	1.259,00	+ 441,00
JUILLET 95	7.646,00	6.603,00	+ 1.043,00
AOUT 1995	1.800,00	2.020,00	- 220,00
SEPTEMBRE 95	6.444,00	6.315,00	+ 129,00
TOTAUX:	22.570,00	20.431,00	+ 2.139,00

5

4. RELEVE DES DETTES ENVERS LA TRESORERIE

HIGIRO Léonidas	:	120 $	- lors de la vente du CA.MITSUBISHI à KATALE
	:	100 $	- faux billet gardé lors de la même vente
	:	100 $	- faux billet lui remis pour échange par AFRIKA Alexis
	:	300 $	- faux billets lui remis pour échange/IYAMUREMYE G.
	:	40 $	- emprunt
	:	40 $	- frais taxi Août 1995 non justifiés
	:	50 $	- prime agent GOAL non justifiée
	:	4 $	- transport non justifié
		754 $	
TWAGIRAYEZU Materne	:	50 $	- emprunt
BAHEMBERA Célestin	:	50 $	- "
HABYARIMANA J.B.	:	20 $	- "
HABYARIMANA J.B.	:	20 $	- "
TOTAL DES DETTES	:	894 $	

5. ENCAISSE AU 30 SEPTEMBRE 1995: a) Théorique : 2.139 $
  b) Réelle   : 2.139 $ - 894 $ = 1.245 $/

6. REMARQUES

   a. Le résultat financier relatif à la période considérée est très minime pour
      pouvoir venir en aide à nos réfugiés.
      Le poste "Mission" et les primes diverses engloutissent beaucoup d'argent
      eu égard aux recettes modérées perçues en dehors de celles émanant du Bus A9225.

   b. Les produits de vente des véhicules par la Sous-Commission de RUTSHURU dans
      son ressort restent sous la responsabilité de Mr HIGIRO Léonidas, Président
      de la Commission du Patrimoine, jusqu'au jour de leur remise au Trésorier de
      la Commission devant tous les membres de la Commission.

   c. Les dettes envers la trésorerie doivent être remboursées sans délais sans quoi
      les mesures disciplinaires devraient être prises à l'encontre des fautifs.

   d. Les maigres résultats financiers enregistrés au cours de la période écoulée
      devraient nous inciter à redoubler d'efforts pour balayer tous les obstacles
      qui handicapent l'accomplissement digne et honnête de la mission qui nous est
      assignée. Le patrimoine à rechercher et à gérer appartient à la Communauté
      Rwandaise en Exil et à elle seule.

                              Fait à Mugunga, le 30 Septembre 1995
                                   IYAMUREMYE Gaston
                          Trésorier de la Commission du Patrimoine.

COMPLÉMENT DU RAPPORT DE GESTION FINANCIÈRE DE LA COMMISSION DU PATRIMOINE
RELATIF A LA PÉRIODE ALLANT DU 01 OCTOBRE AU 06 NOVEMBRE 1995.

1. Le 06/11/1995 correspond à la date à laquelle j'ai présenté ma démission au
   sein de la Commission du Patrimoine.

2. Les opérations comptables reprises dans le rapport sont celles ordonnées par
   le Bureau de la Commission du Patrimoine lors de sa séance du 05/11/1995 au
   Siège de l'ONATRACOM en Exil et exécutées le 06/11/1995.
   Je signale à la Commission du Patrimoine que le 05/11/95, j'ai versé dans la
   Caisse de Solidarité de la Communauté Rwandaise en Exil une somme minable de
   Six cents Dollars (600 $US) représentant la moitié de l'encaisse réelle
   justifiée dans mon précédent rapport.

3. Ordonnancement des recettes et des dépenses
   a) Mois d'Octobre 1995
      1° Recettes = Néant
      2° Dépenses = Néant
      3° Solde   = Néant   *1°) Recettes : Néant*
   b) Mois de Novembre 1995   { *2°) Dépenses :*

POSTE	DATE	L I B E L L E	MONTANT ($)	SOMME CUMULEE ($)
120/D/95	05/11	Versement à la Caisse de Solidarité	600	600
121/D/95	06/11	Payement à TERERAHO	50	650
122/D/95	"	Payement à NSENGIYUMVA (F.R.)	15	665
123/D/95	"	Payement à BANDIKURE Sudi	200	865
124/D/95	"	Payement à HABYARIMANA J.B. (F.R.)	20	885
125/D/95	"	Frais de Prison pour SIBOMANA	20	905
126/D/95	"	Frais de transport	32	937
127/D/95	"	Achat 30 l de mazout	13	950
128/D/95	"	Primes Personnel ONATRACOM	144	1.094
129/D/95	"	Prime de dactylographe	64	1.158

   3° Solde = 0 - 1.158 = - 1.158 $.

4. Synthèse de la situation mensuelle comptable du 14/04 au 06/11/1995

M O I S	RECETTES ($)	DEPENSES ($)	SOLDES ($)
AVRIL	2.530,00	2.394,50	+ 135,50
MAI	2.450,00	1.839,50	+ 610,50
JUIN	1.700,00	1.259,00	+ 441,00
JUILLET	7.646,00	6.603,00	+ 1.043,00

.../...

AOUT	1.800,00	2.020,00	-	220,00
SEPTEMBRE	6.444,00	6.315,00	+	129,00
OCTOBRE	0,00	0,00	+	0,00
NOVEMBRE	0,00	1.158,00	-	1.158,00
TOTAUX:	22.570,00	21.589,00	+	981,00

a) Encaisse théorique = 981 $.

b) Dettes envers la trésorerie = 894 $

c) Encaisse réelle = 87 $

d) Remarques:

1. Mr HIGIRO Léonidas, Président de la Commission du Patrimoine, n'a jamais versé chez le Trésorier le produit global de ± dix ventes de véhicules effectuées dans la zone de KATALE. Il lui revient donc de présenter son rapport à la Commission du Patrimoine.

2. Il est demandé aux membres de la Commission du Patrimoine ayant contracté une dette envers la trésorerie de la rembourser dans les meilleurs délais.

3. Les remarques reprises dans mon précédent rapport restent toujours valables.

Fait à Mugunga, le 06 Novembre 1995

IYAMUREMYE Gaston

Trésorier de la Commission du Patrimoine,

Démissionnaire

Index